THE ENCYCLOPEDIA OF WOOD

THE ENCYCLOPEDIA OF WOOD

A TREE-BY-TREE GUIDE TO THE WORLD'S MOST VERSATILE RESOURCE

General Editor: Aidan Walker

NEW BURLINGTON BOOKS

A QUARTO BOOK

Published by
New Burlington Books
6 Blundell Street
London N7 9BH

ISBN 1 84566 1583

Conceived, designed, and produced by
Quarto Publishing plc
The Old Brewery
6 Blundell Street
London N7 9BH

QUA: EWO

Art editor: Claire van Rhyn
Designer: Karin Skånberg
Illustrators: Martin Brown, John Woodcock
Photographers: Paul Forrester, Martin Norris
Picture researcher: Claudia Tate
Assistant art director: Penny Cobb

Art director: Moira Clinch
Publisher: Piers Spence

Color separation by Universal Graphic (PTE) Ltd, Singapore
Printed by SNP Leefung Printer Ltd, China

CONTENTS

No single form of plant life means so much to humanity as the tree. Highly complex biosystems, providers of oxygen for us to breathe, shade for us to rest in, nuts and fruit for us to eat, habitats for birds and insects, wood to burn and wood to build; the inter-relationship between humankind and tree life is as old as humanity itself.

FROM **TREE** TO **WOOD**

1.1 ANATOMY OF THE TREE

Trees have the longest lifespan of all the higher forms of life. Perhaps the greatest survivors among them are the bristlecone pines (*Pinus longeava*) of California's White Mountains. One specimen there, known appropriately as Methuselah, is estimated to be around 5,000 years old: it was a mere seedling when the Egyptians built their pyramids.

Coniferous or broad-leaved?

All trees are classified into one of two botanical divisions: the *Gymnospermae*, which includes the conifers, as well as the cycads and ginkgo; and the *Angiospermae*, a very large group of flowering plants, among which are the broad-leaved, flowering, fruit-bearing trees.

Conifers are also known as evergreens because (with the exception of spruce) they retain their needles or scale-like leaves throughout the year. They grow in cool, temperate, northern regions and supply the bulk of the world's commercial timber. Conifers emerged 275 million years ago, towering over other land plants and eventually covering two-thirds of the earth's surface. The Latin name for this group of trees means "naked seed," as their seeds are not enclosed in an ovary or fruit, but borne on a modified leaf.

Broad-leaved trees, most of which are deciduous and drop their leaves in cool-climate winters, first emerged about 140 million years after the conifers. Upheaval of the earth's crust and subsequent severe climatic changes drastically reduced their numbers and extensive treeless savannah plains and prairies took their place.

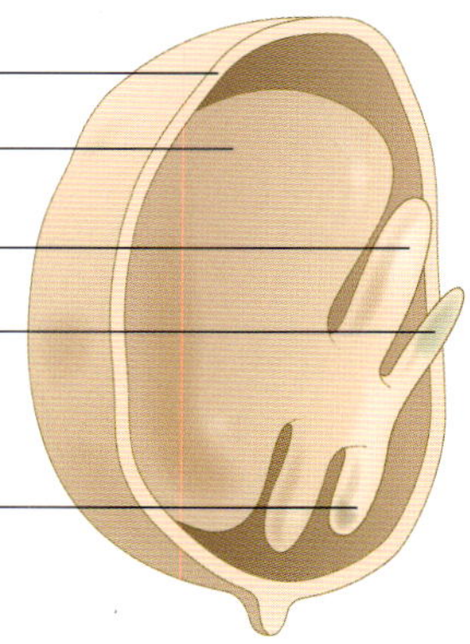

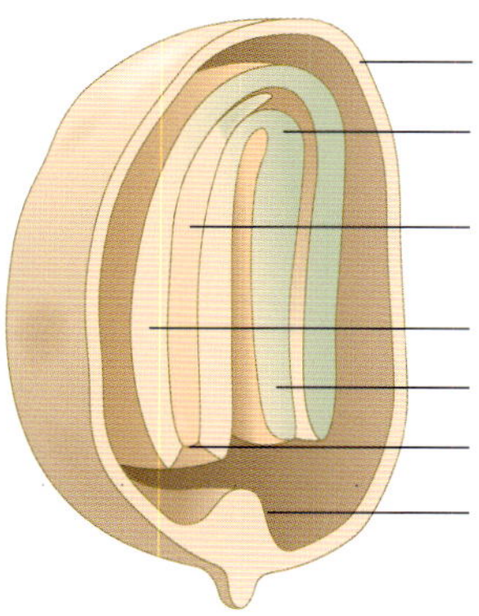

SEED STRUCTURE *Seeds of all higher plants comprise an embryo and an endosperm, or reserve of stored food, enclosed in a protective casing. When the seed germinates, the radicle, or embryonic root, bursts through the seed case and begins to grow down into the soil. What happens next varies by class: in dicots, the hypocotyl emerges and lifts the shoot tip, often including the seed coat, above the ground, bearing the cotyledons or seed leaves. In monocots, the seed tends to remain in the soil, and the growing shoot or epicotyl emerges through the soil bearing the single cotyledon.*

Softwoods and hardwoods

Somewhat confusingly, the terms "softwoods" and "hardwoods" are regularly used as synonyms for coniferous and broad-leaved trees as a group, rather than referring to the softness or hardness of the wood obtained from them. While it is true to say that, broadly speaking, conifers produce softwood and broad-leaved trees produce hardwood, the wood obtained from some "hardwoods," such as balsa and poplar, is much softer than that from botanical "softwoods" like yew or pitch pine.

Angiosperm plants are divided into two classes based on the structure of their seeds: those whose seeds have one seed leaf, such as palms, are called *monocotyledoneae*, or monocots; those whose seeds have two seed leaves are known as *dicotyledoneae*, or dicots. Since most monocots are herbs and none has true wood, this book concentrates

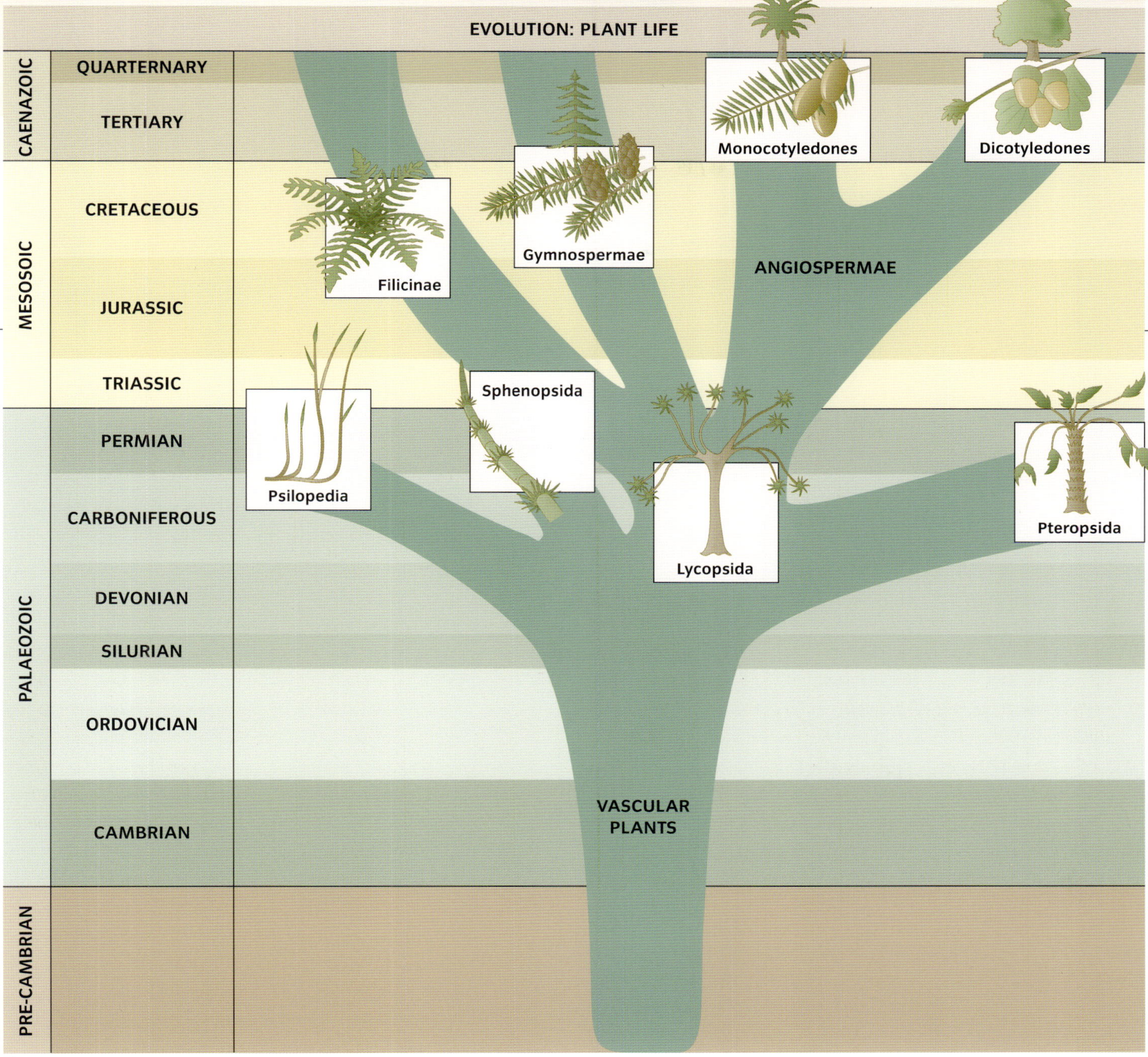

principally on the dicots, which represent the vast majority of valuable commercial hardwoods.

Dicots themselves subdivide into two types. Polypetalous species possess both a calyx and a multipetaled corolla, and produce beautiful flowers and fruits. Apple, almond, pear, peach, and cherry are polypetalous, as are horse chestnut, maple, and mahogany. Trees in the apetalous group have inconspicuous flowers, lacking the corolla and often the calyx too, but tend to produce the strongest and most durable woods. Timbers such as hickory, birch, alder, beech, oak, elm, and walnut all come from apetalous trees.

SOFTWOODS AND HARDWOODS *Softwoods generally come from coniferous trees (far left) and hardwoods from broad-leaved trees (left).*

1.2 How a Tree Grows

Trees use a range of strategies to ensure fertilization and the continuation of the genetic line. Some have flowers scented to attract pollinating bees and birds. In others, hanging, tassel-shaped clusters of male catkins release clouds of pollen that are collected on the exposed stigmas of bud-shaped female catkins. The development of seed follows.

From seed to shoot

The seeds of angiosperms are contained in a hard and/or fleshy structure called a fruit. Gymnosperm seeds develop on the bracts of cones. For the best chance of survival, seeds must be dispersed as widely as possible, and plants have evolved various ingenious ways to bring this about. Some seeds are attached to feather-light fiber parachutes—think of the dandelion—while others have broad-bladed wings to aid wind dispersal: the woody cones of a pine tree contain numerous winged seeds. Some seeds float in water; some are covered in hooks or burrs that attach themselves to the skin of passing animals. Many catkin-bearing trees yield large nuts, relying on squirrels or birds to disperse them. Other seeds are contained within a sweet and juicy fruit that invites consumption. These seeds have a tough protective outer coating so that, while the fruit is digested, the seeds will pass through their animal host's digestive tract intact, and grow wherever they fall. For the majority of seeds, successful growth is impossible. They may land on hard, rocky, or infertile ground, thick turf, or grazing or farming land tilled by the plow. Very few find a niche on the forest floor.

The seedling lies dormant until conditions for sprouting are right. Surrounding the embryo is the endosperm, a supply of stored fats, starch, and protein necessary to start the growth process. When this food supply runs out, the seed needs light to make its own food. Water is absorbed, and after a few days the latent plantlet splits the seed case and rapidly grows a root tip and a shoot tip. The shoot tip grows up toward the light (it is said to be phototropic), while the geotropic root tip grows into the soil to perform its function of anchorage, food storage, and absorption of water and nutrients.

The seed leaves are storage organs. Some, like oak, remain within the husk beneath the ground, and the first shoot grows out from a bud between them. With other trees, such as maple and all pines, the seed leaves are raised into the air on an expanding stalk while the husk that enclosed them falls away. At the tip of the shoot is the growing point (apical meristem).

Root tips also possess a growing point and develop short-lived root hairs. Via these, inorganic ions permeate freely through the cell walls and air spaces of outside root cells. Water enters by osmosis, the flow from a solution of low salt concentration (the ground water) to high salt concentration (the root hair cell). The water carries in solution salts and elements essential for life.

Within a few weeks the root system develops, either in the form of fibrous spreading roots growing near the surface, or taproots that can grow 20ft (6m) deep in mature trees. Fir, maple, and beech have fibrous roots, but pine, hickory, and oak have taproots.

ROOT SYSTEM *The root hairs absorb water and mineral salts; a cortex of large, thin-walled parenchyma cells surrounds the single layer of box-like endodermis cells, inside which is the pericycle, another single layer. This contains the two food systems: xylem carrying water and phloem carrying organic food. The pith is right in the center.*

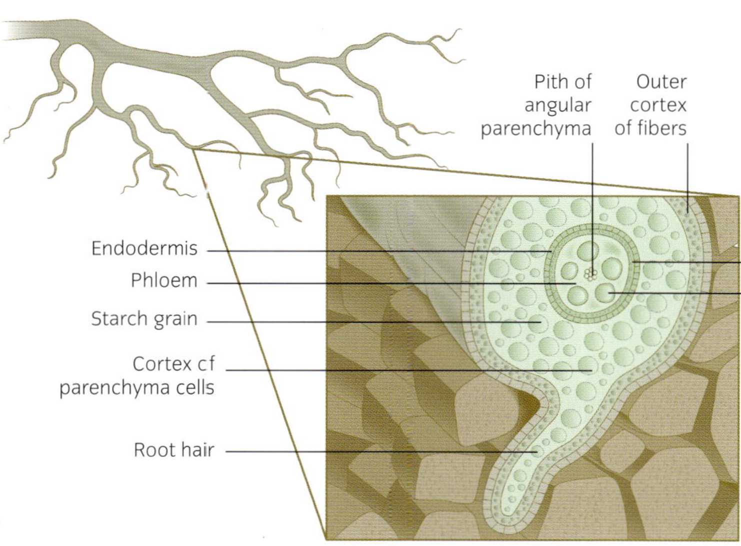

OAK TREE TAPROOTS *Trees such as the oak have taproots that can grow 20ft (6m) deep and amount to 10 percent of the tree' s mass.*

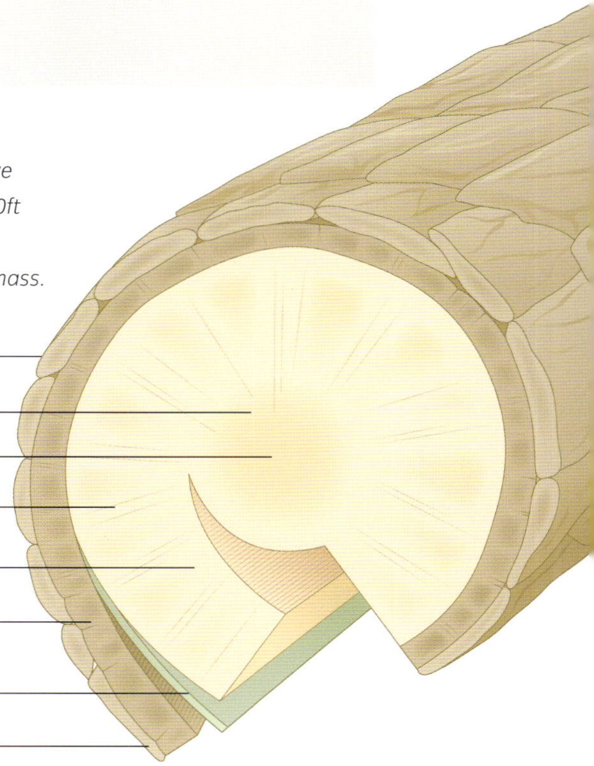

STEM STRUCTURE *The crucial single-cell layer of growth, the cambium; xylem (sapwood) is inside this, and phloem (inner bast and outer bark) outside it. Sapwood becomes hard, inert heartwood as growth develops. Vascular rays carry food from the center to the outside.*

Early development

During the first year of its life, the sapling develops a layer of internal generative cells called the vascular cambium, which forms a continuous sheath completely enclosing all living parts of the tree. This single, simple layer, one cell thick, is the crucial element in the tree's growth. During periods of activity the cambial cells cause the tree to increase in diameter; they multiply and divide into new cells, forming xylem on the inside of the sheath, or phloem on the outside, making a layer of bast.

Large volumes of air, consisting of nitrogen, oxygen, and a tiny fraction of carbon dioxide, are filtered into the organism through the leaves. Departing air carries with it large amounts of water. This constant evaporation, known as transpiration, is passed through perforations in the leaf surface called stomata. In a constant stream, lost water is replaced by more, carried from the roots via the xylem. On a summer's day, a large tree may take up 100 gallons of water from the roots, and lose 90 percent of that through the leaf stomata by evaporation.

In the leaf cells are particles called chloroplasts containing chlorophyll. The solar energy absorbed by the leaves activates this photosynthetic green pigment, which gives the leaves their color, to create carbohydrates from carbon dioxide and water. Oxygen is formed as a by-product. These combine with the water and mineral nutrients drawn up from the roots in the complex chemical process known as photosynthesis, which produces sucrose sugar, a soluble carbohydrate that can flow freely through the leaf veins. Thus the

WILLOW SAPLING *This young willow has new leaf buds and catkins developing along its stems.*

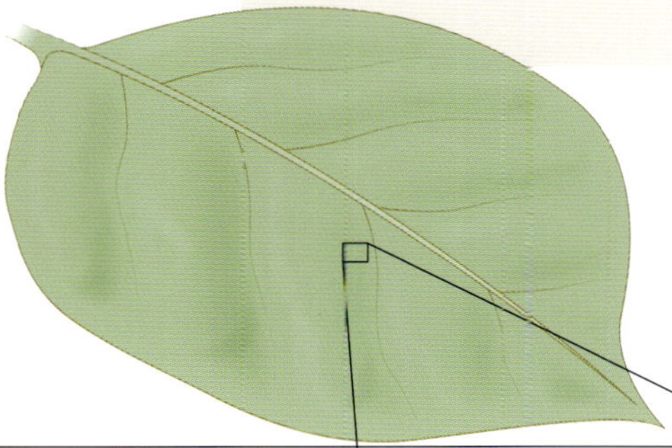

LEAF STRUCTURE *Both surfaces contain stomata—pores; epidermal guard cells control water flow. The spongy mesophyll lies beneath the vertical "palisade" of thin-walled parenchyma cells, which contain green chloroplasts for photosynthesis.*

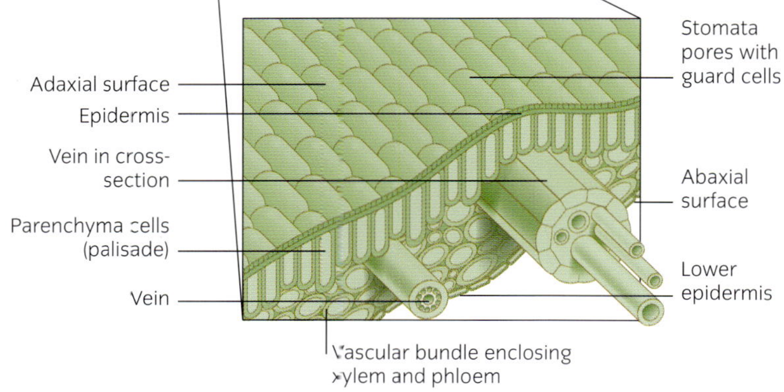

leaves feed vital energy back down to all parts of the growing tree to create new tissue.

The tree now has a two-way system. Dissolved mineral salts ascend from the roots through the xylem tissues of the sapwood, and the energy-giving sugar leaf sap travels down to the roots and throughout the tree in the outer phloem tissues, or bast. The resulting wood is a chemical compound of cellulose and lignin and various minerals that contribute to its density and hardness. The tree also develops a protective coating of cork cells called bark, which is waterproof so that the underlying tissues do not dry out. It has pores called lenticels to admit air and shield the nutritious bast beneath it from gnawing birds and beasts; it also acts as a barrier to fungal spores and as a buffer to temperature changes.

Growth rings

As the sap rises in the spring and ends in the fall in temperate climates, this interrupted growth cycle causes a distinctive wood layer to form that is called a growth ring. These are not annual rings by which to count the age of a tree, because cold winters or periodic droughts can interrupt the growth cycle. In the tropics the growth may be continuous, and the wood may appear not to have any growth rings at all.

Each growth ring has two distinct zones. Earlywood cells formed in the spring have thin walls and large cavities, while latewood cells formed in the summer have small cavities with thick walls. It is the contrast

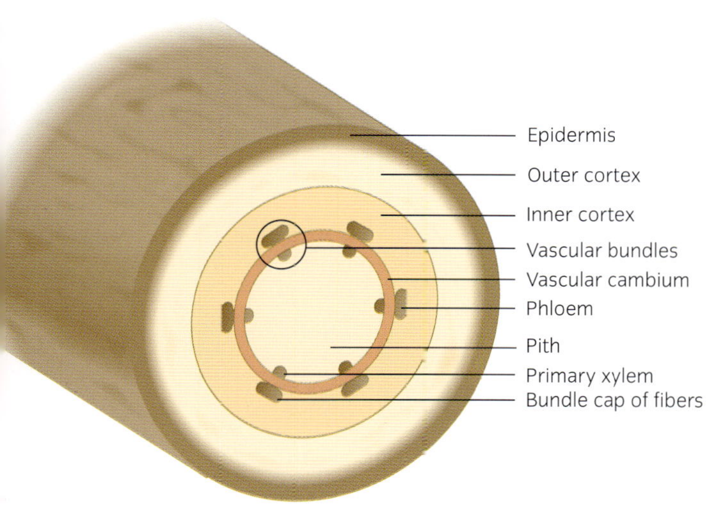

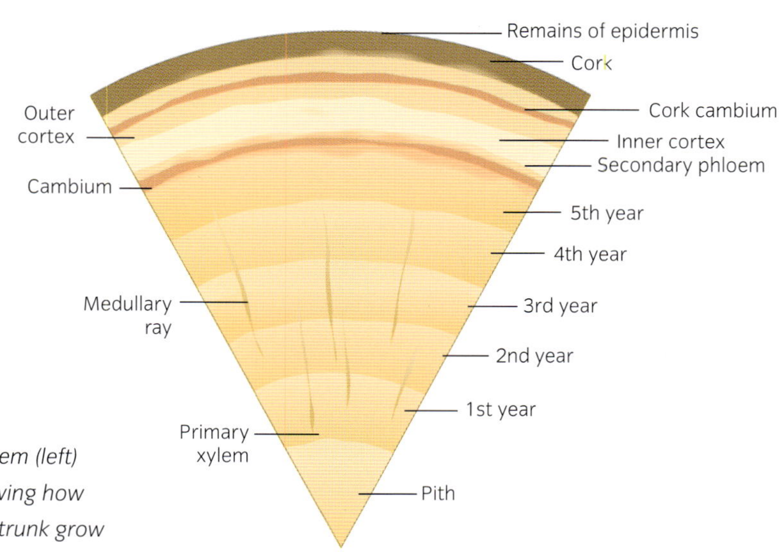

STEM GROWTH *A one-year-old stem (left) and a six-year-old stem (right), showing how the cambial cells make the stem or trunk grow in diameter each year.*

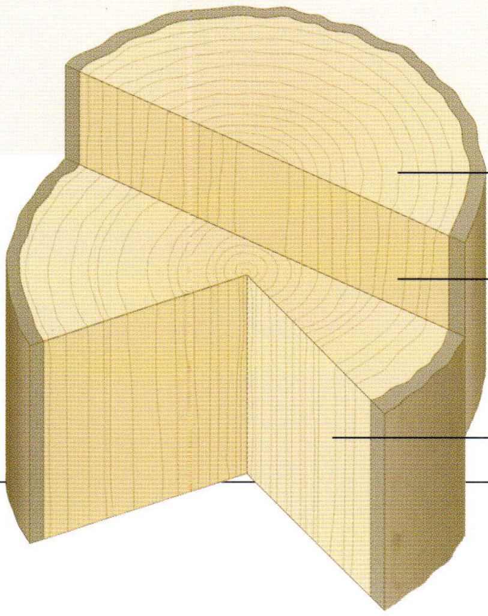

TYPES OF CUT *The trunk of a tree showing some of the ways in which it can be cut. A transverse section is a straight cross-section across the trunk; a tangential section gives an idea of vertical structures; and a radial section shows vascular rays to best advantage.*

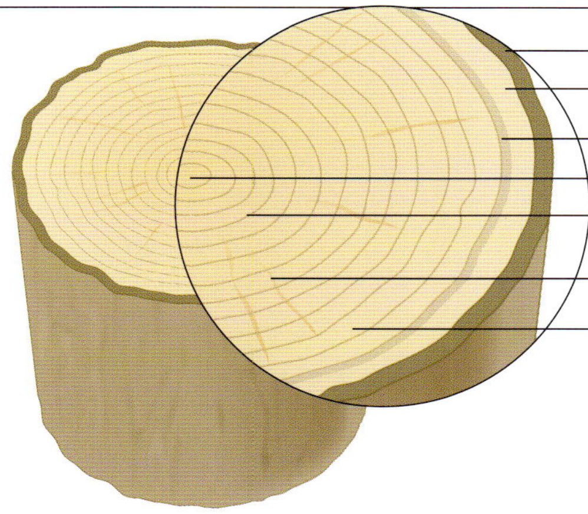

TRUNK STRUCTURE *A section of trunk showing cambium, pith, and rays. Poor conditions cause slow growth and close rings; faster growth can be detected because the rings are farther apart and the proportion of dense "summer wood" or latewood is smaller. Quick-grown timber is generally less structurally strong than slow-grown.*

between these two layers that enables us to identify the tree with the naked eye, when viewing the end section of a piece of timber. A color difference between earlywood and latewood can also be seen on the longitudinal or tangential surface in some woods.

The wood scientist studies the number of growth rings to the inch and the proportion of earlywood to latewood cells to determine the wood's strength, toughness, and durability. The width of the growth rings varies according to the moisture absorbed by the tree, and will show the annual variations in climate, and all the hardships such as forest fires or insect or fungal attack endured during the tree's lifetime.

Growth rings will also show the presence of "reaction wood," which forms with a special structure and chemical composition to help the tree overcome mechanical stresses—near the base of the trunk where the weight is carried, or if it is growing on a hillside, for example, the rings will be wider spaced on the uphill side, indicating an extra pull to make the tree grow upright; such "tension wood" occurs more usually in hardwoods. Softwoods exhibit an equivalent reaction, by producing "compression wood" with much tighter growth rings on the downhill side of the tree for a pushing effect. Strong branches, high winds, stones, or foreign objects that become included in the body of the tree all produce reaction wood; it is characteristically difficult to work, becoming unpredictable under the saw or blade because of the release of stresses, and showing disproportionate longitudinal shrinkage.

As the tree increases in diameter, the cambium layer just below the bast grows farther away from the inner sapwood cells, which become inactive, cease to conduct sap, and die. Only the parenchyma, the food storage cells, are left alive as the wood transforms into a darker color and becomes what is known as heartwood, which provides strength and support to the tree. It is far more valuable commercially than the weaker sapwood.

GROWTH RINGS *Each growth ring has two distinct zones: thin, light earlywood cells and dense, darker latewood cells.*

1.3 Cell Structure

All wood is formed of tube-like cells that differ in appearance according to their three main functions. Vessel cells carry the sap throughout the tree; supportive cells provide the tree's strength; and food storage cells appear in the form of soft tissues that comprise up to a fifth of the tree's total volume.

Sap transport and mechanical support

Viewed under a microscope, softwood cells appear to have a honeycomb structure. There is a special type of cell, the tracheid, that functions as both a vessel and a supportive cell. Tracheids are thin and blunt-tipped, with pitted side walls and large open cavities with rounded ends. They overlap each other so that the pits of adjoining tracheids connect, enabling the sap to flow between them. Earlywood tracheids are thinner walled, with larger internal cavities and more pitting for better sap conduction; latewood tracheids develop much thicker walls, with smaller pits in their sidewalls and very small cavities. Their function is to provide strength rather than sap transport. In all softwoods, sap conduction and mechanical support are performed by both earlywood and latewood tracheids that measure about ⅛in (3mm) long.

Hardwoods, in contrast, have two entirely different types of cell for sap carrying and mechanical support. The "vessel" cells have thin walls, are open-ended, and piled one on top of the other like short lengths of drainpipe. In cross-section, vessel cells are visible as pores that on endgrain

SOFTWOOD CELL STRUCTURE (CEDAR)

Thick-walled latewood tracheids give strength, while thin-walled earlywood tracheids are better for sap conduction. The fine medullary rays, for food storage, travel across the tracheids; the large opening is a resin duct.

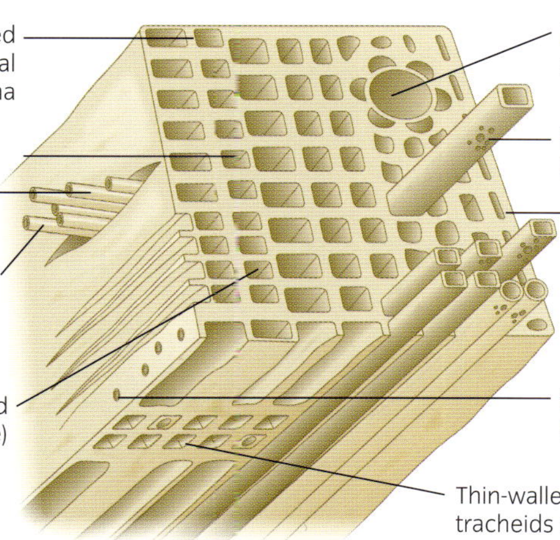

RING-POROUS WOOD CELL STRUCTURE (OAK)

There is a marked difference between the earlywood, with its large pores, and the small pores of latewood. Strength is gained from the large number of fiber cells in latewood; parenchyma tissue, laid in rays at right angles to the rings, holds food.

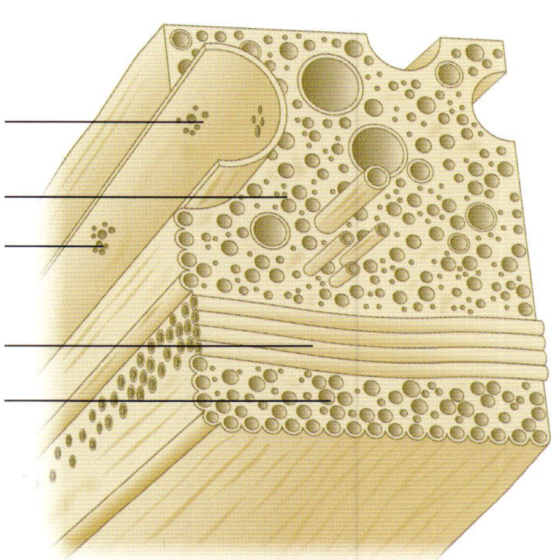

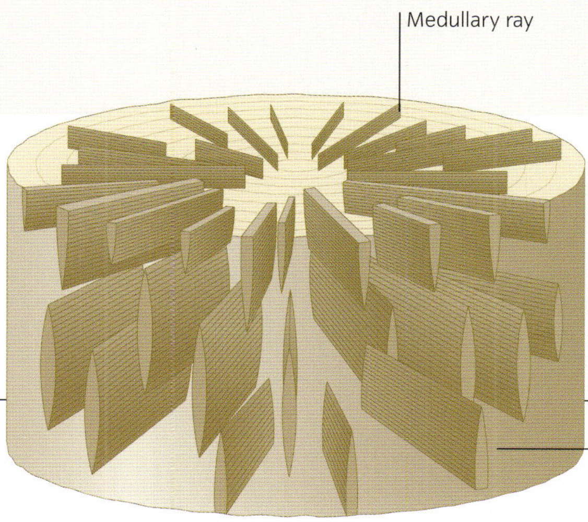

FOOD STORAGE SYSTEM *Medullary or vascular rays are collections of parenchyma, cells that store food, characteristically arranged radially across the vertical lie of fibers and vessels (pores).*

surfaces can be seen as very tiny holes. In fine-textured wood, pores can only be seen with a magnifying glass.

Where the earlywood pores are much larger than the latewood ones and form well-defined growth rings, the tree is known as "ring-porous"—for instance, ash or elm. When the pores are scattered across the growth ring with little difference between early and latewood pores, the wood is described as "diffuse-porous"; beech, birch, cherry, and willow are examples. Pore arrangements in hardwoods are described as "solitary" if they are isolated from each other; "clustered" if they are of a given number; or in "chains," in which case the direction of the chain is a diagnostic feature.

The mechanical support of hardwoods is performed by fibers that are long, narrow, minutely pitted, thick-walled cells, sharply tapered at each end. They make up the bulk of the woody tissue and are similar in structure to the latewood tracheids of softwoods, except that they are only about $\frac{1}{32}$in (1mm) long. The vessel cells of hardwoods do similar work to the earlywood tracheids of softwoods, and the hardwood fibers are the equivalent of the softwood latewood tracheids. The major difference between the woods is the complete absence of pores in softwood growth rings, and the presence of pores in hardwoods.

DIFFUSE-POROUS WOOD CELL STRUCTURE (BEECH) *There is little or no gradation in size between early and latewood pores or vessels, which are surrounded by fine strength-giving fibers. Storage tissue, which is not as pronounced as in ring-porous wood, lies in the form of rays across the pores and fibers.*

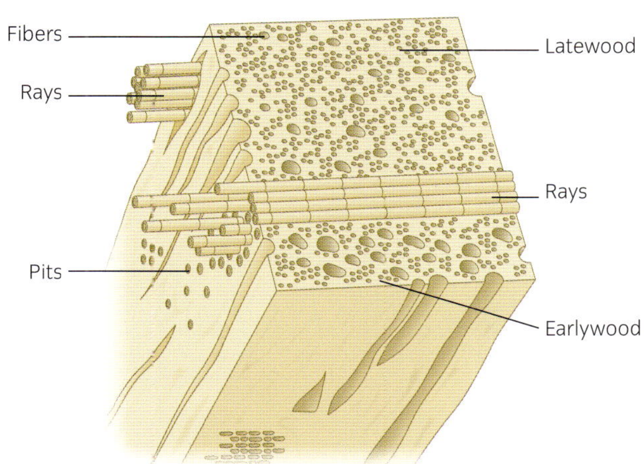

Food storage

This function in both softwoods and hardwoods is carried out by thin, brick-shaped cells of soft tissue called "parenchyma" that form into rays running radially to the tree's vertical axis, horizontally and at right angles to the growth rings. They originate at the cambium and run toward the pith at the center of the tree—the wood formed in its first year.

These rays vary from extremely fine to wide and broad. They might be of the same width, as in chestnut, or of two different widths, as in oak; they may combine to form an aggregate ray formation, as in alder. There are many different groups of parenchyma, and its absence or presence, its type, form, and distribution are valuable diagnostic features for wood identification.

Many softwoods, such as spruce, larch, Douglas fir, and pine, have resin ducts, surrounded by secretory parenchyma cells that exude resin into channels. Sometimes resin ducts are found in hardwoods such as meranti, seraya, and mahogany.

1.4 Grain and Figure

If you say a piece of wood has beautiful grain, you are more likely to be talking about the surface pattern. This is correctly known as the figure, and is produced by the wood's natural features and the way it has been cut. Grain, strictly speaking, refers to the lines visible on a cut board that show the intersection of the growth rings and the plane of the board itself.

Types of grain

The natural arrangement of the wood fibers in relation to the main axis of the tree produces eight types of grain. Straight grain is where the fibers run parallel to the vertical axis of the tree; irregular grain is caused where the fibers contort around knots, swollen buttresses, or crotches.

Cross grain occurs where the fibers are not parallel to the main axis of the tree, and wavy grain where the fibers form short waves in a regular pattern. Curly grain forms where these waves are in irregular sequence. Spiral grain develops when the fibers form a spiral around the circumference of the tree. Diagonal grain results from a flat cut board of spiral grain. Interlocked grain occurs when the fibers change direction at intervals from a right-handed spiral to a left-handed one and back again.

MASK AND BOWL *A mask carved from white pine and a bowl carved from apple wood.*

Types of figure

The pattern on the surface of wood—the figure—results from the interaction of combined natural features and the way the log is cut to achieve an effect. Natural features include the scarcity or frequency of growth rings; color and tonal variations between early and latewood cells; pigments and markings in the structure; contortions around knots and butts, and so on.

A fine striped figure can result on a radially cut board when there is a marked variation in density between early and latewood cells. Wavy-grained timber provides fiddleback figure or, when combined with spiral growth, a block-mottled figure as in avodiré.

Roe figure is obtained when both interlocked and wavy grain combine, as in afrormosia. Sometimes reverse spiral

TYPES OF GRAIN AND FIGURE *The many different grain and figure patterns of wood are exploited by woodworkers to add visual interest to their creations.*

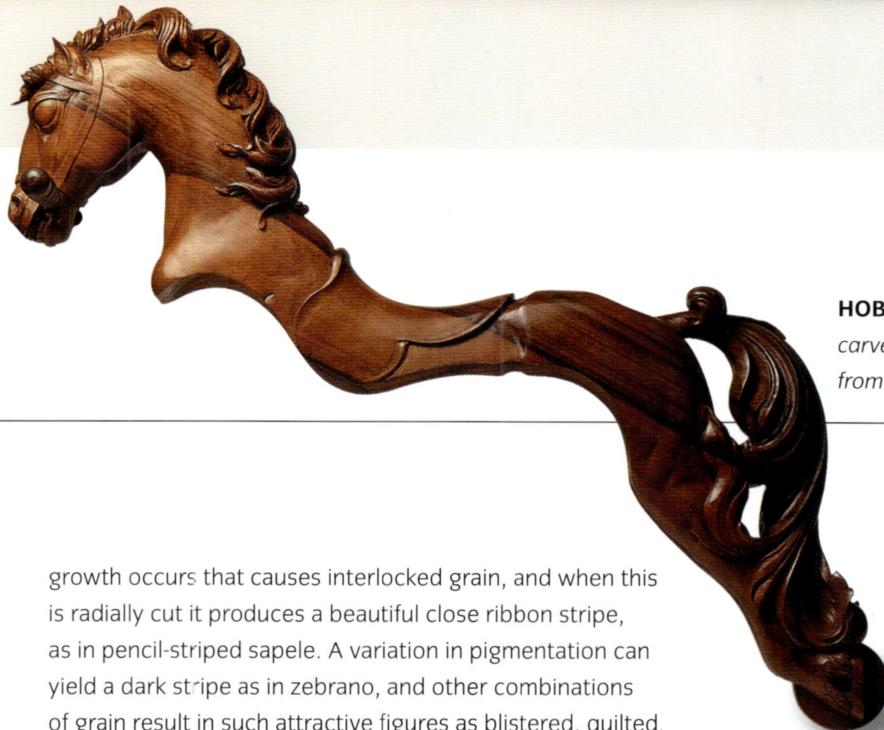

HOBBY HORSE *This decoratively carved child's toy was carved from American black walnut.*

WINDSOR CHAIR *The classic Windsor chair traditionally has a seat carved from elm with yew bentwork.*

growth occurs that causes interlocked grain, and when this is radially cut it produces a beautiful close ribbon stripe, as in pencil-striped sapele. A variation in pigmentation can yield a dark stripe as in zebrano, and other combinations of grain result in such attractive figures as blistered, quilted, plum pudding, pommelle, moiré, and snail quilt. Wood that is radially cut, the faces of the boards parallel with the rays, produces a strong or deep ray figure as in raindrop-figured oak, lacewood from the plane tree, lace-figured sycamore, and Australian silky oak.

Other distinctive features

There are several other features that affect both the appearance of wood and how it is used. Burls, or burrs, are wart-like growths that affect some trees. They give the appearance of tight clusters of dormant buds, each with a dark pith caused by stunted growth, that failed to develop into branches. For turners especially, burls are the most highly treasured of all woods.

Crotch, or curl, logs are cut from a point just above the root buttress, to a point below the first limb or fork of the tree. When this is cut through, it forms an attractive crotch or curl figure, sometimes called feather, that is elliptical in outline with a strong central plume.

The texture of wood is governed by the variation in size of the early and latewood cells. Diffuse-porous woods like boxwood, with narrow vessels and fine rays, are fine-textured; ring-porous woods like oak, with wide vessels and broad rays, are coarse-textured. Mahogany is medium-textured.

Luster is the ability of the wood cells to reflect light and is related to texture. Smooth, fine-textured woods are more lustrous than coarse-textured ones. Many woods, such as resinous pines, have a strong natural odor. Camphorwood is used to line the interior of clothes closets, and cigar-box cedar to make humidifiers.

2.1 WORLD FORESTS

The main types of forest are determined by climate, which means location in relation to the equator, and altitude. They are generally delineated in band zones, but of course there is great overlap: conifers, for instance, grow from just below the polar regions right into areas of Mediterranean climate.

Coniferous forests

Above a latitude of 60 degrees north, the great coniferous evergreen forests encircle the polar regions. Cone-bearing trees also grow in temperate zones. The southern pines of the United States survive the winter by restricting water loss through their exceptionally long and tough, narrow needle-shaped leaves with blue waxy surfaces. Conifers can withstand drought because they adjust to a climate where precipitation falls as snow and the ground water freezes for a great part of the year. The lack of water is just as severe as it would be in the drought conditions of a hot desert. Xerophytic or water-conserving conifers can grow in the frozen north, on limestone mountains, or in the Mediterranean. Douglas firs grow from Mexico to Alaska.

Hardwood and coniferous forests

Forests of mixed hardwood and coniferous trees occur in the northern temperate zone. Farther north, coniferous trees predominate and, conversely, there are more hardwood trees in southern areas.

Temperate hardwood forests

Broad-leaved forests stretch across the temperate zones of Europe, Asia, and America, broken only by the high mountain ranges or arid prairies. Oak, beech, ash, birch, and maple occur in the most northern regions.

Mediterranean forests

To the south of the temperate region, mixed forests of conifers and broad-leaved evergreen trees occur.

CONIFEROUS FORESTS

Great coniferous forests, or taiga, stretch from Siberia across northern Europe and Scandinavia, into Canada and Alaska, to within 2,000 miles (3,200km) of the North Pole.

HARDWOOD AND CONIFEROUS FORESTS

In mixed northern temperate forests, coniferous trees predominate in the colder northern areas, with more hardwoods growing in warmer southern climates.

KEY

- Coniferous forests
- Hardwood and coniferous forests
- Temperate hardwood forests
- Mediterranean forests

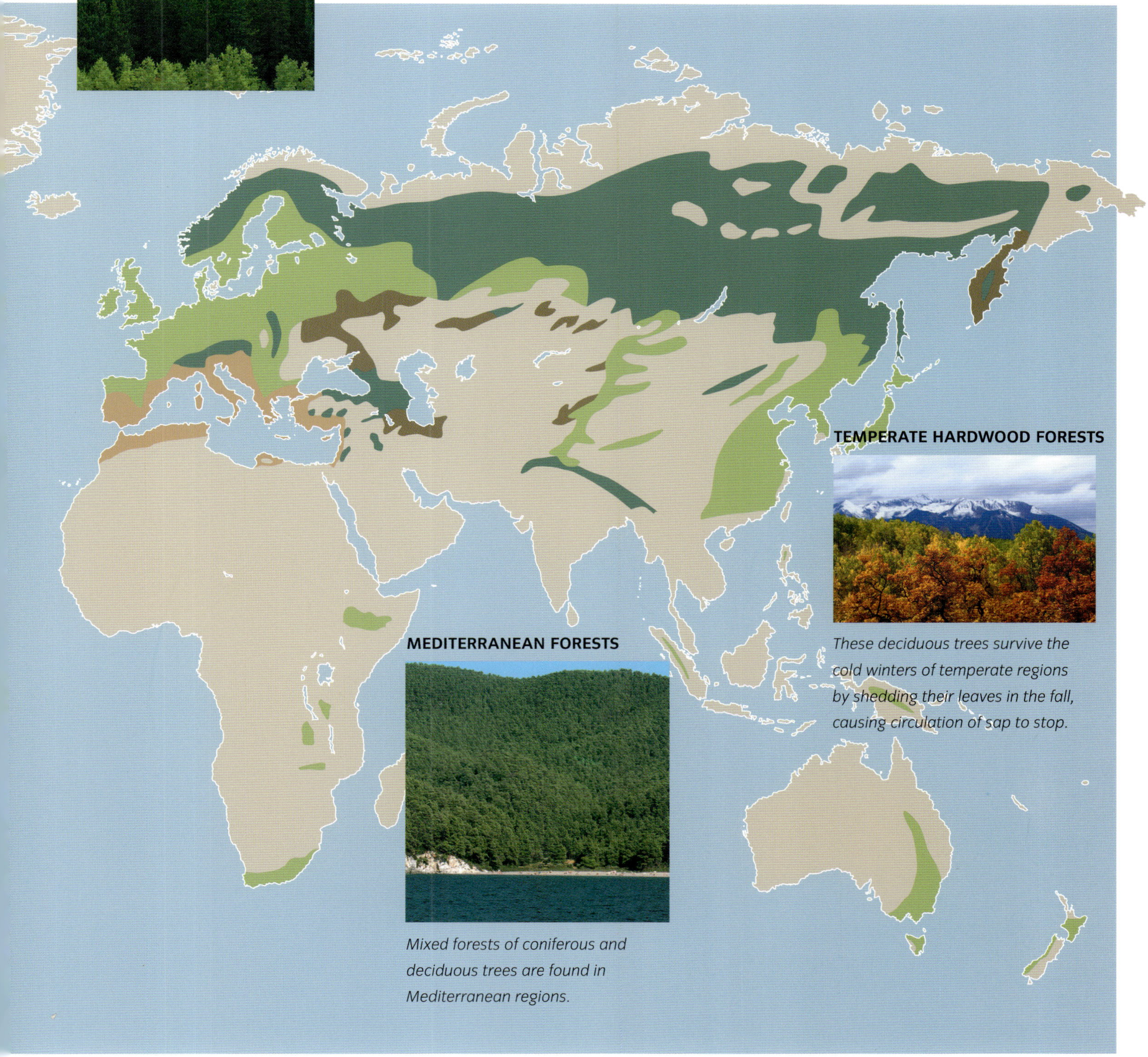

TEMPERATE HARDWOOD FORESTS

These deciduous trees survive the cold winters of temperate regions by shedding their leaves in the fall, causing circulation of sap to stop.

MEDITERRANEAN FORESTS

Mixed forests of coniferous and deciduous trees are found in Mediterranean regions.

Subtropical forests

Below the temperate zones are the subtropical forests of Europe, central and west Africa, India, Asia, South Africa, Central and South America, and southern and western Australia. Each has its own characteristic forest types, designed to resist summer drought rather than winter cold.

Savannah forests

Almost a third of the land surface of the world is arid, with high daytime temperatures and very cold night-time ones. Such deserts occur in Australia, India, southern Arabia, Africa, and in both North and South America. Not all deserts are flat; some are mountainous like the Painted Desert in the United States. Savannah-type forests occur in North America where there is heavy rainfall: on the open prairies of Canada east of the Rockies, and on the plains of the United States as far south as the Gulf of Mexico.

Tropical rainforests

In South America, west, central, and east Africa, and from India, Malaysia, and Indonesia throughout southeast Asia to Papua New Guinea, very high temperatures and high annual rainfall encourage a dense growth of lush forest in a wide belt around the equator. There is an extraordinary variety of trees, hundreds of different species per square mile. In tropical forests leaf fall and flowering and fruiting are not seasonal but continuous. These mature "high forests" are typical of tropical rainforests, where rainfall exceeds 60in (1,500mm) per year with no prolonged dry spells.

Montane forests

The band zoning of forest from the North to South Poles is paralleled by changes in altitude. One can travel from the hot desert scrub, too dry for tropical forest, up through broad-leaved trees to coniferous forest, up above the treeline, through alpine tundra into the snow. The treeline varies according to the annual rainfall, shelter, temperature, and soil conditions. Montane forests occur in Mexico, Peru, Chile, east Africa, China, Tibet, and western Australia.

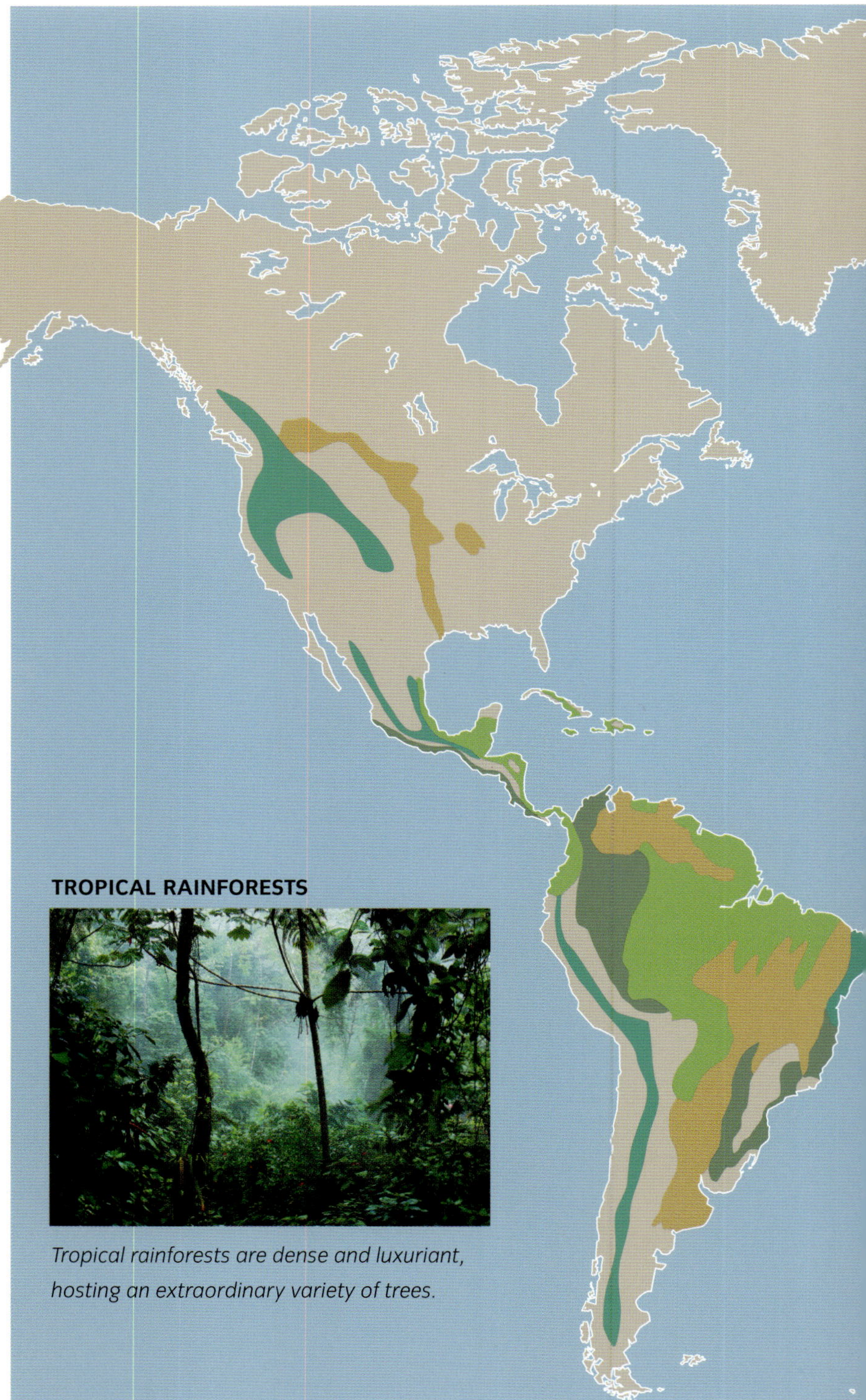

TROPICAL RAINFORESTS

Tropical rainforests are dense and luxuriant, hosting an extraordinary variety of trees.

SAVANNAH FORESTS

These forests occur throughout the world, from the prairies of North America to the deserts of Australia.

KEY

- Subtropical forests
- Savannah forests
- Tropical rainforests
- Montane forests

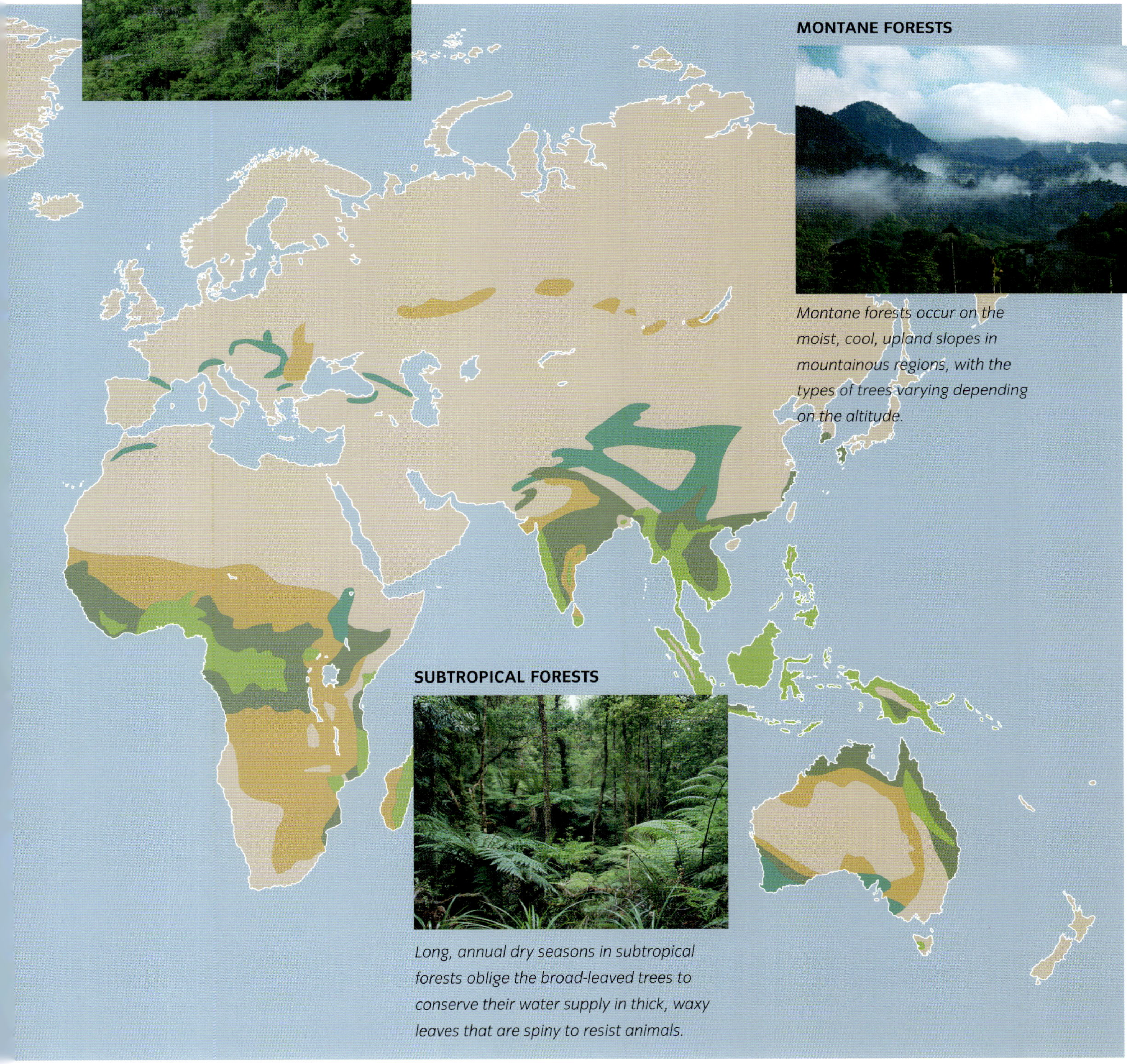

MONTANE FORESTS

Montane forests occur on the moist, cool, upland slopes in mountainous regions, with the types of trees varying depending on the altitude.

SUBTROPICAL FORESTS

Long, annual dry seasons in subtropical forests oblige the broad-leaved trees to conserve their water supply in thick, waxy leaves that are spiny to resist animals.

2.2 Environmental Issues

The world's tropical rainforests have existed in much the same form for millions of years, but researchers say that at least 50 percent have been lost in the past century. The ecological implications are dire. Rainforests are home to half our plant and animal species, and changing climate, soil erosion, and lost water resources will affect billions of people.

Destruction of the rainforests

Rainforests are extraordinarily diverse, and there may be over 200 species of tree in a single acre of ground. Madagascar alone supports 2,000 tree species; Canada and the continental United States together boast a total of 700 species, yet just ten 1-hectare plots of Borneo forest have yielded the same number. Rainforest has a fragile structure. The soils are poor, and all the contents of the forest depend on constant recycling of nutrients and a complex interdependence between species. While it can recover from selective culling of its "crops," too great a disturbance upsets the balance to a point where regeneration becomes impossible.

The effects of the loss of rainforest are already being felt, such as the greenhouse effect—the gradual warming of the atmosphere caused by a build-up of carbon monoxide, which traps the sun's heat. The vast forests become contributors to that build-up by burning, rather than playing their natural role of consuming the gas.

Sources of many useful products have also been found in the rainforest. In addition to timber, local communities harvest rattan, rubber, nuts, and fruits, while agriculturalists and scientists have developed chocolate, coffee, and medicinal drugs. Destruction removes the chances of discovering more of these important substances and destroys the habitat of many animal species as well.

Assessing the problem

Vast and remote areas, primitive conditions, difficult communications, and political problems all make it hard to compile accurate information on what is actually going on. In addition, much of the information available is filtered, interpreted, and presented with inbuilt bias. For example, a government recommendation to extract no more than 10 percent of the timber from the Amazon in order to allow for natural regeneration may appear sensible. Local companies claim that in any case it is not economic to take more than this because 90 percent of the trees are too small, too big, or the wrong species. However, heavy bulldozers and tractors need large areas for access, thereby increasing the amount removed for a given amount extracted. In addition, up to 50 percent of the forest can be damaged in the process of extracting 10 percent of the timber.

Although timber use is often identified as a main cause of deforestation, logging is in fact only one of the many

DEFORESTATION *The accelerating rate of disappearance of the world's forests is as fearful as the disappearance itself—it is a geometric progression, like the population growth that causes the main bulk of the destruction.*

ENDANGERED SPECIES *Animals such as the orangutan are under threat due to the destruction of their forest habitat.*

CASH CROPS *Crops such as coffee beans and coconuts can necessitate large areas of forest clearance.*

reasons for land clearance. Rapidly increasing populations, coupled with increasing awareness of the apparent advantages of a cash economy, put constant pressure on land. Agricultural needs for subsistence and the possibilities of cash crops such as coffee, cocoa, and palm oil mean that large areas of forest land are cleared, frequently by burning rather than using the timber.

Apart from the need for a source of timber, conserving the forest has many other useful functions ecologically and environmentally. Several disasters caused by large-scale flooding and drought in different parts of the world have been blamed on deforestation. The trees act as an environmental regulator, gradually absorbing and releasing moisture like a giant sponge. Remove the tree cover and violent storms flood an area, washing away the precious topsoil in one rapid and uncontrolled burst followed by periods of no water at all.

Then there is the downward spiral; wood is scarce, so animal dung and crop residue are burned, thus further reducing soil fertility. As one area of land becomes desert, so groups of people move on and clear others. In more developed areas, where land is scarcer, the infrastructure is there to distribute fertilizer to sustain the land artificially and to distribute the results in the form of crops, but impoverished areas do not have this option.

In underdeveloped countries, governments often trade natural resources with foreign investors in exchange for development of the infrastructure—roads, schools, health posts, and so on. Even the apparent benefits of this trade can have an adverse effect on the forest. For example, shifting cultivation is carried out by about 200 million people worldwide. In Papua New Guinea this is in the form of slash-and-burn on rotating small garden plots. These work well if 10- to 15-year fallow periods are left between uses, but now that larger numbers of people are moving closer together to be near services like medical aid posts, the fallow period is often reduced to around five years. This is not enough time for the soil to recover its fertility, so yields fall and more land must be cleared. Thus indirectly the provision of aid and services can cause a drop in nutritional standards and an increase in forest clearance.

FLOODING AND SOIL EROSION *Areas of deforestation are vulnerable to flooding that can cause devastating soil erosion, not only in the immediate area but for miles around.*

2.3 Conservation and Management

The key to preserving the rainforest is the possibility of sustainable timber yield through efficient, long-term forest management. Experiments have shown that it is possible to use the forest for the sustainable yield of timber and other products in perpetuity without disrupting its function as a natural ecological habitat and environmental protector.

Forest management

Management consists of a series of different techniques, including enrichment planting with indigenous species in degraded areas of natural forest, the planting of buffer zones of trees for local use around the forest, selective clearance to encourage particular locally suited species, and careful methods of felling to minimize soil erosion and damage to the canopy.

It is necessary to encourage such sustainable timber harvesting as an alternative to other cash crops and then to devise a system by which we can identify timber so produced. A decision to patronize only those producers acting responsibly would be an irrefutable economic argument in favor of conservation. However, this will mean an increase in the price of the raw material. For far too long timber has been a relatively cheap commodity. Its price should come to reflect not just the cost of extracting and transporting it now, but of replacing it for the future.

One of the crucial questions for impoverished third-world producer countries is whether their tropical forests can be sustainably managed and still give adequate revenue. Many countries have introduced regulations requiring the processing of timber locally, several banning the export of round logs altogether. Converting them into planks on the spot, or better still plywood that involves even more work and thus added value, means that the loggers (usually international companies) have to become processors as well. Investment like this involves a much greater financial stake in the country concerned, and in order to justify that there must be medium- to long-term future use of the equipment. This in turn leads to more careful use of the available forest since it must be made to yield indefinitely.

Planting and plantations

Total preservation of the rainforest is not practical where land is scarce, but utilizing rather than destroying it can contribute to conserving it. The answer lies in easing the economic pressures on its owners first—exploitation zones can help pay for reserves, and both will protect the environment.

In the past loggers ranged over wide areas to find particular trees, damaging many others in the process. Extracting only one product in this way is very wasteful.

RAINFOREST REGENERATION *Agro-forestry projects optimize the production of crops as well as the protection of the environment, and thus benefit the local economy.*

TREE PLANTING *Fast-growing species such as* Morus alba *provide a wide variety of benefits, from fruit and firewood to soil enrichment.*

PLANTATIONS *Young banana saplings (left) growing in a rainforest plantation project.*

By fully using one small area, taking all possible timbers and other products, the economic gain can be sufficient to leave the rest alone. Changing technology and research have resulted in more species becoming known, so smaller areas can be more intensively exploited.

Successful experiments with agro-forestry point out another hopeful direction. Here, tree planting is used in conjunction with other crops. Particular species have been developed that give a wide range of benefits to subsistence farmers. One type of rapidly growing tree—*Morus alba*—can give fruit, firewood, animal fodder, and building poles. Such species contribute to anti-erosion measures, shade crops, and can even enrich the soil. All this helps to relieve the pressure on the natural forest.

In many cases if the natural forest will not sustain the required timber output, then harvesting is combined with new plantations. Plantations are labor intensive in the early stages—rapid growth of the trees is matched by that of the weeds—and can look very untidy at the beginning, typical of what you imagine the worst clear-felled devastation would look like. However, this mess of hacked and burned stumps and crushed vegetation rots down rapidly and the nutrients are returned to the soil. Ash from burning provides additional nutrients, and large stumps protect seedlings from sunlight and anchor the soil.

In selective felling the devastation frequently looks much worse than it is. The same huge stumps and mangled crowns litter the ground, but later provide natural fertilizer. Controlled selective felling by humans copies the effects of natural tree fall that is common in the undisturbed forest. The trees have evolved to recover from damage from cyclones, floods, landslides, and fires. The structure of the forest is such that the saplings that have been waiting beneath shoot up after a mature tree has been removed, competing for the light flooding in through the hole in the canopy. This environment, and the trees' genetic composition, make them grow tall and straight in crowded conditions. These regeneration qualities are the basis on which sustainable yield policies are built, but they are only possible if the forest is not overexploited and the processes of nature can take their course.

FELLING *Areas of felling may look terrible, but the roots, trunks, and branches rot back into the soil, adding nutrients for future plantings.*

3.1 LOGGING AND EXTRACTION

From the huge coniferous forests of the Pacific northwest of the United States to the tropical rainforests of Papua New Guinea, there is a huge industry at work transforming the uncut tree into regular, regimented timber. Having been transported from the forest, the log is skillfully cut to maximize the yield of planks. The planks are then carefully dried.

Mechanization and efficiency

Mechanization and cost-efficiency are at a premium in commercial logging operations, and nowhere more so than in the Pacific northwest United States, where giant paper companies and sawmills can invest in the most advanced equipment. In these mountainous areas, self-powered mobile tower yarders, with telescopic steel poles from which lines to haul the felled trunks are rigged, have replaced the old spar tree system, in which a selected centrally located tree would be topped and trimmed, rigged with an elaborate system of lines and pulleys, and used as a point to which the logs were hauled. Smaller mobile yarders with a cranelike jib are also used for skylines—cables that float overhead and along which pulleys heave the trunks to be loaded onto trucks.

In tropical forests, too, especially in areas of comparatively high accessibility, cutting and extraction can be achieved with a degree of mechanization. In difficult terrain there is little or no alternative to the intensive use of human labor, although chainsaws replace the ax, and transporting the enormous trunks, here as everywhere, is a matter of controversial roadbuilding for the heavy trucks.

Although tropical hardwoods reach a high value by the time they arrive in the destination country, third-world economics entails comparatively small investment in logging operations unless foreign companies are involved, and even then the sophisticated equipment seen in the softwood forests of the northwest US has insignificant presence in Borneo or Papua New Guinea. Scandinavian softwood forests, on the other hand, are highly mechanized because of expensive labor; here, machinery fells the trees, trims them, debarks, and even crosscuts—bucks—them to length on site. Thus transport is made easier and cheaper.

Management and processing

For timber as well as pulp and paper production, softwood and even temperate hardwood forests in developed countries are sustainably managed to a degree only dreamed of in the tropics. Timber is not just logged but harvested; as many seedlings are planted as trees are felled each year; the forests are managed to a plan that ensures continuing production. In the plantations, such techniques as multiple cropping—planting agricultural crops to grow with the trees—or underplanting—where one species acts as a nurse to encourage growth of another—are brought into use to maximize profit.

MILLING *Processing timber as much as possible in the country of origin allows maximum profits to benefit the local economy.*

LOG PILE *Logs stripped of branches and piled together, ready for transportation.*

TRANSPORTATION *Felled logs being transported by river to a mill for additional processing.*

Pulp and paper mills, chipboard and plywood plants, and sawmills are often close to the forests themselves. For third-world tropical timber producers, it is of course sound economics to gain as much added value as possible for the indigenous crop before it leaves the country. This is why almost every timber-producing country in the world is now also a chipboard producer, because the technology and investment needed are both comparatively accessible.

Traditionally, major softwood exporters such as Canada and the Scandinavian countries have sawn their timber to size before it is shipped, and stamped the endgrain with shipping marks that show precisely where the wood came from; hardwoods have been chiefly exported in logs, but now, more and more tropical timber does not leave the producing country until it has been through the sawmill. It travels either in the form of boards—wide planks, 1 or 2in (25 or 50mm) thick, and usually waney-edged (that is, with the bark still on them)—or dimensional lumber—material that is left in greater thicknesses and lengths for constructional purposes. An average section of dimensional lumber might be 4 x 8in (100 x 200mm), and for a structural hardwood such as jarrah the length can reach 27ft (8m).

Temperate hardwoods do not come in such great heights as tropical species, and so board length will usually be less for, say, oak or ash than it will for ramin or mahogany. However, transport can be a limiting factor in tropical timber extraction, and despite the original tree growing to perhaps 200ft (60m), the logs might be disproportionately short by the time the timber is on the market. Tropical timbers tend to come in much wider boards, however.

LOGGING METHODS *Different methods of mechanization are employed to increase the cost-efficiency of logging, including chainsaws (far left) and telescopic pole and pulley systems for transporting felled logs in mountainous areas (left).*

3.2 Conversion and Grading

Conversion is the name given to the process of turning a log into usable form, either in the shape of dimensional lumber (material that is left in greater thicknesses and lengths for structural purposes) or sawn boards. As the wood is sawn it is graded to distinguish which pieces are suitable for which jobs, both in terms of appearance and strength.

The fine art of the sawyer

The way a tree is cut affects the way the wood absorbs and releases moisture, and shrinks and expands as it does so. Appearance, too, is a major consideration during conversion; the faces of a tangentially cut board look very different from those of one cut radially. The method of conversion also affects the wood's strength: it is crucial that constructional timber is not weakened by knots. The sawyer's skill lies in deciding how to get the best out of a log to achieve the optimum combination of strength, appearance, and stability.

There are many variations on the basic methods of log conversion, all of which come down to whether cuts are made radially or at a tangent to the log. The first—known in different forms as through and through, flat sawn, or slash sawn—produces the widest but least stable boards, some of which may be severely weakened by knots running from edge to edge. It is, however, the most economical conversion method. Refinements such as billet sawing or plain sawing attempt to limit the worst disadvantages of the tangential cut, perhaps by boxing out the unreliable heart, where rot, splits, and shakes are most likely to appear. Growth rings almost always meet the face of flat-sawn boards at less than a 45-degree angle, giving the boards a strong tendency to cup away from the center of the tree's original trunk. On the positive side, the figure on the face of softwood boards cut in this way will be strong and attractive.

Radial sawing, or quarter sawing, always makes cuts at maximum perpendicularity to the growth rings. It produces the most dimensionally stable boards, and is most often made use of in musical instrument soundboards, where stability, great strength, and clear tonal quality are needed from wide, thin pieces. It is, however, very uneconomical, and since the cuts all stop at the center of the trunk, it limits board width. Timbers with a pronounced medullary ray system, such as oak, benefit greatly in terms of appearance from quarter sawing.

CUTTING METHODS

Methods of conversion of the tree to timber, chosen to minimize distortion or knots, or to maximize appearance or board width.

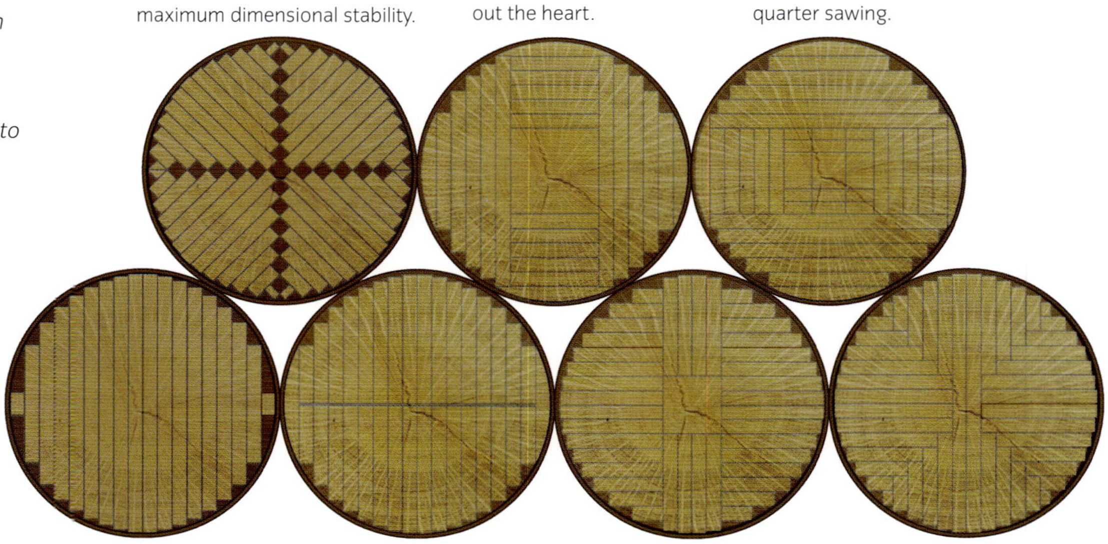

1 True radial cutting for maximum dimensional stability.

2 Plain sawing boxes out the heart.

3 More economic quarter sawing.

4 Through and through, or slash sawing.

5 Billet sawing.

6 Cutting for both board and structural lumber.

7 Cutting to maximize radial faces.

THE SAWMILL *Opening up a log with an industrial bandsaw to produce wide, knot-free, and "clear" boards (top). Some logs are cut to maximize the radial faces of the lumber (middle). It is the sawyer's skill to "read" the logs as they are being cut and make decisions on how best to cut the lumber on the basis of economy or appearance (bottom).*

MULTIPURPOSE CONVERSION *This log has been sawn for both board and dimensional lumber.*

Grading wood

Timber is destined for many different uses, some of which set appearance at a premium, like fine furniture making, and some of which place the most importance on strength. Deciding which wood should be used for what purpose is known as grading, the two types of which—visual quality and stress grading—make assessments on the basis of the two criteria.

Systems differ from country to country, but there are accepted standards that form the basis for a general understanding of what a batch of timber will be like. This holds more for softwood than hardwood.

Visual grading of a board or batch takes into account the number and direction of knots, the amount of wane—or unsquared tree-edge—the amount of surface splits and checks, and the grain direction. Knot area ratio is one of the standards applied to timber; in other words, the proportion of knot as a whole area against clear timber. A ratio of 1:6 for the face and 1:12 for the edge puts timber in the best grades, while a ratio of 1:3 on the face and 1:6 on the edge is low-grade.

Stress grading looks at bending strength and stiffness, measuring the force required to break a piece of horizontally held timber, and the force to deflect it by a certain amount. Timber so graded is marked so that specifiers and site staff can identify it immediately. This is normally done by machine, but there is also visual stress grading, which includes examination of the slope angles of the grain to face or edge. A grain slope angle of 1/10 or 1/12 signifies a top-grade wood, while an angle of 1/8 or 1/6 is low-grade.

GRADING MARKS *Cut lumber showing marks to identify the grade of the wood and other technical information.*

3.3 Seasoning and Preservatives

Timber absorbs and releases moisture from the surrounding air. Once the moisture content drops below about 30 percent, water begins leaving the cell walls, causing them to shrink. Seasoning is the process of drying wood ready for use. The life of timber can be extended by the use of preservatives to guard against stain, decay, mold growth, and insect attack.

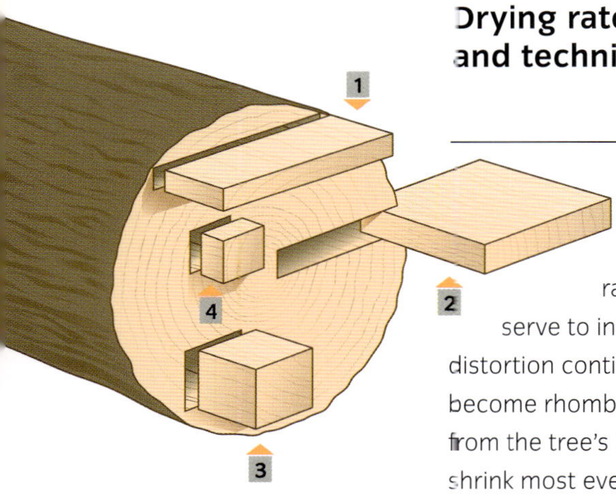

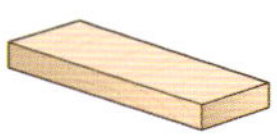
1 Wide boards shrink more in width than in length or thickness, and cup away from the tree's original heart.

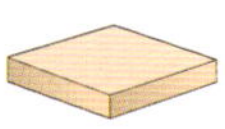
2 Growth rings at right angles to the surface cause minimum shrinkage and distortion.

3 Perpendicular rings give optimum dimensional stability.

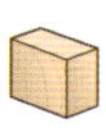
4 Square sections with growth rings running diagonally across them tend to go rhomboid.

Drying rates and techniques

Different woods dry at different rates, and there are differentials in drying rates and amounts within the wood itself; denser latewood with thicker cell walls shrinks proportionately more than thin-walled earlywood, for instance, and pronounced radial cell systems such as the rays in oak serve to inhibit radial shrinkage, while tangential distortion continues apace. A square section of timber will become rhomboid while drying, flat-sawn boards cup away from the tree's heart, and quarter-sawn boards (radially cut) shrink most evenly.

Such differentials cause enormous stresses inside the wood, and it is practically impossible to season a log in the round without at least a radial shake or split across the rings and along the grain. Ring or cup shakes, which follow the rings, and heart shake, which occurs in the center of the log, are also likely.

There are two methods of drying wood: air drying and kiln drying. Air drying is the traditional method of reducing the moisture content of freshly felled—or green—timber. It seeks to maximize the drying effect of wind, while reducing the effect of fog and wind-blown rain. Clearly, this is simpler in some climates than in others and, as a result, many countries in the northern hemisphere now use air drying mainly for predrying sawn timber before it is treated with

METHODS OF DRYING
Sawn timber being air dried (above) prior to preservative treatment. Stacks of timber in a large commercial kiln (left).

WOOD FINISHES *Wood can be treated with a clear preservative, as used on this garden bench, or with wood stains in a wide variety of colors.*

preservative and kilned, and for drying items such as fence posts where low moisture contents are not essential.

While most kiln drying of timber is carried out in bulk by professional timber dryers, since the method involves the use of expensive and sophisticated equipment, there are smaller workshop-sized methods that involve temperature-controlled dehumidification. The timber is stacked, each layer separated by smaller pieces of dry, clean softwood placed at regular intervals to support the timber and help prevent distortion. This is known as sticking and enables air to flow all around the timber. The stacks are then placed in the kilns, which are sealed units within which both temperature and humidity levels can be controlled.

Preservatives and finishes

Before deciding to use preservative treatment, the natural resistance of the timber species to decay and insect attack should be considered. A timber that is naturally durable can, without preservative treatment, give an effective service life of anything between a few years and infinity, depending on the degree of exposure. Regardless of how durable the heartwood is, however, the sapwood of any species is low in natural durability. Even a naturally durable species of timber will require preservative treatment if it has substantial amounts of sapwood. Another consideration is how long the component must last. Wood does not decay immediately, even when it is in contact with the ground. If only a limited life is required, and the component is considered expendable, treatment may be unnecessary.

The three main types of preservative in common use today are tar oils, water-borne preservatives, and solvent-borne preservatives.

Traditional creosote belongs to the first group; used mainly on fences and outbuildings, it gives excellent durability but has environmental disadvantages. Its oily nature also slows down weathering. Most water-borne preservatives are applied by vacuum/pressure impregnation. This fixes the most common copper-chrome-arsenic (CCA) types as insoluble in the timber, giving high levels of protection. Some softwoods take on a greenish color after treatment, although this tones down with weathering. No maintenance is required, but timber treated in this way will tend to become gray after prolonged exposure to the elements.

Organic solvent-borne preservatives can be applied by double-vacuum, by vacuum-pressure impregnation, or by dip. Brushing provides only minimal protection. It is generally preferable to cover them with some sort of finish—a wood stain, paint, or varnish—and this is essential if they are to perform well in exterior situations. The development of microporous or breather paints, stains, and varnishes has given such finishes a protective dimension they did not have before; instead of cracking and peeling, they allow moisture in the wood to evaporate, but do not allow the passage of free water. Moisture can leave the timber but not enter it, so the risk of paint failure and decay is dramatically reduced.

PRESERVATIVE PRODUCTS *Modern preservatives and finishes allow moisture to evaporate from the timber but not enter it.*

3.4 Veneers and Manufactured Boards

Veneering—the use of a thin layer of fine wood applied over a base of more common wood—is a method of maximizing the use of rare, exotic, and expensive timber. Modern technological processes have also turned wood waste into an enormous variety of panel products, the three major categories being plywood, particleboard, and fiber building board.

Veneers

Until comparatively recently, saw-cutting was the only method of producing veneers, which would usually be as thick as $\frac{1}{8}$ in (3mm). With sophisticated modern production methods, thickness can be brought down to as little as $\frac{1}{32}$ in (1mm), which obviously achieves great efficiency in terms of area covered.

Veneers also have a conservation side-effect in that timber species under threat of extinction can be made to last far longer. For the exporting country, veneer production means work for local labor, added value, and a higher return on an indigenous resource. For the individual furniture maker, the relative cheapness of the material makes it attractive, an advantage with especially exotic timbers.

VENEERS *Thin slices of wood veneer (far left) maximize the use of decorative timbers to make a wide range of crafted objects, such as box (above).*

Constructional veneers go into the production of plywood, blockboard, and other laminated timber products, but appearance is not the main criterion in such uses, and manufactured boards do not depend on valuable woods, other than visual selection for the facing plys, which are better quality than the internal ones. There is, however, a high demand for pre-veneered plys and blockboards that are faced with high-value and exotic timbers. Used in furniture and paneling, they combine the advantages of beautiful hardwoods with the structural stability and comparative cheapness of sheet material.

The wonderful figuring of truly decorative veneers is a quality for which the best logs of a batch are often earmarked. Other characteristics that would be considered defects in a log for conversion into timber can make a veneer yet more highly prized; color variation, growth irregularities, even diseases, can be turned to advantage.

PLYWOOD TABLE *This plywood table top has been finished with a veneer of teakwood to give an attractive result at a fraction of the cost of a solid teak top.*

Plywood

The practice of cross-laminating veneers for special uses can be traced back to the pre-Christian Egyptian empire, when crude forms of plywood were bonded with natural adhesives such as animal glue and blood albumen. Plywood was developed to provide panels with dimensional stability and good strength properties both along and across the sheet. Made up of successive veneers glued and assembled at right angles to one another, plywood is a comparatively light, strong sheet material, whose size and thickness can be varied easily during manufacture. It combines an attractive surface appearance with excellent performance under strenuous conditions such as marine applications and building construction.

CHIPBOARD *This variety is made from laminated planer shavings, making a light and relatively inexpensive board with an unusual finish.*

Particleboards

Wood chipboard was developed during World War II, with the advent of thermosetting adhesives. Its manufacture uses wood residues such as forest thinnings, planer shavings, and other joinery chip residues. The product is not as demanding as plywood in terms of raw materials and skilled labor, and wood chipboard mills are now found in most countries.

Particleboards like wood chipboard are made from small particles of wood, mixed with adhesives, and formed into a mat. They come in 1/8–2in (3–50mm) thicknesses, and vary in quality; they can be of uniform construction through their thickness, of graded density, or of distinct three- or five-layer construction, to give enhanced properties without excessive weight. The differences in constructional quality allow chipboard to be used in various situations, from furniture to flooring, and some boards are designed to give a certain amount of moisture resistance. Generally, chipboard has a sponge-like reputation when it comes to water contact.

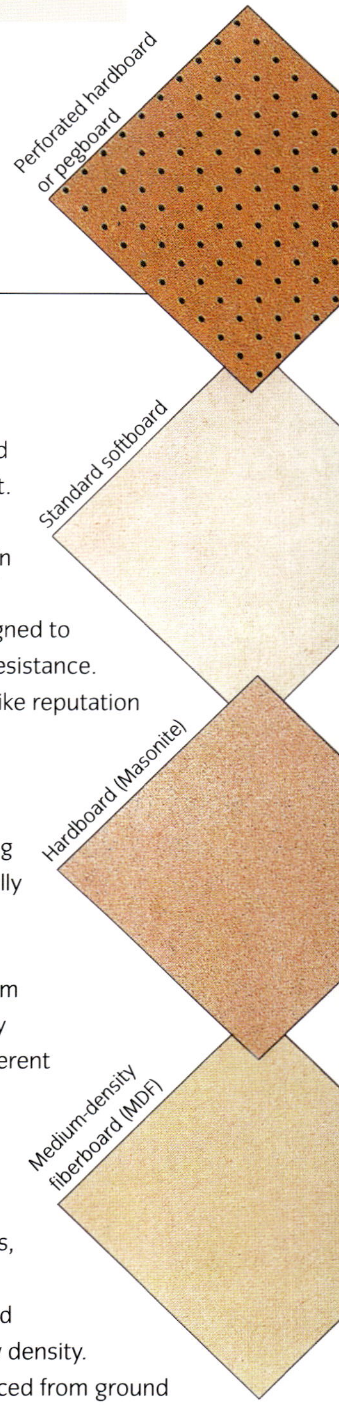

Fiber building boards

Fiber building boards usually exceed 1/16in (1.5mm) in thickness, and are manufactured from ligno-cellulosic material. The primary bond is usually derived from the inherent adhesive properties of the material, when the fibers are formed into a mat under pressure—a process known as felting.

The earliest fiber building boards, produced in the late 19th century, contained large amounts of repulped newsprint and were of relatively low density. Later, insulating boards were produced from ground wood pulp. During the 1920s and early 1930s, techniques were developed to break solid wood down into fibers and reconstitute them under heat and pressure as a strong and durable panel—hardboard or Masonite. Medium-density fiberboard (MDF) is a furniture-grade board with superior characteristics in terms of surface texture, smoothness, and machinability. Fiber building boards are used in a very wide range of applications, from pinboards, sheathing panels, and insulating boards through to high-class joinery and shopfitting.

From the many different species of trees comes a huge variety of timbers for numerous different purposes—delicate turnery wood to timber for railway sleepers. This chapter describes in detail 150 of the world's top commercial timbers, together with an illustration showing each wood's typical grain. Where it grows, its special properties, its resistance to insect attack, and its commercial and creative uses are also covered.

THE **DIRECTORY** OF **WOOD**

CONTENTS

HOW WOODS ARE NAMED

Names in common usage are often misleading because they allude to some prominent characteristic of the tree. For example, a very heavy tree may be called "ironwood," but there are more than 80 species, of completely different families, all known as ironwood. Hornbeam is one example.

Sometimes the common name of a tree is quite simply untrue. Black Italian poplar is not black but white, nor is it Italian—it grows in Britain. Indian silver graywood likewise is not from India, nor is it silver or gray.

Vernacular names are those by which the wood is known in its country of origin, and are naturally in the same language. Trade names are sometimes given to a wood by traders who seek to glamorize an otherwise ordinary species such as ayan by calling it Nigerian satinwood; another example is afara, which is sold as korina in the US.

There is also a remarkable difference in the naming of woods between nations in the English-speaking world. In Australia, for example, oak, ash, and elm are entirely different species from those recognized in Europe and the United States. For instance, Australian silky oak (*Cardwellia sublimis*) is not a true oak and is known as lacewood in the US and UK. Another example of differences in nomenclature is *Acer pseudoplatanus*, which known as maple in the US but sycamore in the UK.

112 *Heritiera spp.* MENGKULANG
113 *Hymenaea courbaril* COURBARIL
114 *Ilex spp.* HOLLY
115 *Juglans nigra* BLACK WALNUT
116 *Juglans regia* EUROPEAN WALNUT
117 *Kalopanax pictus* SEN
118 *Khaya spp.* AFRICAN MAHOGANY
119 *Knightia excelsa* REWAREWA
120 *Laburnum anagyroides* LABURNUM
121 *Larix spp.* LARCH
122 *Laurelia sempervirens* CHILEAN LAUREL
123 *Liriodendron tulipifera* AMERICAN WHITEWOOD
124 *Lovoa trichilioides* AFRICAN WALNUT
125 *Machaerium villosum* JACARANDA PARDO
126 *Magnolia grandiflora* MAGNOLIA
127 *Mansonia altissima* MANSONIA
128 *Metopium brownii* CHECHEN
129 *Microberlinia brazzavillensis* ZEBRANO
130 *Millettia laurentii* WENGE
131 *Mitragyna ciliata* ABURA
132 *Myroxylon balsamum* BALSAMO
133 *Nesogordonia papaverifera* DANTA
134 *Nothofagus cunninghamii* TASMANIAN MYRTLE
135 *Nothofagus spp.* NEW ZEALAND BEECH
136 *Ochroma pyramidale* BALSA
137 *Ocotea bullata* STINKWOOD
138 *Ocotea rodiaei* GREENHEART
139 *Olea spp.* OLIVEWOOD
140 *Paratecoma peroba* WHITE PEROBA
141 *Peltogyne spp.* PURPLEHEART
142 *Pericopsis elata* AFRORMOSIA
143 *Phoebe porosa* IMBUIA
144 *Picea abies* EUROPEAN SPRUCE/WHITEWOOD
145 *Pinus monticola* WESTERN WHITE PINE
146 *Pinus ponderosa* PONDEROSA PINE
147 *Pinus spp.* AMERICAN PITCH PINE
148 *Pinus strobus* YELLOW PINE
149 *Pinus sylvestris* REDWOOD/SCOTS PINE
150 *Piratinera guianensis* SNAKEWOOD
151 *Platanus hybrida* EUROPEAN PLANE
152 *Podocarpus spp.* PODO
153 *Podocarpus totara* TOTARA
154 *Populus spp.* POPLAR
155 *Populus tremuloides* CANADIAN ASPEN
156 *Prunus spp.* CHERRY
157 *Pseudotsuga menziesii* DOUGLAS FIR
158 *Pterocarpus angolensis* MUNINGA
159 *Pterocarpus dalbergoides* ANDAMAN PADAUK
160 *Pterocarpus indicus* NARRA
161 *Pterocarpus soyauxii* AFRICAN PADAUK
162 *Pterygota spp.* AFRICAN PTERYGOTA
163 *Pyrus communis* PEAR
164 *Quercus alba* AMERICAN WHITE OAK
165 *Quercus rubra* AMERICAN RED OAK
166 *Quercus spp.* EUROPEAN WHITE OAK
167 *Salix spp.* WILLOW
168 *Sequoia sempervirens* SEQUOIA
169 *Shorea spp.* RED MERANTI/SERAYA/LAUAN
170 *Shorea spp.* WHITE/YELLOW MERANTI/SERAYA
171 *Swietenia spp.* AMERICAN MAHOGANY
172 *Tabebuia spp.* IPE
173 *Taxus baccata* YEW
174 *Tectona grandis* TEAK
175 *Terminalia bialata* INDIAN SILVER GRAYWOOD
176 *Terminalia ivorensis* IDIGBO
177 *Terminalia spp.* INDIAN LAUREL
178 *Terminalia superba* AFARA/LIMBA
179 *Tetraclinis articulata* THUYA BURL
180 *Thuya plicata* WESTERN RED CEDAR
181 *Tieghemella heckelii* MAKORE
182 *Tilia spp.* LIME/BASSWOOD
183 *Triplochiton scleroxylon* OBECHE
184 *Tsuga heterophylla* WESTERN HEMLOCK
185 *Turreanthus africanus* AVODIRE
186 *Ulmus spp.* AMERICAN ELM
187 *Ulmus spp.* EUROPEAN ELM

The International Code of Botanical Nomenclature is the standarized code of Latin names to enable people who work, study, or play with wood in all parts of the world, whatever their native tongue, to identify a species correctly.

The first name is assigned to a genus and the second to a specific epithet to indicate the particular species within the genus. Thus we can see, for example, that parana pine (*Araucaria angustifolia*) is not a pine at all; it belongs neither to the *Pinus* genus, nor even to the family (*Pinaceae*).

Botanically, every tree has a classification from which the generic and specific names are taken, as in the following example of American black walnut:

Kingdom	*Vegetable*
Division	*Angiospermae*
Class	*Dicotyledoneae*
Order	*Juglandales*
Family	*Juglandaceae*
Genus	*Juglans*
Species	*Nigra*

In the following directory, we have provided the family, genus, and species names of each of the 150 woods for positive identification, plus the most well-known common names.

***Abies* spp.** | Family: *Pinaceae* | **SILVER FIR/WHITEWOOD** | Softwood

Growth

Only *Abies* spp. produces true fir trees. *A.lasiocarpa* provides alpine fir and grows to 130ft (40m). *A.procera* produces noble fir and can reach up to 230ft (70m). *A.alba*, the common silver fir, grows in the range of 125–150ft (38–45m). *A.grandis*, a closely related species, has topped 185ft (56m) and is the tallest tree in the UK. The silver fir is included with hemlock in supplies from western Canada, and with European spruce in shipments of whitewood from central and southern Europe. It is known by the trade name of European silver pine, as white deal in the UK, and as Baltic fir, Finnish fir, and so on, according to its port of shipment.

Appearance

The color varies from creamy white to pale yellow-brown, closely resembling European spruce (*Picea abies*), but is slightly less lustrous. The timber is straight grained with a fine texture.

Properties

Silver fir is slightly resinous, and weighs 30lb/ft^3 (480kg/m^3) when dry. It should be kiln dried for best results. It will air dry very rapidly with little tendency to warp, but may split or check, and knots may loosen and split. There is medium movement in service. Silver fir has low stiffness and resistance to shock loads, with medium bending and crushing strengths, but a very poor steam-bending classification. Fir works well with both hand and machine tools, and has little dulling effect on cutters if they are kept reasonably sharp. It nails satisfactorily, can be glued without difficulty, and can be brought to a smooth finish; it takes stain, paint, and varnish well. There is often damage by pinhole borer, longhorn and *Buprestid* beetles, and sometimes by *Sirex*. The wood is nondurable and moderately resistant to preservative treatment, but the sapwood is permeable.

Uses

Fir is excellent for building work, carcassing, interior construction, carpentry, boxes, pallets, and crates. Small trees are used in the round for scaffolding, poles, and masts; it is used in conjunction with *Pinus sylvestris* for plywood manufacture.

Where it grows

Fir is distributed widely across the world. Silver fir grows extensively in the UK and mid-Europe, from Corsica and the Balkans through Poland to the Carpathian Mountains and western Russia. Alpine fir occurs from Alaska to New Mexico, while noble fir grows in the western US.

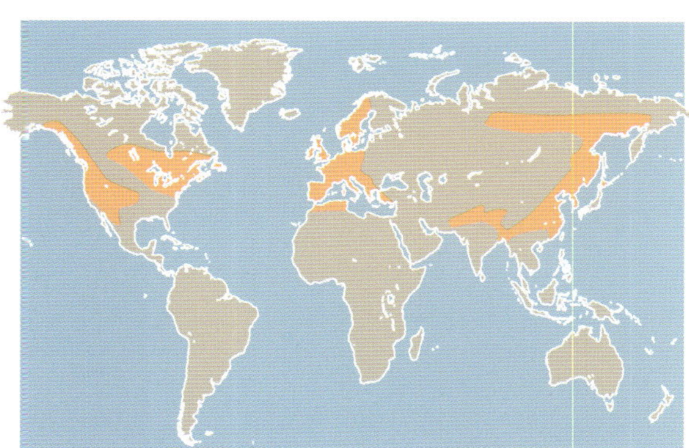

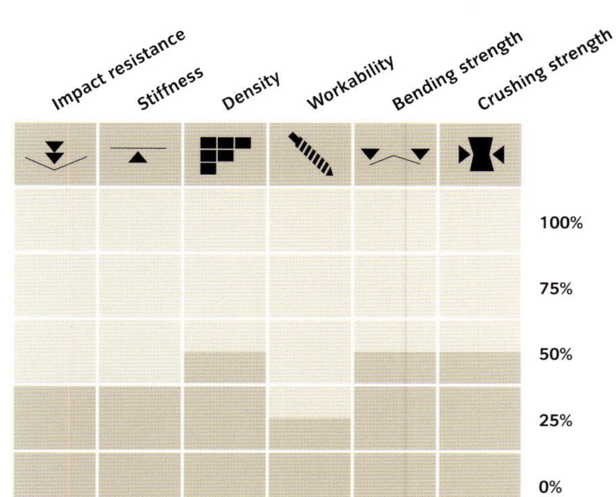

AT A GLANCE

Impact resistance is a measure of the wood's toughness. It describes its resistance to suddenly applied shock loads.

Stiffness is a measure of the wood's elasticity. It is considered in conjunction with bending strength.

Density is measured as specific gravity, the ratio of the density of a substance to that of water.

Acacia koa | Family: *Leguminosae* | **KOA** | Hardwood

Growth

Koa adapts to it surroundings, and is able ito grow high up in the mountains or lower down the slopes. However, the most successful trees tend to be found higher up, where there is more rain and where they can reach around 85ft (25m) in height, with a diameter up to 4ft (1.2m). It is higher up in the hills that the top-quality construction lumber is produced.

Appearance

Light brown to reddish brown in color, *Acacia koa* is distinguished by its golden luster and has a fine texture with a wavy grain. Not surprisingly, it is sometimes referred to as Hawaiian mahogany, because it shares some of the characteristics of true mahogany (*Swietenia macrophylla*). Growth rings reveal themselves as darker lines, and there can be some fiddleback figure.

Properties

Koa is heavy, weighing 42lb/ft^3 (670kg/m^3), and reasonably dense. It is hard and tough, and working across the end grain of the wood can be difficult. Although koa is far from the best timber to be found in the Hawaiian islands, it is still counted as valuable. Koa seasons well and is stable once dry. It is relatively easy to work by hand or machine, and finishes superbly to a good luster. It is durable to damp and insects.

Uses

Traditionally, koa is used in the production of Hawaiian ukeleles because it is resonant and looks attractive. In addition to this, it is employed in a range of professions, from furniture making and joinery to turning and carving.

Where it grows

Koa is a native of the Hawaiian islands.

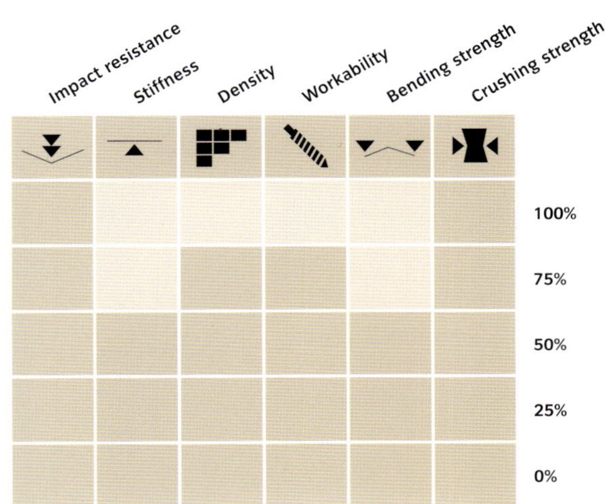

Workability describes how easy a wood is to work and whether it has a significant blunting effect on tools.

Bending strength is also known as maximum bending strength. Pressure is applied to each end of a board until it cracks.

Crushing strength is the ability of wood to withstand loads applied to the end grain, a critical test for wood used as short columns or props.

Acacia melanoxylon	Family: *Leguminosae*	**AUSTRALIAN BLACKWOOD**	Hardwood

Growth

Acacia melanoxylon is the most attractive of hundreds of species of wattle. It is one of the largest of the wattles, reaching a height of 85–100ft (25–30m); the diameter of the bole, which is known as black wattle, is about 3ft (1m).

Appearance

The sapwood of Australian blackwood is straw colored. The heartwood timber is not black, despite its name, but reddish brown to almost black, with attractive bands of golden to dark brown with a reddish tint. Regular dark brown zones mark the growth rings. It is usually straight grained, but with a handsome fiddleback figure when the grain is interlocked or wavy. It is medium and even textured with a lustrous appearance.

Properties

Blackwood weighs about 41lb/ft^3 (660kg/m^3) when seasoned. It is a fairly heavy, dense timber with medium bending strength and stiffness, and a high crushing strength. It has good resistance to impact loads and a very good steam-bending classification. The wood dries fairly easily and is stable in service. It works satisfactorily with both hand and power tools, and offers only a moderate blunting effect on cutting edges. The grain tends to pick up when planing or molding interlocked or wavy grain on quartered stock, and a reduction of the cutting angle is recommended. Wattle can be nailed and screwed satisfactorily, and takes stain and polish for an excellent finish. The heartwood is durable, but liable to attack by the common furniture beetle and termites, while the sapwood is liable to attack by powder post beetle. It is extremely resistant to preservative treatment.

Uses

This is a highly decorative timber, in great demand for top-quality furniture, cabinets, and paneling. It is also used for shop, office, and bank fitting as well as interior joinery. Billiard tables, tool handles, and gunstocks are made of wattle; ornamental turnery, bentwork for cooperage, coach, and boat building, and wood-block flooring are other applications. Selected logs are sliced to make beautiful decorative veneers for use in plywood faces and flush doors, cabinets, and architectural paneling.

Where it grows

Australian blackwood grows as an understory tree in forests of giant mountain ash in New South Wales, Queensland, southeast Australia, and Victoria, and is also found in Tasmania, India, South Africa, and South America.

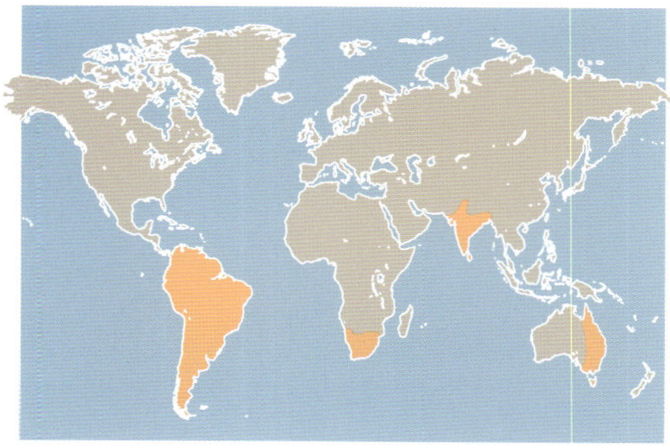

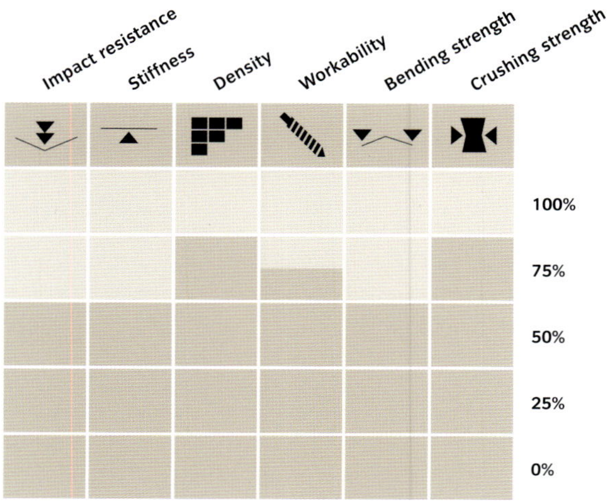

AT A GLANCE

Impact resistance is a measure of the wood's toughness. It describes its resistance to suddenly applied shock loads.

Stiffness is a measure of the wood's elasticity. It is considered in conjunction with bending strength.

Density is measured as specific gravity, the ratio of the density of a substance to that of water.

Acer pseudoplatanus | Family: *Aceraceae* | **SYCAMORE** | Hardwood

Growth
The sycamore reaches about 115ft (35m) in height with a large broad-domed crown, and the bole is 5ft (1.5m) in diameter. It is variously known as sycamore plane, great maple (England), or plane (Scotland). Field maple (*Acer campestre*) and Norway maple (*A.platanoides*) are similar and both grow in Europe.

Appearance
There is little difference between the sapwood and heartwood; both are creamy white in color with a natural luster. Slowly dried timber changes to a light tan color and is known as weathered sycamore. It is usually straight grained, but curly or wavy grain produces a very attractive fiddleback or lace ray figure on quartered surfaces. The texture is fine and even.

Properties
The wood is of medium density and weighs about 38lb/ft^3 (610kg/m^3) when seasoned. It air dries fairly rapidly and well, but is inclined to stain unless end stacked; it kiln dries well. There is medium movement in service. Sycamore has medium bending and crushing strength, low shock resistance, and very low stiffness, giving it good steam-bending properties. The wood has a moderate blunting effect on tools and cutting edges; the grain tends to pick up when planing or molding interlocked or wavy grain on quartered stock, so a reduction of the cutting angle is recommended. It has good nailing and gluing properties and can be given an excellent finish. Sycamore is perishable and the sapwood is liable to attack by the common furniture beetle and by *Ptilinus pectinicornis*, but it is permeable for preservation treatment.

Uses
Sycamore is the traditional wood for the fingerboards and ribs of lutes—the chief instrument in 15th- and 16th-century court music—and is still used for violin backs. It is an excellent turnery wood for textile rollers and bobbins, brush handles, domestic and dairy utensils, laundry appliances, and food containers. It is also the traditional wood for chemical treatment into various shades of silver gray, sold as harewood. Selected logs are sliced to produce attractive figure for cabinets and paneling, and it is dyed for marquetry and inlays.

Where it grows
This medium-height tree grows in widely differing soil and exposure conditions in the UK, but is a native of central and southern Europe and parts of Asia.

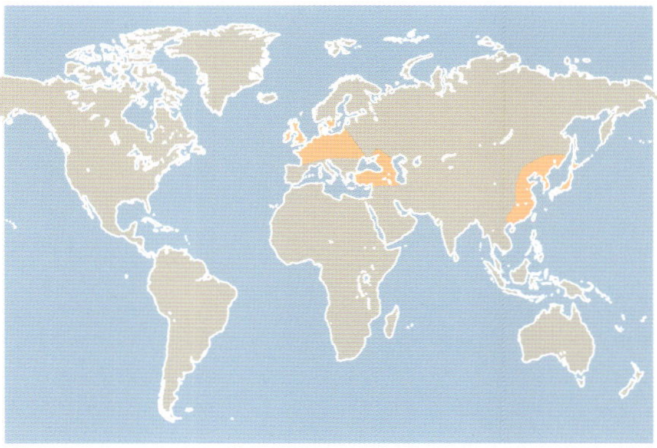

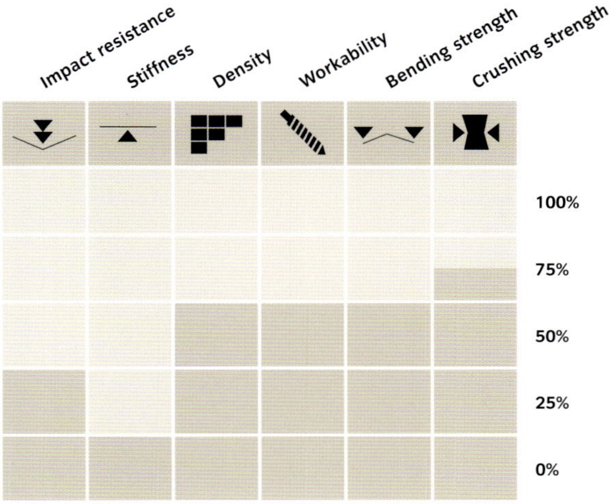

Workability describes how easy a wood is to work and whether it has a significant blunting effect on tools.

Bending strength is also known as maximum bending strength. Pressure is applied to each end of a board until it cracks.

Crushing strength is the ability of wood to withstand loads applied to the end grain, a critical test for wood used as short columns or props.

Acer saccharum | Family: *Aceraceae* | **ROCK MAPLE** | Hardwood

Growth

Rock maple grows to 130ft (40m) tall with a diameter of 2–3ft (0.6–1m). *Acer saccharum* and *A.nigrum*, jointly sold as rock maple, are also known as hard maple (US, Canada, and UK); the sapwood as white maple (US); and black maple. Canada displays the red leaf of *A.saccharum* on its national flag, and it is also known as sugar maple because it is the source of maple sugar and maple syrup, obtained by tapping the sap in spring.

Appearance

The wood is creamy white with a reddish tinge, sometimes with a dark brown heart. It is usually straight grained but often curly or wavy, with fine brown lines marking the growth rings on plain-sawn surfaces. The texture is even, fine, and lustrous. Pith flecks are sometimes present.

Properties

Rock maple weighs about 45lb/ft^3 (720kg/m^3) when seasoned. It dries fairly slowly with little degrade, and there is medium movement in service. The wood is of medium density, has good bending and crushing strengths, with low stiffness and shock resistance, and a good steam-bending classification. It has a moderate blunting effect on tools, with a tendency to create tooth vibration when sawing. Irregular grain can pick up when planing or molding on quartered surfaces, and a reduced cutter angle is recommended. The wood has a tendency to ride on cutters and burn during end-grain working. Rock maple requires pre-boring for nailing, but it glues very well and polishes to an excellent finish. The wood is nondurable, liable to beetle attack, and subject to growth defects, known as pith flecks, caused by insects. The heartwood is resistant to preservation treatment, but the sapwood is permeable.

Uses

Rock maple makes excellent heavy industrial flooring for roller-skating rinks, dance halls, squash courts, and bowling alleys. It is used for textile rollers, dairy and laundry equipment, butchers' blocks, piano actions and musical instruments, and sports goods. It is also a valuable turnery wood. Selected logs are peeled for bird's eye figure, or sliced to produce fiddleback, curly or blistered, and mottled maple veneers for cabinets and architectural paneling.

Where it grows

Rock maple is one of the most valuable timbers growing east of the Rocky Mountains in Canada and in northern and eastern US.

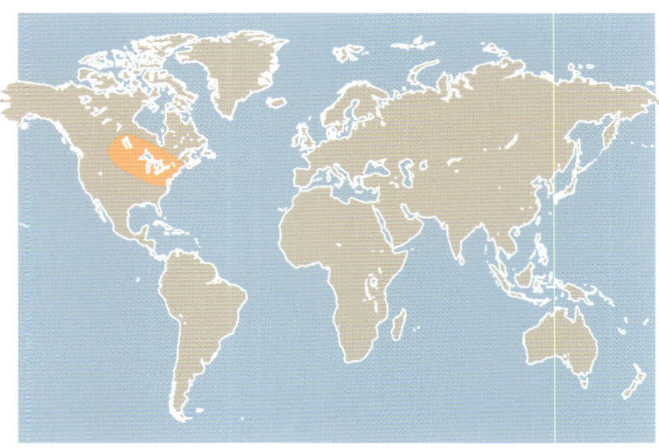

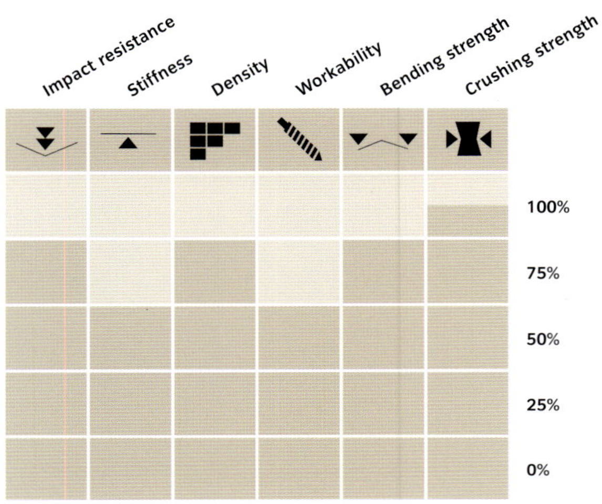

AT A GLANCE

Impact resistance is a measure of the wood's toughness. It describes its resistance to suddenly applied shock loads.

Stiffness is a measure of the wood's elasticity. It is considered in conjunction with bending strength.

Density is measured as specific gravity, the ratio of the density of a substance to that of water.

***Acer* spp.** | Family: *Aceraceae* | **SOFT MAPLE** | Hardwood

Growth

Maples are famed for their brilliant spectrum of multicolored autumn leaves of yellow, golden orange, and red. Soft maple is provided by both *Acer rubrum*, which produces red maple, and *A.saccharinum*, which provides silver maple, one of the largest and fastest growing of all the maples. It reaches a height of 130ft (40m), but red maple is smaller, reaching only 100ft (30m) with a diameter 2–4ft (0.6–1.2m). *A.macrophyllum* produces Pacific maple.

Appearance

The sapwood is indistinguishable from the heartwood; both are creamy white in color with a close, straight grain and indistinct growth rings on plain-sawn surfaces. The texture is even, fine, and slightly less lustrous than rock maple (*A.saccharum*).

Properties

The weight of *A.rubrum* is about 38lb/ft^3 (610kg/m^3), while *A.saccharinum* and *A.macrophyllum* are about 34lb/ft^3 (540kg/m^3) when seasoned. The wood dries rather slowly with little degrade and there is medium movement in service. Soft maple is of medium density, with good bending and crushing strengths, and low stiffness and shock resistance. It has a good steam-bending classification and works well with both hand and machine tools in all operations, offering only a moderate blunting effect on cutting edges. Nailing and screwing are satisfactory but require care; gluing is variable. The wood can be brought to a good finish. Soft maple is nondurable and moderately resistant to preservation treatment; the sapwood is liable to insect attack but is permeable.

Uses

This attractive timber is softer and lower in strength than rock maple, but is eminently suitable for furniture making, interior joinery, turnery, and domestic woodware. Numerous specialized uses include the manufacture of shoe lasts, dairy and laundry equipment, musical instruments and piano actions, and sports goods. Soft maple also makes an excellent light domestic flooring. Selected logs are peeled for plywood manufacture and sliced to produce a range of excellently figured veneers for cabinets, flush doors, and architectural paneling.

Where it grows

More than 10 species of this genus grow in the northern temperate regions of Canada and the eastern US as well as on the Pacific coast, but only about five are important sources of timber. Some species also occur in Asia.

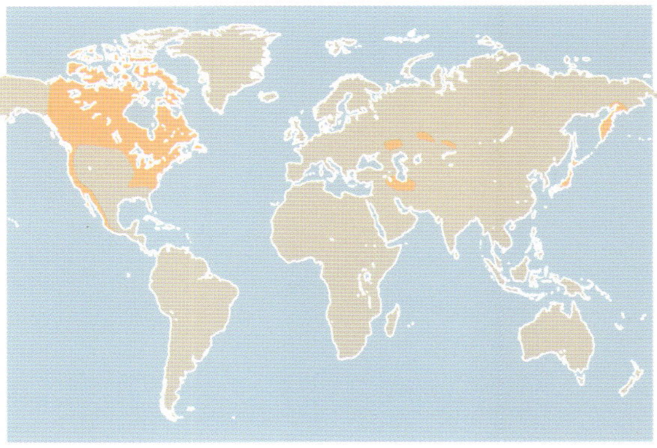

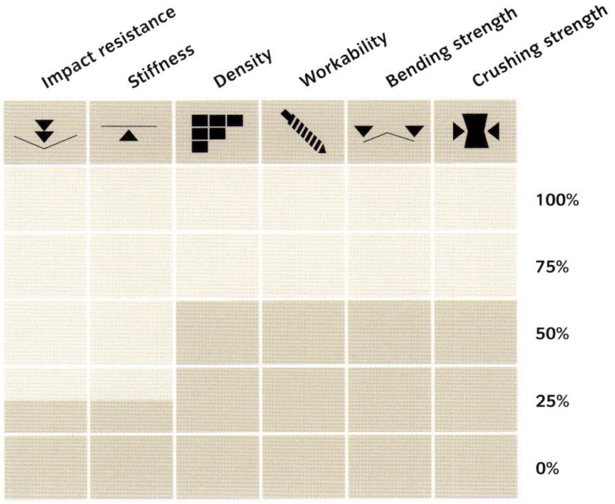

Workability describes how easy a wood is to work and whether it has a significant blunting effect on tools.

Bending strength is also known as maximum bending strength. Pressure is applied to each end of a board until it cracks.

Crushing strength is the ability of wood to withstand loads applied to the end grain, a critical test for wood used as short columns or props.

Aesculus hippocastanum | Family: *Hippocastanaceae* | **HORSE CHESTNUT** | Hardwood

Growth

More than 20 species of horse chestnut occur in the US, where it is called buckeye because the base of the nuts resemble the eyes of a deer. The tree is grown as an ornamental parkland tree in Europe. In cultivated positions it attains a grand stature of 130ft (40m) in height, but in parklands it has a short bole that rarely exceeds about 20ft (6m), with its low branches hung with lanterns. The diameter is 5–6ft (1.5–1.8m).

Appearance

If the tree is felled in early winter it is extremely white like holly (*Ilex spp.*), but timber felled later in the year is a pale yellow-brown color. Spiral grain is usually present, and the wood is inclined to be cross or wavy grained. It has a very fine, close, uniform texture, however, caused by minute pores and fine-storied rays that give the surface a lustrous sheen. Longitudinal surfaces sometimes show a subdued mottle.

Properties

This medium-density wood weighs about 32lb/ft³ (510kg/m³) when seasoned. It dries well with little degrade, and has small movement in service. It has a low bending strength, very low stiffness, and low to medium crushing strength, with a good steam-bending classification. It can be worked easily with both hand and machine tools, with only a slight blunting effect on cutting edges, which must be kept very sharp. Nailing, screwing, and gluing are satisfactory, and the wood can be brought to a good finish when stained and polished. The sapwood is liable to attack by the common furniture beetle. The wood is perishable, but permeable for preservation treatment.

Uses

Horse chestnut is extensively used as a substitute for holly for cabinet making, furniture making, and carving, and is popular for general turnery for brush backs and handles, dairy and kitchen utensils, fruit storage trays and racks, and engineering and molders' patterns. It is also used for the hand pieces of tennis, badminton, and squash rackets. Selected logs are sliced for handsome decorative veneers, and dyed for marquetry veneers sold as harewood.

Where it grows

Native to Albania, horse chestnut thrives in the mountain regions of northern Greece, Bulgaria, Iran, and northern India. It is now widespread throughout Europe and North America, and is also grown in China, Japan, and the Himalayas.

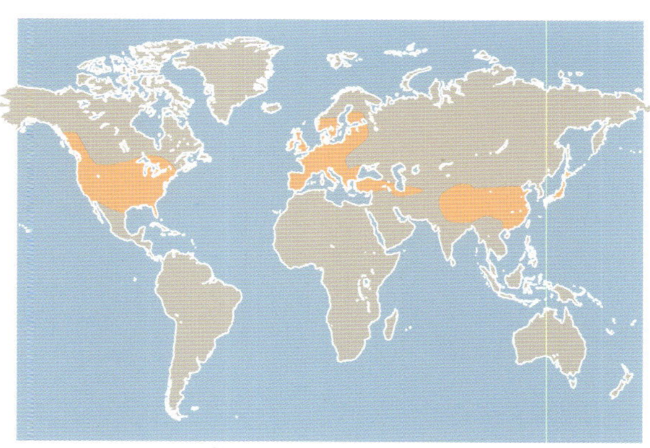

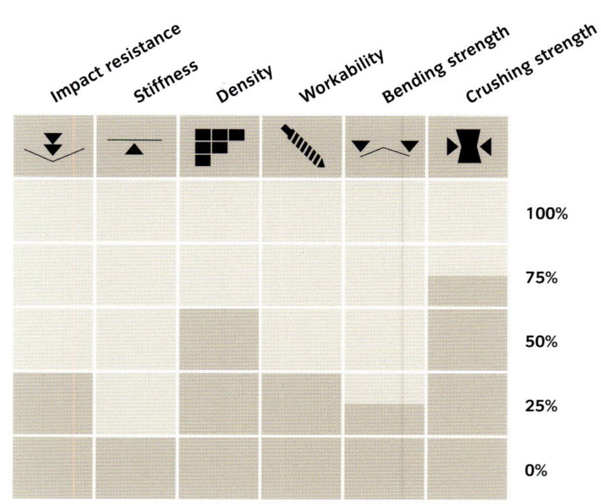

AT A GLANCE

Impact resistance is a measure of the wood's toughness. It describes its resistance to suddenly applied shock loads.

Stiffness is a measure of the wood's elasticity. It is considered in conjunction with bending strength.

Density is measured as specific gravity, the ratio of the density of a substance to that of water.

Afzelia spp. | Family: *Leguminosae* | **AFZELIA** | Hardwood

Growth

Sold as a single commercial timber, *Afzelia africana* (Smith), *A.bipindenis* (Harms), and *A.pachyloba* (Harms), from west Africa, are known as doussié. *A.quanzensis* (Welw.), from Mozambique and Tanzania, is known as chamfuta and marketed separately. Other names include apa and aligna (Nigeria); mkora and mbembakofi (Tanzania); and mussacossa (Mozambique). Trees from the moist deciduous forests reach a maximum height of about 100ft (30m), and east African trees grow to 70–80ft (21–24m). The diameter averages 4ft (1.2m).

Appearance

The sapwood is a pale straw color and quite sharply demarcated from the light brown heartwood, which matures to a rich red-brown mahogany color on exposure. Yellow or white deposits in the grain may cause staining. The grain is often irregular and interlocked, with a coarse but even texture.

Properties

This dense timber weighs 39–59lb/ft^3 (620–950kg/m^3), averaging 51lb/ft^3 (820kg/m^3) when seasoned. Afzelia can be kiln dried satisfactorily but very slowly from green, and there may be some distortion in the extension of existing shakes and fine checking. It is an exceptionally stable timber, comparable to teak (*Tectona grandis*). The wood has high strength and outstanding durability and stability. It is fairly hard to work and has a moderate blunting effect on cutting edges. Gluing can be difficult. Afzelia has a moderate bending classification because it distorts and exudes resin during steaming, but *A.quanzensis* can be bent to a small radius. A satisfactory finish can be obtained when the grain is filled. The sapwood is liable to attack by powder post beetle; the heartwood has outstanding durability, with extreme resistance to preservation treatment.

Uses

Afzelia is highly valued for interior and exterior joinery, window frames, doors and doorframes, staircase work, bank and shop counters, and ships' rails. It is used for heavy construction, dock and harbor work, and bridge building. It is popular for school, office, and garden furniture, and is especially useful for laboratory benches as well as vats and presses for acids and chemicals. It is used for flooring in public buildings.

Where it grows

Afzelia grows between the savannah forests of the dry areas of eastern Africa and the dense deciduous forests of the more humid regions of west Africa.

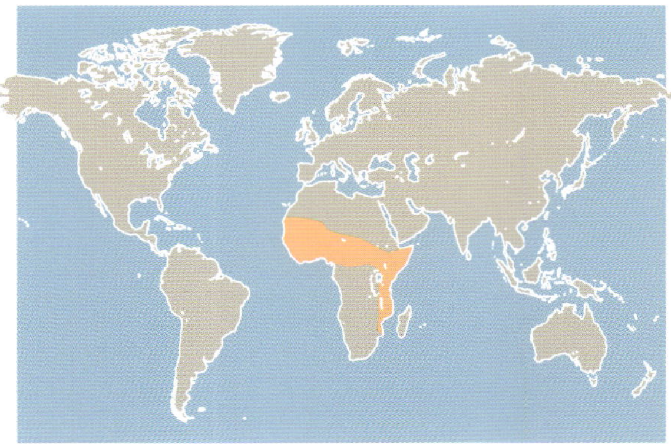

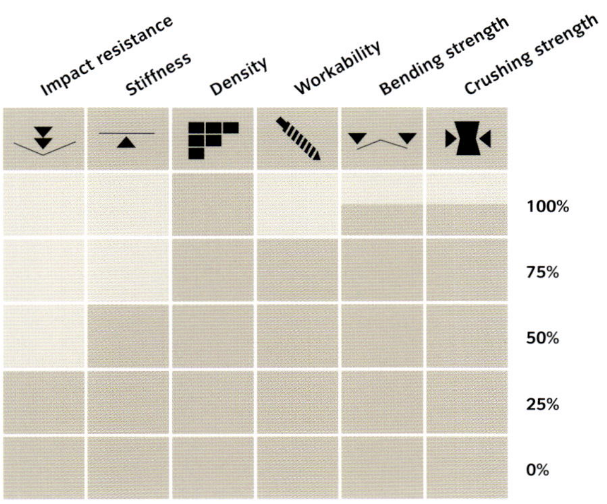

Workability describes how easy a wood is to work and whether it has a significant blunting effect on tools.

Bending strength is also known as maximum bending strength. Pressure is applied to each end of a board until it cracks.

Crushing strength is the ability of wood to withstand loads applied to the end grain, a critical test for wood used as short columns or props.

Agathis spp.	Family: *Araucariaceae*	**KAURI PINE**	Softwood

Growth

Agathis australis produces New Zealand kauri; *A.robusta*, *A.palmerstonii* and *A.microstachya* provide Queensland kauri; *A.dammara* produces East Indian kauri; and *A.vitiensis* provides Fijian kauri. The Maoris from the North Island of New Zealand call kauri pine tanemahuta (king of the forest) because the trees soar up to 150ft (45m) above the forest canopy, with a diameter of 5–13ft (1.5–4m).

Appearance

These valuable straight-grained timbers are not true pines (*Pinus spp.*). In appearance they resemble the botanically related parana pine, *Araucaria angustifolia*, but are darker in color and coarser in texture. The heartwood color varies from pale biscuit to pink or even dark red-brown. The darker wood contains the most resin, though kauri pine does not contain either resin cells or resin canals. It comes from the ray cells, and in vertical tracheids near the rays, in the form of hard resin plugs that do not affect the wood's finishing properties. Kauri pine has a fine, even, silky texture and a lustrous surface.

Properties

The weight of New Zealand kauri is 36lb/ft^3 (580kg/m^3); Queensland kauri is lighter at 30lb/ft^3 (480kg/m^3) when seasoned. It dries at a moderate rate with a tendency to warp, but is stable in use. The wood has high stiffness, medium bending and crushing strength and resistance to shock loads, but it is not suitable for steam bending. It works easily with both hand and machine tools, and has only a very slight dulling effect on cutters. The wood planes or molds to a smooth finish, but when boring or mortising it needs to be properly supported at the tool exit. The wood holds nails and screws well. It glues easily and can be brought to an excellent finish. Kauri is subject to attack by the common furniture beetle, but is moderately durable and resistant to preservation treatment.

Uses

Top grades of kauri pine are used for vats, wooden machinery, and boat building; the lower grades are utilized for building construction. Queensland and Fijian kauri are employed for high-class joinery and cabinet work, battery separators, pattern making, and butter boxes and churns. Cheap plywood manufacture, boxes, and crates are made from lower grades.

Where it grows

The cone-bearing softwood kauris occur singly or in small groves intermingled with broad-leaved trees, and are distributed from Malaysia to Australia, and from New Guinea to New Zealand and Fiji.

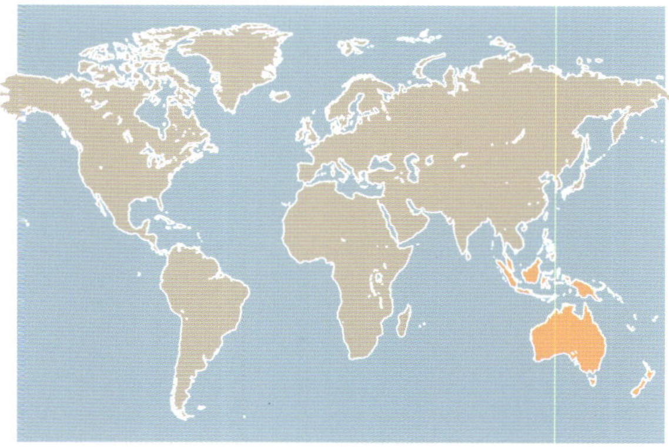

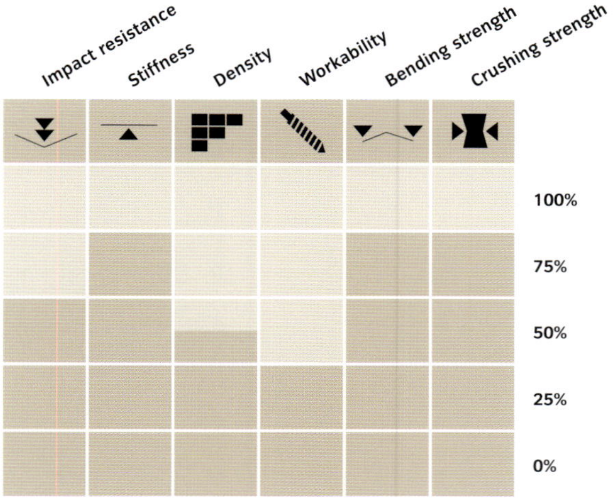

AT A GLANCE

Impact resistance is a measure of the wood's toughness. It describes its resistance to suddenly applied shock loads.

Stiffness is a measure of the wood's elasticity. It is considered in conjunction with bending strength.

Density is measured as specific gravity, the ratio of the density of a substance to that of water.

Albizia spp. | Family: *Leguminosae* | **ALBIZIA** | Hardwood

Growth

West African albiz a comprises *Albizia adianthifolia* (Schum) W.F. Wright; *A.ferruginea* (Guill. & Perr.) Benth.; and *A.zygia* (D.C.) McBride. *A.ferruginea* produces heavy albizia. East African albizia is sold as red or white nongo according to color and includes *A.grandibracteata* Taub and *A.zygia* (D.C.) McBride.The trees grow to an average height of about 120ft (37m) or more, with a diameter of about 3ft (1m). The wood is known as okuro in Ghana, ayinre in Nigeria, and sifou in Zaire.

Appearance

The sapwood is clearly demarcated from the heartwood and is pale yellow to straw in color and about 2in (5cm) wide. The valuable heartwood color varies from red-brown to chocolate-brown, often with a purplish tinge. The grain is irregular and often interlocked and variable in direction, with a coarse texture.

Properties

This dense wood weighs on average 44lb/ft^3 (700kg/m^3) when seasoned. Kiln drying must be carried out very slowly to avoid checking or twisting, but there is small movement in service. It has a medium bending strength, low stiffness, and very low shock resistance, but a high crushing strength and a moderate steam-bending classification. The wood requires care in machining, and fine dust can cause nasal irritation. It has a moderate blunting effect on tools, and irregular grain tends to pick up when planing or molding on quartered surfaces. A reduced cutter angle is recommended in this case. It also tends to break out when machining across the grain, when recessing, or on arrises. Pre-boring is required for nailing. The grain must be filled before the surface can be brought to a good finish. The sapwood is liable to powder post beetle attack. The heartwood is very durable and extremely resistant to preservative treatment, but the sapwood is permeable.

Uses

Heavy albizia is used for marine construction and piling. The lighter species are used for utility and general joinery, domestic flooring, general carpentry, and vehicle bodywork. Selected logs are sliced for veneers.

Where it grows

The genus *Albizia* includes more than 30 species in Africa, many from the savannah forests. Commercial timbers come from the high forests and occur from Sierra Leone through central and east Africa down to Zimbabwe.

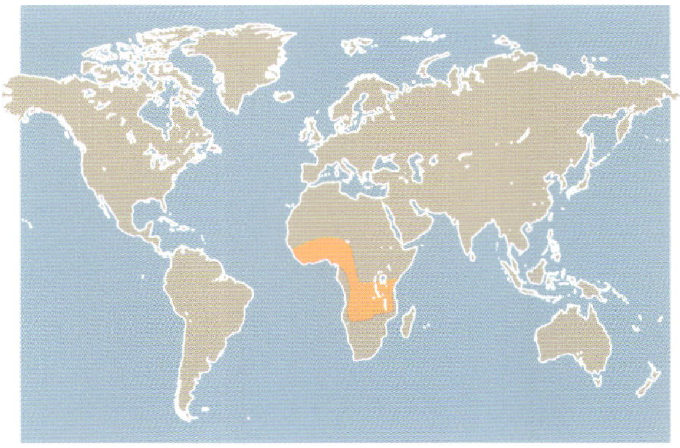

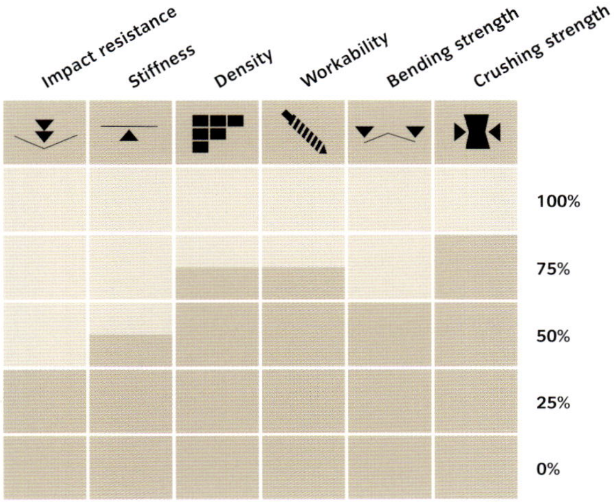

Workability describes how easy a wood is to work and whether it has a significant blunting effect on tools.

Bending strength is also known as maximum bending strength. Pressure is applied to each end of a board until it cracks.

Crushing strength is the ability of wood to withstand loads applied to the end grain, a critical test for wood used as short columns or props.

Alnus spp. | Family: *Betulaceae* | **ALDER** | Hardwood

Growth
Alders grow on stream-side, damp, and moist sites to a modest height of 50–90ft (15–27m), with a diameter of 1–4ft (0.3–1.2m). Common alder (*Alnus glutinosa*) and gray alder (*A.incana* Moench) are found in northern Europe and western Siberia. Red alder (*A.rubra* Bong.) is one of the most common commercial hardwoods in the US and Canada.

Appearance
There is little difference in color between the sapwood and heartwood of the alder, which is a dull, lusterless, bright orange-brown when freshly cut, maturing to light reddish brown, with darker lines or streaks formed by the broad rays. It is straight grained except near the butts, and has a fine texture.

Properties
The medium-density heartwood of the alder dries fairly rapidly and well, and weighs about 33lb/ft^3 (530kg/m^3) when seasoned. It can be machined easily if the cutting edges are kept sharp, with only a slight blunting effect on tools. Alder possesses a low bending strength and shock resistance, a medium crushing strength, and very low stiffness, which earns it a moderate steam-bending classification. It is inferior to many other hardwoods, such as beech (*Fagus spp.*). Nailing and screw holding are satisfactory, and the wood can be glued without difficulty. The timber can be stained and polished to a good finish. The sapwood is liable to attack by the common furniture beetle. The wood is perishable but permeable for preservation treatment.

Uses
Alder is widely used for wood carving and turnery for domestic woodware, broom handles, brush backs, hat blocks, textile rollers, and wooden toys. It is the traditional wood for clog making and is highly regarded as ideal for the manufacture of artificial limbs. It is also a source of charcoal for making gunpowder. Gnarled pieces of the tree are highly prized in Japan for decorative sculpture and carving. It is also rotary cut to make utility plywood for packing crates, while selected logs are sliced to provide an attractive figure suitable for decorative veneers for furniture and paneling.

Where it grows
Common alder is native to Europe, but has a wide distribution throughout the northern hemisphere in Russia, western Asia, and Japan. Red alder is widely distributed on the Pacific coast of Canada and the US.

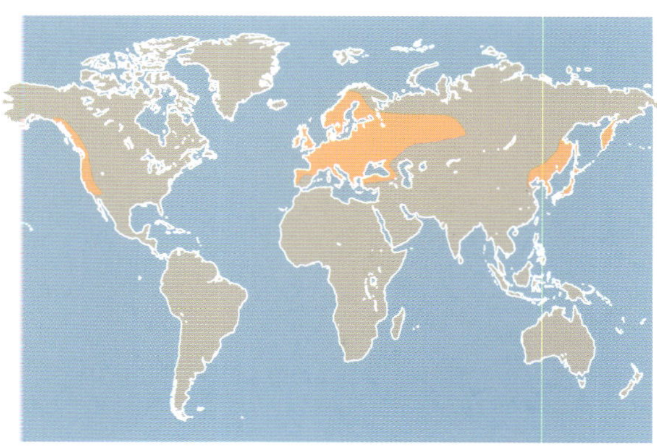

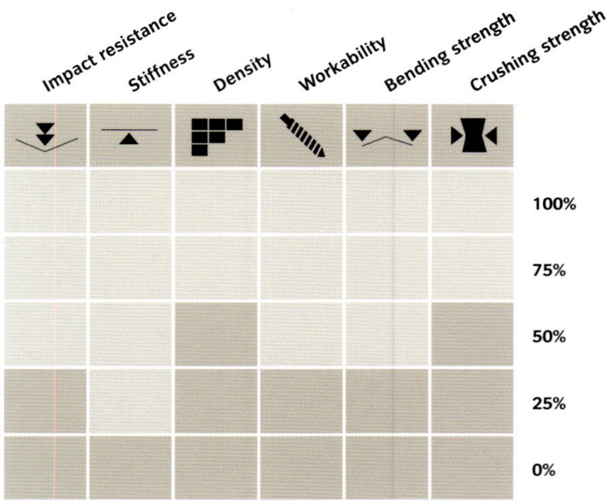

AT A GLANCE

Impact resistance is a measure of the wood's toughness. It describes its resistance to suddenly applied shock loads.

Stiffness is a measure of the wood's elasticity. It is considered in conjunction with bending strength.

Density is measured as specific gravity, the ratio of the density of a substance to that of water.

Aniba duckei	Family: *Lauraceae*	**PAU ROSA**	Hardwood

Growth

Aniba duckei is a reasonably sized tree that grows up to 100ft (30m) in height, with a fair stem of clean wood and a trunk of about 2½ft (0.8m) in diameter. When growing, the trunk is buttressed at the ground, but not significantly.

Appearance

Pau rosa heartwood is a strange dusty brown color, sometimes with a green hue, but generally a mid-honey shade. The grain is straightish, and the quarter-sawn surfaces have attractive lines, with a gradual border between the thin bands of early and latewood. It is not uncommon to find ray flecks on quarter-sawn sides. It is a little lighter in color than teak (*Tectona grandis*) and has a slightly more defined pattern, but is so similar that it is often misidentified.

Properties

Like teak, pau rosa is very durable. It is relatively heavy at 51lb/ft^3 (820kg/m^3), with a medium texture. It also has a medium luster, though you can work pau rosa to a good finish without too much difficulty. In fact, it works well by hand and machine, but tends to degrade as it is seasoned, and moves a fair amount once dry.

Uses

Pau rosa is employed for a range of tasks, but that does not make it a utility lumber. It is often chosen for quality furniture, turning, and cabinet making. Its high durability means that it is also tough enough to be used for flooring and implements, as well as for boat building.

Where it grows

Pau rosa grows in Brazil. A synonym of *Aniba duckei* is *A.rosaeodora*, hinting at the use of pau rosa in the manufacture of perfume.

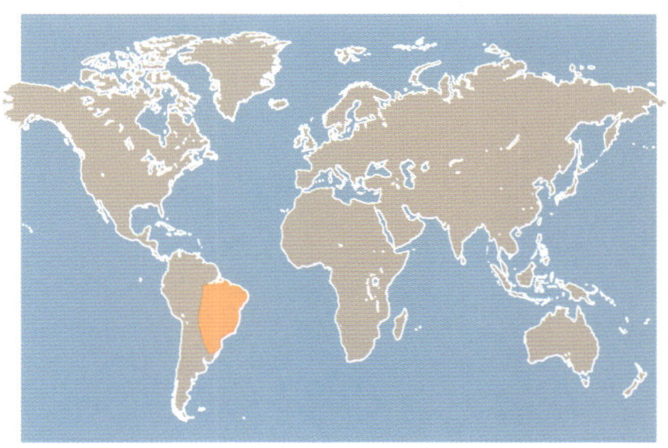

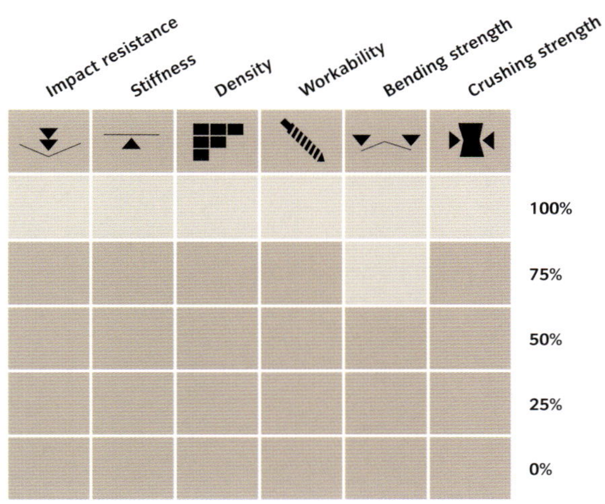

Workability describes how easy a wood is to work and whether it has a significant blunting effect on tools.

Bending strength is also known as maximum bending strength. Pressure is applied to each end of a board until it cracks.

Crushing strength is the ability of wood to withstand loads applied to the end grain, a critical test for wood used as short columns or props.

Anisoptera spp. | Family: *Dipterocarpaceae* | **MERSAWA/KRABAK** | Hardwood

Growth
There are many species of the genus *Anisoptera*, with different common names depending on the country of origin. They are usually mixed together and exported in a group under the trade name of mersawa or krabak. Mersawa comprises principally *A.costata* Korth.; *A.laevis* Ridl.; *A.scaphula* Pierre; *A.curtisii* Dyer; and *A.marginata* Korth. Krabak from Thailand comprises *A.curtisii* Dyer; *A.oblonga* Dyer; and *A.scaphula* Pierre. Kaunghmu from Burma is *A.scaphula* Pierre; palosapis from the Philippines is *A.thurifera*. The trees vary in size but generally reach a height of 150ft (45m) with a diameter of 3–5ft (1–1.5m).

Appearance
The sapwood, not clearly different from the heartwood, is usually attacked by a blue fungus that stains it. The heartwood varies from pale yellow to yellow-brown with a pinkish tinge, and is moderately coarse but even in texture. The timber is rather plain, but with a slight silver-flecked figure and ribbon stripe on quartered surfaces from prominent rays. Generally, the grain varies from straight to interlocked, and it has a fairly coarse, even texture.

Properties
The weight of this wood averages 40lb/ft^3 (640kg/m^3) when seasoned. The timber dries very slowly from green, and it is difficult to extract moisture from the center of thick stock. The interlocked grain and silica content affect machining, causing severe blunting of cutting edges. It possesses a low bending strength and shock resistance, with medium crushing strength; it has very low stiffness and a poor steam-bending rating. It can be glued and nailed satisfactorily and brought to a good finish. The sapwood is liable to attack by the powder post beetle. The wood is moderately durable and resistant to preservation treatment.

Uses
Mersawa/krabak is used for furniture making and general construction, for interior joinery, domestic flooring, vehicle bodies, and in boat building for planking. It is rotary cut for utility plywood, and sliced for decorative veneers.

Where it grows
Mersawa grows in Malaya, Brunei, Sarawak, and Sabah (it is also known as pengiran in Sabah). Other regions of growth include Thailand (where it is known as krabak); Burma (known as kaunghmu); and the Philippines (known as palopsapis).

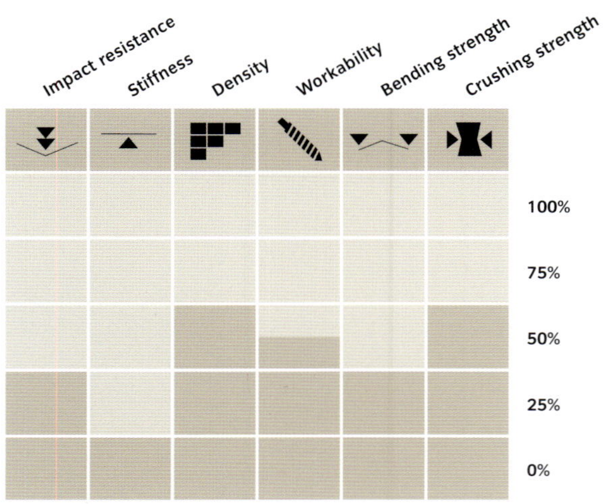

AT A GLANCE

Impact resistance is a measure of the wood's toughness. It describes its resistance to suddenly applied shock loads.

Stiffness is a measure of the wood's elasticity. It is considered in conjunction with bending strength.

Density is measured as specific gravity, the ratio of the density of a substance to that of water.

Araucaria angustifolia	Family: *Araucariaceae*	**PARANA PINE**	Softwood

Growth

Parana pine, also known as Brazilian pine, is not a true pine of the *Pinaceae* family, but is closely related to *Araucaria araucana* (known as Chile pine or monkeypuzzle tree). It grows to a height of 130ft (40m) with a flat-topped crown, and has a diameter of about 4ft (1.2m), with a clear, straight bole.

Appearance

Parana pine's very close density, unusual coloring, and almost complete absence of growth rings make it an extremely attractive wood. It is mainly straight grained and honey colored, although dark gray patches appear at the inner core of the heartwood, along with (sometimes vivid) red streaks that fade with age. The texture is fine and uniform.

Properties

You can get a very light or a very heavy piece of parana pine. The weight varies widely, between about 30 and 40lb/ft^3 (480 and 640kg/m^3) when seasoned. The timber has only medium bending and crushing strengths, with a very low resistance to shock loads. It is extremely difficult to dry, showing a marked tendency to split in the darker areas, and needs to be monitored constantly. If it is not well dried it can distort alarmingly in service, particularly if the commonly available wide boards are used. It works extremely well with both hand and machine tools, and planes and molds cleanly to a very smooth finish. It also glues and finishes nicely. The sapwood is liable to attack by the pinhole borer beetle and the common furniture beetle. The heartwood is nondurable and moderately resistant to preservation treatment, but the sapwood is permeable and can be injected with preservative.

Uses

This is Brazil's major export timber and only the higher grades are shipped. It is used for internal joinery (especially staircases), cabinet framing, drawer sides, shop fitting, and vehicle building. It is not tough enough, however, for applications such as long ladder strings. Locally it is used for joinery, furniture, turnery, sleepers, and general constructional work. It is also employed for plywood manufacture and sliced for decorative veneers. Its availability in larger sizes, its freedom from knots, and its ease of working make parana pine an attractive DIY timber, but its moisture level must be carefully checked.

Where it grows

All members of the *Araucariaceae* family originate in the southern hemisphere and parana pine is no exception. It grows mainly in the Brazilian state of Parana, and is also found in Paraguay and northern Argentina.

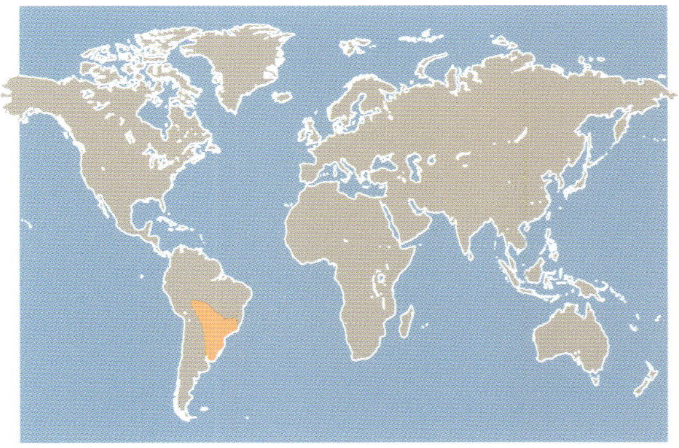

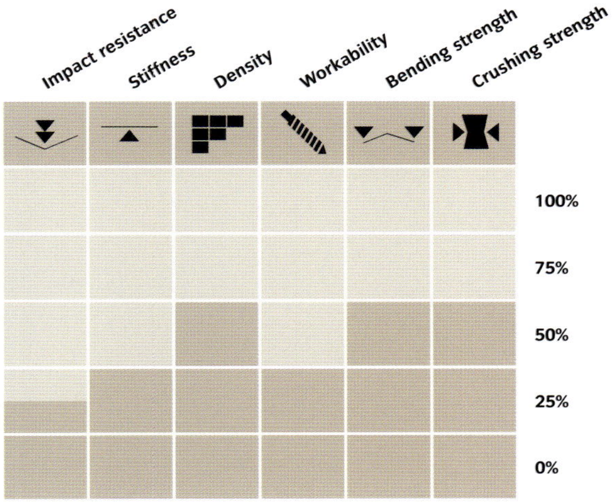

Workability describes how easy a wood is to work and whether it has a significant blunting effect on tools.

Bending strength is also known as maximum bending strength. Pressure is applied to each end of a board until it cracks.

Crushing strength is the ability of wood to withstand loads applied to the end grain, a critical test for wood used as short columns or props.

Aspidosperma spp. | Family: *Apocynaceae* | **ROSA PEROBA** | Hardwood

Growth

Derived principally from *Aspidosperma peroba* Fr.Al. (*A.polyneuron* M.uell.Arg.), this wood is known as both rosa peroba and red peroba. Its height varies from 50ft (15m) up to about 125ft (38m), averaging around 90ft (27m), with a well-formed straight bole of an average diameter of 4–5ft (1.2–1.5m).

Appearance

The creamy yellow sapwood blends gradually into the rose-red heartwood, which varies considerably from tree to tree. Sometimes it has purplish brown streaks and patches that turn orange-brown on exposure. Although the grain is extremely variable, from straight to very irregular, the texture is fine and uniform but without luster. Peroba preta is rose-red with black streaks; peroba revesa has bird's eye figuring; peroba muida is red with darker patches; peroba poca is almost white; peroba rajada is pink-red with large black patches; and peroba tremida is yellow with golden patches.

Properties

This wood is hard, heavy, and very dense. It varies in weight between about 44 and 53lb/ft^3 (700 and 850kg/m^3), averaging 47lb/ft^3 (750kg/m^3) when seasoned. Special care is needed in drying to avoid distortion and splitting. Its irregular grain means that there is considerable variation in strength properties. On average, the timber has medium to high bending strength, medium resistance to shock loads, low stiffness, and a high crushing strength, but it is not normally used for steam bending. This durable wood is fairly easy to work, with a slight blunting effect on cutting edges. A reduced cutter angle is recommended. The wood requires pre-boring for screwing and nailing. It can be glued easily and takes stain and polish finishes excellently. The sapwood is liable to insect attack. The heartwood is durable and extremely resistant to preservative treatment, but the sapwood is permeable.

Uses

In Brazil, rosa peroba is used externally for construction work, joinery, ship building, superior furniture and cabinet making, paneling, strip and parquet flooring, and turnery. Selected logs are sliced to produce a beautiful range of decorative veneers for architectural paneling and marquetry.

Where it grows

Rosa peroba occurs in the southeast regions of Brazil, chiefly in Goias, Minais Gerais, and São Paulo.

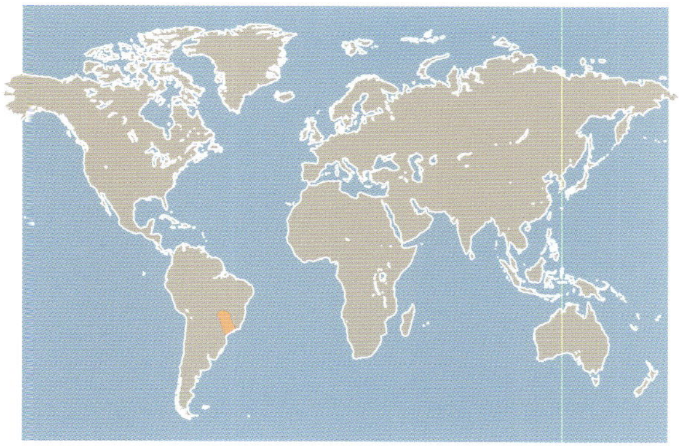

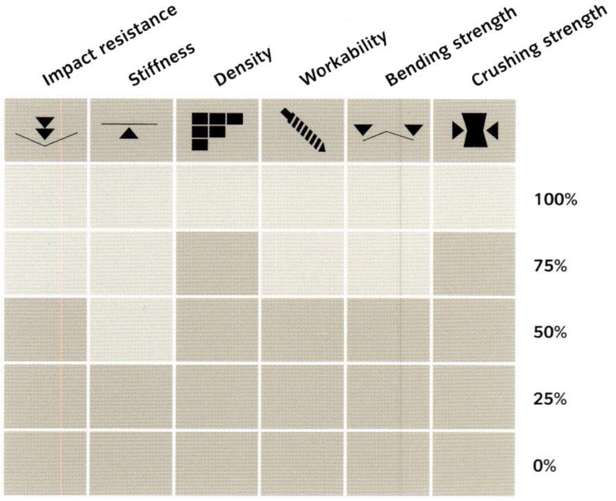

AT A GLANCE

Impact resistance is a measure of the wood's toughness. It describes its resistance to suddenly applied shock loads.

Stiffness is a measure of the wood's elasticity. It is considered in conjunction with bending strength.

Density is measured as specific gravity, the ratio of the density of a substance to that of water.

Astronium fraxifolium | Family: *Anacardiaceae* | **GONCALO ALVES** | Hardwood

Growth

A tidy tree that grows up to 100ft (30m) in height with a consistent diameter of up to 3ft (1m), gonçalo alvez is also commonly known as zebrawood, tigerwood, and kingwood, though the latter name is generally used to identify its rosewood cousin, *Dalbergia cearensis*. Gonçalo alvez is often used as a cutlery handle substitute for cocobolo (*D.retusa*), another of the rosewood clan.

Appearance

Resembling many of the rosewoods, gonçalo alvez tends to have contrasting pale and dark bands that curve casually across the surface—hence its alternative names of zebrawood and tigerwood. It also has the spots and black lines that are typical of rosewood.

Properties

The grain of gonçalo alves is irregular and often interlocking, and the density varies accordingly. It is heavy, hard, and dense, and although it is difficult to season, it is very stable once dry. Gonçalo alvez is strong, cannot easily be bent, and is generally difficult to use because it blunts tool edges, which will often chatter as they cross the contrasting densities of the bands. It does, at least, have a high luster and is very durable.

Uses

The durability of gonçalo alvez means that it is often used for boat building and construction, but furniture makers and cabinet makers also find it interesting enough to employ. In addition, it is utilized for flooring, veneers, and turning.

Where it grows

Although the main source is Brazil, gonçalo alvez can be found across Latin America, from Mexico, Guatemala, and Honduras as far south as Peru.

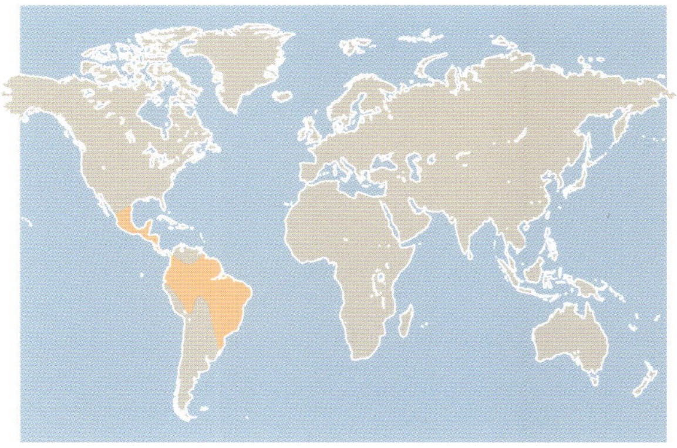

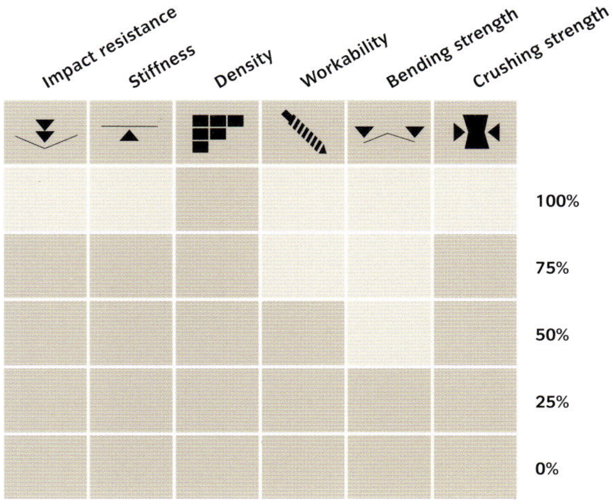

Workability describes how easy a wood is to work and whether it has a significant blunting effect on tools.

Bending strength is also known as maximum bending strength. Pressure is applied to each end of a board until it cracks.

Crushing strength is the ability of wood to withstand loads applied to the end grain, a critical test for wood used as short columns or props.

Aucoumea klaineana | Family: *Burseraceae* | **GABOON** | Hardwood

Growth

More gaboon is exported from Africa than any other native wood. *Aucoumea klaineana* is known under several names: okoum and angouma (Gabon); combogala (Congo); and mofoumou and n'goumi (Equatorial Guinea). It grows to a height of around 200ft (60m) and has a slightly curved but clear cylindrical bole with a diameter of 3–7ft (1–2m).

Appearance

The heartwood of gaboon is light pink, toning to pink-brown on exposure. It is commonly straight grained and sometimes shallowly interlocked or slightly wavy, producing an attractive stripe on quartered surfaces. Gaboon has a medium, uniform, even texture with an attractive natural luster.

Properties

Gaboon is a weak timber of light density, weighing 23–35lb/ft^3 (370–560kg/m^3), with an average of around 27lb/ft^3 (430kg/m^3) when seasoned. It dries fairly rapidly, without difficulty and with little degrade, and there is medium movement in service. It has low bending strength, very low stiffness, a medium crushing strength, and a poor steam-bending classification. It is generally a weak wood that is not durable or resistant to decay, but because it is mostly used internally these faults are not critically important. Although the timber works fairly well with both hand and machine tools, it is rather wooly and its silica content can result in moderate to severe blunting of cutting edges. The grain tends to pick up when planing or molding irregular grain on quartered surfaces. It nails without difficulty and glues easily. The wood can be polished to a lustrous finish if the surface is scraped and sanded well. The sapwood is liable to attack by the powder post beetle. The wood is nondurable and resistant to preservation treatment.

Uses

This very important timber is usually rotary cut into constructional veneers for the manufacture of plywood, blockboard, and laminboard, which are used for flush doors, cabinet making, and paneling. The solid timber is utilized for edge lippings, facings, and moldings as a substitute for mahogany, and for interior frames for furniture construction. It is also used for cigar boxes and sports goods. Selected logs are sliced for mottled and striped decorative veneers for cabinet work, wall paneling, and so on.

Where it grows

This large tree grows mostly in Equatorial Guinea, Gabon, and the Congo Republic.

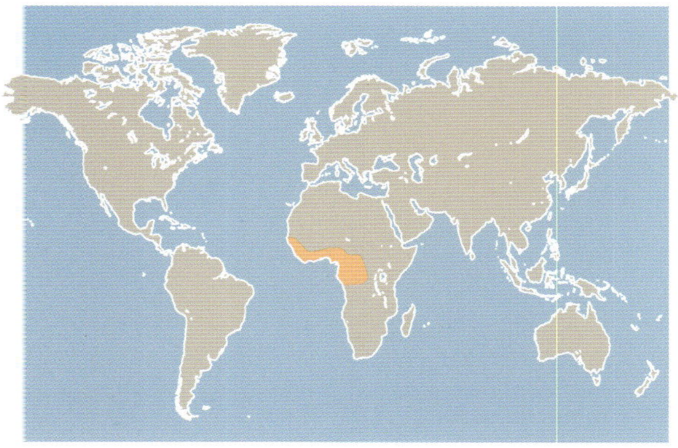

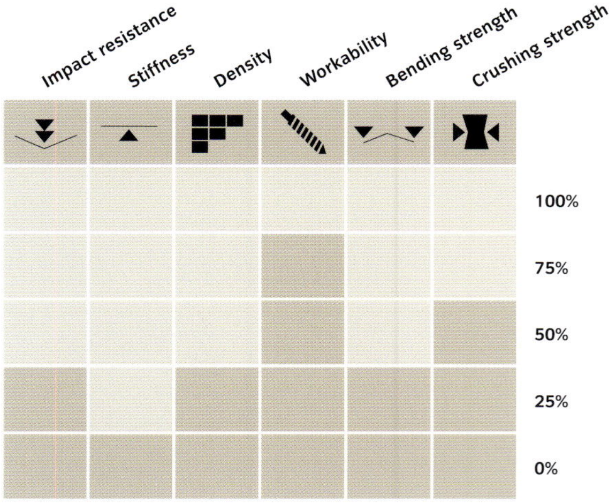

AT A GLANCE

Impact resistance is a measure of the wood's toughness. It describes its resistance to suddenly applied shock loads.

Stiffness is a measure of the wood's elasticity. It is considered in conjunction with bending strength.

Density is measured as specific gravity, the ratio of the density of a substance to that of water.

Baillonella toxisperma | Family: *Sapotaceae* | **MOABI** | Hardwood

Growth
Although moabi is an African tree, its Latin name *Baillonella toxisperma* is derived from the name of Australian botanist F.M. Bailey. Moabi can grow to great heights—up to 200ft (60m)—and some trunks are supported by buttressing. The largest trees grow to 10ft (3m) in diameter.

Appearance
When it comes to patterning, woods do not get much more uninteresting than moabi, although you can find some boards with attractive figure. This is certainly a species that you would want to use when the shape and design of the item you are making is more important than the appearance of the lumber. The color can vary considerably, ranging from a light red to a rich red-brown.

Properties
Moabi makes up for its lack of pattern by being very strong, hard, and tough. It is heavy at 50lb/ft^3 (800kg/m^3), very durable, and fairly stable once dry, though there is a small risk of checking when the wood is being seasoned, which can be done relatively quickly. However, you only have to hold a piece to the light to notice the flecks of silica, which means that moabi is tough on tools and the dust can irritate the eyes and nose. Although it has a good luster, moabi is not particularly enjoyable to work with. It is very similar to makore (*Tieghemella heckelii*), which comes from the same regions of Africa.

Uses
With its reddish brown color, moabi is a natural choice for anyone who wants to replicate the appearance of mahogany, and is used for furniture making, carving, turning, cabinet making, and flooring. It is also employed for exterior construction and building work.

Where it grows
Moabi grows in Nigeria, Gabon, and the Congo.

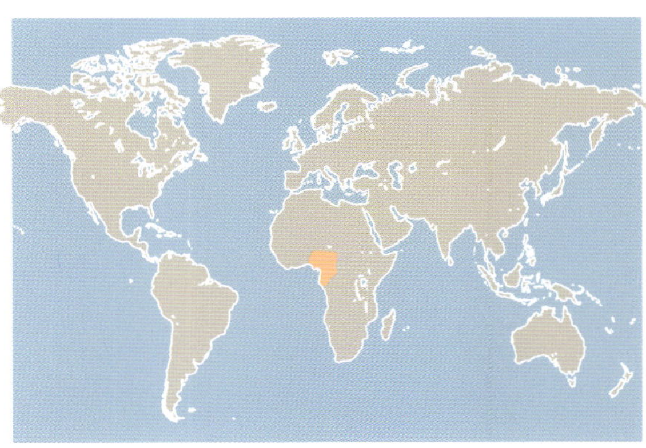

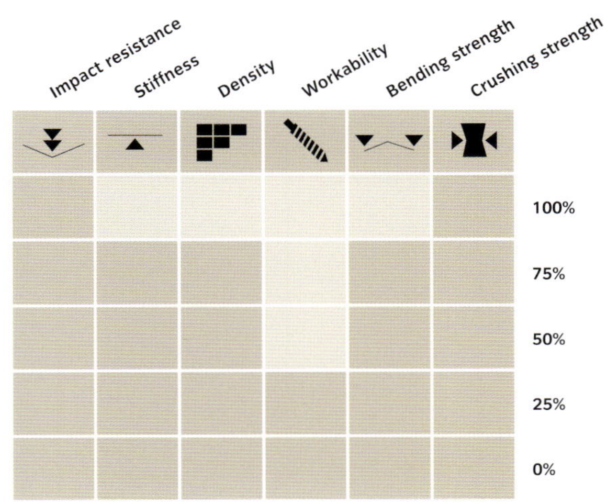

Workability describes how easy a wood is to work and whether it has a significant blunting effect on tools.

Bending strength is also known as maximum bending strength. Pressure is applied to each end of a board until it cracks.

Crushing strength is the ability of wood to withstand loads applied to the end grain, a critical test for wood used as short columns or props.

Balfourodendron riedelianum | Family: *Rutaceae* | **PAU MARFIM** | Hardwood

Growth

Pau marfim may reach a height of 80ft (24m), and a rather slender diameter of 2½ft (0.8m). It is usually shipped as sawn lumber and squares. It is also known as moroti and guatambu moroti (Brazil and Argentina); quatamba, farinha seca, and pau liso (Brazil); kyrandy (Paraguay); quillo bordon (Peru); yomo de huero (Colombia); and ivorywood (US). Other pale, fine-textured woods in South America, especially species of *Aspidosperma*, are also called pau marfim.

Appearance

Pau marfim has an almost featureless appearance and a pale creamy lemon-yellow color. There is very little difference between the sapwood and heartwood, the latter sometimes having darker streaks and a very fine, even texture. The growth rings are visible on flat-sawn surfaces. The grain is mostly straight, but sometimes irregular or occasionally interlocked, with a medium natural luster.

Properties

This heavy, dense wood weighs around 50lb/ft^3 (800kg/m^3) when seasoned. It dries without difficulty and is stable in use and easy to work, although it may quickly blunt the cutting edges of tools. It can be brought to a smooth, fine finish. It is a really tough, strong timber and has high strength properties in all categories, especially resistance to shock loads. It is considered too tough for steam bending. Irregular grain tends to pick up when planing or molding on quartered surfaces, and a reduced cutter angle is recommended. The wood can be nailed and screwed without difficulty and glues readily. It can be stained and polished to a fine, smooth finish. The sapwood is permeable and liable to insect attack, while the heartwood is both nondurable and resistant to preservative treatment.

Uses

This tough wood is ideal for uses such as striking tool handles and oars. It is employed in the countries of origin for construction, furniture, and cabinet work. It is also an excellent turnery wood, being fine textured and compact; it is used for shoe lasts, textile rollers, drawing instruments, and rulers, and is also an ideal substitute for maple (*Acer spp.*) for hard-wearing floors. Selected logs are sliced for highly decorative veneers that are suitable for cabinets, paneling, and marquetry.

Where it grows

This moderately sized tree grows chiefly in southern Brazil, around Rio Paranapamena, São Paulo, and Rio de Sul. It also occurs in Paraguay and northern Argentina.

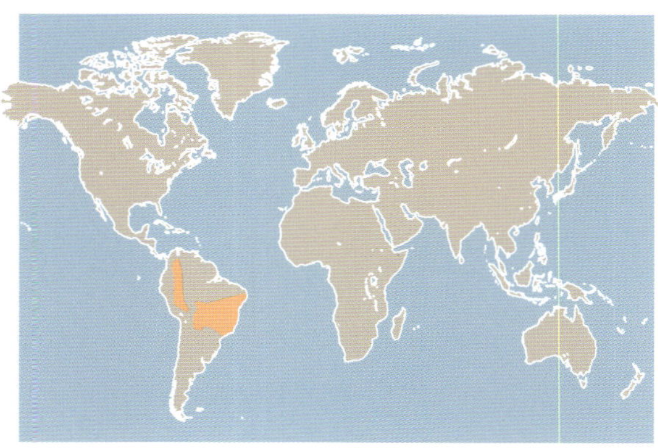

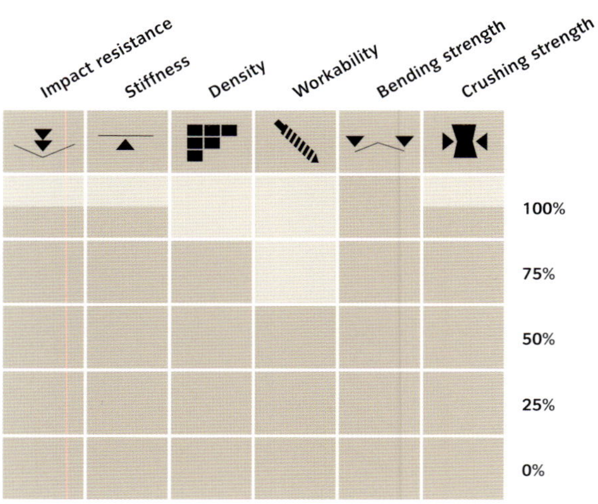

AT A GLANCE

Impact resistance is a measure of the wood's toughness. It describes its resistance to suddenly applied shock loads.

Stiffness is a measure of the wood's elasticity. It is considered in conjunction with bending strength.

Density is measured as specific gravity, the ratio of the density of a substance to that of water.

Betula alleghaniensis | Family: *Betulaceae* | **YELLOW BIRCH** | Hardwood

Growth

Betula alleghaniensis—syn. *B.lutea* Michx.f. (principally) and *B.lenta* L.—is also known as Quebec birch or American birch (UK), and hard birch or betula wood (Canada). The wood is graded and named by uniformity of color; for example, strongly figured woods are sometimes called Canadian silky wood, sapwood may be called white birch (occasionally confused with paper birch), and heartwood may be known as red birch. The tree grows straight and upright to a maximum height of 100ft (30m), with a diameter of 3–4ft (1–1.2m).

Appearance

The light yellow sapwood is distinct from the heartwood, which is reddish brown, with growth rings marked with dark reddish brown lines. This is a straight-grained wood with a fine, even texture. The sapwood and heartwood often contain growth defects known as pith flecks caused by insect attack.

Properties

This dense, heavy wood weighs about 43lb/ft^3 (690kg/m^3) when seasoned, and dries rather slowly with little degrade, but suffers from considerable movement in use. It is as tough as ash (*Fraxinus spp.*), with high bending, shock resistance, and crushing strengths, medium stiffness, and a very good steam-bending rating. It works well with both hand and machine tools, with only a moderate blunting effect on cutting edges. Pre-boring is required for screwing or nailing. It glues well. This timber is liable to attack by the common furniture beetle. It is perishable and moderately resistant to preservative treatment, but the sapwood is permeable.

Uses

Yellow birch is used for high-grade, best-quality plywood. It is highly valued for furniture and upholstery frames, and is excellent for turnery, bobbins, shuttles, and spools. It is also used for cooperage and parts of agricultural instruments. Its high resistance to wear makes it ideal for light-duty flooring in factories, schools, dance halls, and gymnasia. Selected logs are sliced for highly decorative veneers for high-quality cabinets and paneling.

Where it grows

Yellow birch is a very important and common tree in Canada and the eastern US, growing in the Canadian Maritime Provinces from Lake Superior down into the US as far as Tennessee.

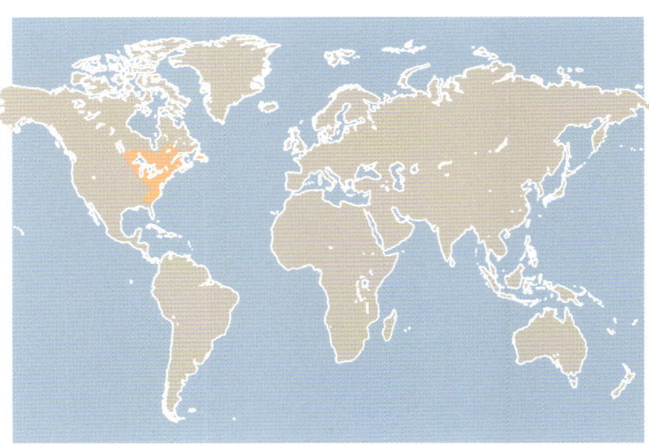

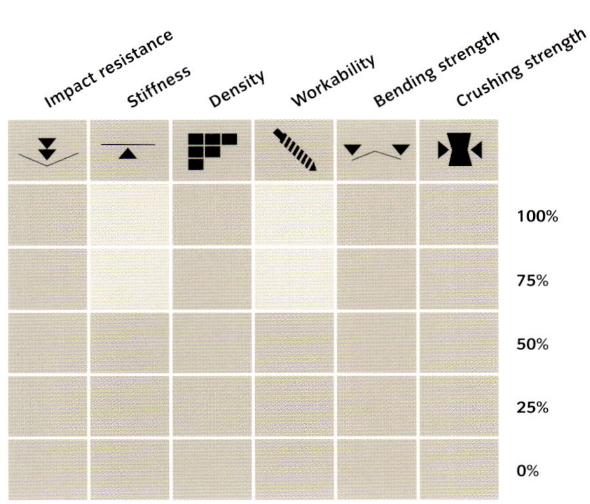

Workability describes how easy a wood is to work and whether it has a significant blunting effect on tools.

Bending strength is also known as maximum bending strength. Pressure is applied to each end of a board until it cracks.

Crushing strength is the ability of wood to withstand loads applied to the end grain, a critical test for wood used as short columns or props.

Betula papyrifera | Family: *Betulaceae* | **PAPER BIRCH** | Hardwood

Growth
Paper birch is also known as American birch (UK) and white birch (Canada). The tree grows to a height of 60–70ft (18–21m), with a long, clear cylindrical bole, and an average diameter of 1½ft (0.5m).

Appearance
Paper birch has a wide, creamy white sapwood with a pale brown heartwood, normally with a straight grain and fine, uniform texture. A good proportion of the logs produce a lovely curly figure known as flame birch. Growth defects known as pith flecks caused by insects sometimes form a decorative feature.

Properties
This medium-density tree weighs about 39lb/ft^3 (620kg/m^3) when seasoned. It dries rather slowly with little degrade. Paper birch is closer to European birch (*Betula pendula*) in characteristics than yellow birch (*B.alleghaniensis*), and is slightly inferior in strength properties but shrinks less. Paper birch has medium strength in all categories except stiffness, which is rated low, and has only a moderately good steam-bending rating. It works reasonably well with both hand and machine tools, with a moderate blunting effect on the cutting edges of tools; sometimes curly grain may pick up when planing or molding on quartered surfaces, and a reduced cutter angle is recommended. The wood glues well, takes stain and polish easily, and can be brought to an excellent finish. It is nondurable and moderately resistant to preservative treatment, but the sapwood is permeable.

Uses
The bulk of the timber is rotary cut for plywood manufacture. It is also an excellent turnery wood, and is used for spools, bobbins, dowels, domestic woodware, hoops, crates, toys, and parts of agricultural machinery. Selected logs are sliced for attractive decorative veneers for cabinets and architectural paneling. It is also valuable as a pulp wood for writing paper, and is used for fruit basket making, ice cream spoons, and medical spatulas. The World War II Mosquito fighter bomber aircraft was built from Canadian birch plywood made principally from paper and yellow birch.

Where it grows
Native Americans made their canoes from the bark of this tree. Today, it is an important commercial timber growing from the Yukon to Hudson Bay, and Newfoundland down to the eastern US.

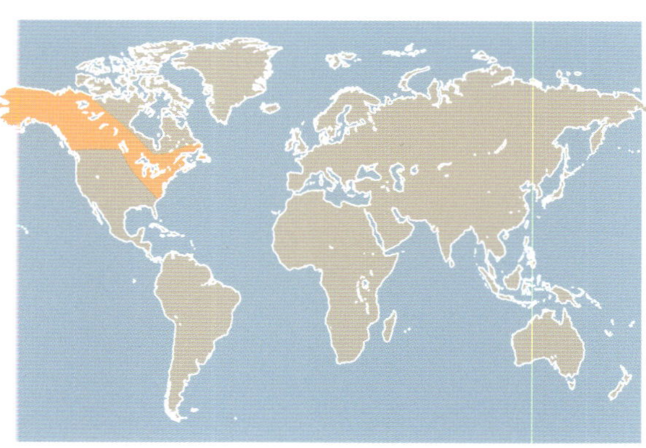

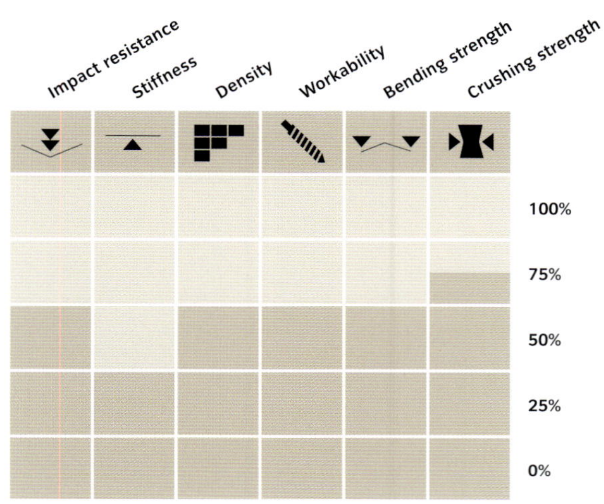

AT A GLANCE

Impact resistance is a measure of the wood's toughness. It describes its resistance to suddenly applied shock loads.

Stiffness is a measure of the wood's elasticity. It is considered in conjunction with bending strength.

Density is measured as specific gravity, the ratio of the density of a substance to that of water.

Betula pendula | Family: *Betulaceae* | **EUROPEAN BIRCH** | Hardwood

Growth

European birch is sold according to its country of origin—English, Finnish, Swedish birch, and so on. Two forms are valuable commercially: *Betula pendula* (*B.alba* L. partly) and *B.pubescens* Ehrh. European birch attains a height of 60–70ft (18–21m), with a diameter of 2–3ft (0.6–1m).

Appearance

There is no distinction in color between the sapwood and heartwood, both being a featureless creamy white to pale brown. The wood is straight grained and fine textured. The larvae of burrowing insects create pith flecks that show as irregular dark markings and local grain disturbance. When this happens, the timber is called masur birch when peeled into veneer. Grain deviation causes flame and curly figure.

Properties

Birch is a heavy, dense wood and weighs about 41lb/ft^3 (660kg/m^3) when seasoned. It dries fairly rapidly with a slight tendency to warp. The wood is moderately stable in use and possesses high bending and crushing strengths, with medium stiffness and shock resistance. Knots and irregular grain are commonly present, limiting the wood's use for steam bending. The wood works easily with both hand and machine tools, but is inclined to be wooly. To prevent tearing of cross- or irregular-grained material when planing or molding, use a reduced cutter angle. The wood requires pre-boring for nailing and screwing, can be glued satisfactorily, and can be stained and polished to a good finish. The sapwood is liable to attack by the common furniture beetle. The heartwood is moderately resistant to preservative treatment, but the sapwood is permeable.

Uses

This is the major material for birch plywood in Finland and Russia. In solid form, it is used for upholstery framing, interior joinery, and furniture making. It is an excellent wood for turnery and is also suitable for brushes, brooms, bobbins, and dowels. Selected logs are peeled or sliced for highly decorative veneers for doors and paneling.

Where it grows

Birch, which will endure extremes of cold and heat, can be found farther north than any other broad-leaved tree, as far as Lapland. It also grows throughout Europe, from Scandinavia down to central Spain.

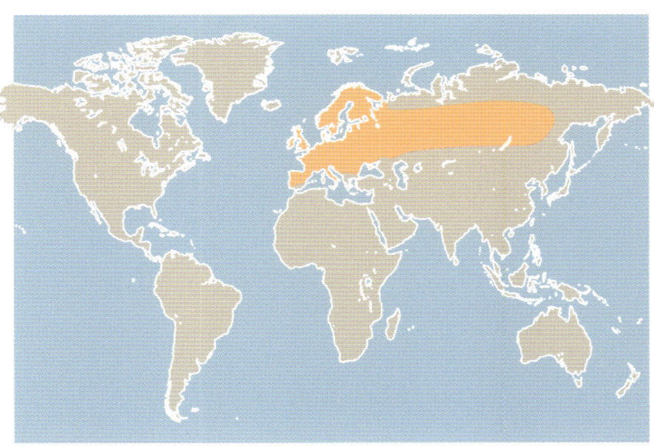

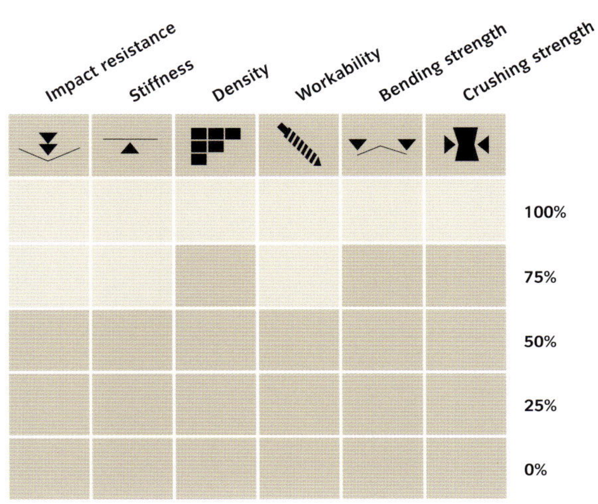

Workability describes how easy a wood is to work and whether it has a significant blunting effect on tools.

Bending strength is also known as maximum bending strength. Pressure is applied to each end of a board until it cracks.

Crushing strength is the ability of wood to withstand loads applied to the end grain, a critical test for wood used as short columns or props.

Brachylaena hutchinsii	Family: *Compositae*	**MUHUHU**	Hardwood

Growth

Muhuhu is medium sized, growing to a height of about 80ft (24m), with a diameter of 1½–2ft (0.5–0.6m). The tree is often twisted or fluted and difficult to get in large sizes.

Appearance

The narrow gray-white sapwood is quite distinct from the heartwood, which is orange-brown in color, sometimes with a greenish tinge. It matures to a medium brown on exposure, and although usually straight grained, can also contain closely interlocked or wavy grain. It has a very fine, even texture and a pleasant odor when cut.

Properties

This very heavy, dense wood varies in weight from 52 to 62lb/ft³ (830 to 1,000kg/m³), but averages around 57–60lb/ft³ (910–960kg/m³) when dry. The timber needs to be dried slowly and carefully in order to avoid a tendency for hair checking and end splitting. When dry, however, muhuhu is stable in use. It has medium bending strength, low stiffness, very low shock resistance, and a high crushing strength. Unless pin knots are present, it has a medium steam-bending rating. It also has a high resistance to indentation and abrasion. The wood is difficult to machine, and will moderately blunt any cutting edges, on which gum tends to build up. This extremely durable timber requires pre-boring for nailing, but it glues well and a very good finish is obtained when stained and polished. Muhuhu is extremely resistant to preservative treatment.

Uses

This attractive, very hard-wearing timber is available only in short lengths, which tends to limit its usefulness. It is used for flooring blocks and strips for high-quality floors in public buildings like hotels, where there is heavy pedestrian traffic, and in factories and warehouses where it is exposed to industrial traffic such as fork lift trucks. In east Africa it is employed for carving animals, and is a very fine turnery wood. When longer lengths are available, it is used for heavy construction, bridge decking, girders, and railway sleepers. It has a spicy, aromatic oil that is distilled and sold as a substitute for sandalwood oil, and the timber has been exported to India for use in crematoria instead of sandalwood.

Where it grows

Muhuhu grows in the semi-evergreen and lowland dry forests of the east African coastal belt, and also occurs in the highland forests of Tanzania and Kenya.

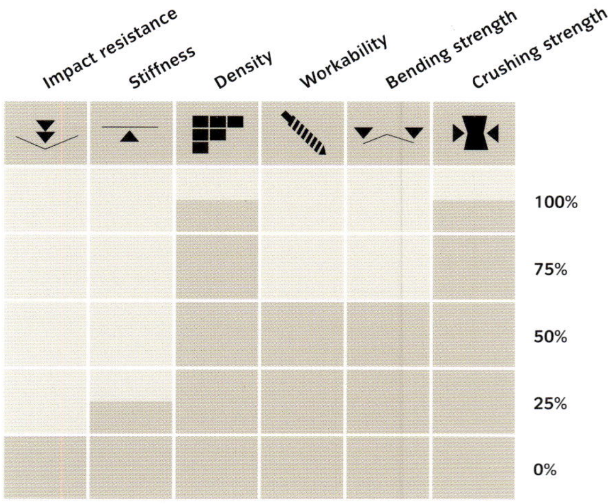

AT A GLANCE

Impact resistance is a measure of the wood's toughness. It describes its resistance to suddenly applied shock loads.

Stiffness is a measure of the wood's elasticity. It is considered in conjunction with bending strength.

Density is measured as specific gravity, the ratio of the density of a substance to that of water.

Brosimum paraense | Family: *Moraceae* | **BLOODWOOD** | Hardwood

Growth

Although frequently referred to as satine, bloodwood is the most appropriate name for *Brosimum paraense* because the lumber is so dramatically red. This is a tall rainforest tree, growing up to 130ft (40m) in height, with clean, unbuttressed stems stretching far into the canopy, at least half the height of the tree. A synonym of this species is *B.rubescens*.

Appearance

Wonderfully smooth and even in texture, bloodwood has startling red heartwood when first cut, although this does darken with age. The wide sapwood is yellow-white in color, and there is a harsh line between the sapwood and the heartwood. You can also sometimes find honey-gold streaks, but this is a species that wins popularity by having remarkable color rather than distinctive patterning.

Properties

The texture and grain of bloodwood varies greatly. It can be straight grained, but also interlocking and wavy. Equally, the texture tends to be fine or medium, though that can vary from board to board. Although it tends to warp during seasoning, the lumber dries quickly and is relatively stable once dry, but only fairly narrow sections of heartwood are usually available. It is very durable and finishes to a high luster.

Uses

The uses of bloodwood tend to fall into two camps. The heartwood on its own tends to be narrow in dimension and is therefore employed for specific jobs, such as bows, inlay, and fishing rods. With the sapwood intact, the lumber is used for a wider range of jobs, for which its durability is an asset.

Where it grows

Do not be confused that bloodwood is sometimes referred to as brazilwood, although it does grow in Brazil as well as Peru, French Guiana, Panama, and Venezuela.

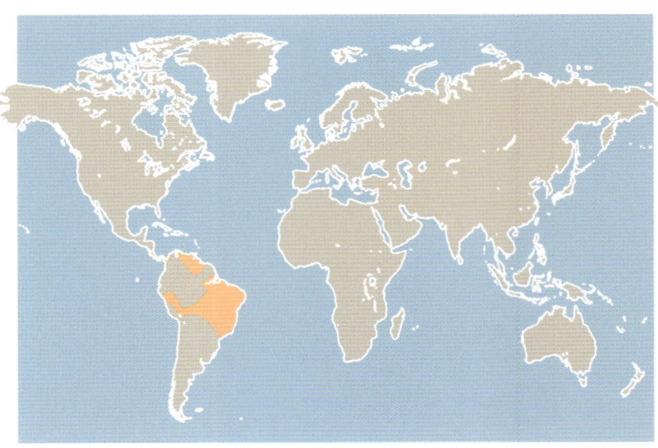

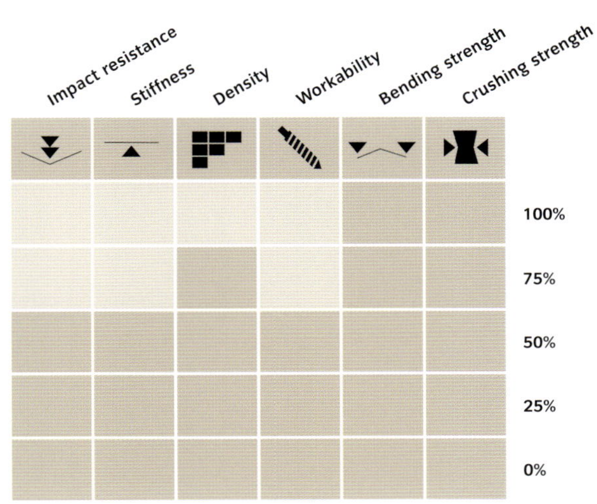

Workability describes how easy a wood is to work and whether it has a significant blunting effect on tools.

Bending strength is also known as maximum bending strength. Pressure is applied to each end of a board until it cracks.

Crushing strength is the ability of wood to withstand loads applied to the end grain, a critical test for wood used as short columns or props.

Buxus sempervirens	Family: *Buxaceae*	**BOXWOOD**	Hardwood

Growth

Buxus sempervirens is known as European, Abassian, Iranian, Persian, and Turkish boxwood, according to its place of origin. It is a small tree, growing to a height of 20–30ft (6–9m). Imported billets are only 3–4ft (1–1.2m) long and 4–8in (10–20cm) in diameter.

Appearance

The wood is a pale orange-yellow color, occasionally straight grained but often irregular, especially from small trees grown in the UK. It has a very compact, very fine, and even texture.

Properties

The weight varies from 52 to 71 lb/ft^3 (830 to 1140kg/m^3), averaging about 57lb/ft^3 (910kg/m^3) when seasoned. Boxwood dries very slowly, with a strong tendency to develop surface checks or split badly if dried in the round. The billets are usually soaked in a solution of common salt or urea before being dried and end coatings applied. Billets should be converted into half-rounds and dried under covered storage conditions. It is a very dense, hard, durable wood with a high resistance to cutters, which should be kept very sharp to prevent the wood from burning when boring or recessing. The irregular grain tends to tear in planing. It is an excellent turnery wood and has a good steam-bending rating, with high stiffness, good crushing strength, and resistance to shock loads. Pre-boring is required for nailing. It glues very well, and when stained and polished gives an excellent finish. The sapwood is liable to attack by the common furniture beetle. The heartwood is durable and resistant to preservative treatment.

Uses

Boxwood has an outstanding reputation for its fine, smooth texture and excellent turning properties. It is used for textile rollers, shuttles, pulley blocks, skittles, croquet mallets, and especially tool handles. It is also in demand for wood sculpture and carving. Specialized uses include measuring instruments, rulers, engraving blocks, parts of musical instruments, chessmen, corkscrews, and so on. It is also employed for inlay lines and bandings in marquetry, the reproduction of period furniture, and the repair of antiques.

Where it grows

This is one of the very few evergreen broad-leaved trees that occur in mild temperate climates. It grows in the UK, Europe, north Africa, Asia Minor, and other parts of Asia.

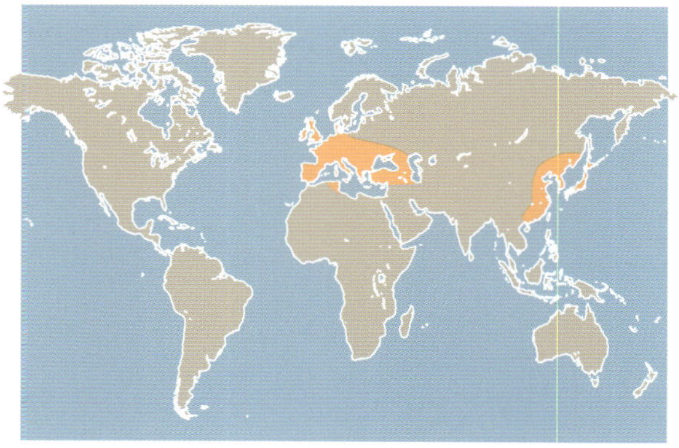

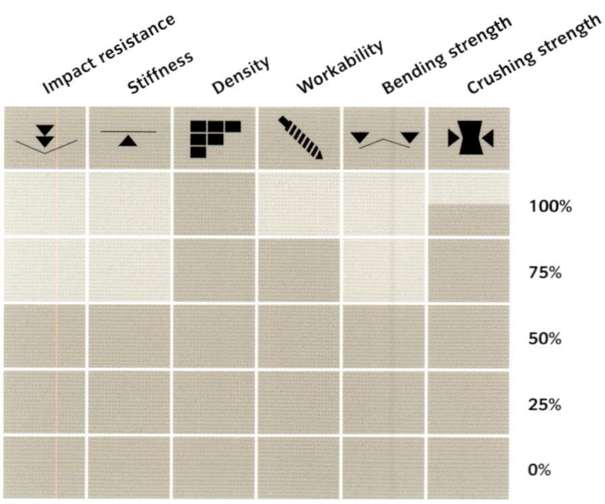

AT A GLANCE

Impact resistance is a measure of the wood's toughness. It describes its resistance to suddenly applied shock loads.

Stiffness is a measure of the wood's elasticity. It is considered in conjunction with bending strength.

Density is measured as specific gravity, the ratio of the density of a substance to that of water.

Caesalpinia echinata	Family: *Leguminosae*	**BRAZILWOOD**	Hardwood

Growth

The name brazil (*brasa* in Portuguese) had been used since the Middle Ages to describe a red dye with the color of glowing fire embers that came from the east Indian wood *Caesalpinia sappan*. The Portuguese gave the name of the wood to the country when they came to Brazil. This timber is also known as bahia wood, para wood, and pernambuco wood (UK); Brazil ironwood (US); and hypernic, brasilette, brasilete, and brasiletto (Brazil). It grows to a height of 20–30ft (6–9m), yielding short billets 3ft (1m) long and up to 8in (20cm) in diameter.

Appearance

The almost white sapwood is sharply distinct from the heartwood, which matures from bright orange to a rich, deep, dark red. It has a marble-like figure of dark red-brown variegated stripes, sometimes dotted with pin knots. It can be selected for straight grain, but is often interlocked, and has a fine, compact, smooth, even texture with a natural luster.

Properties

Brazilwood is a very hard, heavy wood, weighing in the region of 75–80lb/ft^3 (1200–1280kg/m^3) when seasoned. It needs to be dried very slowly to avoid degrade, but is very stable in service. It has high strength properties in all categories, but is unsuitable for steam bending. It is sometimes difficult to work, with a severe blunting effect on cutting edges, which must be kept very sharp, but it finishes well. It needs pre-boring for nailing but has good screw-holding properties. The very durable wood can be glued easily and brought to a very smooth, lustrous, brilliant finish, often showing a snake-like ripple. It is resistant both to insect attack and to fungal decay.

Uses

Brazilwood has a richly deserved worldwide reputation as a dye wood, but it is also regarded as the world's finest timber for violin bows because of its weight, flexibility, strength, and resilience. It is also highly prized for ornamental turnery and for high-quality gun butts and rifle stocks. It is used locally for exterior joinery, and it makes excellent heavy-duty parquetry flooring. Selected logs are sliced to make decorative veneers for paneling and sawn for inlays in reproduction antique furniture.

Where it grows

This small tree grows along the coastal forests of eastern Brazil, from Bahia toward the south.

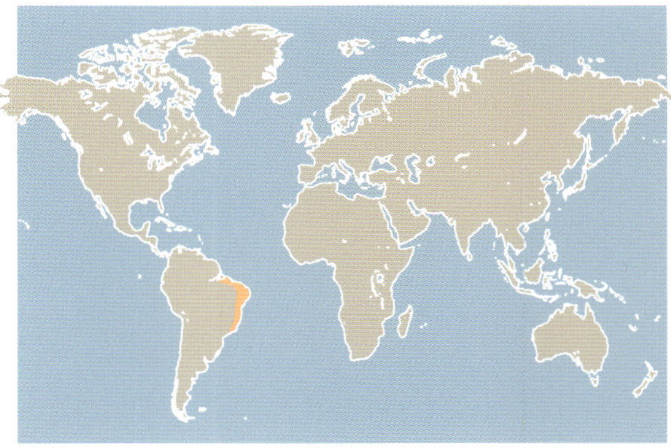

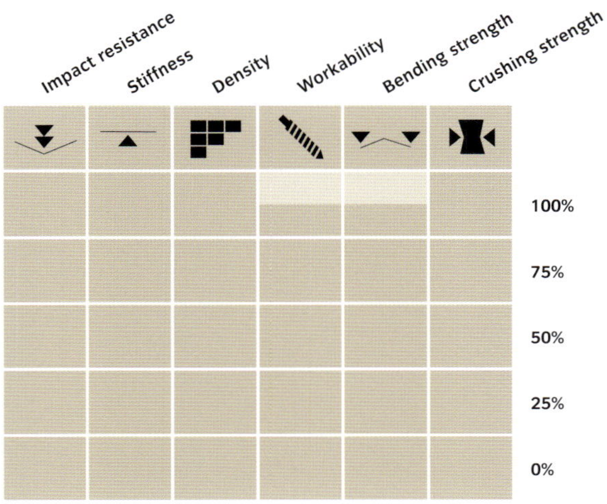

Workability describes how easy a wood is to work and whether it has a significant blunting effect on tools.

Bending strength is also known as maximum bending strength. Pressure is applied to each end of a board until it cracks.

Crushing strength is the ability of wood to withstand loads applied to the end grain, a critical test for wood used as short columns or props.

Calophyllum brasiliense | Family: *Guttiferae* | **JACAREUBA/SANTA MARIA** | Hardwood

Growth
Calophyllum brasiliense Camb. (*var. rekoi* Standl.) produces santa maria from Central America and the West Indies, and is known as jacareuba in Brazil. It is also known as guanandi and pau de Maria (Brazil); krassa (Nicaragua); and koerahara (Surinam). The tree grows to a height of 100–150ft (30–45m) and has a diameter of 3–5ft (1–1.5m), with a clear cylindrical bole for around 65ft (20m).

Appearance
The heartwood of jacareuba varies from yellow-pink to rich red-brown. Its grain is commonly interlocked, sometimes straight, often with fine dark red parenchyma stripes that show on flat-sawn surfaces, and an attractive ribbon-striped figure on quartered surfaces. The indistinct band of narrow sapwood is lighter in color. The wood has a fairly uniform, medium texture.

Properties
The weight of jacareuba varies from about 34 to 44lb/ft^3 (540 to 700kg/m^3), averaging about 37lb/ft^3 (590kg/m^3) when seasoned. The timber is difficult to air dry because it dries slowly with a considerable amount of warping and splitting, and it is especially difficult to extract moisture from the center of thick material. There is medium movement in use. It has medium bending strength and shock resistance, with low stiffness, and high crushing strength. It has a moderate steam-bending rating. The timber is moderately easy to machine, but the soft parenchyma tissue tends to pick up badly, and brown gum streaks can cause rapid blunting of cutting edges when planing or molding quarter-sawn surfaces. A reduction of cutting angle is advised here. It requires pre-boring for screwing or nailing. This very durable wood glues well, and stains and polishes to a good finish. The heartwood is extremely resistant to preservation treatment, but the sapwood is permeable.

Uses
Jacareuba is used locally for exterior joinery, general construction, bridge building, shingles, ship building, and so on. It is also utilized for interior construction and joinery, shop fitting, and furniture making. Selected logs are sliced for decorative veneers for cabinets and paneling.

Where it grows
This genus is widely distributed in the tropics. It grows throughout the West Indies, and from southern Mexico down into the northern parts of South America.

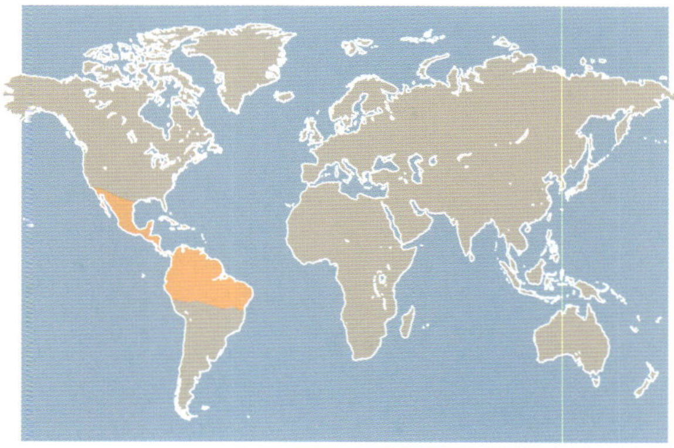

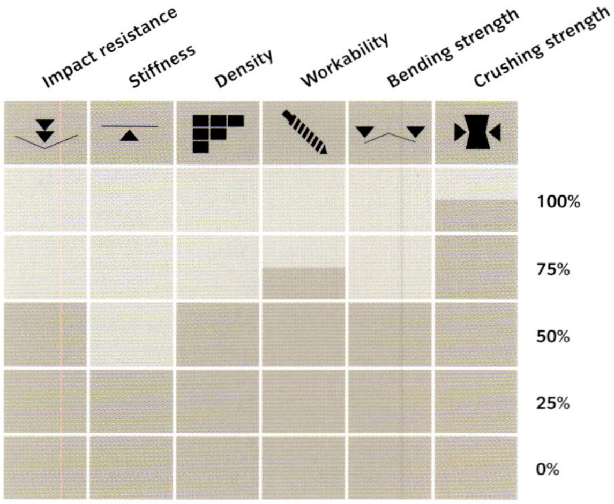

AT A GLANCE

Impact resistance is a measure of the wood's toughness. It describes its resistance to suddenly applied shock loads.

Stiffness is a measure of the wood's elasticity. It is considered in conjunction with bending strength.

Density is measured as specific gravity, the ratio of the density of a substance to that of water.

Calycophyllum candidissimum | Family: *Rubiaceae* | **DEGAME** | Hardwood

Growth
Degame grows to a height of 40–65ft (12–20m), and an average diameter of 16in (0.4m). Exported in small, round, unbarked logs, it is also known as lancewood (US and UK) and lemonwood (US).

Appearance
The wood has a wide, thick sapwood of white to very pale brown, not clearly defined from the heartwood, which is a variegated light olive-brown. The grain is generally straight, occasionally irregular, with an exceedingly fine and even texture.

Properties
Degame's average weight is about 51lb/ft^3 (820kg/m^3) when seasoned. It dries slowly with little degrade, and is stable in use. Degame is a hard, heavy, tough, and resilient timber, and does not split easily. It has high bending and crushing strengths, medium stiffness and shock resistance, and a very good steam-bending rating. The wood is not difficult to work with either hand or machine tools if the cutting edges are kept sharp. It holds screws and nails without difficulty, glues well, takes stain and polish easily, and can be brought to an excellent finish. The wood is not durable or resistant to decay.

Uses
Degame is an excellent wood for sculpture and wood carving, and has a first-class reputation for turnery. It is extensively used as a good alternative for true lancewood (*Oxandra lanceolata*) for tool handles of exceptional hardness and the top joints of fishing rods; it is also used for billiard cues, shuttles, shoe lasts, pulleys, and measuring instruments. It is valued for archery bows because it will bend and not break, and it is also used for parts in organ building and textile machinery. It is a tough flooring timber, and is superior for interior joinery and cabinet work. Locally it is used for agricultural implements, and for internal frames for buildings.

Where it grows
This small- to medium-sized tree occurs in Cuba, and from southern Mexico through Central America, to Colombia and Venezuela in tropical South America.

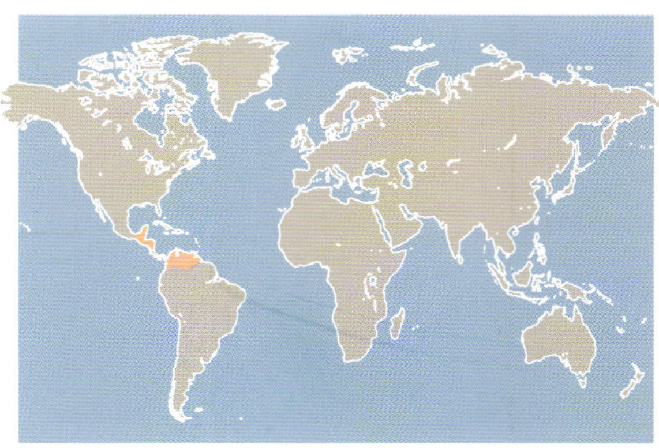

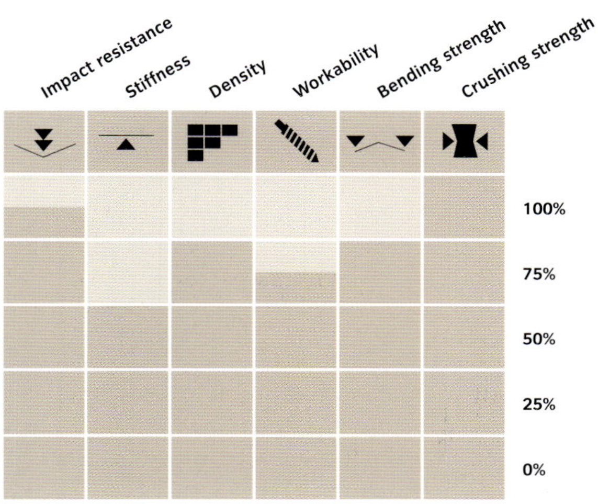

Workability describes how easy a wood is to work and whether it has a significant blunting effect on tools.

Bending strength is also known as maximum bending strength. Pressure is applied to each end of a board until it cracks.

Crushing strength is the ability of wood to withstand loads applied to the end grain, a critical test for wood used as short columns or props.

Cardwellia sublimis | Family: *Proteaceae* | **AUSTRALIAN SILKY OAK** | Hardwood

Growth

The name silky oak originally referred to *Grevillea robusta*, a native of southern Queensland that also occurs in New South Wales. *Cardwellia sublimis*, from north Queensland, has similar characteristics, and became known as silky oak and northern silky oak. Both are large trees, about 120ft (37m) high and 4ft (1.2m) in diameter.

Appearance

This very attractive timber has large rays and a very well-marked silver grain ray figure showing on quartered surfaces, but it is not a true oak (*Quercus spp.*). The heartwood of both main species is pink to reddish brown, maturing into a darker red-brown. *Cardwellia* is generally darker than *Grevillea*, which is a paler pink-brown. They are usually straight grained, except where the wood fibers distort around the rays, and have a coarse but even texture. Narrow gum lines are sometimes present and the wood has an attractive golden sheen.

Properties

When seasoned, the weight of *Grevillea* is about 36lb/ft^3 (580kg/m^3), and *Cardwellia* is about 34lb/ft^3 (540kg/m^3). Silky oak is a difficult timber to dry, and severe cupping of wide boards may occur. It has medium movement in use. The wood works readily with both hand and machine tools, with only a slight blunting effect on cutting edges, but quarter-sawn material tends to pick up when planing or molding and a reduction of the cutting angle is advised. It has good nail-holding properties. Silky oak has below average strength in all categories relative to its density, especially bending and compression, but a good steam-bending classification. The wood glues well, takes stain readily, and provides an excellent finish. The sapwood is liable to attack by the powder post beetle. The heartwood is moderately durable and resistant to preservation treatment.

Uses

Silky oak is used in Australia instead of softwood for building and shuttering. Top grades are used for furniture, interior joinery and paneling, office, bank, and shop fitting, coachwork, and cask staves, and for hard-wearing floors. It is rotary cut for plywood manufacture and sliced for decorative veneers for paneling.

Where it grows

The name silky oak is given to a number of different genera and species in Australia and New Zealand.

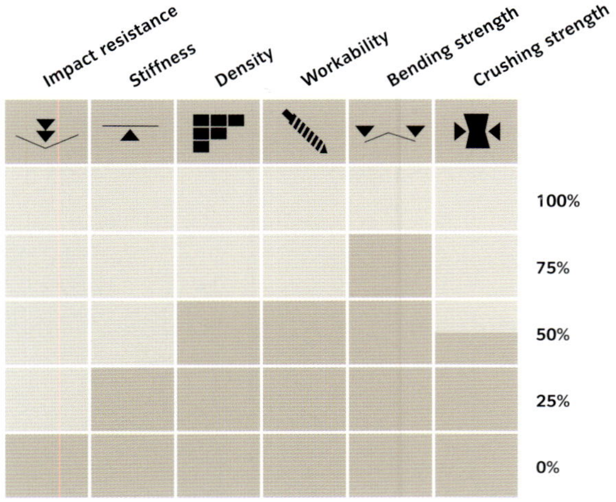

AT A GLANCE

Impact resistance is a measure of the wood's toughness. It describes its resistance to suddenly applied shock loads.

Stiffness is a measure of the wood's elasticity. It is considered in conjunction with bending strength.

Density is measured as specific gravity, the ratio of the density of a substance to that of water.

Carpinus betulus | Family: *Betulaceae* | **HORNBEAM** | Hardwood

Growth
Hornbeam grows to a height of 50–80ft (15–24m), with a fluted bole that is seldom clear of branches. The trunk is usually elliptical instead of round. The diameter is 3–4ft (0.9–1.2m).

Appearance
There is no distinction between the sapwood and heartwood—both are a dull white color marked with gray streaks and flecks caused by the broad ray structure, which produces a flecked figure on quartered surfaces. It is usually irregular or cross grained, but has a fine, even texture.

Properties
The weight averages 47lb/ft^3 (750kg/m^3) when seasoned. Hornbeam dries fairly rapidly and well with little degrade, but with considerable movement in service. This heavy, dense wood has high bending and crushing strength, medium stiffness and resistance to shock loads, and excellent shear strength and resistance to splitting. Similar to ash (*Fraxinus spp.*) in toughness, it has a very good steam-bending classification. It is fairly difficult to work because there is high resistance in cutting, with a moderate blunting effect on tools. The wood finishes very smoothly, glues well, takes stain and polish easily, and can provide an excellent finish. The sapwood is liable to attack by the common furniture beetle and the heartwood is perishable but permeable for preservation treatment.

Uses
Hornbeam is an excellent turnery wood and is used especially for brush backs, drumsticks, the shafts of billiard cues, skittles, and Indian clubs. It is also used for piano actions, clavichords, harpsichords, and other musical instrument parts such as violin bridges; plus wooden cog wheels, pulleys, millwrights' work, dead-eyes, mallets, and wooden pegs. Its high resistance to wear makes it a good flooring timber for light industrial use. Selected logs are sliced for decorative veneers.

Where it grows
About 20 species of hornbeam grow in the northern temperate zones of Europe, in rich soil on low ground. It occurs from Sweden south to Asia Minor, but the species of commercial interest grow in France, Turkey, and Iran. In the UK, it is a woodland and hedgerow tree.

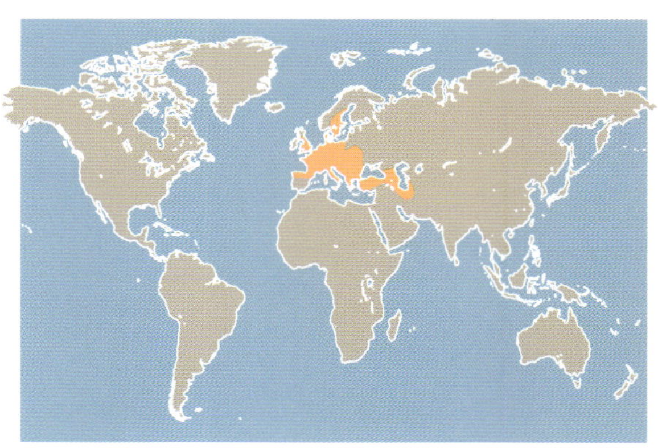

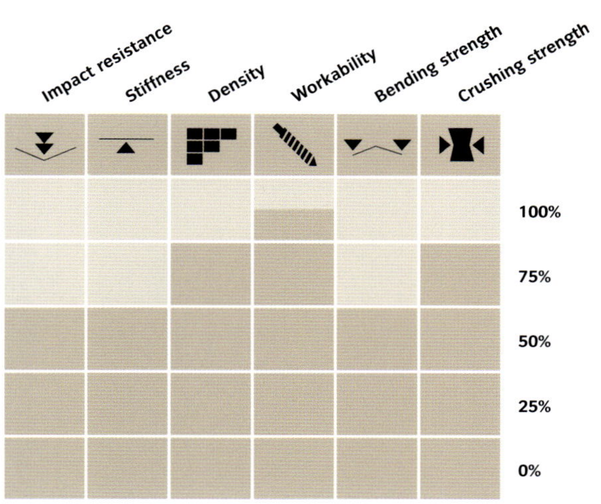

Workability describes how easy a wood is to work and whether it has a significant blunting effect on tools.

Bending strength is also known as maximum bending strength. Pressure is applied to each end of a board until it cracks.

Crushing strength is the ability of wood to withstand loads applied to the end grain, a critical test for wood used as short columns or props.

Carya illinoinensis	Family: *Juglandaceae*	**PECAN**	Hardwood

Growth

Also referred to as *Carya illinoiensis*, pecan is closely related to the many hickory species (*Carya spp.*) and is also known as sweet pecan and pecan hickory. It is a big tree, upward of 50m (165ft) in height and 2m (7ft) in diameter. It lives for a long time, with examples known to last 350 years. Carya is the Greek word for nut.

Appearance

Pecan has an inconsistent color, ranging from pale brown, almost straw-like, to a darker tan color. There is often a tinge of red or pink to its appearance. The grain of pecan wood is varied, but the figuring is attractive without being particularly special. Unusually, the pale sapwood tends to be more valued than the heartwood, and is often referred to as white hickory, while the heartwood is known as red hickory.

Properties

Like other hickories, pecan is a strong wood. The texture is fairly coarse, though variable, with curving bands of much denser wood. It is heavy—47lb/ft^3 (750kg/m^3)—and seasons well and quickly. It does tend to shrink when drying, but it is stable once dry. It works well enough, but for a good finish you will need to sand carefully and for some time. Unfortunately, it is not particularly durable, otherwise it would be used more frequently in construction and for other outdoor projects.

Uses

Like ash (*Fraxinus spp.*), pecan is used largely when strength is important, so it is no surprise that the lumber is used for staircases and drumsticks. It is also employed for handles, chairs, wheels, and vehicles.

Where it grows

Pecan grows from north to south down the center of the US, from Indiana to Texas and even Mexico.

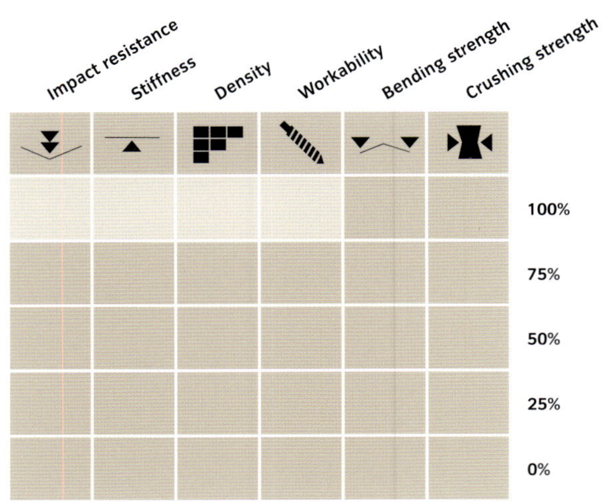

AT A GLANCE

Impact resistance is a measure of the wood's toughness. It describes its resistance to suddenly applied shock loads.

Stiffness is a measure of the wood's elasticity. It is considered in conjunction with bending strength.

Density is measured as specific gravity, the ratio of the density of a substance to that of water.

Carya spp. | Family: *Juglandaceae* | **HICKORY** | Hardwood

Growth

There are four commercial species of hickory: *Carya glabra* (Mill.) Sweet produces pignut hickory; *C.tomentosa* provides mockernut hickory; *C.laciniosa* produces shellbark hickory; and *C.ovata* provides shagbark hickory. The trees vary according to species and grow from 60 to 120ft (18 to 37m) high. They have a straight, cylindrical bole, with a diameter of around 2–3ft (0.6–1m).

Appearance

The wide, very pale gray sapwood, which is sold as white hickory, is generally preferred to the heartwood, which is red to reddish brown in color and referred to as red hickory. It is usually straight grained, but occasionally wavy or irregular, with a rather coarse texture.

Properties

The weight ranges from about 45 to 56lb/ft^3 (720 to 900kg/m^3), but averages 51lb/ft^3 (820kg/m^3) when seasoned. Hickory needs very careful drying but is stable in service. It is very dense and has high toughness, bending, stiffness, and crushing strengths, with exceptional shock resistance. It has excellent steam-bending properties. The wood is difficult to machine, and has a moderate blunting effect on tools. It is also difficult to glue, but stains and polishes very well. Hickory is nondurable. The sapwood is liable to attack by the powder post beetle, and the heartwood is moderately resistant to preservation treatment.

Uses

Hickory is ideal for the handles of striking tools, such as hammers, picks, and axes, as well as for wheel spokes, chairs, and ladder rungs. It is a valuable sculpture and carving wood, and is extensively used for sports equipment such as golf clubs, lacrosse sticks, baseball bats, the backs of longbows, laminae in tennis rackets, and skis. It appears in the tops of heavy sea-fishing rods, drumsticks, picking sticks in the textile industry, and vehicle building. Hickory is rotary cut for plywood faces and sliced for decorative veneers.

Where it grows

Although more than 20 species of hickory grow in the large forests of eastern Canada and the US, there are only four commercial species. These occur in deciduous forests from Ontario in Canada to Minnesota and Florida in the US and down to Mexico.

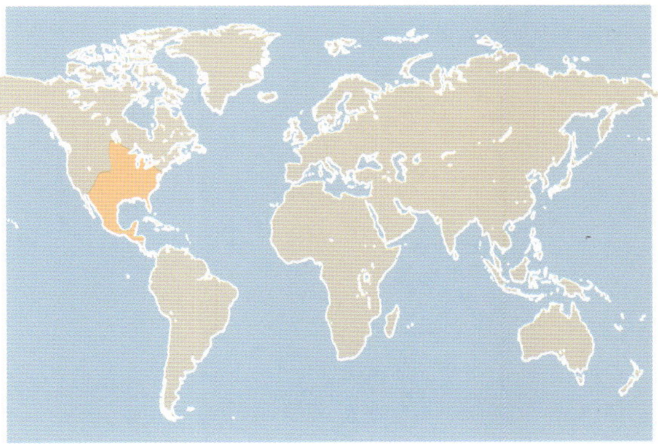

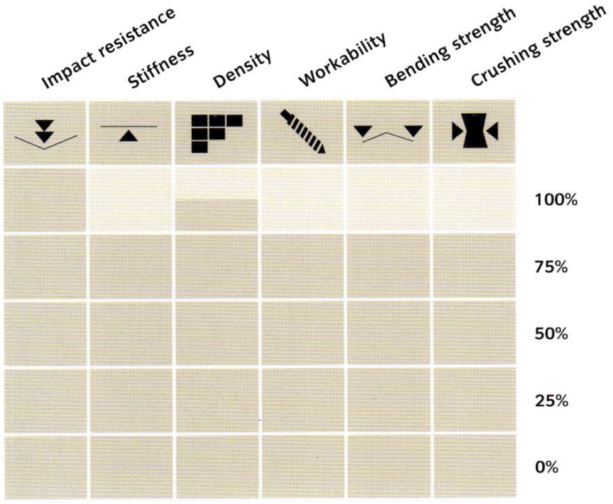

Workability describes how easy a wood is to work and whether it has a significant blunting effect on tools.

Bending strength is also known as maximum bending strength. Pressure is applied to each end of a board until it cracks.

Crushing strength is the ability of wood to withstand loads applied to the end grain, a critical test for wood used as short columns or props.

Castanea sativa | Family: *Fagaceae* | **SWEET CHESTNUT** | Hardwood

Growth

In favorable conditions of growth, the sweet chestnut reaches a height of about 100ft (30m) or more, and has a diameter of 5ft (1.5m). In less favorable sites, the short bole branches into several limbs It is also commonly known as Spanish chestnut and European chestnut.

Appearance

The heartwood of sweet chestnut is a straw to brown color that resembles oak (*Quercus spp.*), distinct from the narrow sapwood. The wood has prominent growth rings but finer rays, so it does not have the silver grain figure of oak on quartered surfaces. The grain is straight but often spiral, especially from mature trees, and has a coarse texture. Many logs are subject to cupping or ring shakes.

Properties

The weight of sweet chestnut averages about 34lb/ft³ (540kg/m³) when seasoned. It is rather difficult to air dry because it retains moisture in patches and tends to collapse or honeycomb; it does not respond well to kiln reconditioning. Its acidic character tends to corrode iron fastenings in damp conditions, and tannin in the wood causes blue-black stains to appear when it is in contact with iron or iron compounds. It is a medium-density wood, possessing low bending strength, very low stiffness and shock resistance, and medium crushing strength. Air-dried wood has a good bending rating if free from knots. It works satisfactorily with both hand and machine tools, to which it offers only a slight blunting effect. It has good screw- and nail-holding properties, glues well, and stains and polishes to an excellent finish. The sapwood is liable to attack by the powder post beetle and the common furniture beetle. The heartwood is durable and extremely resistant to preservation treatment.

Uses

Sweet chestnut is used as a substitute for oak in furniture, and also for coffin boards, domestic woodware, and kitchen utensils. It is utilized for turnery for walking sticks, umbrella handles, bowls, and so on, as well as being cleft for fencing, gates, and hop poles. Staves are used for casks for holding oils, fats, fruit juices, and wines. Selected logs of sweet chestnut are sliced for decorative veneers.

Where it grows

This stately tree is a native of southwest Europe, and grows in the UK, France, Germany, north Africa, and parts of Asia.

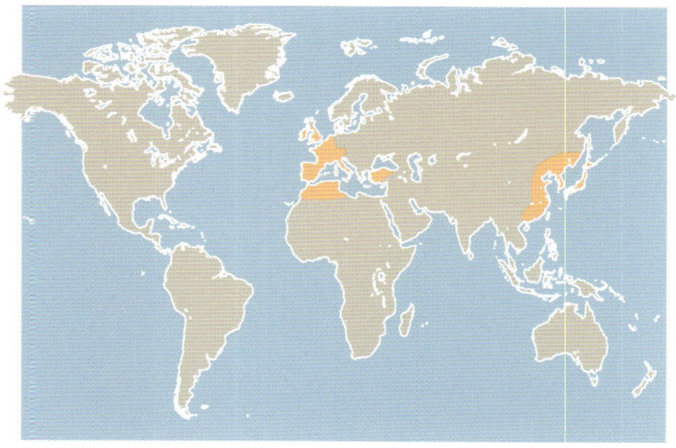

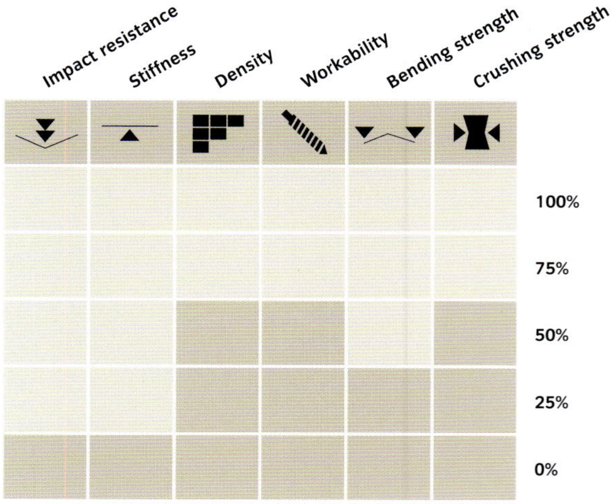

AT A GLANCE

Impact resistance is a measure of the wood's toughness. It describes its resistance to suddenly applied shock loads.

Stiffness is a measure of the wood's elasticity. It is considered in conjunction with bending strength.

Density is measured as specific gravity, the ratio of the density of a substance to that of water.

Cedrela spp.	Family: *Meliaceae*	**SOUTH AMERICAN CEDAR**	Hardwood

Growth

This is not a true cedar (*Cedrus spp.*), which is a softwood. The *Cedrela* species comprises: *C.fissilis* Vell., which produces South American cedar, also known as Brazilian cedar, British Guiana cedar, Peruvian cedar (UK), and cedro (South America); and *C.odorata* L. (*C.mexicana* Roem), which provides Central American cedar, also known as Honduras cedar, Mexican cedar, Nicaraguan cedar, Tabasco cedar, and Spanish cedar according to country of origin, as well as cigar-box cedar. The growth varies according to species and locality from 70 to 100ft (21 to 30m) in height, with a diameter of 3–6ft (1–1.8m).

Appearance

The pale pink-brown young trees are not so straight grained, but have a fine texture; the darker reddish brown types, occasionally with a purplish tinge, are from mature, slow-grown trees, and are more resinous, straight grained, but often interlocked and with a coarser texture. The wood contains gum that gives it a characteristic odor similar to genuine softwood cedar.

Properties

The weight varies from 23 to 47lb/ft³ (370 to 750kg/m³), with an average of about 30lb/ft³ (480kg/m³) when seasoned. It is very stable in use, and dries fairly rapidly and without difficulty. It is an easy wood to work with hand or machine tools, with low resistance to cutters, which should be kept sharp to avoid a tendency to wooliness. There is only slight blunting of cutting edges. The wood has a medium density and strength in all categories, and a moderately good steam-bending rating despite gum exudation. It nails and glues well, and can be brought to an excellent finish. The wood is durable, but the sapwood is liable to attack by the powder post beetle. The heartwood is extremely resistant to preservation treatment but the sapwood is permeable.

Uses

Cedar is used for high-quality cabinets and furniture, clothing chests, interior joinery and paneling, boat building, racing boat skins and canoe decks, organ sound boards, and cigar boxes. It is also rotary cut for plywood and sliced for decorative veneers for cabinets and paneling.

Where it grows

The name cedar has been given to many hardwoods of similar fragrance that occur in practically every country south of the US, with the exception of Chile.

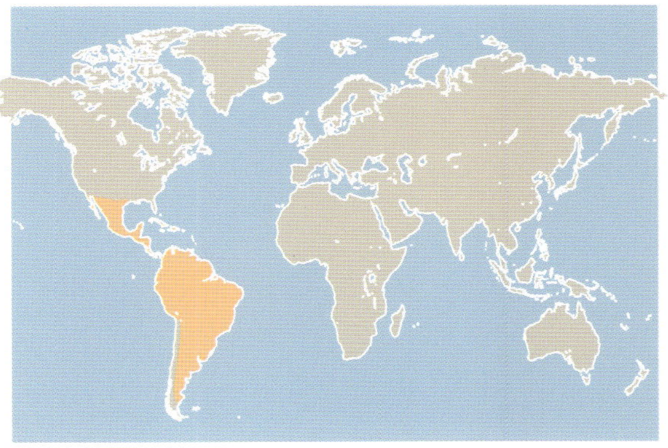

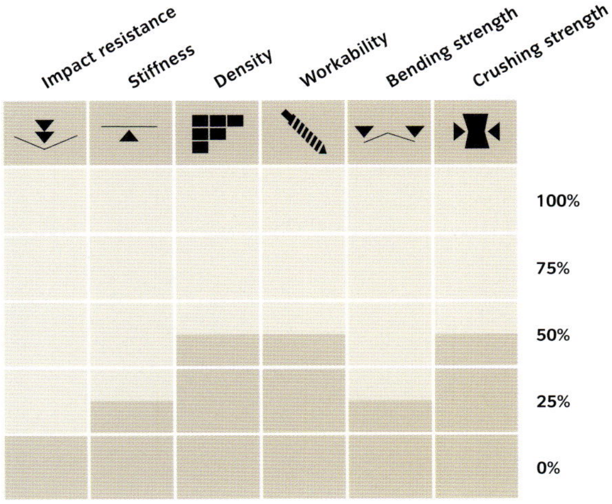

Workability describes how easy a wood is to work and whether it has a significant blunting effect on tools.

Bending strength is also known as maximum bending strength. Pressure is applied to each end of a board until it cracks.

Crushing strength is the ability of wood to withstand loads applied to the end grain, a critical test for wood used as short columns or props.

***Cedrus* spp.** | Family: *Pinaceae* | **CEDAR** | Softwood

Growth

The *Cedrus* species are the true cedars and should not be confused with other softwoods and hardwoods that are called cedar because of their fragrant scent. *C.atlantica* (Endl.) Carr., from Algeria and Morocco, is commonly known as Atlas cedar and Atlantic cedar; *C.deocara* (Roxb.) G.Don. produces deodar cedar from the western Himalayas, and is an important tree in India; *C.libani* A.Rich. produces cedar of Lebanon. The deodar grows to a height of about 200ft (60m) with a diameter of about 7ft (2m); Atlantic and Lebanon cedars vary from 120 to 150ft (37 to 45m) in height, and up to 5ft (1.5m) in diameter. Parkland timbers have a low, flattened crown with large, spreading branches near the ground, often from several stems.

Appearance

The heartwood is resinous, and has a very strong cedar odor. It is light brown in color with a prominent growth ring figure, and is quite distinct from the narrow, lighter colored sapwood. Deodar cedar is straight grained, but Atlantic and Lebanon cedars are usually knotty, with much grain disturbance. These also tend to produce pockets of in-growing bark in the wood. The texture is fairly fine.

Properties

Weight averages about 35lb/ft^3 (560kg/m^3) when seasoned. The wood dries easily, with medium movement in use. It has medium bending strength but is low in other strength properties, and has a very poor steam-bending classification due to resin exudation. Cedar works easily with both hand and machine tools, with only a slight blunting effect on cutters. The large knots and in-growing bark may cause problems in machining, so cutters should be kept sharp. Cedar has good holding properties, and stains, varnishes, paints, and polishes to a good finish. The sapwood is liable to attack by the pinhole borer and longhorn beetle; the heartwood is resistant to preservative treatment. The sapwood varies from moderately resistant to permeable.

Uses

The best grades are employed for furniture, interior joinery, and doors. Lower grades are used for paving blocks, sleepers, bridge building, and house construction. Knotty material is utilized for garden furniture. Selected logs are sliced for decorative veneers for cabinets and paneling.

Where it grows

True cedars grow in Algeria, Morocco, the western Himalayas, and India. King Solomon built his temple with cedar from Mount Lebanon.

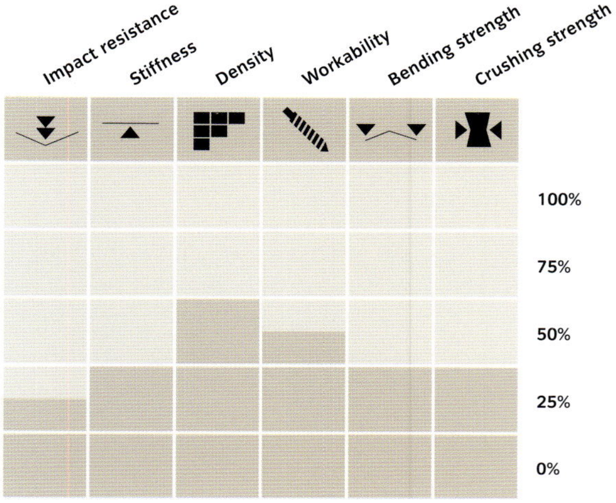

AT A GLANCE

Impact resistance is a measure of the wood's toughness. It describes its resistance to suddenly applied shock loads.

Stiffness is a measure of the wood's elasticity. It is considered in conjunction with bending strength.

Density is measured as specific gravity, the ratio of the density of a substance to that of water.

Ceratopetalum apetalem | Family: *Cunonaceae* | **COACHWOOD** | Hardwood

Growth

Ceratopetalum apetalem grows to a height of 60–80ft (18–24m), and a diameter of 1½–2½ft (0.5–0.8m). Coachwood is also known as scented satinwood.

Appearance

The tree has a light brown to pink-brown colored sapwood, not clearly demarcated from the only slightly darker colored heartwood. It has a close, straight grain with fine rays that produce a flecked figure on quarter-sawn surfaces. This is an attractive timber with a fine, even texture and a fragrant odor.

Properties

The wood weighs about 39lb/ft^3 (620kg/m^3) when seasoned. It dries fairly rapidly, with some tendency to split and warp, and requires slow and careful seasoning to avoid shrinkage. It has medium movement in use. The timber is of medium density, bending strength, stiffness, and shock resistance, but with a high crushing strength and a good steam-bending classification. The wood works fairly easily with both hand and machine tools, and gives a smooth finish. It does tend to chip out at tool exits when drilling or mortising, and nailing requires pre-boring. The wood glues easily, takes stain well, and provides an excellent finish. The sapwood is liable to attack by the powder post beetle. The wood is nondurable, but permeable for preservation treatment.

Uses

Coachwood has a decorative appearance, with a delicate flecked figure and fine texture that is popular for furniture and cabinet making, and is often used for wall paneling where a uniform effect is desired without too much contrast. In Australia it is used extensively for interior joinery and moldings, and is favored for bentwork for boat building and sporting goods. It is also used for gunstocks and parts of musical instruments, appears widely in light domestic flooring and baseboards, and is ideal for turnery for a wide range of uses, including bobbins, shoe heels, domestic woodware, and so on. It is also rotary cut for plywood corestock. Selected logs are sliced to produce decorative veneers for cabinets and architectural paneling.

Where it grows

This medium-sized Australian tree grows in New South Wales and Queensland.

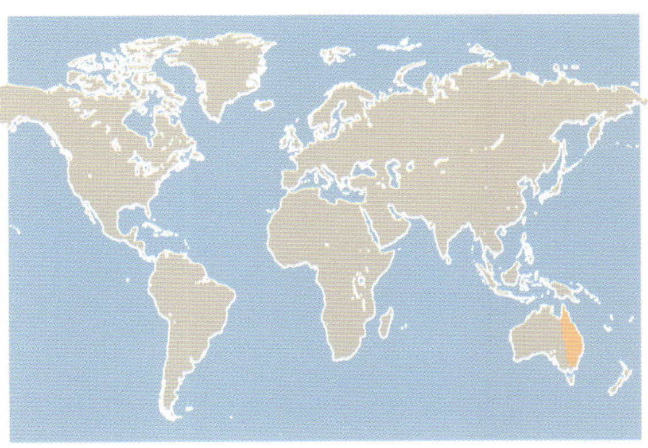

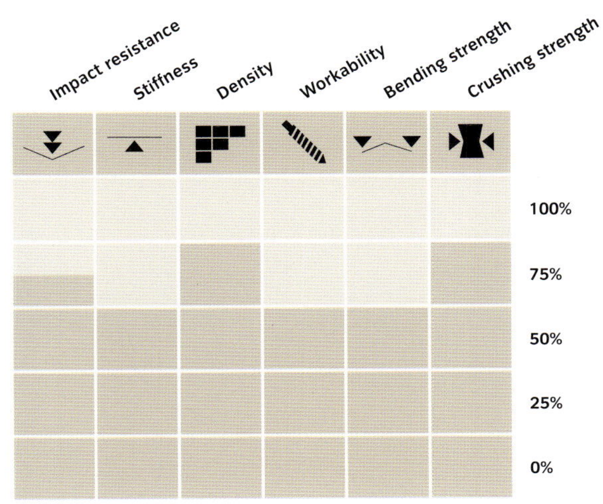

Workability describes how easy a wood is to work and whether it has a significant blunting effect on tools.

Bending strength is also known as maximum bending strength. Pressure is applied to each end of a board until it cracks.

Crushing strength is the ability of wood to withstand loads applied to the end grain, a critical test for wood used as short columns or props.

Chamaecyparis nootkatensis | Family: *Cupressaceae* | **YELLOW CEDAR** | Softwood

Growth

Yellow cedar is also known as Alaska yellow cedar and nootka false cypress (US), and as yellow cypress and Pacific coast yellow cedar (Canada). It grows to a towering 175ft (53m) in height and 7ft (2m) in diameter, but more usually about 80ft (24m) tall with a diameter of 2–3ft (0.6–1m), and a sharply tapering bole. It is not a true cedar (*Cedrus spp.*).

Appearance

This pale yellow wood is straight grained, with a fine, even texture. It has a strong spicy scent when freshly cut, but no appreciable odor when dry.

Properties

Yellow cedar weighs 31lb/ft^3 (500kg/m^3) when seasoned. The wood should be dried slowly to avoid surface checking in thick stock and end splitting if the drying is hurried. Once dry, it is noted for its durability and stability in use. The timber is moderately strong, with medium bending and crushing strengths, and low stiffness and resistance to shock loads. It has a very poor steam-bending rating. It works easily with both hand and machine tools, with only a slight dulling effect on cutting edges. It holds screws and nails without difficulty, glues and takes stain, paint, and varnish satisfactorily, and can be brought to an excellent finish. The wood is durable and resistant to preservative treatment.

Uses

Yellow cedar is extremely stable in use and has a natural durability, especially when exposed to fluctuating atmospheric conditions. It is therefore highly valued locally for high-class joinery, window frames, and finishing in houses. It is also used for furniture and cabinet work. The timber from Alaska trees is heavier and stronger than from those grown in Oregon. It is extensively used for boat and ship building, for exterior joinery, and for cladding and shingles. It is resistant to acids and is considered to be the best wood for battery separators. It is also used for engineers' patterns and surveyors' poles. In the round, the wood is used for posts, poles, and marine piling. Selected logs are sliced for decorative veneers for cabinets, doors, and paneling.

Where it grows

This large forest tree is native to the narrow coastal belt from Alaska down to northern Oregon, but the largest sizes grow in Alaska and north British Columbia.

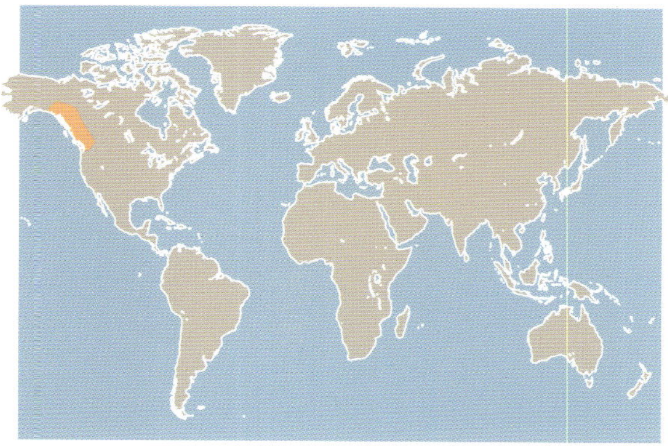

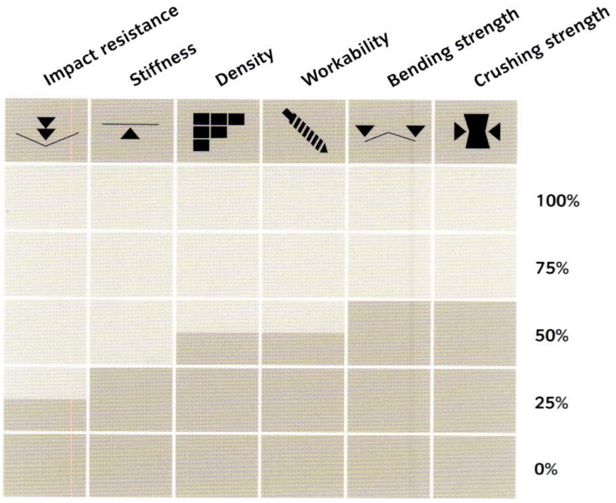

AT A GLANCE

Impact resistance is a measure of the wood's toughness. It describes its resistance to suddenly applied shock loads.

Stiffness is a measure of the wood's elasticity. It is considered in conjunction with bending strength.

Density is measured as specific gravity, the ratio of the density of a substance to that of water.

Chlorophora excelsa | Family: *Moraceae* | **IROKO** | Hardwood

Growth

Chlorophora excelsa reaches 165ft (50m) in height with a diameter of about 8–9ft (2.5m); the bole is clear and cylindrical up to 70ft (21m) or more. The related species *C.regia* A.Chév., which grows in west Africa from Senegal to Ghana, is not quite so tall. Iroko is also known as mvule (east Africa), odum (Ghana and Ivory Coast), kambala (Zaire), tule and intule (Mozambique), and moreira (Angola).

Appearance

The pale sapwood of iroko is clearly defined from the yellow-brown colored heartwood, which matures to a deeper brown, with lighter vessel lines conspicuous on flat-sawn surfaces. The grain of iroko is typically interlocked and sometimes irregular.

Properties

When seasoned, iroko weighs about $40lb/ft^3$ ($640kg/m^3$). The wood dries well and fairly rapidly, with some degrade. This very durable wood of medium density is stable in use, has medium bending and crushing strengths, very low stiffness and shock resistance, and a moderate bending rating. Hard deposits of calcium carbonate known as stone are often completely hidden in the grain and are only detectable from the darker wood surrounding them. They can severely damage the cutting edges of tools, and tipped or hardened saw teeth are required. The fine machining dust can cause nasal and skin irritation. Nailing, screwing, and gluing are satisfactory. When filled, it provides an excellent finish. The sapwood is liable to attack by the powder post beetle. The wood is very durable and extremely resistant to preservation treatment, but the sapwood is classed as permeable.

Uses

Iroko is used for similar purposes to, and as a substitute for, teak (*Tectona grandis*), but lacks teak's greasy feel. Iroko is valued for high-class interior and exterior joinery, counter and laboratory bench tops, and draining boards. It is a favorite wood for sculpture and wood carving, and is also ideal for turnery. It is widely used in ship, boat, and vehicle building (but not for bentwork), and as a structural timber for piling, marine work, and garden and park bench seats. Another popular use is for domestic parquet flooring where underfloor heating is used. Logs are rotary cut for plywood manufacture and sliced for decorative veneers.

Where it grows

This species grows in the moist, semi-deciduous forests of tropical Africa, from Sierra Leone in the west to Tanzania in the east.

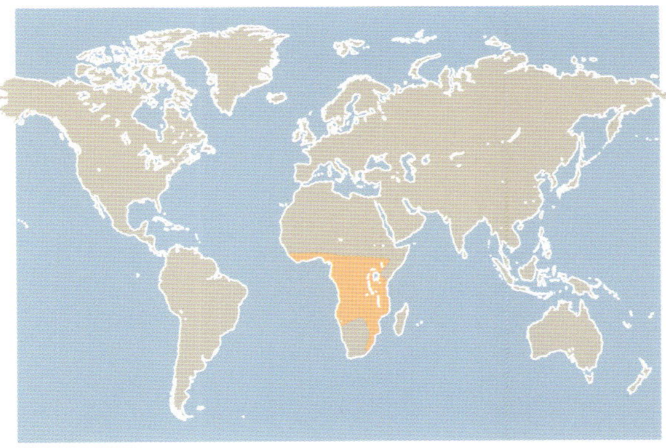

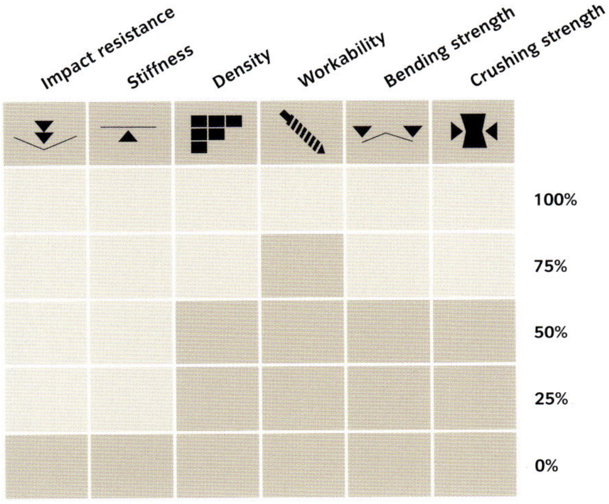

Workability describes how easy a wood is to work and whether it has a significant blunting effect on tools.

Bending strength is also known as maximum bending strength. Pressure is applied to each end of a board until it cracks.

Crushing strength is the ability of wood to withstand loads applied to the end grain, a critical test for wood used as short columns or props.

Chloroxylon swietenia | Family: *Rutaceae* | **CEYLON SATINWOOD** | Hardwood

Growth

Ceylon satinwood is also known as east Indian satinwood (US and UK); burutu (Sri Lanka); and bhera, behra, and mutirai (India). It grows to 45–50ft (14–15m) in height, with a diameter of about 1ft (0.3m) or more, and a cylindrical bole up to around 3m (10ft).

Appearance

There is very little distinction between the sapwood color and the heartwood, which is a beautiful golden yellow. The inner heartwood matures into a slightly darker golden brown. The grain is narrowly interlocked, sometimes wavy or variegated, producing roe or narrow ribbon-striped figure on quartered surfaces. It is often broken striped, or with bee's wing cross-mottled figure. Gum rings can develop thin dark veins on flat-sawn surfaces. The wood is lustrous and fragrant; the texture is fine and very even.

Properties

The average weight is about 61lb/ft^3 (980kg/m^3) when seasoned. The wood should be allowed to air dry slowly to avoid a tendency to surface cracking and distortion, but it kiln dries well with little degrade and is stable in service. This very heavy, dense wood has high bending and crushing strengths, medium stiffness, and low shock resistance, but strength is of little importance for the end uses of this timber. It is fairly difficult to work with machinery and has a moderate blunting effect on cutting edges. Nailing requires pre-boring. It is a difficult wood to glue, but it takes stain and polishes to an excellent finish when filled. The wood is durable, and extremely resistant to preservative treatment.

Uses

This timber has long been highly valued and in great demand for luxury cabinets, fine furniture making, and interior joinery. It is excellent for turnery, for the backs and handles of hair brushes, and is also used for jute bobbins. It appears widely in paneling in office, shop, and bank fitting, and also in the manufacture of traditional inlay motifs, lines, and bandings. Selected logs are sliced to produce extremely attractive decorative veneers with a range of ribbon-striped or mottled surface figure.

Where it grows

This small- to medium-sized tree reaches its best development in Sri Lanka, but also occurs in central and southern India.

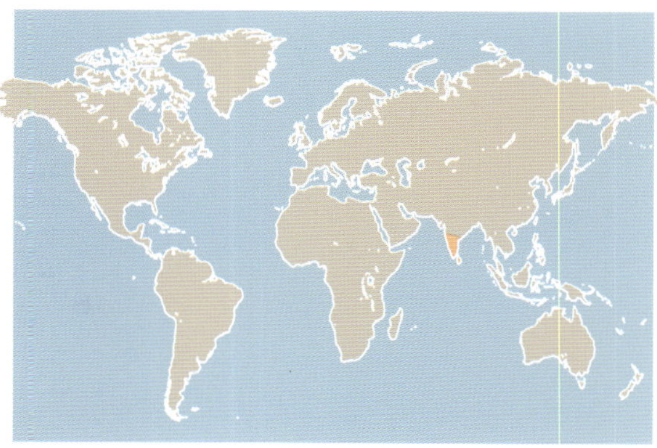

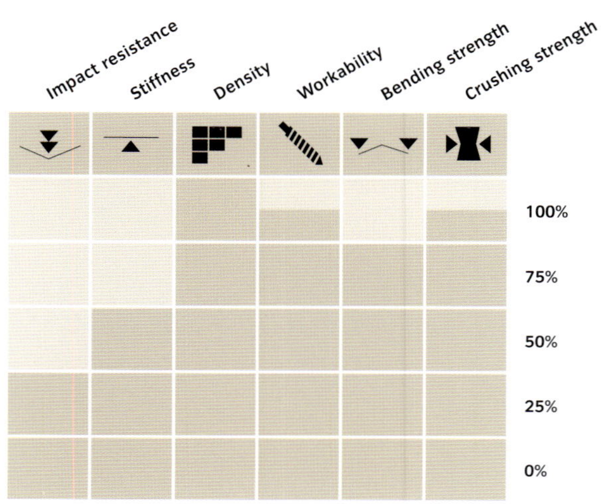

AT A GLANCE

Impact resistance is a measure of the wood's toughness. It describes its resistance to suddenly applied shock loads.

Stiffness is a measure of the wood's elasticity. It is considered in conjunction with bending strength.

Density is measured as specific gravity, the ratio of the density of a substance to that of water.

Cordia dodecandra	Family: *Boraginaceae*	**ZIRICOTE**	Hardwood

Growth

Named after the German botanist Euricius Cordus, whose life spanned the 15th and 16th centuries, the ziricote tree is not particularly large at no more than 90ft (27m) high and 2½ft (0.8m) in diameter, with a straight, clean stem. Frequently, however, it is much smaller and inhibited by its neighbors, and is in short supply. Ziricote is often referred to as sericote.

Appearance

The distinctive grain pattern is in the walnut style, combining the wavy lines of European walnut (*Juglans regia*) with the hardness and color of rosewood (*Dalbergia spp.*). It is very distinctive, and if you can find it from a sustainable source is well worth trying, though it is likely to be expensive. The color is rich dark brown, with thin wavy black lines. There can be some silvery flecking where rays are revealed, and the texture is uniformly fine to medium. The grain tends to be fairly straight, but with some waviness. There is also a contrasting pale sapwood, which is often used for effect.

Properties

Very hard and strong, and fairly heavy at 55lb/ft^3 (880kg/m^3), ziricote is difficult to season because there is a high risk of surface checking, though it is very stable once dry. Its durability is moderate, and because the grain tends to be straight, it is not particularly difficult to use. It turns very well, and polishes to a high luster.

Uses

Increasingly, ziricote is available only as a veneer, and is expensive enough to be used sparingly. It is commonly used for furniture, cabinets, paneling, and interior trim, as well as for gunstocks and flooring.

Where it grows

Ziricote is grown across a relatively small area of southern Mexico, Belize, and Guatemala.

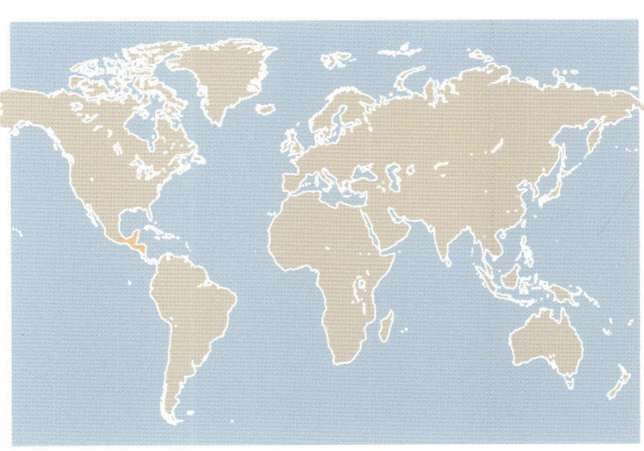

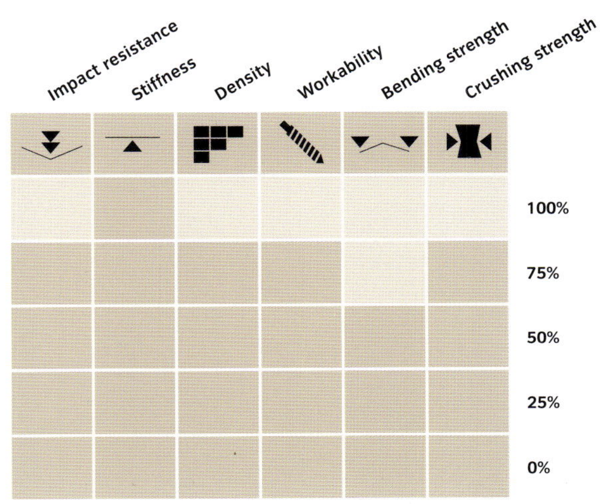

Workability describes how easy a wood is to work and whether it has a significant blunting effect on tools.

Bending strength is also known as maximum bending strength. Pressure is applied to each end of a board until it cracks.

Crushing strength is the ability of wood to withstand loads applied to the end grain, a critical test for wood used as short columns or props.

Cordia spp.	Family: *Boraginaceae*	**AFRICAN CORDIA**	Hardwood

Growth

The species include: *Cordia abyssinica* R.Br., known as mukumari (Kenya) and mringaringa (Tanzania); *C.millenii* Bak., known as mugoma (Kenya) and mukeba (Uganda); and *C.platythyrsa* Bak. Both *C.millenii* and *C.platythyrsa* are known as omo in Nigeria. The trees are medium sized, averaging 60–100ft (18–30m) in height, with an irregularly shaped bole about 3ft (1m) in diameter.

Appearance

The cream-colored sapwood is distinct from the heartwood, which varies in color from golden to medium brown, sometimes with dark streaks and a pink tinge. It usually darkens on maturity to a light red-brown. The grain varies from fairly straight to interlocked or irregular, and the medium-sized rays give an attractive striped or mottled figure on quartered surfaces. The texture is coarse.

Properties

The weight is about 27lb/ft^3 (430kg/m^3) when seasoned. The wood dries well and rapidly, without too much splitting or warping, and is stable in service. It has low density, low bending strength, very low stiffness, medium crushing strength, very low shock resistance, and a poor steam-bending classification. Brittleheart is fairly common in this species. The wood works easily with both hand and machine tools, but cutters should be kept very sharp to prevent the surface from becoming wooly. Nailing and gluing are satisfactory, and when filled the timber can be brought to a good finish. The outer heartwood is very durable, but the inner heartwood is only moderately durable and resistant to preservative treatment.

Uses

This rather weak and soft timber is mainly used for decorative parts of furniture where strength is unimportant, such as interior framing and fitments, library fittings, edge lippings, and so on. It is used locally for making traditional drums and sound boards because of its resonance properties, and is the traditional wood for canoe making and boat building in west Africa. Logs are rotary cut for plywood and laminated corestock, and selected logs are sliced for decorative veneers for cabinets and paneling.

Where it grows

The African species of *Cordia* is a deciduous tree that occurs in the semi-tropical rainforests of Kenya, Tanzania, and Nigeria.

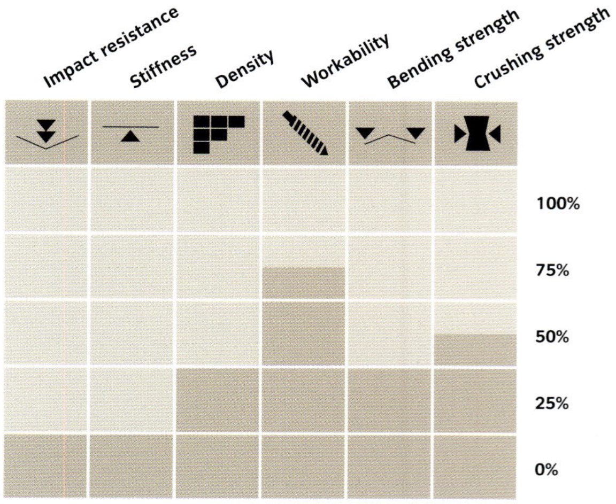

AT A GLANCE

Impact resistance is a measure of the wood's toughness. It describes its resistance to suddenly applied shock loads.

Stiffness is a measure of the wood's elasticity. It is considered in conjunction with bending strength.

Density is measured as specific gravity, the ratio of the density of a substance to that of water.

Dalbergia cearensis	Family: *Leguminosae*	**KINGWOOD**	Hardwood

Growth

Dalbergia cearensis varies in height from 50 to 100ft (15 to 30m). It is exported in small logs that are 3–7ft (1–2m) long and 4–8in (10–20cm) in diameter, with the sapwood removed. Commonly known as kingwood, it is also referred to as violete (Brazil); violetta and violet wood (US); and bois violet (France).

Appearance

The heartwood of *D.cearensis* has a rich violet-brown background color shading almost to black, with variegated stripes or streaks of black, violet-black, or violet-brown, and sometimes golden yellow. The almost white sapwood is clearly defined. The heartwood has a bright luster, a fine uniform texture, and a very smooth surface.

Properties

This very heavy wood weighs about 75lb/ft^3 (1200kg/m^3) when seasoned. Care is needed in air drying to avoid splits, but it kiln dries without degrade, and is stable in use. Kingwood is very strong in all categories. Despite being hard and heavy, it works fairly well with both hand and machine tools, if cutters are kept very sharp. There is a moderate blunting effect on tools. The wood has good nail- and screw-holding properties, but needs pre-boring. Care is needed in gluing, but the wood can be brought to a beautiful high polish because of its natural waxy properties. The timber is durable and resistant to preservative.

Uses

Kingwood is well named, for it is certainly a king among woods. This was a favorite of Parisian cabinet makers during the reigns of Louis XIV and XV of France and in the Georgian period of English furniture; it is in great demand today for restoration and reproduction of antique furniture, and for decorative work generally. Unfortunately, its use is restricted because of the small sizes available. The wood is excellent for turnery for bowls and small fancy items, and is also treasured for sculpture. It is usually saw cut into veneers because the billets are too small for slicing. It is in demand in veneer form for inlay and marquetry work, and oyster veneering for antique repairs and restoration.

Where it grows

This small to medium height member of the rosewood *Dalbergia* species occurs mainly in Brazil.

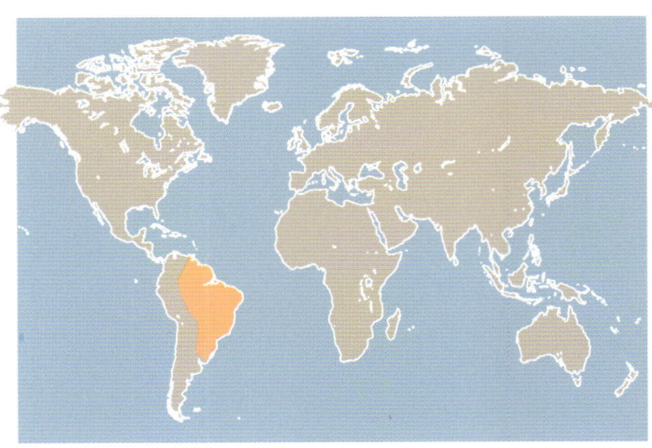

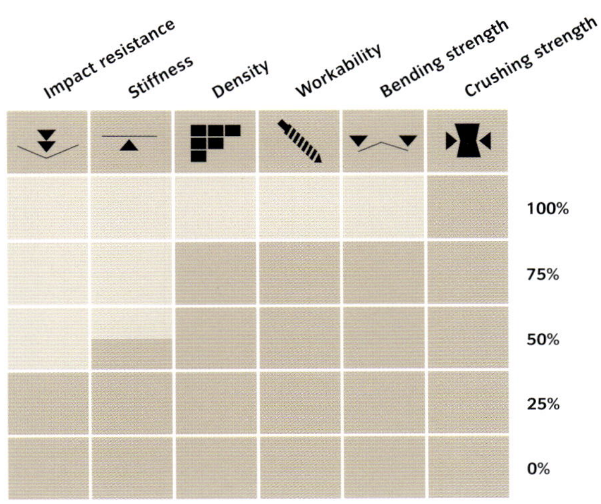

Workability describes how easy a wood is to work and whether it has a significant blunting effect on tools.

Bending strength is also known as maximum bending strength. Pressure is applied to each end of a board until it cracks.

Crushing strength is the ability of wood to withstand loads applied to the end grain, a critical test for wood used as short columns or props.

Dalbergia frutescens | Family: _Leguminosae_ | **BRAZILIAN TULIPWOOD** | Hardwood

Growth
Brazilian tulipwood is exported without sapwood in small billets around 2–4ft (0.6–1.2m) long and 2–8in (5–20cm) in diameter. It is also known as pau rosa, jacaranda rosa, and pau de fuso (Brazil); pinkwood (US); and bois de rose (France). It is not to be confused with the tulip tree, *Liriodendron tulipifera*.

Appearance
The very attractive pink-yellow heartwood of Brazilian tulipwood has a pronounced striped variegated figure in shades of violet-red, salmon-pink, and rose-red. In effect, the coloring of a red and yellow tulip blossom is reproduced by this beautiful wood. As it matures, it tends to lose its original vividness, but it remains a strikingly beautiful timber. The grain is usually interlocked and irregular because of its twisted growth, with a medium to fine texture and a pleasantly mild fragrant scent.

Properties
The heartwood weighs about 60lb/ft^3 (960kg/m^3) when seasoned. It dries fairly easily and is stable in use. It is a very hard, dense, and compact wood, and is liable to split after conversion. It is rather wasteful in conversion because it is extremely hard to work; it is fissile and tends to splinter. There is severe blunting of cutting edges. It also requires pre-boring for screwing or nailing, but it glues well. The wood possesses a very high natural luster and provides an excellent finish. It is nondurable and resists insect and fungal attacks, but is highly resistant to preservative treatment.

Uses
This historical cabinet wood was used extensively in the furniture of the French Kings Louis XV and XVI, and classical English furniture of the 18th century. The billets are usually saw cut for decorative panel crossbandings and marquetry inlay bandings in the restoration and repair of antiques. It is used in Brazil as a turnery wood for brush backs, and for marimba keys, caskets, jewelry boxes, and fancy goods.

Where it grows
This small, often misshapen tree grows in northeast Brazil and around Bahia and Pernambuco.

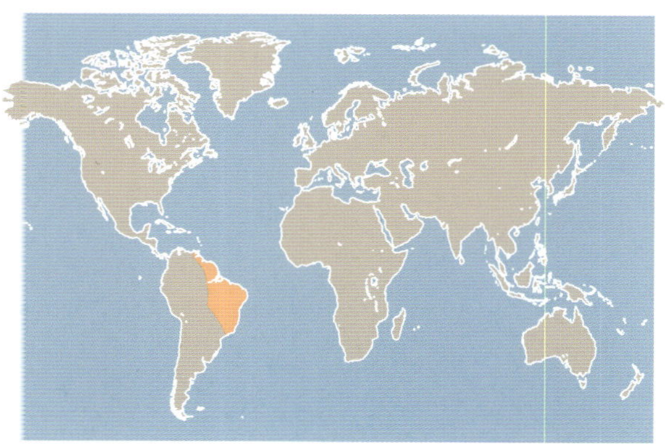

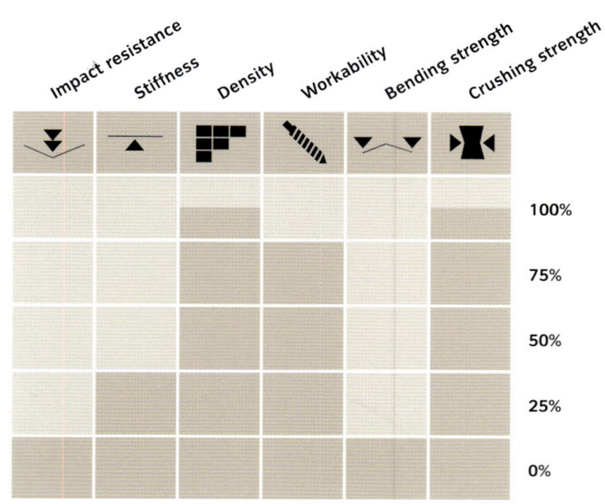

AT A GLANCE

Impact resistance is a measure of the wood's toughness. It describes its resistance to suddenly applied shock loads.

Stiffness is a measure of the wood's elasticity. It is considered in conjunction with bending strength.

Density is measured as specific gravity, the ratio of the density of a substance to that of water.

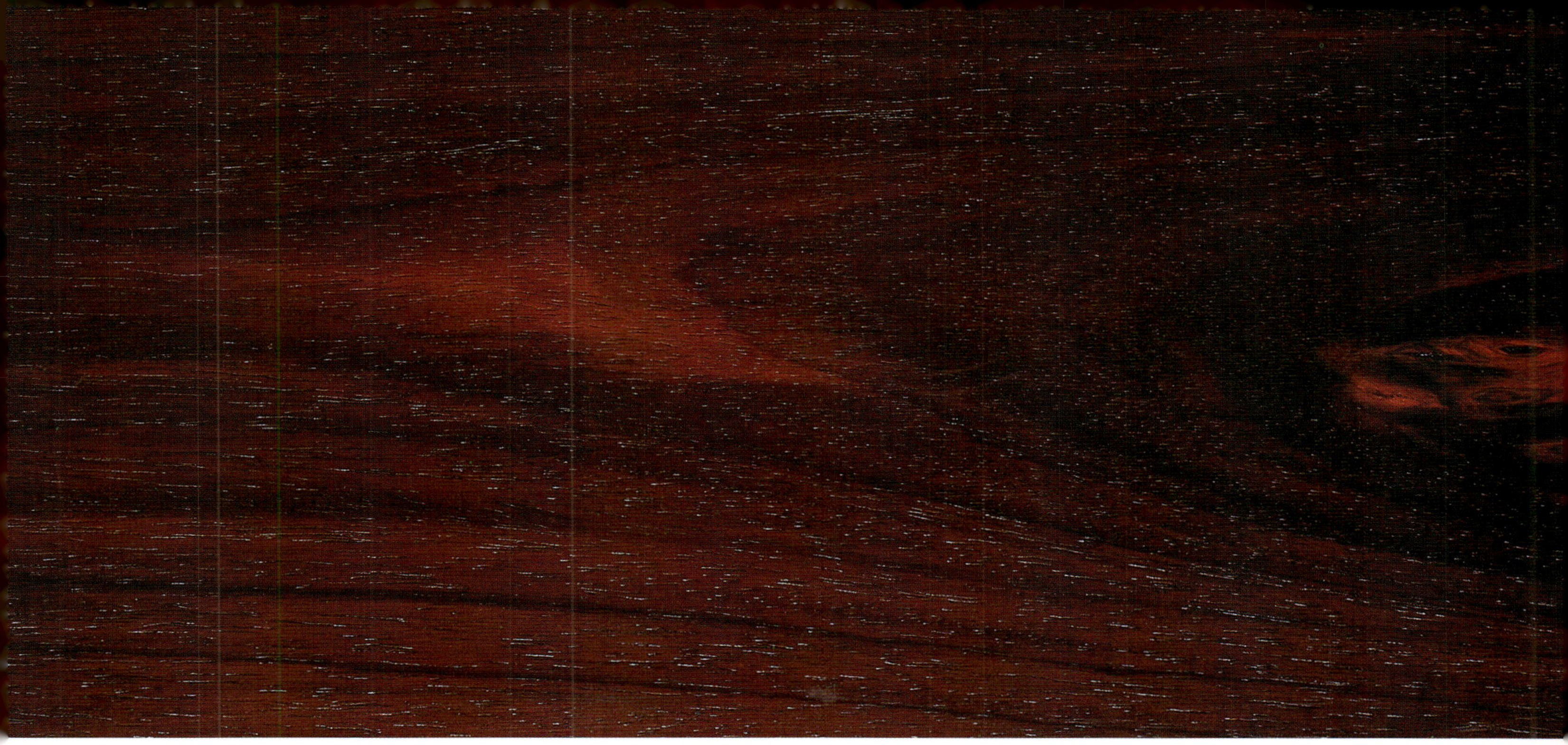

Dalbergia latifolia	Family: *Leguminosae*	**INDIAN ROSEWOOD**	Hardwood

Growth

In southern India where it grows best, *Dalbergia latifolia* can reach a height of 80ft (24m), with diameters varying from 1 to 5ft (0.3 to 1.5m). It averages 2½ft (0.8m) with a cylindrical, fairly straight bole of 20–50ft (6–15m). It is also known as east Indian rosewood and Bombay rosewood (UK), and as Bombay blackwood, shisham, sissoo, biti, ervadi, and kalaruk (India).

Appearance

The narrow, pale yellow-cream sapwood has a purplish tinge and is clearly defined from the heartwood, which is medium to dark purple-brown, with darker streaks terminating the growth zones. Together with the narrowly banded interlocked grain, this produces an attractive ribbon-striped grain figure on quartered surfaces. The texture is uniform and moderately coarse, and the wood has a fragrant scent.

Properties

When seasoned, the weight averages about 53lb/ft^3 (850kg/m^3). This timber responds best by air drying in the round or as square baulks prior to conversion. The wood should be allowed to dry slowly, which improves the color. It is stable in use. This very dense wood has high bending and crushing strengths, with medium resistance to shock loads, low stiffness, and a good steam-bending rating. It is fairly difficult to machine or work with hand tools, severely blunting the cutting edges with calcareous deposits in some of the vessels. It is unsuitable for nailing or screwing, but glues satisfactorily, and when filled, can be polished or waxed to provide an excellent finish. The sapwood is liable to attack by the powder post beetle, but the heartwood is very durable and classified as resistant to preservative.

Uses

This very decorative wood is used for top-class furniture and cabinet work, as well as shop, office, and bank fitting. It makes an excellent turnery wood for small fancy goods, handles, and bowls. It is used for parts of musical instruments, particularly for guitar backs and sides, and is highly valued for sculpture and carving. In India, it is also used for exterior joinery, decorative flooring, boat building, hammer heads, and brake blocks. Selected logs are sliced for highly decorative veneers.

Where it grows

This large Indian tree varies considerably in size according to locality, growing best in the southern part of India.

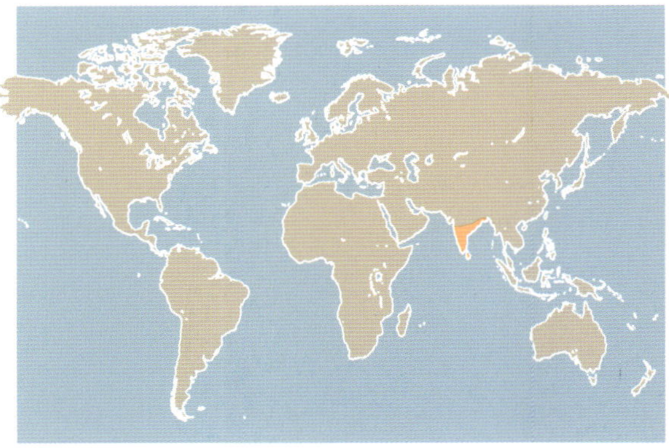

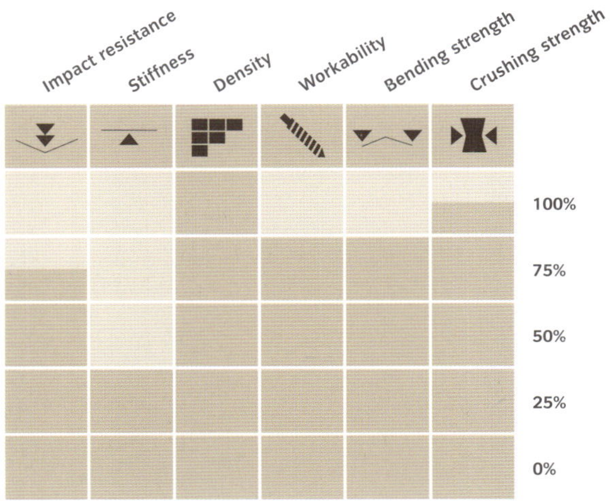

Workability describes how easy a wood is to work and whether it has a significant blunting effect on tools.

Bending strength is also known as maximum bending strength. Pressure is applied to each end of a board until it cracks.

Crushing strength is the ability of wood to withstand loads applied to the end grain, a critical test for wood used as short columns or props.

Dalbergia retusa | Family: *Leguminosae* | **COCOBOLO** | Hardwood

Growth

Also known as granadillo, *Dalbergia retusa* is a medium-sized tree with a fluted trunk that grows to 65–100ft (20–30m), with a diameter of about 3ft (1m). It is shipped in small, round billets, mainly from Costa Rica and Nicaragua.

Appearance

When freshly cut, the heartwood is an array of colors from lemon-orange to deep rich red, with many variegated streaks and zones of yellow, orange, and brick-red. These mature to a deep, mellow orange-red, with darker stripes and mottling. The sapwood, clearly defined from the heartwood, is almost white in color. The grain varies from straight to irregular and is sometimes wavy. It has a fine, medium, uniform texture.

Properties

The weight of cocobolo varies from about 61 to 75lb/ft³ (980 to 1200kg/m³), with an average weight of 68lb/ft³ (1090kg/m³) when seasoned. The wood dries out very slowly, with a tendency to check and split, but it is very stable in service. It is not unduly difficult to work with both hand and machine tools, but there is moderate blunting of cutting edges, which should be kept very sharp. When machined, the wood gives off a mild fragrance from its natural oil. The fine dust can be an irritant and cause a form of dermatitis, staining the skin an orange color. This very tough timber has high mechanical strength in all categories, but this is not important because of the end uses. It is difficult to glue due to its very high natural oiliness, but with care it can be brought to an excellent smooth finish that feels cold, like marble, to the touch. The heartwood is very durable and resistant to preservative treatment.

Uses

Cocobolo is ideal for turnery, and is traditionally used for cutlery handles, knife and tool handles, brush backs, truncheons, and bowling balls. It is also highly valued for sculpture and carving, chessmen, and small decorative items such as inlaid boxes and wooden jewelry. Selected logs are sliced for highly decorative veneers for inlay work, for the decoration of furniture, and for paneling.

Where it grows

Cocobolo occurs along the Pacific seaboard of Central America from Mexico to Panama.

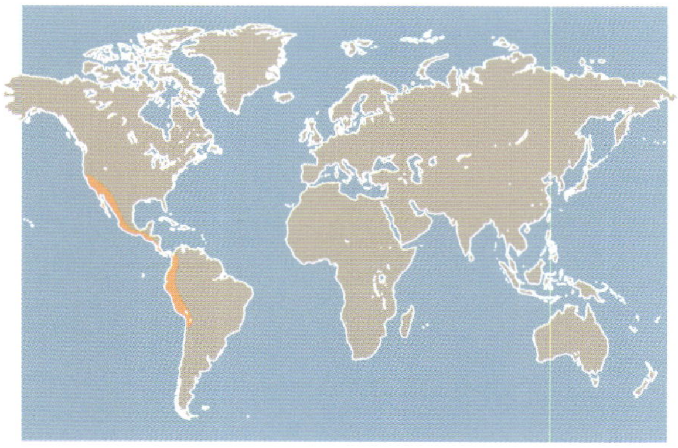

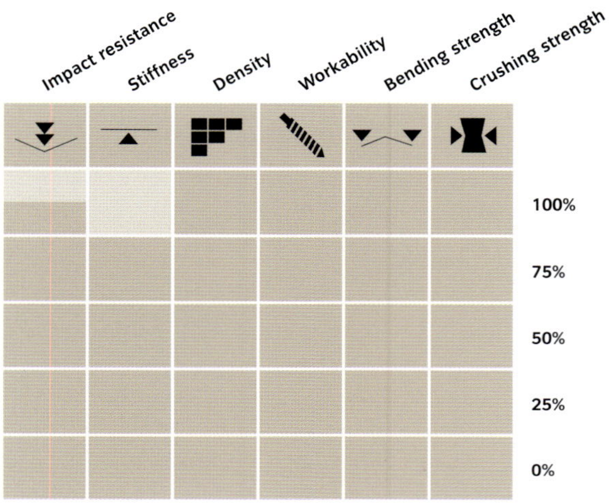

AT A GLANCE

Impact resistance is a measure of the wood's toughness. It describes its resistance to suddenly applied shock loads.

Stiffness is a measure of the wood's elasticity. It is considered in conjunction with bending strength.

Density is measured as specific gravity, the ratio of the density of a substance to that of water.

Dalbergia spp. | Family: *Leguminosae* | **BRAZILIAN/HONDURAS ROSEWOOD** | Hardwood

Growth

Brazilian rosewood has been one of the world's most treasured timbers for centuries. *Dalbergia nigra* Fr.All. is sadly becoming rare. It is also known as Bahia rosewood or Rio rosewood (US and UK), and as jacaranda (Brazil); it grows to a height of about 125ft (38m) and the bole is irregular. When the sapwood is removed, the heartwood is 1½ft (0.5m) in diameter. *D.stevensonii* Standl. produces Honduras rosewood, also known as nogaed (US); it grows to 50–100ft (15–30m) and 3ft (1m) in diameter.

Appearance

The heartwood of Brazilian rosewood is a rich brown color with variegated streaks of golden brown to chocolate-brown and from violet to purple-black, sharply demarcated from the almost cream-colored sapwood. The grain is mostly straight to wavy, the texture coarse, oily, and gritty to the touch, and the timber has a mildly fragrant odor. Honduras rosewood has pinkish to purple-brown heartwood with irregular black markings; it is straight grained and has a medium to fine texture.

Properties

Brazilian rosewood weighs 53lb/ft^3 (850kg/m^3) when seasoned, and Honduras rosewood weighs around 58–68lb/ft^3 (930–1090kg/m^3). Both woods air dry fairly slowly, with a marked tendency to check, but are stable in service. They possess high strength in all categories but are low in stiffness, and have good steam-bending ratings. They are not unduly difficult to work, but have a severe blunting effect on cutting edges. Gluing is no problem if epoxy resin adhesives are used. A smooth, lustrous oil finish can be achieved. Both species are durable, and their heartwood is extremely resistant to preservative.

Uses

Rosewoods, in both solid and veneer forms, have been highly prized for more than 200 years for high-class furniture and superior cabinet making. They are also used for bank and shop fitting, boardroom paneling, tables, furniture, piano cases, and billiard tables. The wood is also in demand for wood carving and sculpture, and is excellent for turnery. Specialized uses include musical instrument fingerboards, percussion bars for xylophones, and marimba keys. Selected logs are sliced for highly decorative veneers.

Where it grows

Brazilian and Honduras rosewood grow, as you might expect, in Brazil and Honduras as well as Mexico.

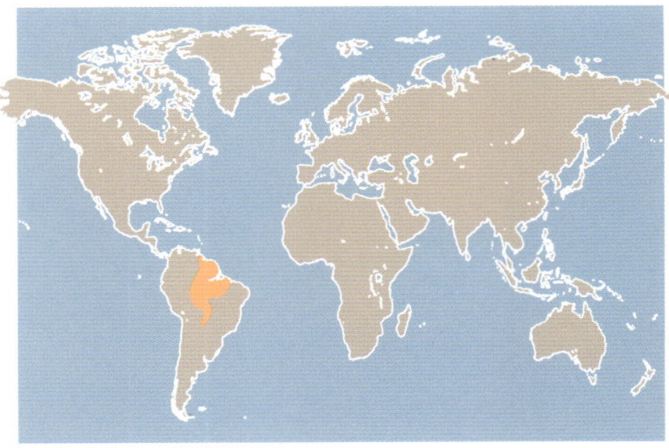

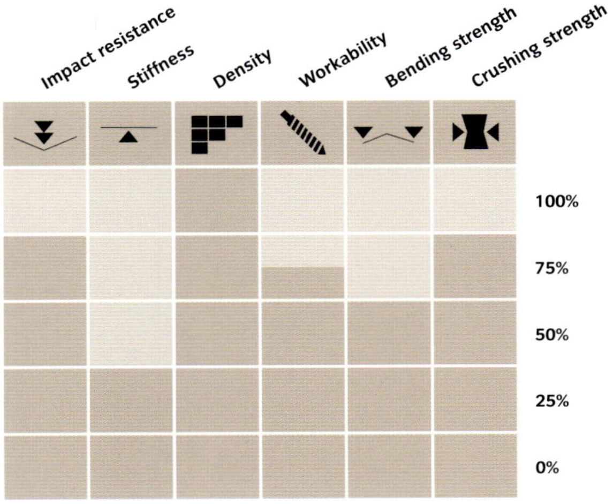

Workability describes how easy a wood is to work and whether it has a significant blunting effect on tools.

Bending strength is also known as maximum bending strength. Pressure is applied to each end of a board until it cracks.

Crushing strength is the ability of wood to withstand loads applied to the end grain, a critical test for wood used as short columns or props.

Diospyrus spp.	Family: *Ebenaceae*	**AFRICAN EBONY**	Hardwood

Growth

The name ebony covers all species of *Diospyrus* with predominantly black heartwood. African ebony includes *D.crassiflora* Hiern and *D.piscatoria* Gürke. The name white ebony refers to the sapwood. The small- to medium-sized tree grows to a height of 50–60ft (15–18m), with an average diameter of about 2ft (0.6m). It is exported as short billets.

Appearance

Since ancient Egyptian times, the black heartwood of ebony has been in great demand. *D.crassiflora* is considered to be the most jet black. Other species have a very attractive black and dark brown striped heartwood. African ebony is usually straight grained to slightly interlocked or curly, and the texture is very fine and even

Properties

This timber weighs about 64lb/ft^3 (1030kg/m^3) when seasoned. The wood air dries fairly rapidly but is liable to surface checking; however, kiln drying produces very little degrade. African ebony is very stable in service. It is very dense, has extremely high strength properties in all categories, and a good steam-bending rating. Ebony is difficult to work with either hand or machine tools because there is a severe blunting of cutting edges. It is also inclined to be brittle, and needs a reduced cutting angle when planing the curly grain of quartered stock. African ebony requires pre-boring for screwing or nailing. The heartwood requires care in gluing, but can be polished to a beautiful finish. The heartwood is very durable and extremely resistant to preservative treatment.

Uses

Ebony has always been used for sculpture and carving, and is an excellent turnery wood for the handles of tools, table cutlery, and pocket knives. It appears as door knobs, brush backs, and the butt ends of billiard cues, as well as for the facings of tee squares. Other specialized uses include piano and organ keys, organ stops, violin fingerboards and pegs, bagpipe chanters, castanets, and guitar backs and sides. It is used for luxury cabinet work, marquetry, and inlay lines and bandings, and is sawcut into veneers for antique repairs.

Where it grows

African ebony occurs in southern Nigeria, Ghana, Cameroon, Zaire, Gabon, Madagascar, and Kribi. It is named after its country or port of origin—for example, Cameroon ebony, Kribi ebony, Gabon ebony, Madagascar ebony, and Nigerian ebony.

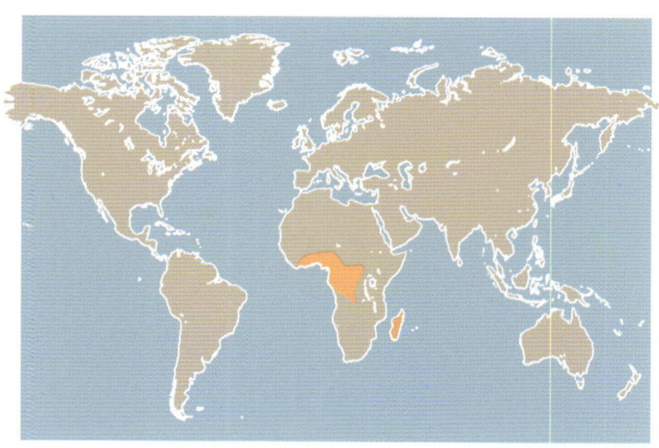

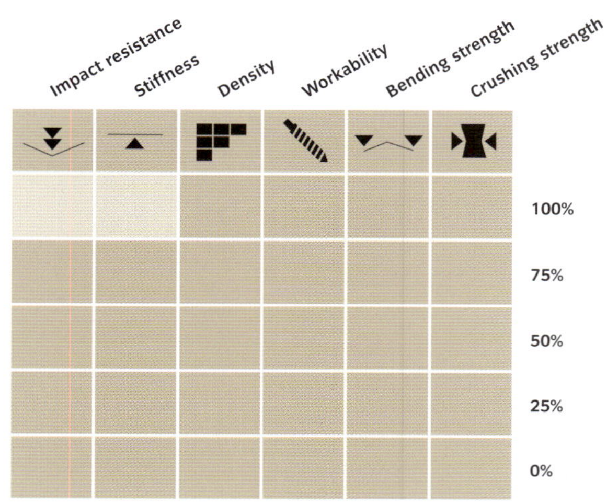

AT A GLANCE

Impact resistance is a measure of the wood's toughness. It describes its resistance to suddenly applied shock loads.

Stiffness is a measure of the wood's elasticity. It is considered in conjunction with bending strength.

Density is measured as specific gravity, the ratio of the density of a substance to that of water.

Diospyrus spp. | Family: *Ebenaceae* | **EAST INDIAN EBONY** | Hardwood

Growth
Ceylon ebony, *Diospyrus ebenum*, Koen., is known as true ebony because its heartwood has a uniform jet black color. *D.melanoxylon* Roxb. and *D.tomentosa* Roxb. provide Indian ebony; *D.celebica* Bakh. produces Macassar ebony from the Celebes Islands; *D.marmorata* Park. provides Andaman marblewood from the Andaman Islands. The various species are smallish trees, with 15–20ft (4.5–6m) long boles and diameters of 1–2ft (0.3–0.6m).

Appearance
The sapwood is a light gray, but the heartwood of Ceylon ebony is jet black. Macassar ebony is medium brown in color with beige and black stripes. Coromandel and calamander ebony refer to heartwood with gray or brown mottled figure. The grain varies from straight to irregular or wavy, with a fine, even texture and a metallic luster.

Properties
Ceylon ebony weighs 73lb/ft^3 (1170kg/m^3); other ebonies weigh between 64 and 68lb/ft^3 (1030 and 1090kg/m^3); Indian ebony is much lighter and weighs 55lb/ft^3 (880kg/m^3) when seasoned. Ebony is difficult to air dry, and unless dried very slowly, develops deep cracks and checks. These exceptionally heavy, dense timbers have very high strength in all categories, but are inclined to be brittle. The sapwood has a good steam-bending rating. The heartwood is extremely difficult to machine and has a very severe blunting effect on cutting edges, so increased pressure should be applied to prevent the wood from rising or chattering on the cutters. Care is required in gluing, but all species provide an excellent finish. The wood is subject to beetle attack but is very durable and extremely resistant to preservative treatment.

Uses
Ever since the times of the ancient courts of Persia and India, ebony has been used for luxury furniture, wood sculpture, and carving. It is used for turnery as tool, cutlery, and knife handles, brush backs, billiard cues, snuff boxes, and combs, as well as for musical instrument parts—piano keys, fingerboards, tail pieces, and saddles for stringed instruments. Ebony also appears as inlay lines and bandings for antique repairs.

Where it grows
East Indian ebony occurs in Sri Lanka, southern India, the Celebes Islands, and the Andaman Islands. Ceylon ebony is also known as tendu, tuki, and ebans in India; other ebonies are named after their country or port of origin.

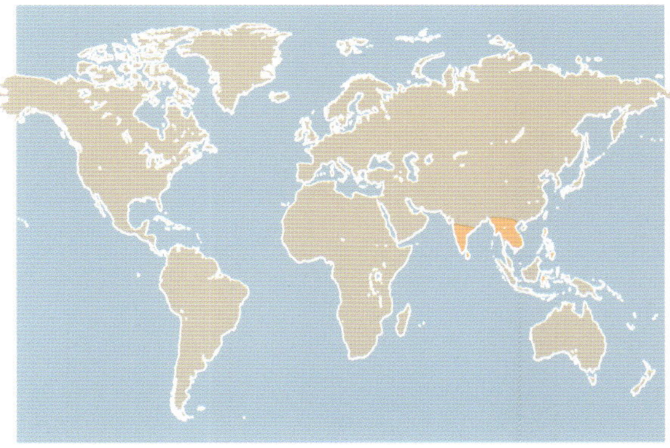

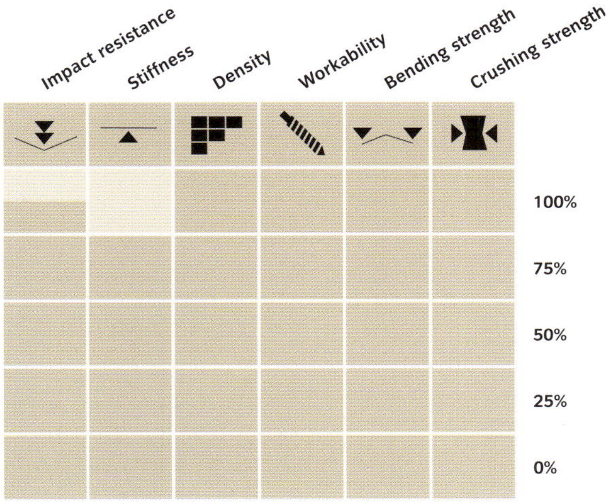

Workability describes how easy a wood is to work and whether it has a significant blunting effect on tools.

Bending strength is also known as maximum bending strength. Pressure is applied to each end of a board until it cracks.

Crushing strength is the ability of wood to withstand loads applied to the end grain, a critical test for wood used as short columns or props.

Diospyrus virginiana	Family: *Ebenaceae*	**PERSIMMON**	Hardwood

Growth

This member of the ebony family is also known as white ebony, because the timber of commercial interest consists almost entirely of pale straw-colored sapwood. It grows to a height of about 100ft (30m), with a diameter of no more than 2½ft (0.8m).

Appearance

Persimmon has a very small heartwood core, with variegated streaks of yellow-brown, orange-brown, dark brown, or black. The valuable sapwood is off-white with a gray tint, and is straight grained with a fine, even texture.

Properties

Persimmon weighs 52lb/ft³ (830kg/m³) when seasoned; there is large movement in service with changes of humidity. The wood dries fairly rapidly, with some tendency to check. It is very dense, has high bending and crushing strengths, and medium stiffness and shock resistance. It is suitable for steam bending to a moderate radius. This is a very tough timber that works readily with both hand and machine tools, but has a moderate blunting effect on cutting edges, which must be kept sharp. The wood requires pre-boring for screwing and nailing. It can be glued without problems, and polished to an exceptionally smooth and lustrous finish. The sapwood is liable to attack by powder post beetle; the heartwood is durable and classified as resistant to preservative treatment.

Uses

Persimmon sapwood is used for textile shuttles, because it can be machined to the intricate detail and very smooth finish required, and is very resistant to wear. It is claimed that these shuttles can be used for more than 1000 hours without replacement. It is also ideal for golf club heads, because it is highly resistant to impact, and for shoe lasts. It is used as a turnery wood for striking tool handles. Selected flitches are cut from logs that contain the variegated heartwood core, showing streaks from orange-brown to black with a wavy grain. These are sliced for ornamental veneers displaying variegated striped or roe figure, for cabinets and architectural paneling.

Where it grows

This small- to medium-sized tree occurs in the central and southern US, where it is known as bara bara, boa wood, butterwood, possum wood, and Virginia date palm.

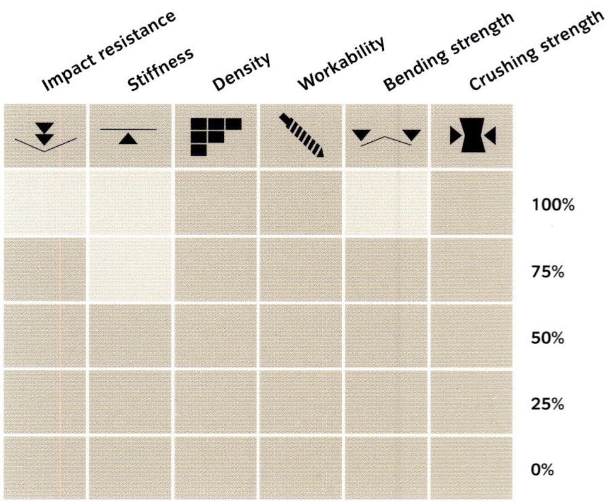

AT A GLANCE

Impact resistance is a measure of the wood's toughness. It describes its resistance to suddenly applied shock loads.

Stiffness is a measure of the wood's elasticity. It is considered in conjunction with bending strength.

Density is measured as specific gravity, the ratio of the density of a substance to that of water.

Distemonanthus benthamianus | Family: *Leguminosae* | **AYAN** | Hardwood

Growth

Ayan grows to between 90 and 125ft (27 and 38m) in height, with a diameter of 2½–5ft (0.8–1.5m). The bole is straight and cylindrical. It is also known as movingue and distemonanthus (UK); Nigerian satinwood (US and UK); barré (Ivory Coast); ayanran (Nigeria); bonsamdua (Ghana); eyen (Cameroon); oguéminia (Gaboon); and okpe (Togo).

Appearance

The sapwood is pale yellow in color and not clearly demarcated from the heartwood, which varies in color from lemon-yellow to golden brown, sometimes with dark streaks. The grain is often irregular and interlocked, and sometimes wavy. It may contain silica. The texture is fine and even, and the surface lustrous.

Properties

The weight varies from 37 to 48lb/ft^3 (590 to 770kg/m^3), averaging about 42lb/ft^3 (670kg/m^3) when seasoned. The heavier wood tends to be slightly darker in color. It dries fairly rapidly and well, with little tendency to split or warp, and has very good dimensional stability. It is dense, has medium bending strength, high crushing strength, low stiffness and shock resistance, and good compression strength along the grain. It has a moderate steam-bending classification. The material is fairly difficult to machine, with moderate to severe blunting of tools caused by silica in the wood; gum build-up on saws requires an increased set. Nailing requires pre-boring. The timber glues well, and if the grain is first filled, a very good finish can be obtained. It is moderately durable, showing some resistance to termites in west Africa. The heartwood is resistant to preservative treatment.

Uses

Ayan is used for exterior joinery, doors, window frames and sills, and ships fittings; it is also utilized for interior joinery, furniture, and cabinet work, and for road and railway vehicle building. Its resilience makes it ideal for domestic and gymnasium floors. Logs are rotary cut for plywood manufacture, and sliced for highly decorative veneers.

Where it grows

Ayan occurs throughout tropical west Africa, from the Ivory Coast to Gabon and Zaire.

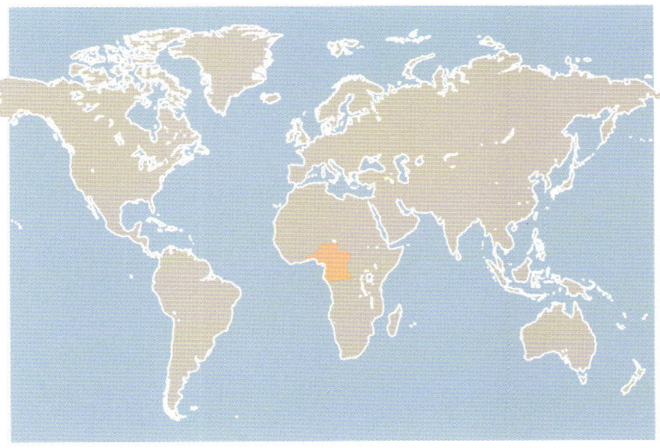

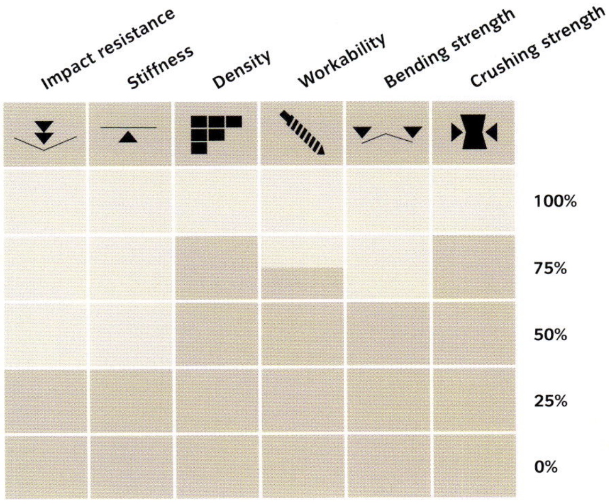

Workability describes how easy a wood is to work and whether it has a significant blunting effect on tools.

Bending strength is also known as maximum bending strength. Pressure is applied to each end of a board until it cracks.

Crushing strength is the ability of wood to withstand loads applied to the end grain, a critical test for wood used as short columns or props.

Dracontomelon dao	Family: *Anacardiaceae*	**PALDAO**	Hardwood

Growth

There is nothing particularly exceptional about paldao, which grows to about 35m (115ft) in height, often with a long, clean stem. The impressive feature of this tree is that it can stretch up to 6m (20ft) in diameter when you take the buttresses into consideration. As a timber, it has many of the qualities of a walnut (*Juglans spp.*), is a bit like butternut (*J.cinerea*) in appearance, and is sometimes marketed as such.

Appearance

Paldao comes in a beautiful range of colors, from straw and tan to a pinkish brown with some green and gray, exhibited with attractive flowing patterns and stripes. It is not uncommon to find much darker, almost black, streaks.

Properties

The texture of paldao is neither fine nor coarse, but is uniform, with a straight grain that is occasionally interlocking or wavy. Paldao weighs about 46lb/ft^3 (740kg/m^3) and is moderately dense. You can season it quite quickly, but it will warp and is likely to continue moving moderately once dry. Although you have to watch out for the interlocking grain, particularly on quarter-sawn surfaces, which can tear, paldao is fine to work, and finishes beautifully. Paldao should not be considered for bending, but is otherwise strong, and is a relatively versatile wood.

Uses

This attractive species is not very well known, but it is counted as a premier wood that is often sliced into veneers for decorative work. It is used for the best furniture, carving, turning, paneling, and interior trim. The buttresses are employed for table tops in its native Philippines.

Where it grows

Paldao is a native of the Philippines, but also grows across southeast Asia and the Pacific islands.

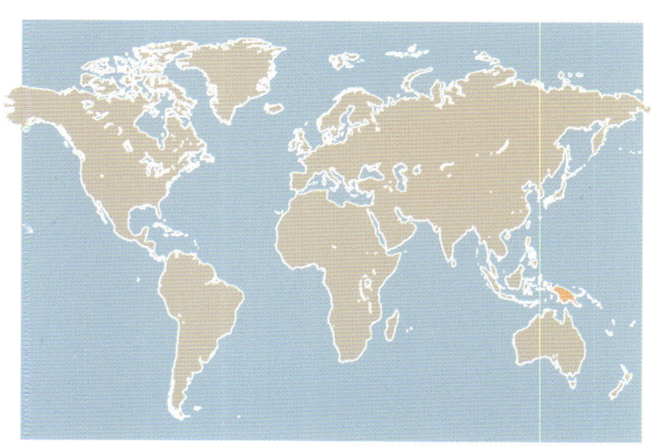

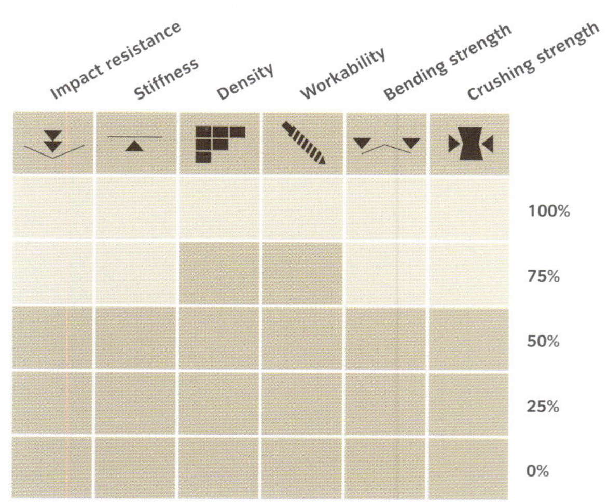

AT A GLANCE

Impact resistance is a measure of the wood's toughness. It describes its resistance to suddenly applied shock loads.

Stiffness is a measure of the wood's elasticity. It is considered in conjunction with bending strength.

Density is measured as specific gravity, the ratio of the density of a substance to that of water.

Dryobalanops spp. | Family: *Dipterocarpaceae* | **KAPUR** | Hardwood

Growth
Several species of *Dryobalanops* are marketed together as kapur. The important commercial species are *D.aromatica* Gaertn.f. and *D.oblongifolia* Dyer., which produce Malayan kapur for export, but the latter species is known locally as keladan. These two species also provide Indonesian kapur shipped from Sumatra. *D.aromatica* and *D.lanceolata* Burck produce Sarawak kapur and Kalimantan kapur. The latter species and *D.beccarii* Dyer. provide Sabah kapur (kapor); *D.aromatica* and *D.fusca* V.S1. produce Indonesian kapur from Borneo. Other names include Borneo camphorwood, Kalimantan kapur, Sabah kapor, and Indonesian kapoer. The various species reach a height of around 200ft (60m), and a diameter of 3–5ft (1–1.5m), with tapering boles above the buttresses.

Appearance
The sapwood is usually white to yellowish brown in color and sharply defined from the heartwood, which is light red-brown to deep red-brown, with straight to shallowly interlocked grain and fairly coarse but even texture. It contains resin, but this does not exude onto the wood surface. The wood has a camphor-like odor.

Properties
Kapur weighs 44–48lb/ft^3 (700–770kg/m^3) when seasoned. The wood dries fairly slowly but well, with little degrade, and there is medium shrinkage in use. This dense wood has high bending and crushing strengths, medium stiffness and shock resistance, and a moderate steam-bending rating because of resin exudation. Machining can produce a fibrous finish, and there is a moderate to severe blunting effect of cutting edges. It glues well and provides a good finish when filled. Kapur is liable to blue stain if it is in contact with iron compounds in damp conditions, and the acidic character may induce the corrosion of metals. The sapwood is durable but liable to attack by powder post beetle; the heartwood is very durable and extremely resistant to preservative treatment.

Uses
Kapur is a good constructional timber for estate and farm buildings, and for wharf decking, exterior joinery, windows, doors, stairs, cladding, garden seats, and vehicle floors. It is used for wharves, dock work, and bridges above the water line. It is rotary cut for plywood manufacture and selected logs are sliced for decorative veneers.

Where it grows
Kapur grows in Malaysia and Indonesia, including Sumatra, Borneo, Sarawak, Kalimantan, and Sabah.

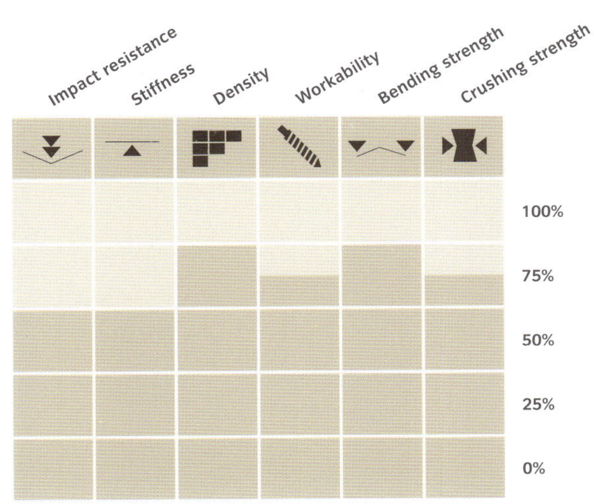

Workability describes how easy a wood is to work and whether it has a significant blunting effect on tools.

Bending strength is also known as maximum bending strength. Pressure is applied to each end of a board until it cracks.

Crushing strength is the ability of wood to withstand loads applied to the end grain, a critical test for wood used as short columns or props.

Dyera costulata | Family: *Apocynaceae* | **JELUTONG** | Hardwood

Growth
Jelutong grows to a substantial size, up to 200ft (60m) in height, with a straight, cylindrical bole up to 90ft (27m) long with a diameter of 8ft (2.5m).

Appearance
Both the sapwood and heartwood are the same creamy white color when first cut, maturing to a pale straw color on exposure, often stained by fungi after the tree has been tapped for latex. The wood is plain, almost straight grained, and has a fine and even texture.

Properties
This figureless wood is very lustrous, but contains slit-like radial latex passages on tangential surfaces, in clusters or rows about 3ft (1m) apart. These passages or canals, which appear lens shaped on flat-sawn surfaces, about ¼in (6mm) wide and ½in (12mm) long, rule out the possibility of using jelutong where sizable pieces are required or where appearance is important. These defects are eliminated in conversion to relatively smaller dimensions. The weight is about 29lb/ft^3 (460kg/m^3) when seasoned. The wood dries fairly easily without degrade, but is difficult to dry in thick stock without staining. There is little shrinkage in service. This soft, weak, and rather brittle timber is perishable, with low strength in most categories and a very poor steam-bending classification. The wood works easily with both hand and machine tools, with only a slight blunting effect on cutting edges, and provides a very smooth surface, taking screws and nails without difficulty. Jelutong can be glued easily, takes stain well, and can be polished or varnished to a good finish. It is nondurable, liable to attack by powder post beetle, but permeable for preservative treatment.

Uses
Ease of working makes jelutong an excellent wood for sculpture and carving, pattern making, architectural models, drawing boards, wooden clogs, and handicraft work. It has specialized uses for battery separators and match splints, and also for lightweight partitions and some parts for interior joinery and fitments. The logs are also rotary cut for corestock for flush doors, plywood, and laminated boards. The latex is extracted for the manufacture of chewing gum.

Where it grows
Jelutong is widely distributed throughout Malaysia and in the Indonesian islands of Sumatra and East Kalimantan.

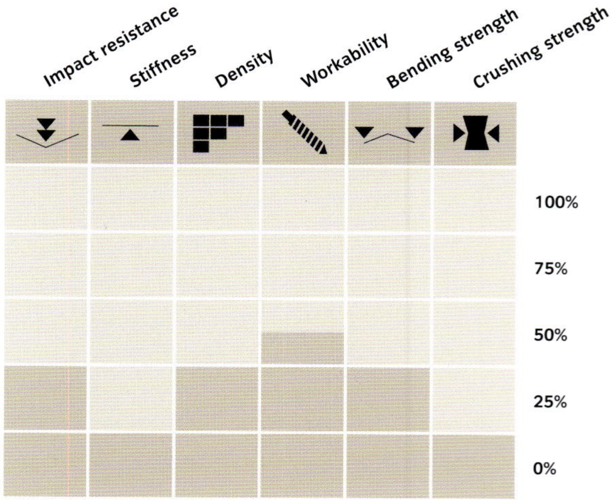

AT A GLANCE

Impact resistance is a measure of the wood's toughness. It describes its resistance to suddenly applied shock loads.

Stiffness is a measure of the wood's elasticity. It is considered in conjunction with bending strength.

Density is measured as specific gravity, the ratio of the density of a substance to that of water.

Endiandra palmerstonii	Family: *Lauracae*	**QUEENSLAND WALNUT**	Hardwood

Growth

Queensland walnut, also known as Australian walnut, walnut bean, and oriental wood, grows to a height of 120–140ft (37–43m) and a diameter of up to 6ft (1.8m). It has a clean bole that can reach up to 80ft (24m).

Appearance

The wood of Queensland walnut bears a striking resemblance to European walnut (*Juglans regia*), but has a more prominent striped figure. The pinkish sapwood is narrow, and the heartwood varies from gray to pale mid-brown, and often to dark brown, with pinkish, gray-green, or purple-black streaks. The grain is interlocked and often wavy, giving a checkered or broken striped figure on quartered surfaces, with a medium texture.

Properties

The wood weighs about 42lb/ft^3 (670kg/m^3) when seasoned. It tends to air dry fairly rapidly, with some tendency to split at the ends; it kiln dries fairly rapidly in thinner sizes without checking, but tends to warp; slight collapse is possible. Thicker boards are liable to split unless quarter sawn. There is medium movement in service. This heavy timber has medium bending strength and shock resistance, low stiffness, and high crushing strength, with a moderate steam-bending classification. Deposits of silica are sometimes present in the form of crystaline aggregates in ray cells. As a result it is a rather difficult timber to work, requiring tipped saws and high-speed cutters to overcome the severe blunting of cutting edges caused by the silica. Gluing is satisfactory and holding properties are good. The wood takes stain and polish well, and can be brought to an excellent standard of finish. The heartwood is nondurable and resistant to preservative treatment, but the sapwood is permeable.

Uses

The wood has high insulation properties and is used for shop, office, and bank fitting, high-class cabinets and furniture, interior joinery, and many forms of decorative work. As a flooring timber it is moderately resistant to wear. Logs are rotary cut for plywood faces, and selected logs are sliced for attractive striped decorative veneers for high-quality cabinets and paneling.

Where it grows

This large buttressed Australian tree, not a true walnut (*Juglans spp.*), grows abundantly in northern Queensland.

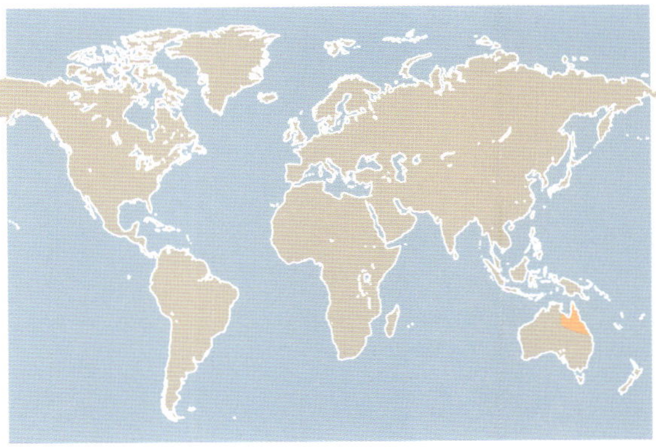

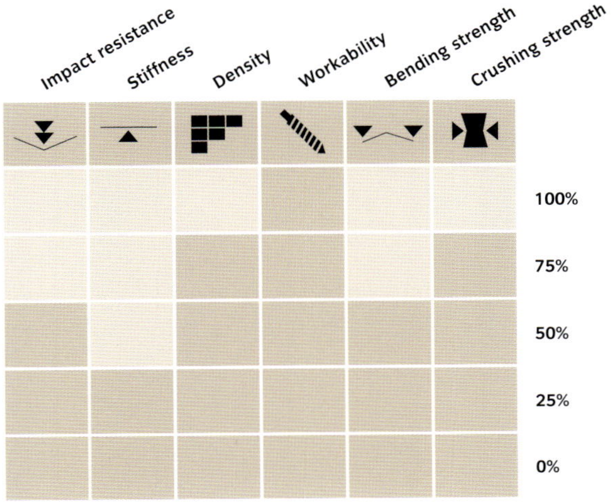

Workability describes how easy a wood is to work and whether it has a significant blunting effect on tools.

Bending strength is also known as maximum bending strength. Pressure is applied to each end of a board until it cracks.

Crushing strength is the ability of wood to withstand loads applied to the end grain, a critical test for wood used as short columns or props.

Entandrophragma angolense | Family: *Meliaceae* | **GEDU NOHOR** | Hardwood

Growth

Other names for gedu nohor include edinam (UK and Ghana); tiama (Ivory Coast); kalungi (Congo and Zaire); gedu lohor and gedu noha (Nigeria); and edoussie (Cameroon). It grows to a height of 160ft (48m), with an average diameter of 4–5ft (1.2–1.5m). It often has strong winged buttresses extending 20ft (6m) up the trunk of the tree.

Appearance

Typically, the heartwood has a rather dull, plain appearance of a light reddish brown color, with a fairly interlocked grain, producing a weak stripe on quartered surfaces, and with a moderately coarse texture. Some logs are a much lighter, pale pinkish gray color similar to the pinkish gray sapwood, which is sometimes about 4in (10cm) wide.

Properties

Gedu nohor weighs 34lb/ft^3 (540kg/m^3) on average when seasoned. It is stable in service and dries fairly rapidly with quite a bit of distortion. It has medium density and crushing strength, low bending strength and shock resistance, and very low stiffness with a poor steam-bending classification. It works fairly easily with hand and machine tools, but the interlocked grain has a moderate blunting effect. It nails, glues, and takes stain well, and can be brought to a good finish. The sapwood is liable to attack by powder post beetle. The heartwood is moderately durable but extremely resistant to preservative treatment.

Uses

Gedu nohor is extensively used as a substitute for mahogany in furniture and cabinet making for interior parts, partitions, edge lippings, and facings; it is also utilized for interior and exterior joinery and shop and office fitting. It makes a good domestic flooring timber. In boat building it is used for cabins, planking, furniture, and fitments. It is also employed for bus bodies and railway carriage construction. Wide boards are used for coffins. The logs are rotary cut for plywood and sliced for decorative veneers.

Where it grows

This large deciduous tree grows in the semi-evergreen forests of west, central, and east Africa, from Uganda in the east across to Angola and the Ivory Coast in the west.

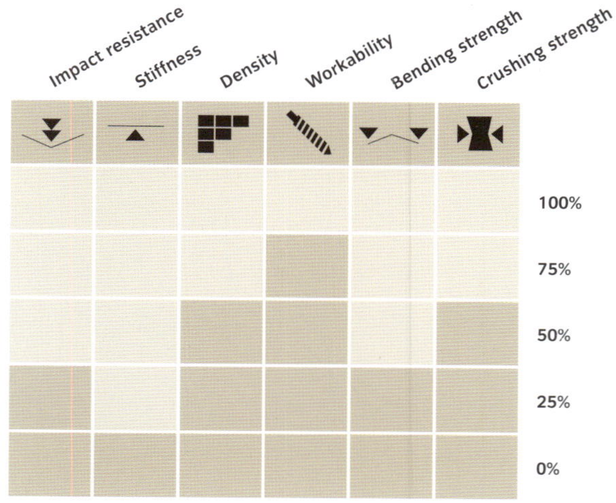

AT A GLANCE

Impact resistance is a measure of the wood's toughness. It describes its resistance to suddenly applied shock loads.

Stiffness is a measure of the wood's elasticity. It is considered in conjunction with bending strength.

Density is measured as specific gravity, the ratio of the density of a substance to that of water.

Entandrophragma cylindricum | Family: *Meliaceae* | **SAPELE** | Hardwood

Growth
Sapele is known as aboudikro on the Ivory Coast. It grows to 150–200ft (45–60m), with a diameter of about 3ft (1m), and a clean bole for 100ft (30m).

Appearance
The narrow sapwood is pale yellow-white; the heartwood is salmon-pink when freshly cut, maturing to reddish brown. It has a closely interlocked grain, resulting in a pronounced and regular pencil-striped or roe figure on quartered surfaces. Wavy grain yields a highly decorative fiddleback or mottled figure with a fine, even texture.

Properties
Sapele weighs in the region of 35–43lb/ft^3 (560–690kg/m^3), averaging about 39lb/ft^3 (620kg/m^3) when seasoned. The wood dries fairly rapidly, with a marked tendency to distort. There is medium movement in service. Sapele has medium density, bending, and shock resistance, high crushing strength, low stiffness, and a poor steam-bending rating. It works fairly well with both hand and machine tools, with moderate blunting of cutting edges caused by the interlocked grain. Nailing and gluing are satisfactory, and care is required when staining. When filled, the surface can be brought to an excellent finish. The sapwood is liable to attack by powder post beetle and is moderately resistant to impregnation. The heartwood is fairly durable but extremely resistant to preservative treatment.

Uses
Sapele enjoys a worldwide reputation as a handsome wood for high-quality furniture and cabinet making, interior and exterior joinery, window frames, shop, office, and bank fitting, counter tops, and solid doors. It is widely used for boat and vehicle building, and for piano cases and sports goods. The wood is ideal for decorative flooring for domestic and public buildings. Logs are rotary cut for plywood, and selected logs are sliced for quartered ribbon-striped decorative veneers that are used in cabinets and paneling.

Where it grows
Sapele grows widely in the tropical rainforests of west, central, and east Africa, from the Ivory Coast through Ghana and Nigeria to Cameroon, and eastwards to Uganda, Zaire, and Tanzania.

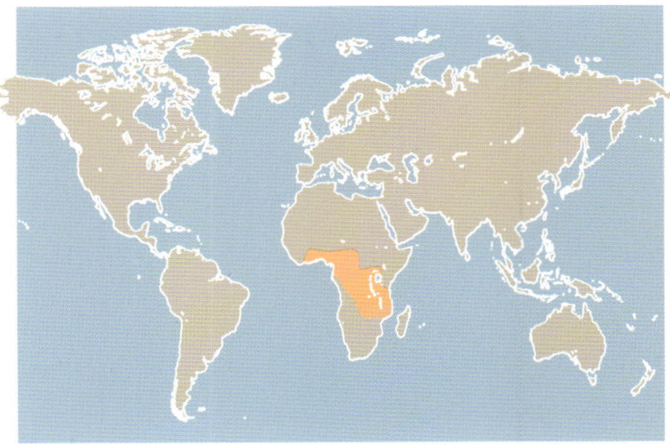

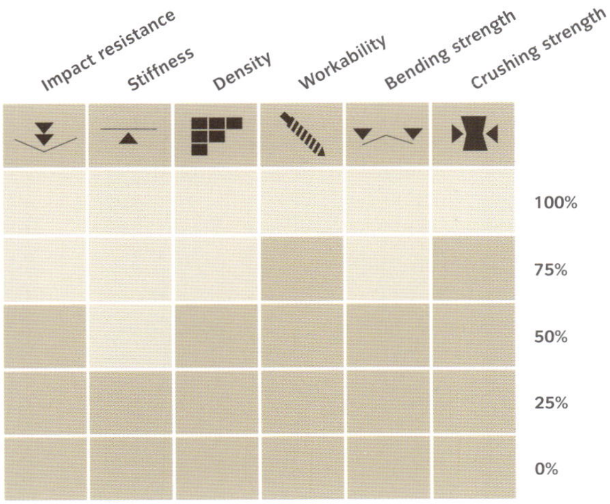

Workability describes how easy a wood is to work and whether it has a significant blunting effect on tools.

Bending strength is also known as maximum bending strength. Pressure is applied to each end of a board until it cracks.

Crushing strength is the ability of wood to withstand loads applied to the end grain, a critical test for wood used as short columns or props.

Entandrophragma utile	Family: *Meliaceae*	**UTILE**	Hardwood

Growth
Entandrophragma utile is known by several different names, depending on its country of origin, including sipo and mebrou zuiri (Ivory Coast); assié (Cameroon); Tshimaje rosso (Zaire); kosi-kosi (Gabon); and afau-konkonti (Ghana). It is a very large tree, reaching a height of 150–200ft (45–60m), with a diameter above the small narrow buttresses of about 8ft (2.5m).

Appearance
The light brown sapwood of utile is distinct from the heartwood, which is a uniform reddish brown mahogany color with an interlocked and rather irregular grain. The quartered surfaces do not possess such a fine ribbon-striped figure as sapele (*E. cylindricum*), and the texture is more open.

Properties
Utile weighs from about 34 to 47lb/ft^3 (540 to 750kg/m^3), with an average of 41lb/ft^3 (660kg/m^3) when seasoned. It dries at a moderate rate with some distortion, but this is not severe. There is medium movement in service. Utile is a dense wood, with high crushing strength, medium bending strength, low stiffness and shock resistance, and a very poor steam-bending rating. Utile works well with both hand and machine tools, with only slight to moderate blunting of cutting edges. The wood takes screws and nails satisfactorily, and is easy to glue. When the grain is filled, it takes stain and polish well and provides an excellent finish. The heartwood is durable but the sapwood is liable to attack by powder post beetle. The heartwood is extremely resistant both to decay and to preservatives.

Uses
Utile is extensively used for furniture and cabinets, counter tops, interior and exterior joinery for doors and window frames, and for interior construction work. It is also used for shop and office fitting, domestic flooring, vehicle and boat building, musical instruments, and sports goods. It is rotary cut for plywood and sliced for decorative furniture and paneling veneers.

Where it grows
Utile grows in the moist, deciduous high forests of tropical west and east Africa, including Sierra Leone, Cameroon, Liberia, Gabon, Uganda, and Angola, with commercial supplies coming from the Ivory Coast and Ghana.

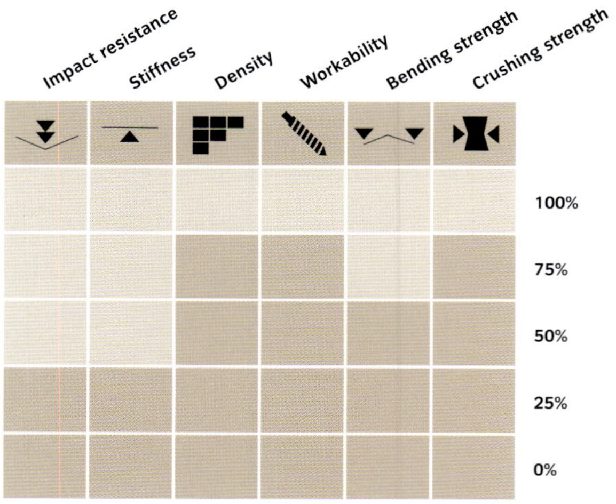

AT A GLANCE

Impact resistance is a measure of the wood's toughness. It describes its resistance to suddenly applied shock loads.

Stiffness is a measure of the wood's elasticity. It is considered in conjunction with bending strength.

Density is measured as specific gravity, the ratio of the density of a substance to that of water.

Eucalyptus diversicolor | Family: *Myrtaceae* | **KARRI** | Hardwood

Growth
Karri grows to an immense 280ft (85m), with a diameter of 6–10ft (1.8–3m) and clear of branches for about 85–100ft (25–30m).

Appearance
The heartwood of karri is a uniform reddish brown color with an interlocked grain, producing a striped figure on quartered surfaces. The texture is moderately coarse but even. Karri is very similar to jarrah (*Eucalyptus marginata*), but the two woods can be distinguished by conducting a splinter test: a small burned splinter of karri forms a thick white ash, while jarrah burns to a black, ashless charcoal.

Properties
The average weight of karri is 55lb/ft^3 (880kg/m^3) when seasoned. Karri requires great care in drying and is prone to deep checking in thick stock and distortion in thin stock. There is also a large movement in service. This very heavy timber is high in all strength categories and has a moderate steam-bending classification, but cannot be bent if small knots are present. It is a difficult wood to work with hand tools and fairly difficult to machine, as the wavy and interlocked grain has a moderate to severe blunting effect on tools. It requires pre-boring for nailing, but glues well and when filled can be brought to an excellent finish. The heartwood is durable and extremely resistant to preservative treatment, but the sapwood is classified as permeable.

Uses
Karri is stronger than jarrah but inferior for underground use if exposed to fungal, marine borer, or termite attack, or when in contact with water for dock and harbor work. It is therefore used above water for wharf and bridge construction, for superstructures, and for ship building. It is ideal for building construction as joists, rafters, and heavy beams. It is also utilized for agricultural implements. Selected pieces are employed for furniture, cabinet fittings, and domestic flooring. When treated, it is used for railway sleepers, poles, and piles. It is rotary cut for plywood manufacture and sliced for decorative cabinet and high-quality paneling veneers.

Where it grows
Karri is an important tree of southwest Australia.

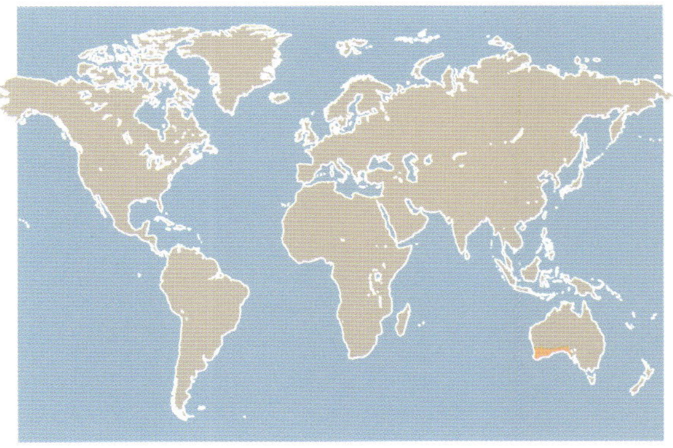

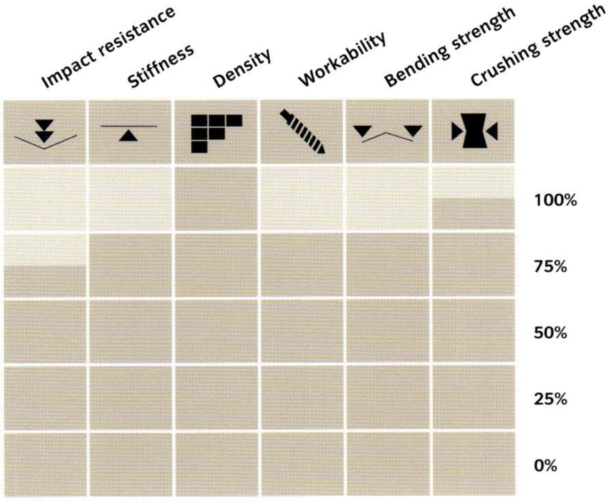

Workability describes how easy a wood is to work and whether it has a significant blunting effect on tools.

Bending strength is also known as maximum bending strength. Pressure is applied to each end of a board until it cracks.

Crushing strength is the ability of wood to withstand loads applied to the end grain, a critical test for wood used as short columns or props.

Eucalyptus marginata | Family: *Myrtaceae* | **JARRAH** | Hardwood

Growth
Jarrah reaches an unremarkable (for eucalyptus) height of 100–150ft (30–45m), with a diameter of 3–5ft (1–1.5m).

Appearance
The heartwood of jarrah is a rich, dark, reddish brown, often with occasional gum veins and pockets that detract from the appearance, and boat-shaped flecks caused by fungus that enhance it. The grain is usually fairly straight, but sometimes interlocked or wavy. The texture is moderately coarse but even.

Properties
The weight of jarrah varies between 43 and 65lb/ft³ (690 and 1040kg/m³), averaging around 51lb/ft³ (820kg/m³) when seasoned. It will distort unless air dried before kilning, particularly in large sizes, which are often air dried only. There is medium shrinkage in service. Jarrah has medium bending strength and stiffness, high crushing strength, and a moderate steam-bending rating. It is fairly hard to machine and not really suitable for working with hand tools because of its hardness and density. There is high resistance in cutting, with a moderate blunting effect on tools. Pre-boring is necessary for nailing and screwing. It glues and finishes well. Jarrah has a very durable heartwood and is highly resistant to insect attack and preservative treatment, but the sapwood is classified as permeable.

Uses
Jarrah is an ideal constructional timber, used in Australia for marine structures like dock pilings and harbor work, wharfs, bridges, and sea defenses; other marine uses include rails and decking for ships. It is utilized throughout the world for railway sleepers. Jarrah makes a good flooring timber and is also employed for shingles, weatherboards, rafters, joists, interior joinery and furniture, chemical vats, and filter presses. As a turnery wood, it is highly valued for striking tool handles. Selected logs are sliced for decorative veneers for architectural paneling.

Where it grows
More jarrah is cut than any other Australian commercial timber. It is found in the coastal region south of Perth in Western Australia, and huge quantities are exported.

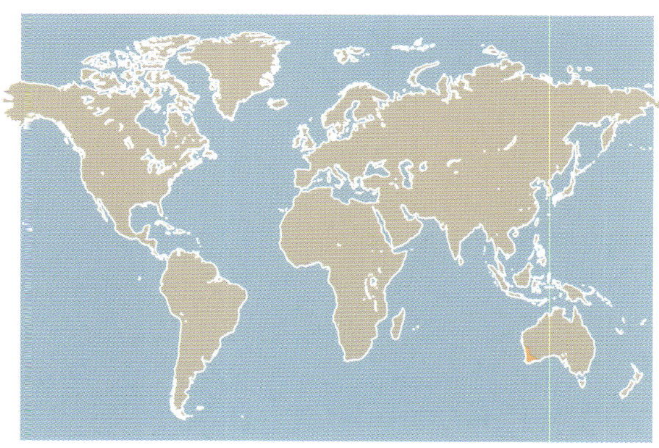

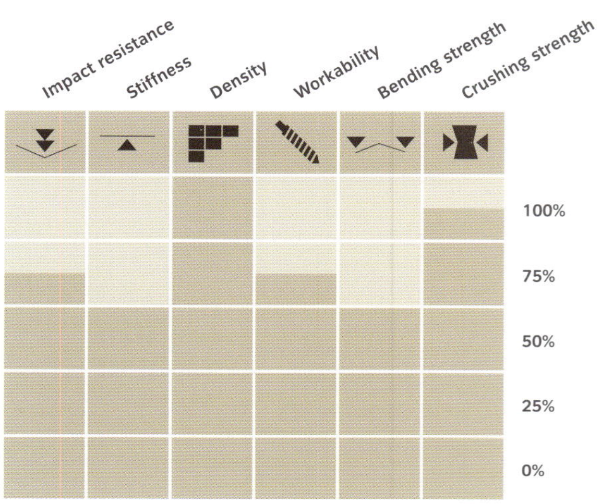

AT A GLANCE

Impact resistance is a measure of the wood's toughness. It describes its resistance to suddenly applied shock loads.

Stiffness is a measure of the wood's elasticity. It is considered in conjunction with bending strength.

Density is measured as specific gravity, the ratio of the density of a substance to that of water.

Eucalyptus spp. | Family: *Myrtaceae* | **AUSTRALIAN OAK** | Hardwood

Growth

There are three species known as Australian oak. *Eucalyptus delegatensis* is sold as alpine ash, white-top or gum-top stringybark, and woollybutt; *E.obliqua* L'Hérit produces messmate stringybark and brown-top stringybark; *E.regnans* F.Muell. provides mountain ash, Victorian ash, stringy gum, and swamp gum. They are marketed together, but are not botanically related either to oak (*Quercus spp.*) or ash (*Fraxinus spp.*). The trees reach a height of 200–300ft (60–90m), with a diameter of 3–7ft (1–2m) or more.

Appearance

The heartwood color of these species varies from a pale biscuit to light brown with a pinkish tinge, and they have a narrow, indistinct, paler sapwood. The wood is usually straight grained, but sometimes interlocked or wavy, and with a coarse texture. Hard gum or kino veins are often present, especially in *E.obliqua*.

Properties

E.delegatensis averages 40lb/ft^3 (640kg/m^3) in weight, *E.obliqua* 49lb/ft^3 (780kg/m^3), and *E.regnans* 39lb/ft^3 (620kg/m^3) when seasoned. The wood dries readily and fairly quickly, but is liable to develop surface checks and to distort. There is medium shrinkage in use. Australian oak has medium bending strength, shock resistance, and stiffness, with high crushing strength. Only *E.obliqua* has a moderate steam-bending rating. The timbers work satisfactorily with both hand and machine tools, and hold nails and screws well. They can be glued easily, take stain and polish well, and can be brought to an excellent finish. The sapwood is liable to attack by powder post beetle; the heartwood is moderately durable and resistant to preservative treatment, but the sapwood is permeable.

Uses

This timber is extensively used for interior and exterior joinery and building construction, and for cladding and weatherboards. It also appears in furniture, cooperage, agricultural implements, handles, coach and truck building, sports goods, and domestic flooring. It is rotary cut in Australia for the manufacture of plywood and sliced for export in decorative veneer form.

Where it grows
The three species of Australian oak occur in southeast Australia from New South Wales to Tasmania.

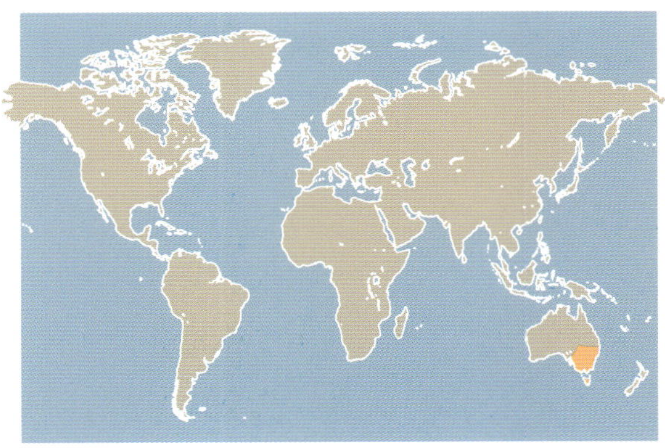

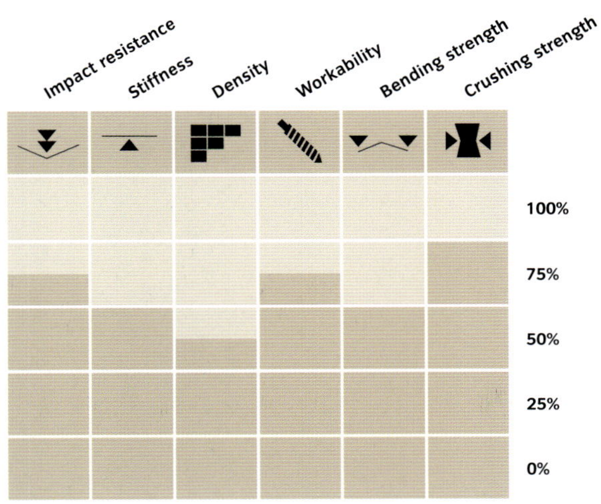

Workability describes how easy a wood is to work and whether it has a significant blunting effect on tools.

Bending strength is also known as maximum bending strength. Pressure is applied to each end of a board until it cracks.

Crushing strength is the ability of wood to withstand loads applied to the end grain, a critical test for wood used as short columns or props.

Fagara flava | Family: *Rutaceae* | **WEST INDIAN SATINWOOD** | Hardwood

Growth

West Indian satinwood should not be confused with Ceylon satinwood (*Chloroxylon swietenia*). Other names by which it is known include Jamaica satinwood and San Domingan satinwood (US); yellow sanders (West Indies); and aceitillo (Cuba). It reaches its best development in Jamaica, where it grows to a height of about 40ft (12m), with a diameter of about 1½ft (0.5m).

Appearance

The heartwood of *Fagara flava* is rich cream to golden yellow, with a straight to interlocked, wavy or irregular grain, producing bee's wing cross-mottled, roe, or broken striped figure on quartered surfaces. The texture is fine and even, with a bright, satin luster. It smells like coconut oil when freshly cut.

Properties

This very heavy and dense timber weighs about 56lb/ft³ (900kg/m³) when seasoned. It requires care in drying to avoid distortion. It works well with both hand and machine tools, but there is high resistance in cutting. Cutting edges have to be kept very sharp where irregular grain is present and a reduced cutting angle is recommended. The fine dust produced in machining operations is liable to cause dermatitis. The timber requires pre-boring for screwing or nailing, but glues well and takes an excellent polish. The timber is nondurable and extremely resistant to impregnation.

Uses

West Indian satinwood was used in England for more than a century before mahogany became the most popular wood for Georgian furniture, and during the 18th century, this beautiful timber was used extensively for the high-class cabinet work of Adam, Sheraton, and Hepplewhite. Today, it is exported only in small quantities and is used for furniture, high-class cabinet making, and reproduction and restoration of period furniture. It is an excellent turnery wood for brush backs, hand mirrors, bobbins, and fancy goods. Selected logs are sliced in a wide range of attractively figured decorative veneers for cabinets, paneling, inlay, and marquetry work.

Where it grows

West Indian satinwood grows in Jamaica, Bermuda, the Bahamas, and southern Florida.

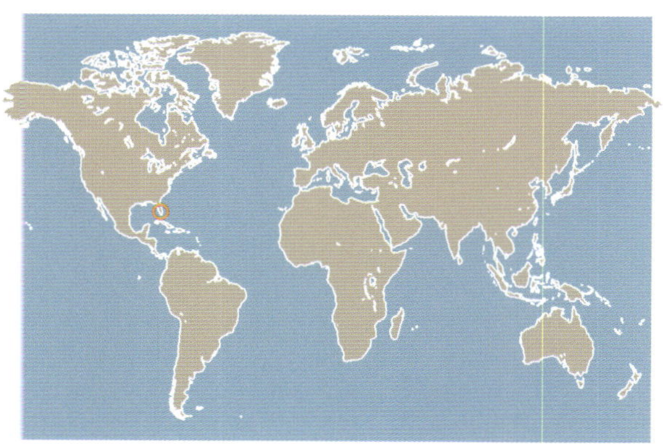

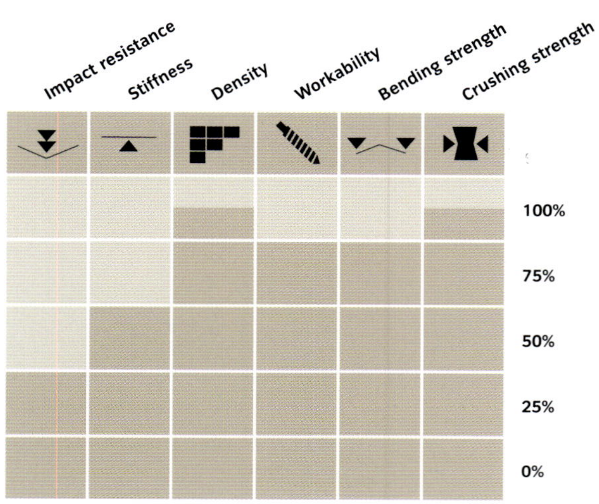

AT A GLANCE

Impact resistance is a measure of the wood's toughness. It describes its resistance to suddenly applied shock loads.

Stiffness is a measure of the wood's elasticity. It is considered in conjunction with bending strength.

Density is measured as specific gravity, the ratio of the density of a substance to that of water.

Fagus spp.	Family: *Fagaceae*	**BEECH**	Hardwood

Growth

Beech is known as the mother of the forest because other hardwoods in mixed broad-leaved forests would struggle to survive without it; its leaf drip kills weeds and its leaf fall provides rich humus for the soil. *Fagus grandifolia* Ehrh. produces American beech; *F.sylvatica* L. European beech; *F.orientalis* Lipsky Turkish beech; and *F.crenata* Bl. Japanese beech. Each is named according to its country of origin. They grow to an average height of 150ft (45m), with a diameter of about 4ft (1.2m).

Appearance

The timber is very pale cream to pinkish brown, and is often weathered to a deep reddish bronze-brown after steaming. It is typically straight grained with broad rays, and has a fine, even texture.

Properties

Japanese beech, the lightest, weighs 39lb/ft^3 (620kg/m^3). Slavonian beech weighs about 42lb/ft^3 (670kg/m^3); European beech 45lb/ft^3 (720kg/m^3); and American beech 46lb/ft^3 (740kg/m^3) when seasoned. Special care is needed in drying because beech dries fairly rapidly and well, but is moderately refractory and shrinks considerably in service. The wood has medium strength in bending, stiffness, and shock resistance, a high crushing strength, and an exceptionally good steam-bending rating. It works readily with hand or machine tools and has good holding properties; it glues very easily and can be brought to an excellent finish. The heartwood is perishable and liable to attack by the common furniture beetle and death watch beetle. The sapwood is affected by the longhorn beetle. Beech is classified as permeable for preservative treatment.

Uses

Beech is perhaps the most popular general-purpose timber for furniture, chairs, school desks, and the like, and for interior joinery and, when treated, exterior joinery. It is a turnery wood for tool handles, brush backs, bobbins, domestic woodware, sports goods, parts of musical instruments, and domestic flooring. It is also used for bentwork and cooperage. It is rotary cut for utility plywood and corestock and sliced for unremarkable decorative veneers.

Where it grows

Beech grows in the northern temperate regions of Europe, Canada, and the United States, as well as parts of Asia, Japan, and northern Africa.

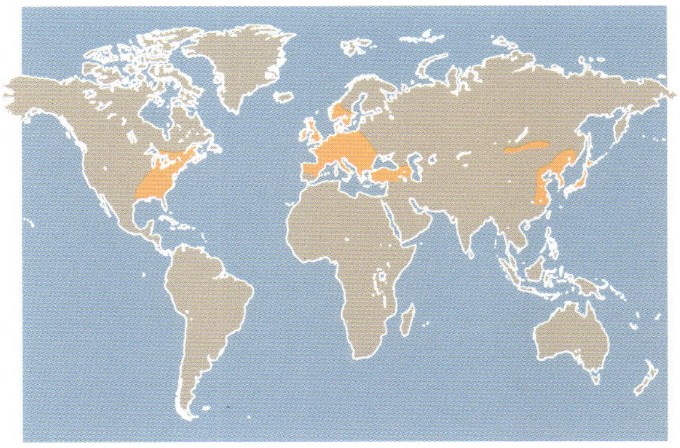

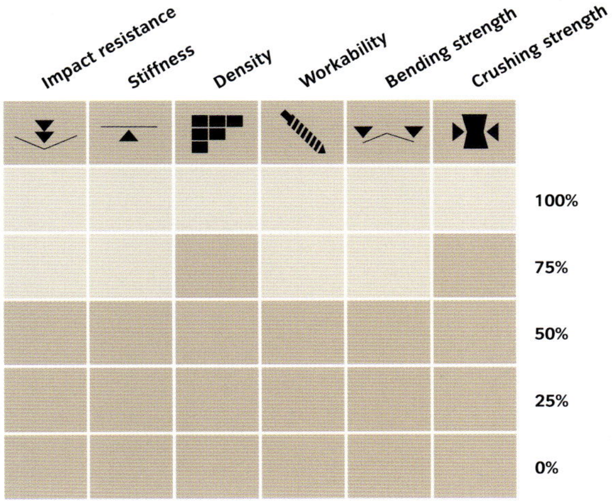

Workability describes how easy a wood is to work and whether it has a significant blunting effect on tools.

Bending strength is also known as maximum bending strength. Pressure is applied to each end of a board until it cracks.

Crushing strength is the ability of wood to withstand loads applied to the end grain, a critical test for wood used as short columns or props.

Flindersia spp.	Family: *Rutaceae*	**AUSTRALIAN MAPLE**	Hardwood

Growth
There are a few closely related species: *Flindersia brayleyana* F.Muell. produces Australian maple, which is also known as Queensland maple and maple silkwood; *F.pimenteliana* F.Muell. and *F.laevicarpa* var. *heterophylla* are both known as scented maple. The trees grow to about 100ft (30m), with a diameter of 3–4ft (1–1.2 m).

Appearance
The heartwood is pale brown to pink with a silken luster and matures to a pale brown. The grain is often interlocked, sometimes wavy or curly, producing a range of attractive figures, with a medium texture.

Properties
The average weight of *F.brayleyana* and *F.pimenteliana* is 34lb/ft^3 (540kg/m^3), while *F.laevicarpa* weighs 43lb/ft^3 (690kg/m^3) when seasoned. They air and kiln dry satisfactorily but with some tendency to collapse; distortion may need kiln reconditioning. There is medium shrinkage in service. The wood has medium bending and crushing strengths, low stiffness and resistance to shock loads, and a poor steam-bending rating. It works readily with both hand and machine tools, but has a moderate blunting effect on cutting edges. Interlocked grain tends to pick up when working on quartered stock, and a reduced angle is necessary. The timber holds screws well, and glues satisfactorily. When filled, stained, and polished, it can be brought to an excellent finish. The heartwood is moderately durable and resistant to preservative treatment, and is not subject to insect attack.

Uses
Australian maple is used for high-class cabinets and furniture, for interior fittings and moldings, and for interior joinery. It has many specialist uses, such as vehicle bodywork, ornamental rifle and gunstocks, and the bases of printing blocks. In boat building, it is widely use for parts, oars, and superstructures. It is also a very good turnery wood. It is often rotary cut for plywood and sliced to produce watered-silk moiré, block mottle, fiddleback, striped, and bird's eye figured veneers for cabinets and paneling.

Where it grows
This decorative Australian timber, not a true maple (*Acer spp.*), is highly valued in northern Queensland. It also occurs in Papua New Guinea.

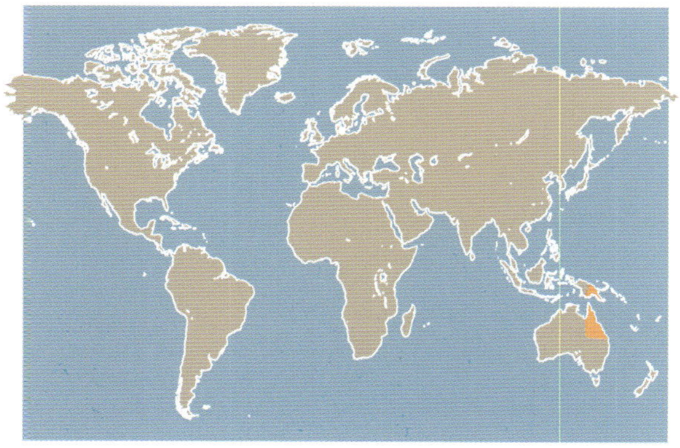

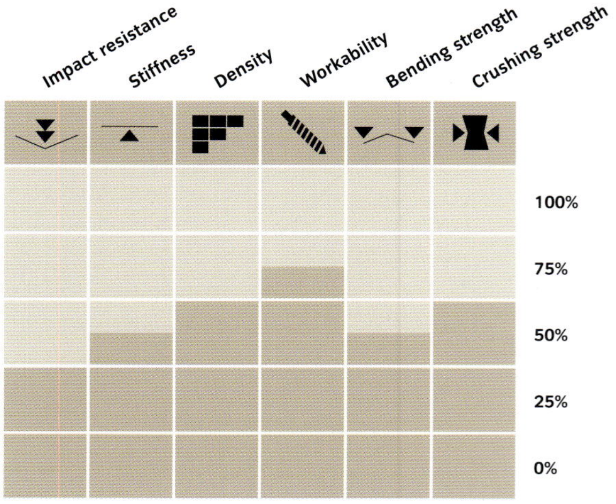

AT A GLANCE

Impact resistance is a measure of the wood's toughness. It describes its resistance to suddenly applied shock loads.

Stiffness is a measure of the wood's elasticity. It is considered in conjunction with bending strength.

Density is measured as specific gravity, the ratio of the density of a substance to that of water.

Flindersia spp. | Family: *Rutaceae* | **AUSTRALIAN SILVER ASH** | Hardwood

Growth

There are many different *Flindersia* species growing in Australia that produce a range of timbers with names such as ash and maple, but that are botanically unrelated to these timbers (*Fraxinus spp.* and *Acer spp.*). *Flindersia schottiana* produces southern silver ash, which is also known as bumpy ash and cudgerie; *F.bourjotiana* provides Queensland silver ash; and *F.pubescens* produces northern silver ash. All three species grow to about 100ft (30m), with a diameter of about 2½ft (0.8m).

Appearance

The pale biscuit-colored heartwood of Australian silver ash is mostly straight grained, but sometimes has a shallowly interlocked or wavy grain. The wood has a medium texture.

Properties

The weight of Australian silver ash varies, but the average is 35lb/ft³ (560kg/m³) when seasoned. The wood dries rather slowly and shows a slight tendency to warp, but it can be air or kiln dried satisfactorily, up to about 2in (5cm) thick, with little degrade. It is stable in service. It has medium bending and crushing strength, and low stiffness and resistance to shock loads. This tough, resilient, and elastic wood has a very good steam-bending classification. It works easily with both hand and machine tools, with only a moderate blunting effect. Quartered surfaces tend to pick up interlocked grain when planing or molding. The material has good nail- and screw-holding properties, and it can be glued without difficulty. If care is taken in grain filling and staining, it can be polished to an excellent finish. The heartwood is very durable above ground and resistant to preservative treatment, but the sapwood is classified as permeable.

Uses

Silver ash is used in Australia for high-class cabinets and furniture, interior trim and fitments, and interior and exterior joinery. It is used for food containers because it is odorless and will not taint. It is extensively employed as a structural timber, for ship and boat building, and vehicle bodies. Its specialist uses include sporting goods and musical instruments, and it is popular for carving and turnery for domestic woodware. It is also rotary cut for plywood and sliced into very attractive decorative veneers for cabinets and paneling.

Where it grows

Southern silver ash is found in New South Wales, Queensland, and Papua New Guinea. Northern silver ash grows in New South Wales and Queensland. Queensland silver ash grows, as can be expected, in Queensland.

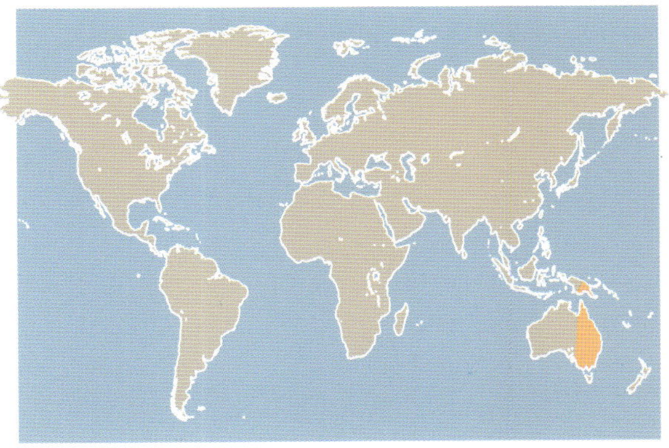

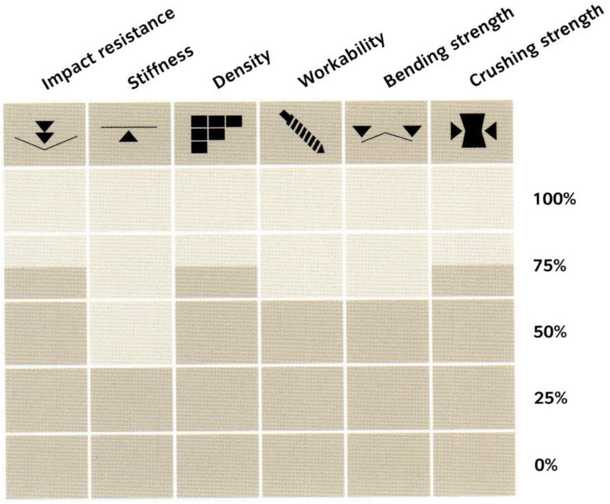

Workability describes how easy a wood is to work and whether it has a significant blunting effect on tools.

Bending strength is also known as maximum bending strength. Pressure is applied to each end of a board until it cracks.

Crushing strength is the ability of wood to withstand loads applied to the end grain, a critical test for wood used as short columns or props.

Fraxinus sieboldiana | Family: *Oleaceae* | **TAMO ASH** | Hardwood

Growth

Tamo ash is one of several species that is also known as Japanese ash. It can grow big and thick, up to 4ft (1.2m) in diameter. *Fraxinus sieboldiana* is named after Philip Franz Siebold, who worked in Japan in the mid-19th century concentrating on the language and natural history of the country from his desk in the Dutch embassy.

Appearance

Tamo ash is remarkable in appearance, resembling the contours of the most convoluted mountain range. It is very pale, with the typical pale brown or beige color of an ash. Tamo ash shares many of the open-grained characteristics of other ash species, but is even wilder and more exciting when plain sawn or rotary cut as a veneer. It has an inconsistent texture, varying from very fine to very open. This can make it awkward to use, but the effect is dramatic, especially when the open grain is highlighted with stain. It has a moderate luster.

Properties

Tamo ash is of medium weight at around 43lb/ft^3 (690kg/m^3). It is stronger than other ash species and very flexible. It seasons well, and considering the complex nature of the patterning, even veneers stay fairly flat. Although tamo trees grow tall, the figured lumber is cut from the lower portion. It is generally only available in the United States as a veneer.

Uses

Like other types of ash wood, tamo ash is used for sporting equipment and tool handles because it is generally whippy and forgiving. However, the patterning is so dramatic that woodworkers and marquetry enthusiasts are likely to want to incorporate it into panels or designs.

Where it grows

Tamo ash grows in Japan, China, Korea, and Siberia. It likes moist alluvial soils in river basins.

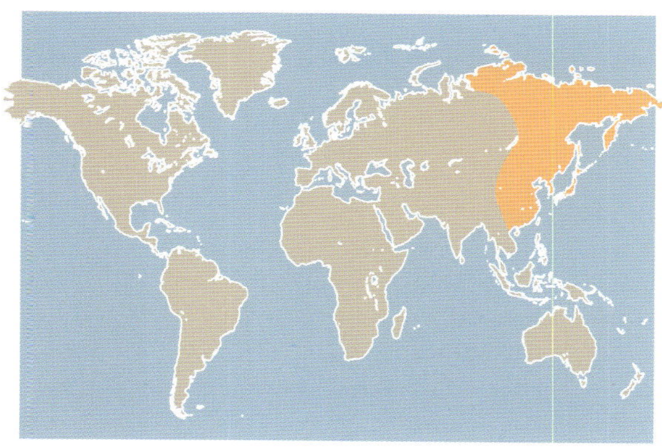

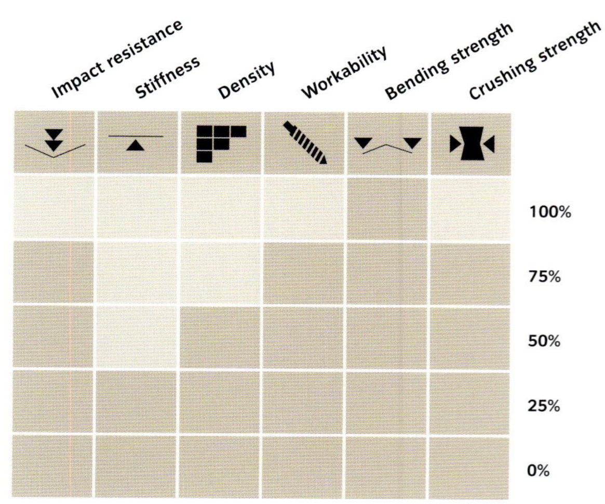

AT A GLANCE

Impact resistance is a measure of the wood's toughness. It describes its resistance to suddenly applied shock loads.

Stiffness is a measure of the wood's elasticity. It is considered in conjunction with bending strength.

Density is measured as specific gravity, the ratio of the density of a substance to that of water.

Fraxinus spp. | Family: *Oleaceae* | **ASH** | Hardwood

Growth

Fraxinus americana L. is known as white ash (Canada); the American species *F.pennsylvania* Marsh. is known as green ash (US) and red ash (Canada); the European species *F.exclesior* L. is named after the country of origin as English ash, French ash, Polish ash, Slavonian ash, and so on. The tree grows to 80–120ft (24–37m) in height, with a diameter of 2–5ft (0.6–1.5m).

Appearance

American ash is gray-brown in color with a reddish tinge. European ash is cream white to light brown, sometimes with a sound dark brown to black heart that is marketed separately as olive ash. Ash is straight grained and coarse textured, and the growth rings produce a very decorative figure on plain-sawn surfaces.

Properties

Weight varies as follows: *F.americana*, 41lb/ft^3 (660kg/m^3); *F.pennsylvania*, 43lb/ft^3 (690kg/m^3); and *F.exclesior*, 36lb/ft^3 (580kg/m^3) when seasoned. The timber dries fairly rapidly, with little degrade and medium shrinkage in use. It has medium bending and crushing strength, medium shock resistance, low stiffness, and an excellent steam-bending classification. It works satisfactorily with both hand and machine tools. Pre-boring is advised for nailing. It glues with ease and takes stains and polishes well to provide a good finish. Ash is nondurable and perishable. It is liable to attack by the powder post beetle and the furniture beetle. The heartwood is moderately resistant to preservative treatment; black heartwood (olive ash) is resistant.

Uses

Ash, one of the very best woods for bending, is used extensively for chairs, cabinet making, furniture, and interior joinery. Specialist uses include bent handles for umbrellas, shop fitting, vehicle building, wheelwrighting, and agricultural implements. It is utilized in boat building for bent parts, frames, canoes, and canvas boats; it is also used for sports goods, tennis rackets, hockey sticks, baseball bats, billiard cues, and gymnasium equipment. It is an excellent turnery wood for tool handles, shovels, and pick axes. It is sliced for decorative furniture and paneling veneers.

Where it grows

Ash thrives throughout Europe, North America, and Japan.

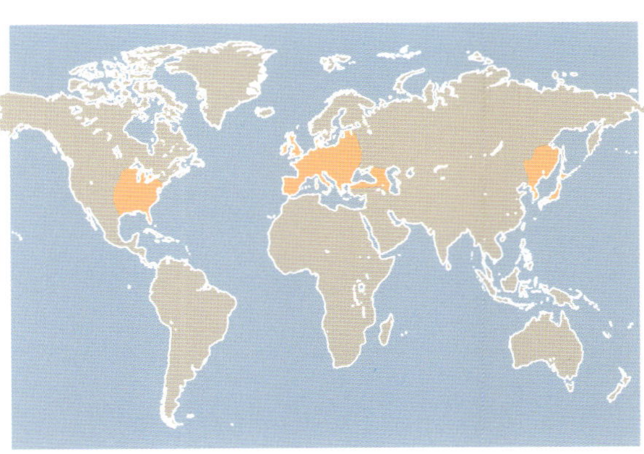

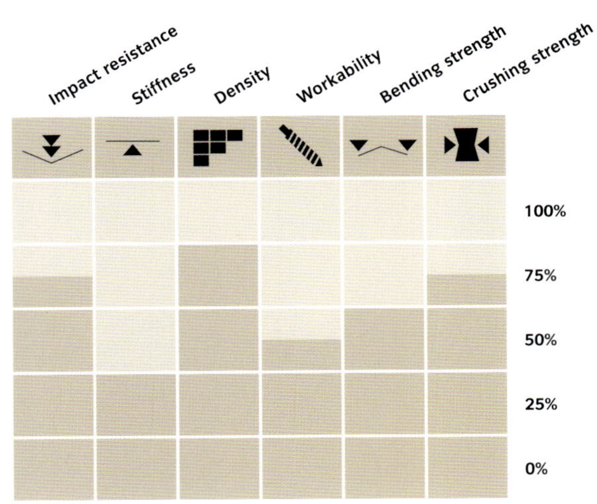

Workability describes how easy a wood is to work and whether it has a significant blunting effect on tools.

Bending strength is also known as maximum bending strength. Pressure is applied to each end of a board until it cracks.

Crushing strength is the ability of wood to withstand loads applied to the end grain, a critical test for wood used as short columns or props.

Gonystylus spp. | Family: *Gonystylaceae* | **RAMIN** | Hardwood

Growth
Ramin is known as ramin telur in Sarawak; *Gonystylus macrophyllum* and *G.bancanus* (Miq.) Kurz. are known as melawis in west Malaysia. The bulk of melawis comprises *G.macrophyllum*, but also includes *G.affinis* and *G.confusus*. These medium-sized trees attain a height of about 80ft (24m), with a diameter of 2–3ft (0.6–1m) and a clear cylindrical bole for 50–60ft (15–18m).

Appearance
The heartwood of ramin is a uniform creamy white to pale straw color, with a featureless straight to shallowly interlocked grain and a moderately fine and even texture. The sapwood is up to 2in (5cm) wide, but is not clearly defined from the heartwood.

Properties
Ramin weighs 40–45lb/ft^3 (640–720kg/m^3), averaging about 41lb/ft^3 (660kg/m^3) when seasoned. Melawis containing *G.affinis* and *G.confusus* weigh about 44lb/ft^3 (700kg/m^3). Air-dried stock is easily kilned without degrade, but is prone to staining and has to be dipped immediately after conversion. There is large movement in service. This dense wood has high bending and crushing strengths, low shock resistance, and medium stiffness, with a very poor steam-bending rating. Ramin works fairly easily by hand and machine, with a moderate blunting effect on tools, but the grain tends to tear on quartered material. It requires pre-boring for nailing, glues well, and when properly filled, can be stained and brought to a good finish. The heartwood is perishable; the sapwood is liable to attack by powder post beetle, but is permeable for preservation treatment.

Uses
Ramin is extensively used as a substitute for beech (*Fagus spp.*) for furniture, fittings, and picture frames, and other moldings. It is used in carving and turnery, for handles of non-striking tools, and for dowels. The wood is also used for interior joinery, shop and office fittings, and wooden toys. It appears in light building work for baseboards, moldings, and domestic flooring. Selected logs are rotary cut for plywood and for corestock in laminated boards, and sliced for decorative veneers.

Where it grows
Ramin grows in the freshwater swamps on the west coasts of Sarawak and throughout Malaysia and southeast Asia.

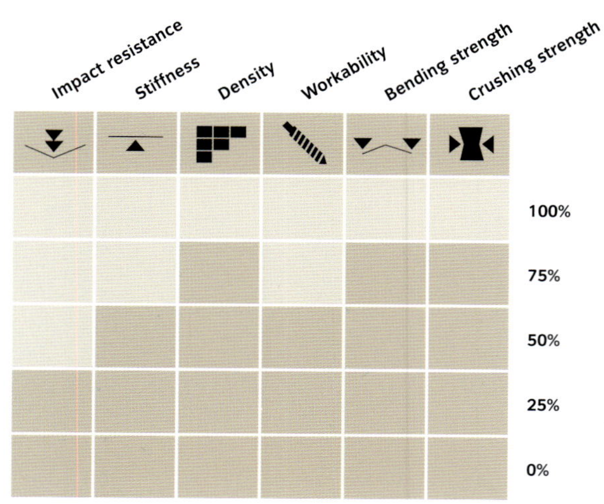

AT A GLANCE

Impact resistance is a measure of the wood's toughness. It describes its resistance to suddenly applied shock loads.

Stiffness is a measure of the wood's elasticity. It is considered in conjunction with bending strength.

Density is measured as specific gravity, the ratio of the density of a substance to that of water.

Gossweilerodendron balsamiferum | Family: *Leguminosae* | **AGBA** | Hardwood

Growth
Agba is also known as tola, ntola, and mutsekamambole (Zaire); moboron, tola branca, and white tola (Angola); Nigerian cedar (UK); mutsekamambole (Nigeria); and nitola (Congo). Trees reach a height of 200ft (60m) and a diameter of over 7ft (2m).

Appearance
The heartwood of agba has a uniform pale straw to tan brown color, with a straight to shallow interlocked or wavy grain that produces a broad striped figure on quartered surfaces. It has a fine texture.

Properties
The wood weighs about 32lb/ft^3 (510kg/m^3) when seasoned. Drying is fairly rapid with little degrade, but exudation of dark oleo resin can occur. This may also affect machining, which is otherwise satisfactory with only slight blunting of tools. The wood is stable with small movement in service. It has a moderately good steam-bending classification, with very low stiffness, low bending strength and shock resistance, and a medium crushing strength. It holds nails well, and it also glues and finishes satisfactorily if the grain is filled. This durable wood is very resistant to decay, but the sapwood is liable to attack by the common furniture beetle. The heartwood is resistant to preservative treatment, but the sapwood is permeable.

Uses
Agba is excellent for interior joinery for table tops, shop fitting, paneling, and chair seats. It is used as a substitute for oak (*Quercus spp.*) for school desks, church furniture, including coffins, and for moldings. It is also a good turnery wood for handles and dowels, domestic hardware, and toymaking, but a slight resinous odor makes it unsuitable for items that may come into contact with food. As domestic flooring, it is ideal over underfloor heating. It is also used for exterior joinery for cladding and planking, the laminated frames of boats, and for motor body coachwork, and truck and trailer flooring. It is rotary cut for constructional veneers for marine plywood and boat building, and for decorative veneers.

Where it grows
Agba is one of the largest trees in tropical west Africa, occurring mainly in western Nigeria and also in Angola and Zaire.

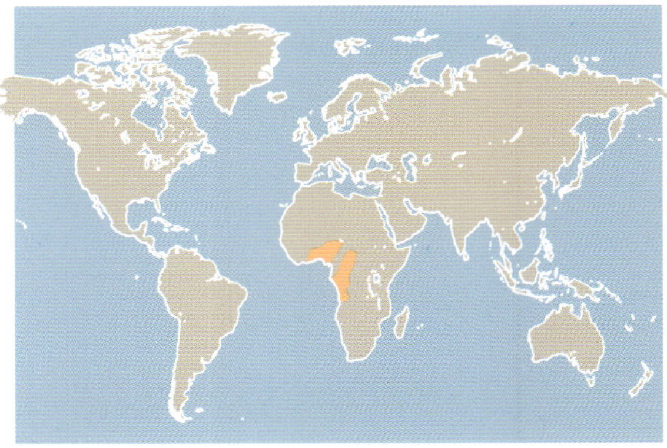

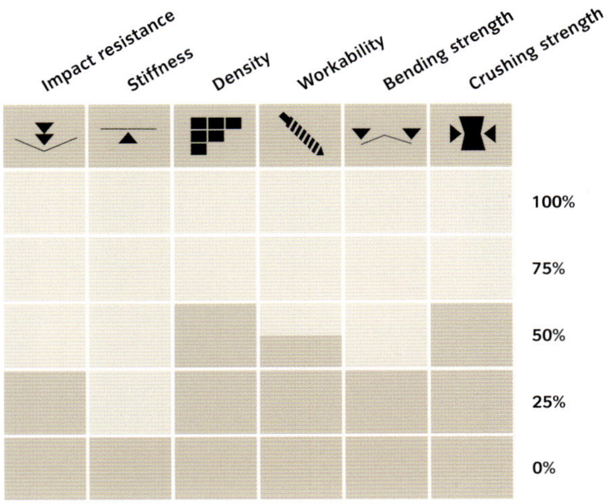

Workability describes how easy a wood is to work and whether it has a significant blunting effect on tools.

Bending strength is also known as maximum bending strength. Pressure is applied to each end of a board until it cracks.

Crushing strength is the ability of wood to withstand loads applied to the end grain, a critical test for wood used as short columns or props.

Gossypiospermum praecox | Family: *Flacourtiaceae* | **MARACAIBO BOXWOOD** | Hardwood

Growth

Maracaibo boxwood is a small tree, producing logs that are around 8–12ft (2.5–3.5m) in length and 6–12in (15–30cm) in diameter. It is also known as Venezuelan boxwood, West Indian boxwood, and Colombian boxwood (UK); zapatero (Venezuela); palo blanco (Dominican Republic); and pau branco, castelo, and zapateiro (Brazil).

Appearance

The timber of *Gossypiospermum praecox* is creamy white to lemon-yellow, with little difference between the heartwood and sapwood, and a high luster. Blue stain is common in timber stored in humid conditions. It is normally straight grained and featureless, with a very fine and uniform texture.

Properties

Maracaibo boxwood weighs 50–56lb/ft^3 (800–900kg/m^3) when seasoned. The timber dries very slowly, with a tendency to split and surface check. It is extremely stable in use. This dense wood is not used for its strength, but it has good steam-bending properties where discoloration is unimportant. It works satisfactorily with both hand and machine tools, but there is high resistance in cutting. The wood glues well and can be brought to a very smooth finish. The sapwood is vulnerable to fungal attack and the common furniture beetle, but the hardwood is durable. The sapwood is permeable for preservative treatment.

Uses

Maracaibo boxwood is outstanding for its very fine, smooth texture and excellent turning properties. It is used for tool handles, skittles, croquet mallet heads, textile rollers, silk industry shuttles, spindles, pulley blocks, and fancy turnery such as chessmen. The wood is ideal for precision rulers, drawing and measuring instruments, and engravers' blocks because of its extreme stability. It is also used for some parts of musical instruments such as pianos. It is sliced for decorative cabinet veneers and dyed black for inlay lines and bandings.

Where it grows

The trade name boxwood originally applied to *Buxus sempervirens* from Europe and eastern Asia, but today covers a wide range of unrelated species. Maracaibo boxwood occurs in Cuba and the Dominican Republic, but commercial supplies come from Colombia and Venezuela.

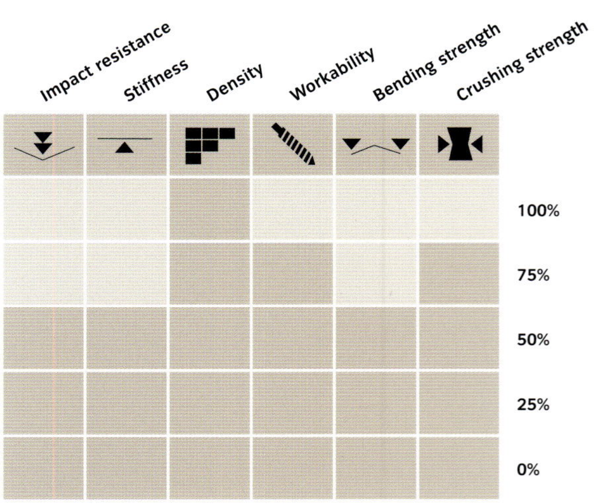

AT A GLANCE

Impact resistance is a measure of the wood's toughness. It describes its resistance to suddenly applied shock loads.

Stiffness is a measure of the wood's elasticity. It is considered in conjunction with bending strength.

Density is measured as specific gravity, the ratio of the density of a substance to that of water.

Guaiacum spp.	Family: *Zygophyllaceae*	**LIGNUM VITAE**	Hardwood

Growth
This wood, known as the wood of life in the 16th century because its resin was believed to cure diseases, is one of the hardest and heaviest timbers in commerce. It is produced from three species: *Guaiacum officinale* L., known as guayacan (Spain), bois de gaiac (France), guayacan negro and palo santo (Cuba), and ironwood (US); *G.sanctum* L., known as guayacan blanco, gaiac femelle, and guayacancillo; and *G.guatemalense* Planch. All three types are exported as lignum vitae. It is a small, slow-growing tree of about 30ft (9m) in height, with a diameter of 10–18in (25–45cm).

Appearance
The timber is dark greenish brown or nearly black, with a closely interlocked grain and a fine, even texture.

Properties
Lignum vitae weighs on average about 77lb/ft^3 (1230kg/m^3) when seasoned. It dries very slowly, is refractory, and is liable to check. There is medium movement in service. The wood has outstanding strength properties in all categories, particularly hardness, and has a very high crushing strengh. Unsuitable for bending, it is a very difficult wood to machine, with its very high resistance to cutting. Gluing can be difficult, but the wood polishes well. Lignum vitae is extremely durable and resistant to preservation treatment.

Uses
The self-lubricating properties of lignum vitae, from its high oil content, make it ideal for marine equipment such as bushing blocks and bearings for ships' propeller shafts, pulley sheaves, and dead-eyes, and as a replacement for metal thrust bearings in steel and tube works. It is used anywhere that lubrication is impractical or unreliable, such as in wheels, guides, rollers, and blocks, and in the textile industry for cotton gins, polishing sticks, and rollers. It is also used in die cutting. Lignum vitae has long been a favorite for wood sculpture and carving as well as an excellent turnery wood for mallet heads and for bowling "woods."

Where it grows
Lignum vitae occurs from southern Florida and the Bahamas through Jamaica, Cuba, and the West Indies, and from Mexico down through Central America to Colombia, Nicaragua, and Venezuela.

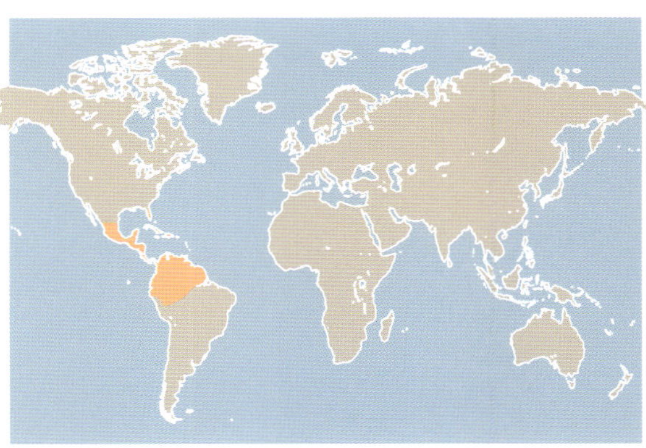

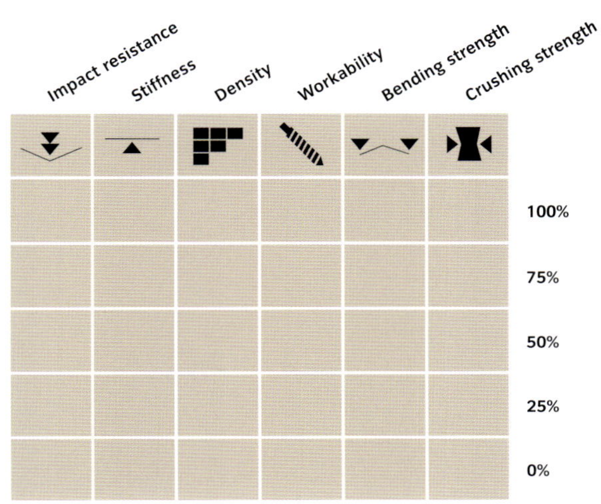

Workability describes how easy a wood is to work and whether it has a significant blunting effect on tools.

Bending strength is also known as maximum bending strength. Pressure is applied to each end of a board until it cracks.

Crushing strength is the ability of wood to withstand loads applied to the end grain, a critical test for wood used as short columns or props.

Guarea spp. | Family: *Meliaceae* | **GUAREA** | Hardwood

Growth

Guarea cedrata produces white guarea, which is also known as obobonufua (Nigeria) and scented guarea (UK). *G.thompsonii* Sprauge and Hutch. provide black guarea, also known as obobonekwi and obobo (Nigeria); bossé (Ivory Coast); diambi (Zaire); ebanghemwa (Cameroon); and divuitii (Gabon). Although the two species are distinguished by the color of their bark, they are sold under a single name. Both species grow to 165ft (50m), with a diameter of 3–4ft (1–1.2m).

Appearance

The wide sapwood is slightly paler than the heartwood, which is a pale pinkish brown mahogany color with straight to interlocked grain. *G.cedrata* produces a mottled or curly figure, and *G.thompsonii* is straighter grained and plainer in appearance, though both have a fine texture.

Properties

G.cedrata weighs 36lb/ft^3 (580kg/m^3) and often contains silica and resin, while silica-free *G.thompsonii* weighs about 39lb/ft^3 (620kg/m^3) when seasoned. It has a lower resin content. They dry fairly rapidly with little tendency to warp, but *G.cedrata* exudes resin, which can mar the appearance, and *G.thompsonii*, tending to split, requires greater care in drying. They are stable in use. Guarea has medium bending strength, and low stiffness and resistance to shock loads. *G.cedrata* has medium crushing strength and a good bending rating, while *G.thompsonii* has high crushing strength and a moderate bending rating. Both work fairly easily with hand and machine tools, but are inclined to be wooly. Both woods glue well, but care is needed in finishing because resin may exude. Machining dust is highly irritating, so efficient dust extraction is important. Guarea is a very durable timber and extremely resistant to preservative treatment, but the sapwood is permeable.

Uses

Guarea, a mahogany-type timber, is used in furniture for chairs, drawer sides and rails, interior fittings, edge lippings and facings, high-class joinery, shop fitting, boat building, vehicle construction, floorboards, and planking in caravans. It also occurs in sports goods, rifle butts, marine piling, exterior plywood, and decorative veneers.

Where it grows

Guarea occurs in tropical west Africa, principally the Ivory Coast and Nigeria.

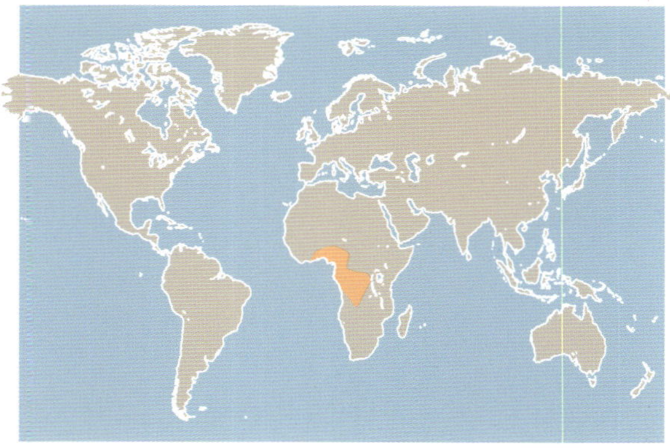

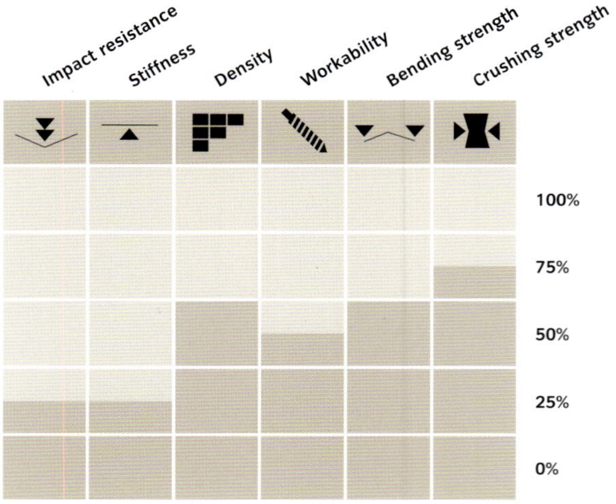

AT A GLANCE

Impact resistance is a measure of the wood's toughness. It describes its resistance to suddenly applied shock loads.

Stiffness is a measure of the wood's elasticity. It is considered in conjunction with bending strength.

Density is measured as specific gravity, the ratio of the density of a substance to that of water.

Guibourtia arnoldiana	Family: *Leguminosae*	**BENGE**	Hardwood

Growth

Known by a number of names, including mozambique, mutenye, and mbenge, *Guibourtia arnoldiana* was named after the French botanist Guibourt and the Arnold Arboretum in Boston, Massachussetts. It is not an ideal lumber tree because the stem is rarely clean and straight for very long, and indeed the tree rarely grows taller than 90ft (27m), with a diameter that is usually no more than 1½ or 2½ft (0.5 or 0.8m).

Appearance

Benge is inconsistent in color, sharing some of the characteristics of European walnut (*Juglans regia*), being a medium chocolate-brown interspersed with curving bands of golden yellow or pink, and dark, black lines. It does, however, have a fantastic figure and is very attractive.

Properties

With a fine, even texture, benge is a very dense and hard wood. Its interlocking grain makes it strong, although perhaps difficult to use as a result. Just as the color and pattern vary, so does the weight of this wood, ranging from 30 to 49lb/ft^3 (480 to 780kg/m^3), but it is at least very stable once dry, with seasoning being slow but not difficult. Although benge is not as durable as its close relative bubinga (*G.demeusii*), it is still moderately so. It is not, however, particularly good for bending because the grain is too wild and the lumber is likely to buckle or burst as it bends.

Uses

Although benge may not be particularly easy to machine, the interlocking grain and hardness make this wood ideal for flooring, while the wild grain makes it popular with turners and furniture makers. It is also sliced for decorative veneer.

Where it grows

The growing region for benge is relatively limited, with the tree notably occurring in western central Africa, specifically in Cameroon, the Congo, and Guinea.

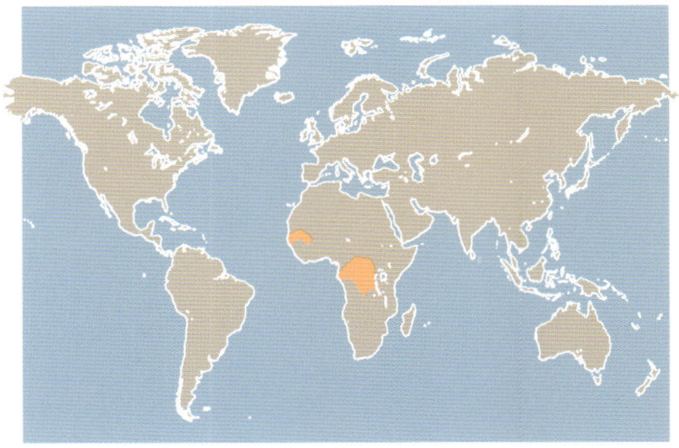

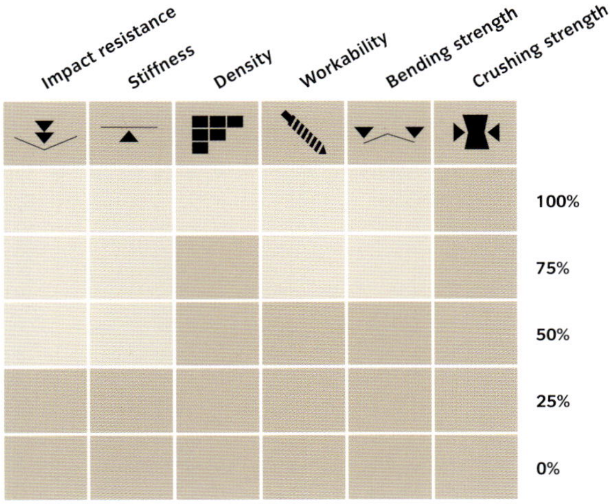

Workability describes how easy a wood is to work and whether it has a significant blunting effect on tools.

Bending strength is also known as maximum bending strength. Pressure is applied to each end of a board until it cracks.

Crushing strength is the ability of wood to withstand loads applied to the end grain, a critical test for wood used as short columns or props.

Guibourtia demeusii | Family: *Leguminosae* | **BUBINGA** | Hardwood

Growth

Also known as *Guibourtia tessmannii*, bubinga is one of the *Leguminosae* family, of which the many rosewood, or *Dalbergia*, species are members. Not surprisingly, it is also known as African rosewood, presumably reflecting its lineage, because it does not immediately strike one as a typical rosewood. Like many tropical hardwoods, the tree has heavy buttressing at the base and a clear bole about 30–60ft (9–20m) high.

Appearance

Bubinga has a distinctive color that tends to darken over the years from pinkish red when it is cut to deep burgundy or purple. Though it can be straight grained, wild whorls of figure are often a characteristic of bubinga, with the pale sapwood contrasting with the dark heartwood. The texture is fairly open but consistent.

Properties

Bubinga is hard and fairly heavy, though its weight has a wide range from about 50 to 60lb/ft^3 (800 to 960kg/m^3). Very stable once dry, it seasons quickly, although you do have to watch out for gum deposits. This is a tricky lumber that can be difficult to work because the grain is often interlocked and there is frequently a fair amount of sapwood to deal with. Watch out for resin pockets that can clog blades. Bubinga is fairly resistant to insect attack, but cannot easily be protected with preservative. It finishes to a high luster, and is relatively easy to work by hand or machine, as long as you are prepared to take shallow cuts to cope with the interlocking grain. It can be glued well into panels.

Uses

Bubinga has many attractions for the furniture maker in the solid form, or for cabinet making and paneling as a veneer. Wood turners love the species because it exhibits such interesting color and figure, but it is dusty to work with. It is also used for knife handles. The most attractive veneer, which is rotary cut, is known as kevasingo, and is identified by its wild, veined grain.

Where it grows

Bubinga is grown mainly in west Africa, particularly in Cameroon, Gabon, and the Ivory Coast.

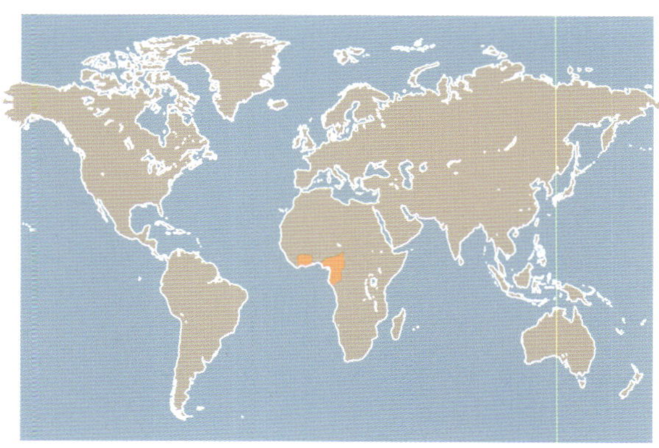

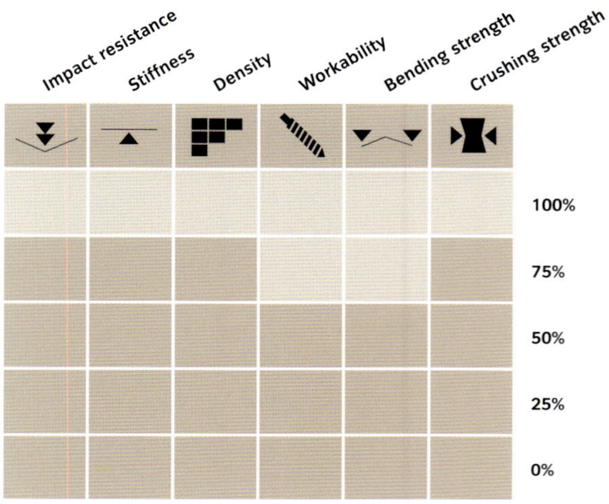

AT A GLANCE

Impact resistance is a measure of the wood's toughness. It describes its resistance to suddenly applied shock loads.

Stiffness is a measure of the wood's elasticity. It is considered in conjunction with bending strength.

Density is measured as specific gravity, the ratio of the density of a substance to that of water.

Guibourtia ehie | Family: *Leguminosae* | **OVANGKOL** | Hardwood

Growth

Ovangkol is also known as amazoué and amazakoué (Ivory Coast), and as ehie, anokye, and hyeduanini (Ghana). It reaches a height of about 100ft (30m), with a diameter of about 2½ft (0.8m). Older stems have a growth of slightly raised horizontal rings that affect the figure in the log.

Appearance

The heartwood is yellow-brown to deep chocolate-brown with grayish black stripes. The grain is interlocked and the texture is moderately coarse.

Properties

The average weight of ovangkol is about 50lb/ft^3 (800kg/m^3) when seasoned. The wood dries rapidly and fairly well, but care is needed in kilning thick stock to avoid collapse. There is medium movement in service. The wood has medium bending and crushing strengths, and medium shock resistance; despite low stiffness, it has a poor steam-bending rating, and only shallow bends are possible. The wood presents a moderate resistance and blunting effect to cutting edges because of its silica content, and tools should be kept very sharp. The wood saws slowly but well and the cutting angle should be reduced, especially when planing or molding quartered stock, to avoid picking up or tearing the interlocked grain. It has good holding properties, glues without difficulty, takes stain and polish well, and can be brought to an excellent finish. The heartwood is moderately durable and resistant to preservative treatment, but the sapwood is permeable.

Uses

Ovangkol is a very attractive wood that is suitable for high-class furniture and cabinet making, interior joinery, and decorative work. It makes hard-wearing domestic flooring and is used for shop, office, and bank fitting. It is an excellent turnery wood for handles and fancy items. Ovangkol logs are rotary cut for plywood faces, and selected logs are sliced for decorative veneers for cabinets, flush doors, and paneling.

Where it grows

This tall tree occurs in tropical west Africa, mainly the Ivory Coast and Ghana. Supplies of ovangkol also come from southern Nigeria and Gabon.

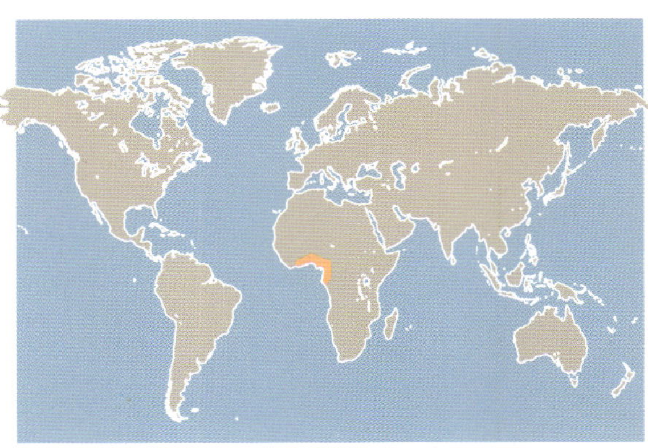

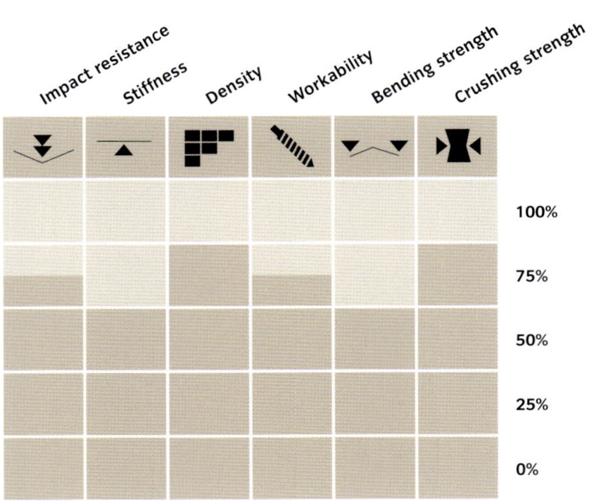

Workability describes how easy a wood is to work and whether it has a significant blunting effect on tools.

Bending strength is also known as maximum bending strength. Pressure is applied to each end of a board until it cracks.

Crushing strength is the ability of wood to withstand loads applied to the end grain, a critical test for wood used as short columns or props.

Heritiera spp.	Family: *Sterculiaceae*	**MENGKULANG**	Hardwood

Growth
Commercial timber is produced from *Heritiera simplicifolia* (Mast.) Kosterm; *H.javanica* (Bl.) Kosterm; and *H.borneensis*. They are also known as niangon (west Africa); kembang (Sabah); chumprak and chumprag (Thailand); lumbayao (Philippines); and gisang (Malaya). Trees reach a height of 100–150ft (30–45m), with a diameter of 2–3ft (0.6–1.0m).

Appearance
The sapwood of mengkulang is pale orange. It blends into the heartwood, which varies from a medium pinkish brown to dark red-brown, often with dark streaks on the longitudinal surfaces. Mengkulang's grain is interlocked and sometimes irregular, producing a broad striped figure on quartered surfaces, often with conspicuous reddish flecks. The texture is moderately coarse and fairly even.

Properties
The weight of mengkulang varies according to the species, but averages 40–45lb/ft^3 (640–720kg/m^3) when seasoned, although kembang is slightly lighter. The wood dries rapidly and well, with a tendency to warping or to surface checking in some species. This dense wood is stable in service, possesses medium bending strength, stiffness, and resistance to shock loads, high crushing strength, and a very poor steam-bending rating. The timber works moderately well, but there is severe blunting of cutting edges, especially saw teeth. It requires pre-boring for nailing, glues well, and with the grain filled can be brought to a good finish. Mengkulang is perishable and the sapwood is liable to attack by powder post beetle. The heartwood is resistant to preservative treatment, while the sapwood is moderately resistant.

Uses
Mengkulang is used locally for cabinet and furniture fitments, wheelwrighting, vehicle framing, paneling, sills, sleepers, boat ribs, and planking; it is also employed for domestic flooring. In addition, the wood appears in general construction, carpentry, and interior joinery. It is rotary cut for plywood for local structural use and sliced for decorative veneers.

Where it grows
A wide number of species of *Heritiera* occur in the tropics, including niangon in west Africa and chumprak in Thailand. *H.javanica* is the principal species found in the Philippines. Mengkulang is a Malayan name for half a dozen or more species that occur in southeast Asia.

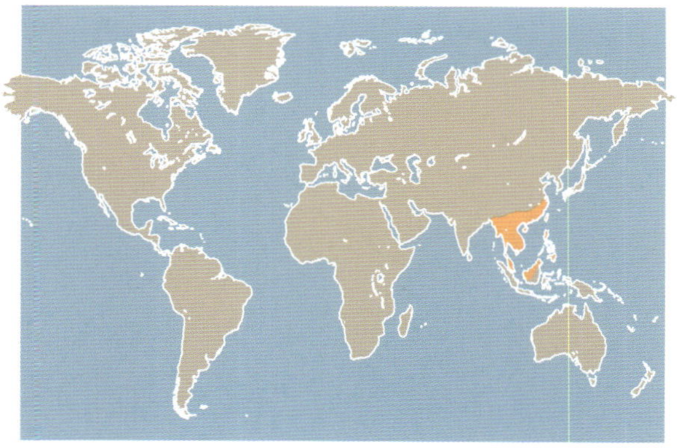

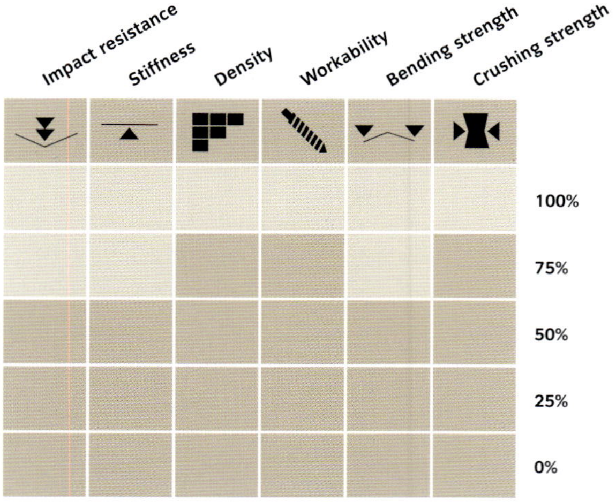

AT A GLANCE

Impact resistance is a measure of the wood's toughness. It describes its resistance to suddenly applied shock loads.

Stiffness is a measure of the wood's elasticity. It is considered in conjunction with bending strength.

Density is measured as specific gravity, the ratio of the density of a substance to that of water.

Hymenaea courbaril | Family: *Leguminosae* | **COURBARIL** | Hardwood

Growth
Courbaril is also known as West Indian locust (UK); rode locust (Surinam); jutaby, jatoba, and jatai amerelo (Brazil); algarrobo (Puerto Rico); guapinal (Mexico); copal (Equador); and marbre (Guadaloupe). Trees reach 100–150ft (30–45m), with a diameter of 3–5ft (1–1.5m).

Appearance
The heartwood matures to an orange-red to reddish brown, marked with russet and dark brown streaks. It often has a golden luster. The grain is usually interlocked with a medium to coarse texture.

Properties
This dense wood weighs about 56lb/ft^3 (900kg/m^3) when seasoned. It is a rather difficult timber to dry, with surface checking, warping, and occasionally case-hardening. It is stable in service and very strong in all categories, but its low stiffness gives it a moderate steam-bending classification. The timber is moderately difficult to work, with a severe blunting effect on tools. It requires pre-boring for nailing, but the wood has good screw-holding properties. It glues well, and can be stained and polished for a very good finish. Courbaril is moderately durable, but nondurable when a high proportion of sapwood is present. It is very resistant to termites and extremely resistant to preservative treatment.

Uses
Courbaril is used locally for general building construction, wheelwrighting, looms, carpentry, and joinery. Its high shock resistance makes it suitable for sports goods and striking tool handles. It is also used for high-class cabinets and furniture, interior joinery, and especially for flooring and stair treads, because of its great resistance to wear. It is ideal for ships' planking, gear cogs, and so on. In boat building it is employed for steam-bent parts. Externally, it is utilized for lock gates in areas free from marine borers. Selected logs are sliced for highly decorative veneers suitable for cabinets and architectural paneling.

Where it grows
This large, almost evergreen tree grows from southern Mexico through Central America and the West Indies, down as far as Brazil, Bolivia, and Peru.

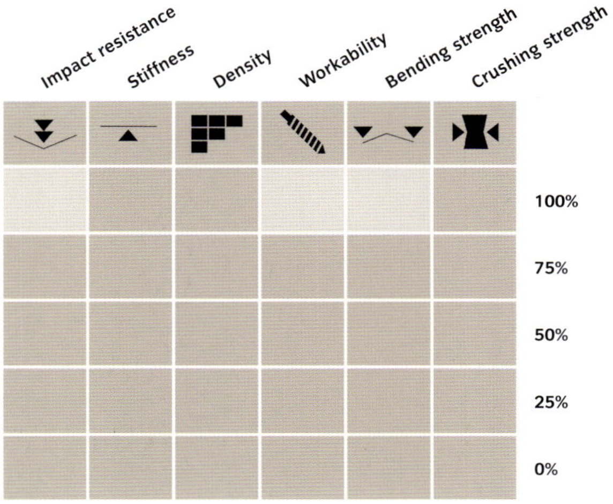

Workability describes how easy a wood is to work and whether it has a significant blunting effect on tools.

Bending strength is also known as maximum bending strength. Pressure is applied to each end of a board until it cracks.

Crushing strength is the ability of wood to withstand loads applied to the end grain, a critical test for wood used as short columns or props.

Ilex spp. | Family: *Aquifoliaceae* | **HOLLY** | Hardwood

Growth
There are about 175 different species of holly, growing most profusely in Europe. *Ilex opaca* produces holly in the United States, reaching a height of approximately 80ft (24m), with a diameter of about 2ft (0.6m). In the UK, *I.aquifolum* has become a small hedgerow tree, about 30ft (9m) tall, with a bole of 10ft (3m) and a diameter of 1½ft (0.5m).

Appearance
Holly is perhaps the whitest known wood in the world. The heartwood ranges from white to gray-white, and sometimes features a greenish gray cast. It has little or no figure. The sapwood of holly is not distinct from the heartwood. The grain tends to be irregular, with a very fine, even texture.

Properties
The weight of holly averages about 49lb/ft^3 (780kg/m^3) when seasoned. The wood is fairly difficult to dry, and it is best to cut the stock into small dimensions and then slowly air dry it under a weighted-down pile. It is stable in use when dry. This heavy, dense wood is tough in all strength categories, but is not suitable for steam bending. Holly has a high resistance to cutting and sawing and a moderate blunting effect on tools, which should be kept very sharp, especially when working with the irregular grain. The wood turns well, requires pre-boring for screwing or nailing, glues easily, and can be brought to an excellent, smooth finish. In the round, logs are liable to attack by forest longhorn or *Buprestid* beetles. The heartwood is perishable and the sapwood is liable to attack by the common furniture beetle, but it is permeable for preservation treatment.

Uses
Holly is available in limited quantities, in small dimensions, and as narrow veneers. It is mainly used as a substitute for boxwood. When dyed black, it is a substitute for ebony for marquetry inlay motifs, lines, bandings, and stringings in antique repair, and for restoration and reproduction furniture. It is excellent for fancy turnery and engraving blocks. It is used for musical instrument parts, piano and organ keys, parts of harpsichords and clavichords, and billiard cue butts.

Where it grows
Holly occurs in Europe, from Norway, Denmark, and Germany down to the Mediterranean. It also occurs in the southeast of the United States and parts of Asia.

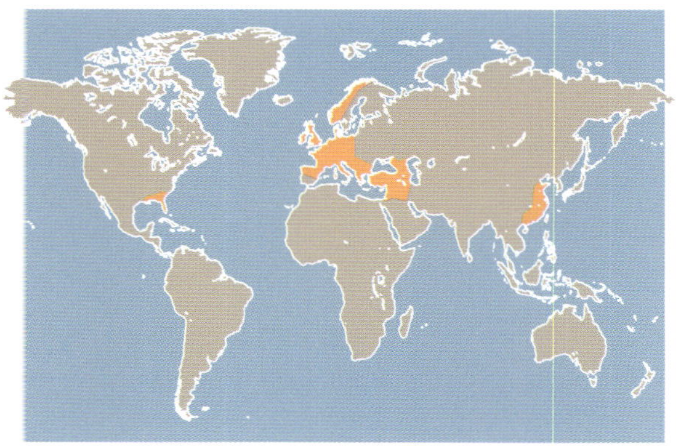

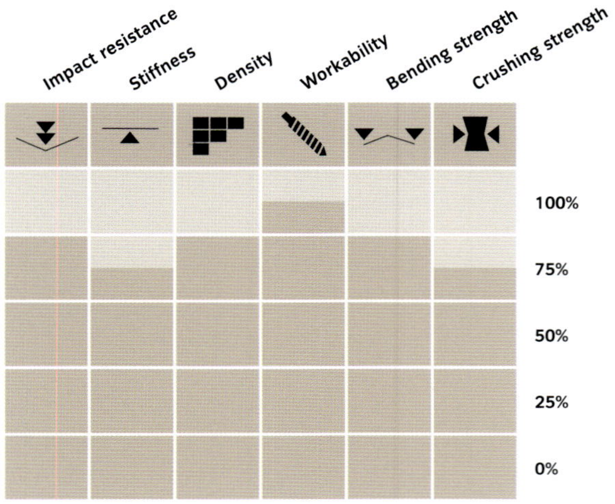

AT A GLANCE

Impact resistance is a measure of the wood's toughness. It describes its resistance to suddenly applied shock loads.

Stiffness is a measure of the wood's elasticity. It is considered in conjunction with bending strength.

Density is measured as specific gravity, the ratio of the density of a substance to that of water.

Juglans nigra | Family: *Juglandaceae* | **BLACK WALNUT** | Hardwood

Growth

Juglans nigra is one of the true walnut trees. It is also known as American walnut and Virginia walnut (UK); walnut, canaletto, black hickory nut, and walnut tree (US); and Canadian walnut (Canada and US). In favorable conditions, the trees reach a height of 100–150ft (30–45m), with a diameter of about 4–6ft (1.2–1.8m) and a straight, clear bole. Related species include the South American *J.neotropica*, *J.columbiensis*, and *J.australis* (called Peruvian walnut in the UK and US).

Appearance

The sapwood of black walnut is almost white, while the attractive heartwood is light brown maturing to a rich, dark chocolate-brown to black, often with purplish streaks. It is usually straight grained, but occasionally wavy or curly. The texture of black walnut is rather coarse, but uniform.

Properties

Black walnut is a heavy wood, weighing about 40lb/ft^3 (640kg/m^3) when seasoned. The wood must be dried carefully to avoid checking and degradation, but once seasoned there is little movement in service. Black walnut is of medium density, with moderate bending and crushing strength, and low stiffness and shock resistance; it has a good steam-bending rating. The wood works well with hand and machine tools, and has a moderate blunting effect on cutting edges. It holds nails and screws well, and can be glued satisfactorily. It is a delight to work, takes stain and polish with ease, and can be brought to an excellent finish. Black walnut is very durable. The sapwood is liable to attack by powder post beetle. The heartwood is resistant to preservative treatment and biodegradation, but the sapwood is permeable.

Uses

Black walnut and its related South American species are extensively used for rifle butts and gunstocks, high-class cabinets and furniture, interior joinery, boat building, musical instruments, clock cases, turnery, carving, and wood sculpture. It is a major timber for plywood manufacture, and selected logs are sliced for decorative veneers of all kinds for cabinets and paneling.

Where it grows

Black walnut is widely distributed throughout North America, from southern Ontario in Canada down to Texas, and in the east from Maine to Florida. Related species occur in South America, including Peru, Colombia, Ecuador, Venezuela, Argentina, and Mexico.

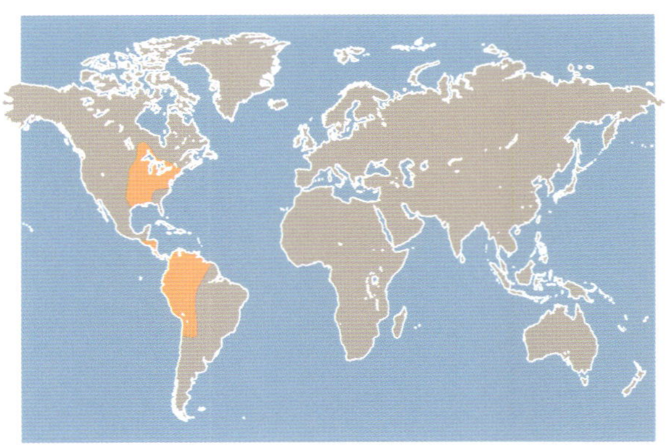

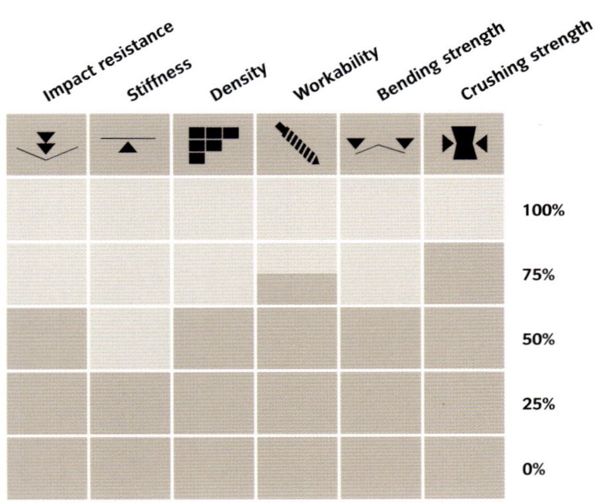

Workability describes how easy a wood is to work and whether it has a significant blunting effect on tools.

Bending strength is also known as maximum bending strength. Pressure is applied to each end of a board until it cracks.

Crushing strength is the ability of wood to withstand loads applied to the end grain, a critical test for wood used as short columns or props.

Juglans regia | Family: *Juglandaceae* | **EUROPEAN WALNUT** | Hardwood

Growth
The European walnut—also known as Ancona, Black Sea, English, French, Italian, and Persian walnut, according to the country of origin—attains, in favorable conditions, a height of 80–100ft (24–30m) and a diameter of 2–5ft (0.6–1.5m), with a rugged bole about 20ft (6m) long.

Appearance
The heartwood is usually gray-brown, with irregular dark brown streaks accentuated by a natural wavy grain. This highly figured wood often forms a central core, sharply defined from the remaining plain heartwood, and this feature is more pronounced in Italian than in English walnut. French walnut is even paler and grayer than English walnut. It is straight to wavy grained, with a rather coarse texture.

Properties
European walnut weighs an average of about 40lb/ft^3 (640kg/m^3) when seasoned. Walnut dries well, but thicker material has a tendency to check. There is medium shrinkage in service. It has medium bending strength and resistance to shock loads, with a high crushing strength and low stiffness. It has a very good steam-bending rating. The wood works easily and well with hand and machine tools, glues satisfactorily, and can be brought to an excellent finish. The heartwood is moderately durable. The sapwood is liable to attack by powder post beetle and the common furniture beetle. The heartwood is resistant to preservative treatment, but the sapwood is permeable. Blue-black stains can appear if the wood comes into contact with iron compounds in damp conditions.

Uses
Ever since the late 17th century, this beautiful timber has been used for high-class cabinets and furniture, interior joinery, and bank, office, and shop fittings. It is also popular for making attractive rifle butts and gunstocks, and for all sorts of sports goods. It is a favorite for carving, wood sculpture, and turnery, and for the fascias and cappings of expensive cars. Highly decorative figured veneers of stumpwood, crotches, and burls are used for plywood, doors, and paneling.

Where it grows
The European walnut is native to the Carpathian Mountains of eastern Europe, but is often found growing wild eastward through Asia Minor to the Himalayas and China. Today's commercial supplies mainly come from France, Italy, Turkey, and the Balkans.

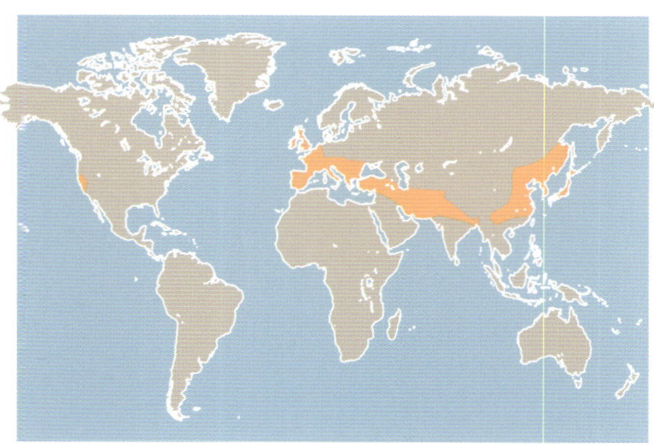

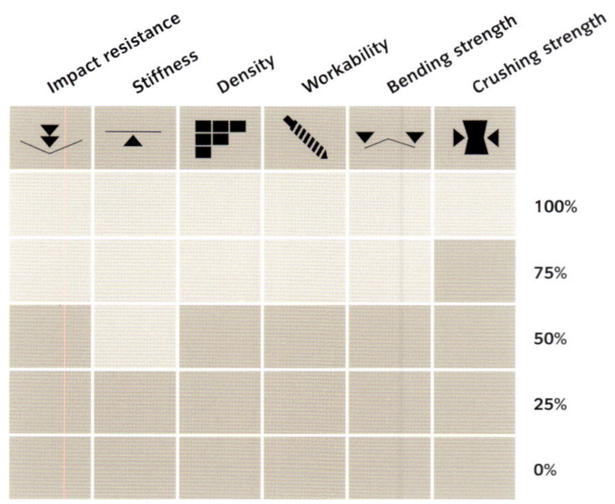

AT A GLANCE

Impact resistance is a measure of the wood's toughness. It describes its resistance to suddenly applied shock loads.

Stiffness is a measure of the wood's elasticity. It is considered in conjunction with bending strength.

Density is measured as specific gravity, the ratio of the density of a substance to that of water.

Kalopanax pictus | Family: _Araliaceae_ | **SEN** | Hardwood

Growth

Also known as _Kalopanax septemlobus_ or _Acanthopanax ricinofolius_, sen is a thick-branched tree with prickly leaves. It normally grows to about 80ft (24m) in height, and is sometimes referred to as Japanese ash, so it is easy to confuse it with tamo ash (_Fraxinus sieboldiana_).

Appearance

Sen looks very similar to some of the more strongly colored ash species, or to the diseased olive ash, which features darker streaks. The color varies from straw to mid-brown, with a gentle transition between the heartwood and the paler sapwood. The grain patterning tends to be fairly straight, but it can be very attractive with shimmering colors. It has a coarse texture and high luster.

Properties

Sen is not particularly strong, has a coarse and moderately uneven texture, and is difficult to season, although it does dry quickly. Unfortunately, it is likely to move considerably once seasoned, thereby limiting its likely range of uses. It is not a durable wood, but can be worked easily by hand or machine, although it will not bend because it tends to be fairly brittle. Sen finishes well enough, but you do have to accept that the open pores will suck in any application, so you will need to use a filler if you want to achieve a mirror-smooth result.

Uses

The coarse texture and high luster of sen combine to produce a wonderful surface for furniture cabinets. Although it is used for interior trim, furniture, and paneling, it is most frequently employed for decoration rather than as a structural component. It is often sliced into veneer or used for plywood, and is especially popular for turnery.

Where it grows

Sen grows in some parts of Japan, and also in China, Korea, and Manchuria.

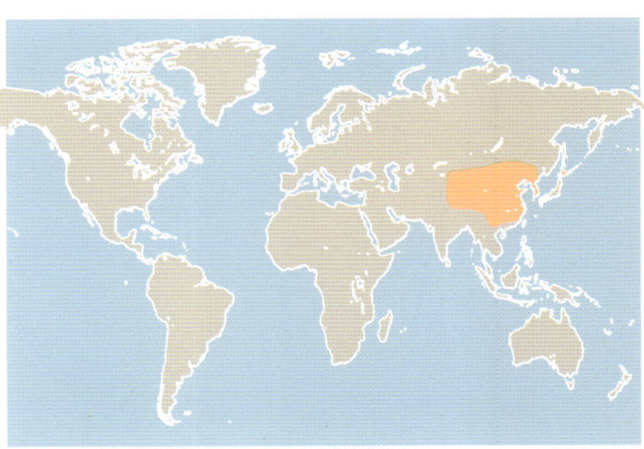

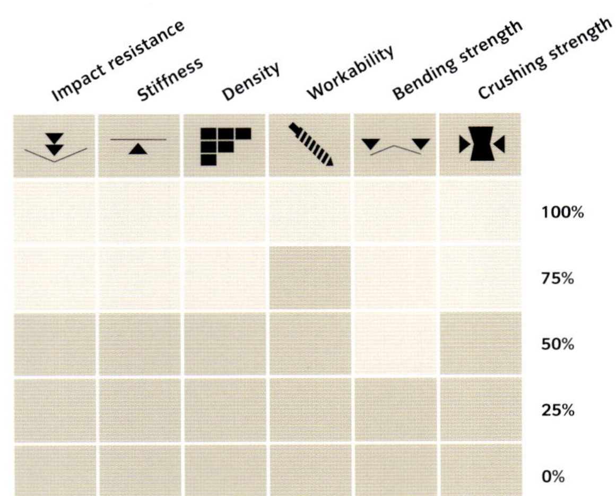

Workability describes how easy a wood is to work and whether it has a significant blunting effect on tools.

Bending strength is also known as maximum bending strength. Pressure is applied to each end of a board until it cracks.

Crushing strength is the ability of wood to withstand loads applied to the end grain, a critical test for wood used as short columns or props.

Khaya spp.	Family: *Meliaceae*	**AFRICAN MAHOGANY**	Hardwood

Growth

The name African mahogany covers all trees of the *Khaya* species. The bulk of commercial timber is produced by: *K.ivorensis* A.Chév., which is also known as Benin, Degema, Lagos, and Nigerian mahogany; *K.anthotheca* (Welw.) C.DC., which is known as krala (Ivory Coast), mangona (Cameroon), munyama (Uganda), mbaua (Mozambique), mbawa (Malawi), and mkangazi (Tanzania); and *K.nyasica* Stapf. ex Bakerf. African mahogany reaches a height of 180–200ft (55–60m) and a diameter of 4–6ft (1.2–1.8m).

Appearance

African mahogany has a typically reddish brown heartwood. The grain can be straight but is usually interlocked, producing a striped or roe figure on quartered surfaces.

Properties

The weight of *K.ivorensis* averages about 33lb/ft³ (530kg/m³), *K.anthotheca* around 34lb/ft³ (540kg/m³), and *K.nyasica* approximately 37lb/ft³ (590kg/m³) when seasoned. The wood dries fairly rapidly with little degrade and is stable in use. The timber is of medium density and crushing strength, has a low bending strength, very low stiffness and resistance to shock loads, and a very poor steam-bending rating. African mahogany works easily with both hand and machine tools. Nailing is satisfactory, the wood glues well, and it can be stained and polished to an excellent finish. The heartwood of African mahogany is moderately durable and the sapwood, which is liable to attack by powder post beetle, is resistant to impregnation.

Uses

African mahogany is a very important timber for furniture, office desks, cabinet making, shop and bank fitting, and for high-quality joinery for staircases, banisters, handrails, and paneling. It is also utilized for domestic flooring, boat building, and vehicle bodies. Logs are rotary cut for plywood and selected logs are sliced for decorative veneers for cabinets and paneling.

Where it grows

Khaya ivorensis occurs in the coastal rainforests of west Africa from the Ivory Coast to Cameroon and Gabon. *K.anthotheca* and *K.nyasica* are not found in the coastal belt but grow in areas of lower rainfall, including Uganda and Tanzania.

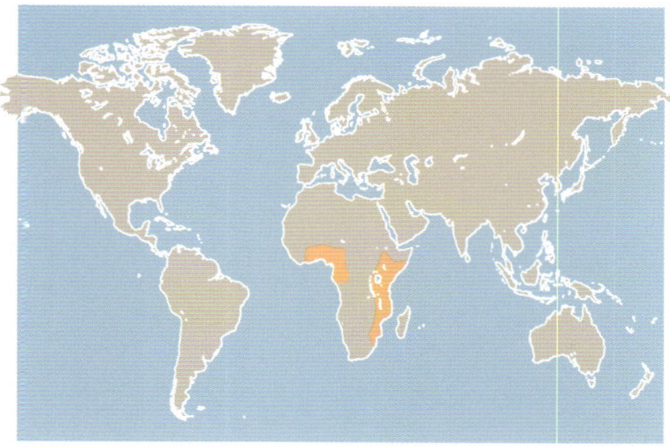

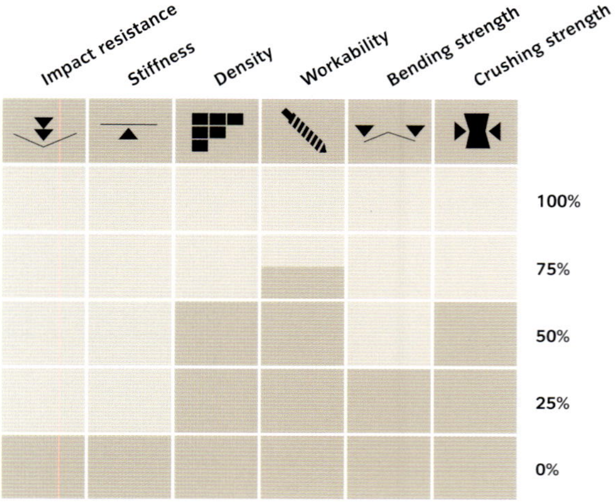

AT A GLANCE

Impact resistance is a measure of the wood's toughness. It describes its resistance to suddenly applied shock loads.

Stiffness is a measure of the wood's elasticity. It is considered in conjunction with bending strength.

Density is measured as specific gravity, the ratio of the density of a substance to that of water.

Knightia excelsa | Family: *Proteaceae* | **REWAREWA** | Hardwood

Growth
This crooked tree provides only clean, straight, cylindrical boles of about 20ft (6m), with a diameter of about 16in (40cm).

Appearance
The heartwood of rewarewa is a deep red color, strongly marked with a dark red-brown ray figure. It is strikingly mottled on the quartered surfaces, with a more subdued growth ring figure on the flat-sawn ones. The grain is irregular and the texture is fine and lustrous.

Properties
Rewarewa weighs approximately 46lb/ft^3 (740kg/m^3) when seasoned. Reaction wood is often present, making it a rather difficult wood to dry. It requires very accurate conversion to avoid serious distortion. There is large movement in service. The wood has medium density and bending strength, but high stiffness, shock resistance, and crushing strength. It is not suitable for steam bending. It works readily with both hand and machine tools, with moderately severe blunting of cutting edges. Nailing requires pre-boring, but it has good holding properties for screws. It glues satisfactorily. Oil finishes and varnish should be avoided, as they are absorbed to the detriment of the finely marked grain. With care, the wood can be brought to an excellent finish. The heartwood is nondurable and resistant to preservative treatment, but the sapwood is permeable.

Uses
Rewarewa is one of the most attractive hardwoods in New Zealand, in demand for ornamental cabinet and furniture making. It is also widely used for interior joinery, flooring, staircases, banisters, and handrails. It is often utilized for carved fireplaces because it is incombustible. It is a firm favorite for ornamental turnery for fancy items, handles, and bowls. Logs given preservative treatment are employed for house blocks, decking, gates, rails, piling, and railway sleepers. Selected logs are rotary cut for plywood faces and for corestock of laminated boards, but rewarewa is best when sliced into the most beautiful decorative veneers for cabinets, paneling, and marquetry.

Where it grows
Rewarewa, which grows in New Zealand, is also known as New Zealand honeysuckle.

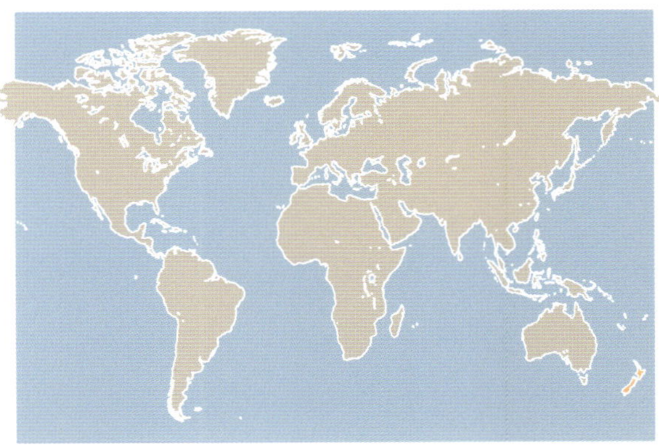

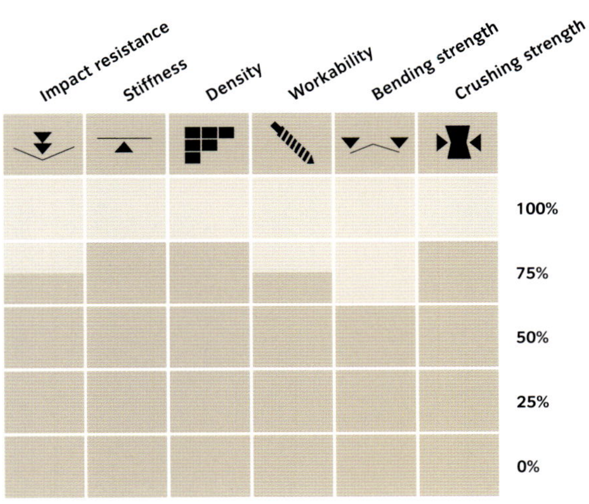

Workability describes how easy a wood is to work and whether it has a significant blunting effect on tools.

Bending strength is also known as maximum bending strength. Pressure is applied to each end of a board until it cracks.

Crushing strength is the ability of wood to withstand loads applied to the end grain, a critical test for wood used as short columns or props.

Laburnum anagyroides | Family: *Leguminosae* | **LABURNUM** | Hardwood

Growth

Never very large—at its maximum 30ft (9m) in height—laburnum is commonly planted as an ornamental tree in gardens and parks. Laburnum is also not a very broad tree, with the trunk rarely thicker than 1ft (0.3m) in diameter, and the few branches do not usually produce much by way of useful lumber.

Appearance

Laburnum has a beautiful, lustrous surface with a heartwood of deep greenish brown, dissimilar to lignum vitae (*Guaiacum spp.*), but with the grain patterning of ash (*Fraxinus spp.*), oak (*Quercus spp.*), or elm (*Ulmus spp.*). When first cut, the heartwood is much lighter, even yellow, but this darkens quite quickly. The contrast between the dark heartwood and pale sapwood can be used to great effect, particularly by turners and carvers.

Properties

Not very much is known about the working properties of laburnum because it is so rarely used as a commercial wood. It is usually only harvested by keen amateurs for turning, although there is trade in veneer, especially end-grain veneer for marquetry and decorative uses. It is, however, hard, dense, and strong, and can be polished to a high finish. It is durable, but prone to some insect attack.

Uses

Branches of laburnum are often sliced across the grain to produce thin disks (known as oysters), from veneer thickness upward. These are used either for decorative veneering to imitate the look of open oysters, or as coasters, often with some sapwood attached for contrast. Turners love laburnum (although the dust can be an irritant), and make a feature of the sapwood/heartwood contrast, particularly for cutlery handles and musical instruments.

Where it grows

Laburnum grows naturally in southern and central Europe, but can be found in gardens around the world.

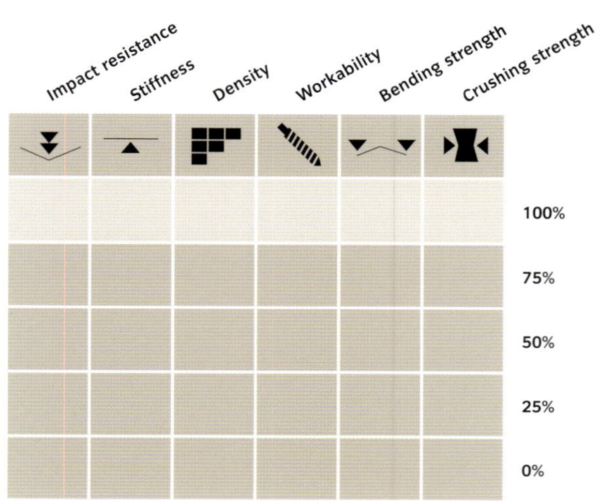

AT A GLANCE

Impact resistance is a measure of the wood's toughness. It describes its resistance to suddenly applied shock loads.

Stiffness is a measure of the wood's elasticity. It is considered in conjunction with bending strength.

Density is measured as specific gravity, the ratio of the density of a substance to that of water.

***Larix* spp.** | Family: *Pinaceae* | **LARCH** | Softwood

Growth
Larch is unusual among the softwoods because it casts its leaves in winter. The chief species are: *Larix decidua* Mill. (*L.europaea* DC), which is known European larch; *L.kaempferi* (Lamb.) Carr., known as Japanese larch and red larch (UK); *L.eurolepis* A.Henry, known as Dunkeld larch; *L.laricina* (Du Roi) K.Koch., known as Tamarak larch (Canada and US); *L.russica* (Endl.) Sabine, known as Siberian larch (northeast Russia); and *L.occidentalis* Nutt., known as western larch (British Columbia and western US). Larch reaches an average height of 100–150ft (30–45m), with a diameter of 3–4ft (1–1.2m).

Appearance
The heartwood of larch is pale reddish brown to brick-red in color, with clearly marked annual rings. The wood has straight grain and a fine, uniform texture.

Properties
Larch varies in weight from 30lb/ft^3 (480kg/m^3) for the lightest species to about 38lb/ft^3 (610kg/m^3) for the heaviest species when seasoned. This resinous wood dries fairly rapidly with some distortion but is stable in use. It has medium bending strength, low stiffness, medium crushing strength and resistance to shock loads, and a moderate steam-bending rating. It works fairly readily with both hand and machine tools. It requires pre-boring for nailing and takes stain, paint, and varnish satisfactorily for a good finish. The wood is moderately durable and liable to insect attack by pinhole borer beetle, longhorn beetle, sometimes *Sirex*, and the common furniture beetle. The heartwood is resistant to preservative treatment and the sapwood is moderately resistant.

Uses
When treated, larch is chiefly used externally for pit props, stakes, transmission poles, and piles. The heartwood is suitable for work where durability is of prime importance, such as boat planking, bridge construction, railway sleepers, and exterior joinery in contact with the ground. Selected logs are also rotary cut for plywood faces and sliced to provide ornamental veneers for flush doors and architectural paneling.

Where it grows
Larch occurs in mountainous districts from the Swiss Alps to the Carpathian Mountains of Russia. Other varieties occur in Canada, the United States, and Japan.

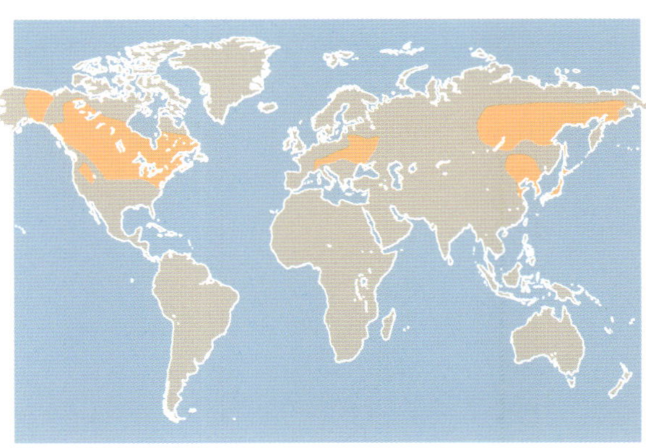

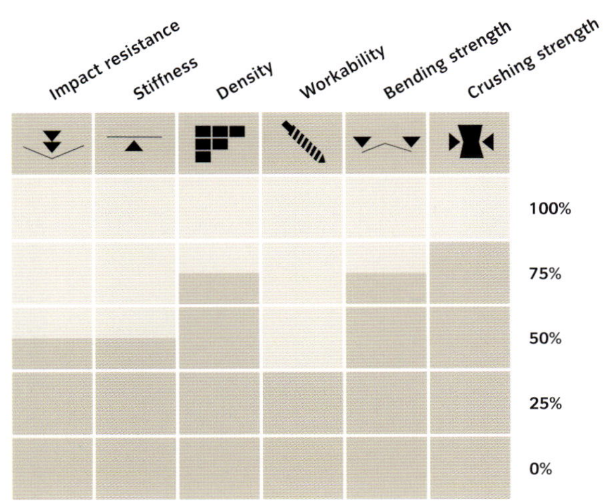

Workability describes how easy a wood is to work and whether it has a significant blunting effect on tools.

Bending strength is also known as maximum bending strength. Pressure is applied to each end of a board until it cracks.

Crushing strength is the ability of wood to withstand loads applied to the end grain, a critical test for wood used as short columns or props.

Laurelia sempervirens | Family: *Monimiaceae* | **CHILEAN LAUREL** | Hardwood

Growth

Chilean laurel is also known as huahuan. It grows to a height of 45–50ft (14–15m), with a diameter of 2–3ft (0.6–1m).

Appearance

The sapwood is a uniform grayish brown, and the heartwood a yellowish brown with darker streaks of green-brown, gray, or purple. The timber has straight grain and a moderately fine texture.

Properties

The weight of Chilean laurel averages about 32lb/ft³ (510kg/m³) when seasoned. The wood dries fairly rapidly, but with a strong tendency to collapse; it responds well to reconditioning in the kiln. There is large movement in service. The wood has medium bending and crushing strengths, with very low stiffness and resistance to shock loads. It has a moderate steam-bending classification; it is suitable for bends of a medium radius, but at the risk of distortion and fracture. The timber works readily with both hand and machine tools, but cutters should be kept very sharp for a clean finish. It can be nailed and glued without problems, and can be stained and polished satisfactorily to a good finish. The heartwood is nondurable and moderately resistant to preservation treatment, although the sapwood is permeable.

Uses

This is a very good general-purpose timber, suitable for the interior parts of furniture, drawer sides, partitions, shelves, and for edge lipping and facings of panels. It is also widely used for interior joinery, doors, light domestic flooring, light construction, and corestock for plywood and laminated board manufacture. Selected logs are sliced for very attractive decorative veneers for paneling. A related Chilean species, *L.philippiana* Looser. (*L.serrata* Ph.), produces tepa, which is also known as laurela. It is used locally for making beehives, boxes, crates, turnery, and plywood. It is a major source of wood pulp.

Where it grows

This relatively small tree occurs in small stands in the mixed forests of Chile.

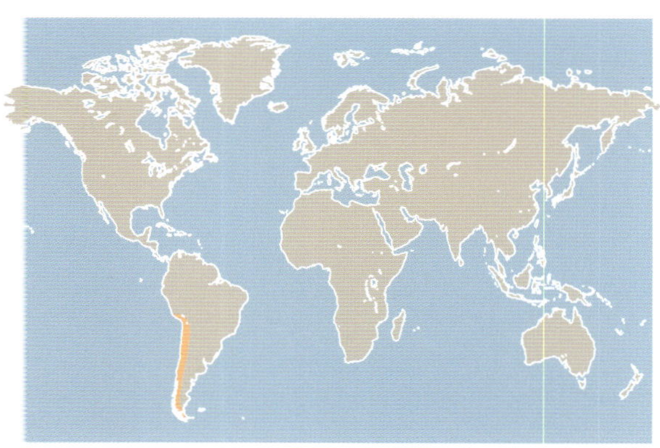

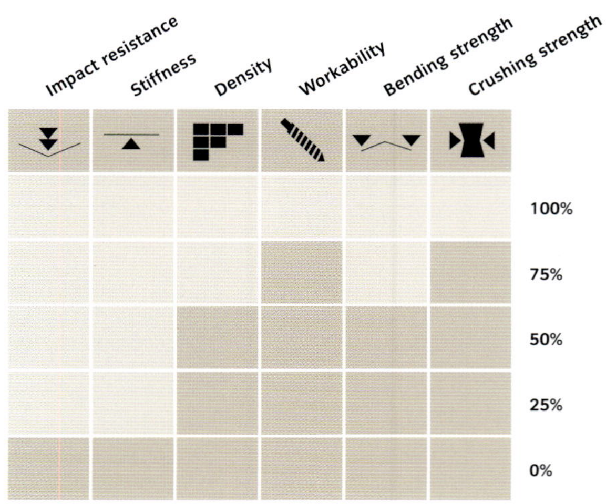

AT A GLANCE

Impact resistance is a measure of the wood's toughness. It describes its resistance to suddenly applied shock loads.

Stiffness is a measure of the wood's elasticity. It is considered in conjunction with bending strength.

Density is measured as specific gravity, the ratio of the density of a substance to that of water.

Liriodendron tulipifera | Family: *Magnoliaceae* | **AMERICAN WHITEWOOD** | Hardwood

Growth

American whitewood is also known as tulip tree (US and UK), poplar and yellow poplar (US), canary wood (Canada), and canary whitewood (UK). The magnificent burl from this tree may be marketed under the name green cypress burr. It grows to a height of 100–150ft (30–45m), with a long, clear, cylindrical bole of 6–8ft (1.8–2.5m) in diameter.

Appearance

The wide sapwood is creamy white, while the heartwood varies from yellow-brown to pale olive-brown, streaked with olive-green, dark gray, black, pinkish brown, red, and sometimes mineral stains of steel blue. A wide band of parenchyma shows as pale veins on flat-sawn surfaces. It is straight grained, with a fine, even texture.

Properties

American whitewood varies in weight from 28 to 32lb/ft^3 (450 to 510kg/m^3) when seasoned. The wood kiln dries easily and well, and also air dries easily with little degrade. There is little movement in service. The timber has medium crushing strength, low bending strength, stiffness, and resistance to shock loads, and a medium steam-bending rating. American whitewood works easily by hand and machine, has good nailing properties, glued joints hold together well, and the wood can be stained, painted, or polished to a good finish. The heartwood is nondurable, and the sapwood is liable to attack by the common furniture beetle. Although the heartwood is moderately resistant to preservative treatment, the sapwood is permeable.

Uses

American whitewood is a favorite wood for pattern making, sculpture, and wood carving. It is used for interior parts of furniture, joinery, and doors, for dry cooperage, packaging, and pallets, and for interior trim for boats. It is extensively utilized for plywood manufacture and corestock for laminated boards. Sliced for decorative veneers, it appears in cabinets, marquetry, and paneling. When treated, it is used for external joinery not in contact with the ground. It is also employed for wood pulp and wood flour.

Where it grows

This large yellow poplar tree, not a true poplar (*Populus spp.*), occurs in the eastern United States and Canada.

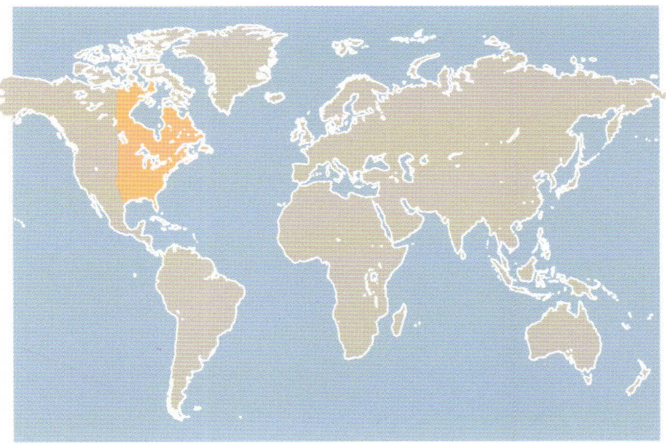

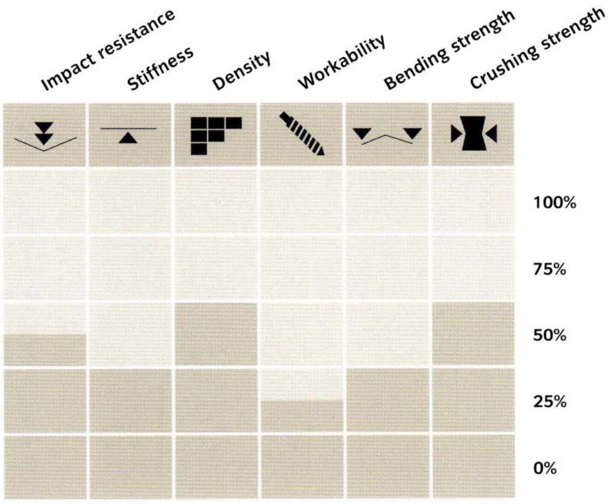

Workability describes how easy a wood is to work and whether it has a significant blunting effect on tools.

Bending strength is also known as maximum bending strength. Pressure is applied to each end of a board until it cracks.

Crushing strength is the ability of wood to withstand loads applied to the end grain, a critical test for wood used as short columns or props.

Lovoa trichilioides | Family: *Meliaceae* | **AFRICAN WALNUT** | Hardwood

Growth
African walnut is known by a number of names, including alona wood, congowood, lovoa wood, and tigerwood (US); Benin walnut, Nigerian golden walnut, Nigerian walnut, and Ghana walnut (UK); apopo and sida (Nigeria); bibolo (Cameroon); dibétou, noyer d'Afrique, and noyer de Gabon (Ivory Coast); eyan (Gabon); nvero and embero (Spanish Guinea); bombolu (Zaire); and dilolo (France). It grows to a height of 150ft (45m) with a clear cylindrical bole of 60ft (18m) and 4ft (1.2m) in diameter.

Appearance
The sapwood is pale brown to buff, clearly demarcated from the golden brown-bronze heartwood, which is marked with black streaks caused by gum lines. The grain is interlocked, sometimes spiral, producing a beautiful ribbon-striped figure on quartered surfaces. The texture is moderately fine and lustrous.

Properties
The weight of African walnut averages 35lb/ft^3 (560kg/m^3) when seasoned. The wood dries fairly well; existing shakes may extend slightly and some distortion may occur, but the degrade is not serious. There is small movement in service. The timber has low bending strength and resistance to shock loads, very low stiffness, medium crushing strength, and a moderate steam-bending classification. It works well with hand or machine tools. The wood tends to split when nailed and needs pre-boring. By sanding and scraping before filling, the surface can be brought to an excellent finish. African walnut is fairly durable, and the sapwood is liable to attack by powder post beetle and dry wood termites in Africa. The heartwood is extremely resistant to preservative treatment, while the sapwood is moderately resistant.

Uses
African walnut is a decorative timber used extensively for furniture and cabinet making, edge lippings and facings, billiard tables, and chairs. It also appears in flush doors, decorative interior joinery, paneling, and domestic flooring. It is an ideal turnery wood for bowls and lamp standards; it is used for gun and rifle stocks, car window and door cappings, and is sliced for decorative veneers.

Where it grows
This tall tree, not a true walnut (*Juglans spp.*), occurs in Nigeria, Ghana, Cameroon, Zaire, and Gabon.

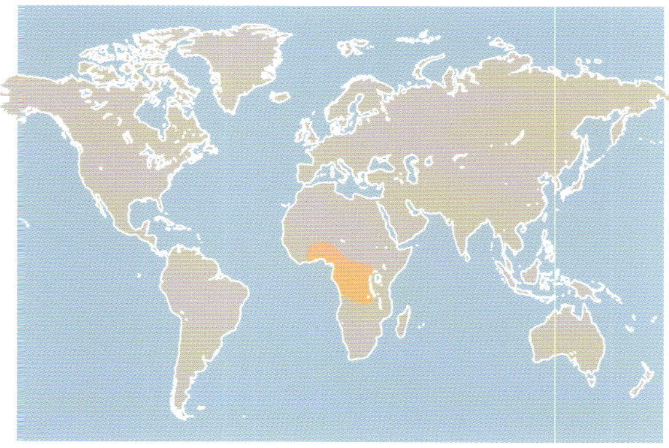

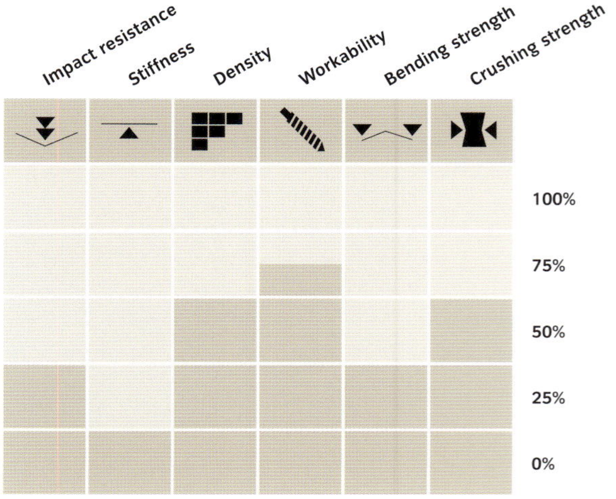

AT A GLANCE

Impact resistance is a measure of the wood's toughness. It describes its resistance to suddenly applied shock loads.

Stiffness is a measure of the wood's elasticity. It is considered in conjunction with bending strength.

Density is measured as specific gravity, the ratio of the density of a substance to that of water.

Machaerium villosum | Family: *Leguminosae* | **JACARANDA PARDO** | Hardwood

Growth
The jacaranda pardo tree is not particularly tall, growing to between 50 and 100ft (15 and 30m) in height, with a trunk of no more than 1–2ft (0.3–0.6m) in diameter. Known by many different names linked to jacaranda, and sometimes as pau ferro, the tree is related to the rosewoods, and shares many of the characteristics of Brazilian rosewood (*Dalbergia nigra*).

Appearance
The similarity of jacaranda pardo to Brazilian rosewood is obvious in its appearance, with the heartwood typically striped with various shades of golden brown, red-brown, and violet-brown, though generally it is lighter in color. The grain tends to be straight but is sometimes gently curving. Jacaranda pardo takes some finishing because it is fairly fibrous, but is a superb woodworking lumber with good luster.

Properties
This wood is heavy, averaging 53lb/ft^3 (850kg/m^3) when seasoned. Hard and strong, jacaranda pardo shares many of the working characteristics and qualities of Brazilian rosewood. Woodworkers tend to consider it to have slightly less figure, and the texture is perhaps a little more coarse and fibrous. In common with its rosewood counterpart, it is also rated as difficult to use, with a tendency to be abrasive and to tear. Jacaranda pardo is, however, durable, but is slow to season with a risk of checking.

Uses
Jacaranda pardo is used as a substitute for rosewood for the making of musical instruments, furniture, and cabinets. It is also popular for cutlery handles and is sliced for veneer for marquetry.

Where it grows
Jacaranda pardo grows in Brazil.

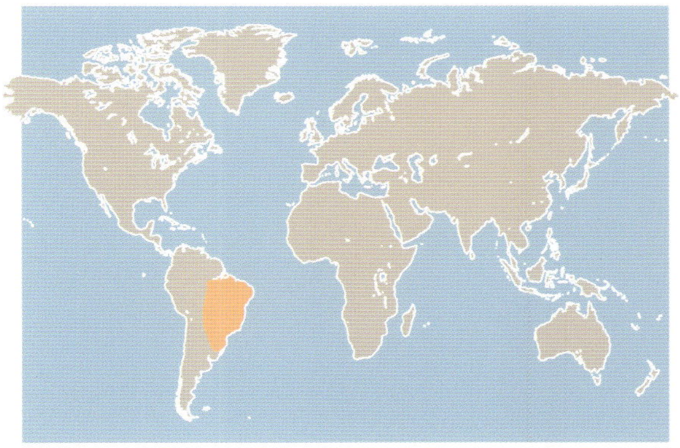

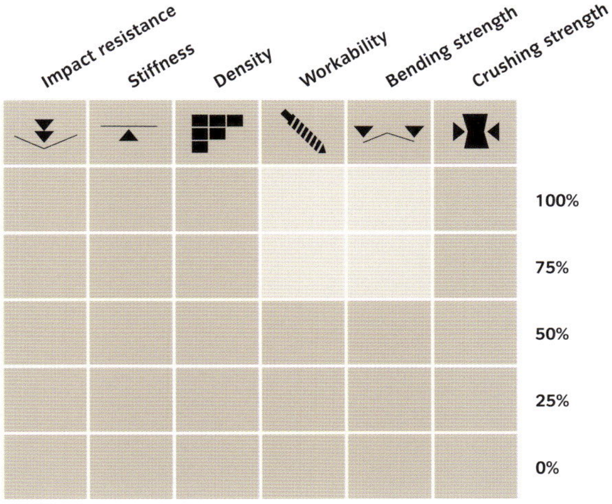

Workability describes how easy a wood is to work and whether it has a significant blunting effect on tools.

Bending strength is also known as maximum bending strength. Pressure is applied to each end of a board until it cracks.

Crushing strength is the ability of wood to withstand loads applied to the end grain, a critical test for wood used as short columns or props.

Magnolia grandiflora	Family: *Magnoliaceae*	**MAGNOLIA**	Hardwood

Growth
Often referred to as the southern magnolia, this species is the state tree of Mississippi and has, not surprisingly, a large flower—one of its many names is the large-flowered evergreen magnolia. It is generally grown as an ornamental tree, reaching 90ft (27m) in height and up to 4ft (1.2m) in diameter.

Appearance
Magnolia is not a particularly notable lumber in appearance, with a slightly yellowy green hue and unexceptional figure. It is quite similar to American whitewood (*Liriodendron tulipifera*), but is not as fibrous and has a more consistent color. Occasionally magnolia can be stained with mineral streaks, and these cuts are valued for decorative veneers. The sapwood is narrow and very pale.

Properties
Magnolia is a medium-weight wood averaging 35lb/ft^3 (560kg/m^3) when seasoned. Magnolia seasons well and finishes to a good luster. Its consistent grain and texture make it easy to work by hand or machine. Although the texture is fine and uniform, magnolia is not durable outdoors. However, it does nail, screw, and glue well. The grain is usually straight, and the wood is tougher and denser than some other utility lumbers.

Uses
Because of its fine, even texture and its bending qualities, magnolia is often selected for the production of venetian blinds and other thin components. It is used for the making of furniture, though more often than not in the mass-production industries rather than by individual designer/makers. It is also employed for utility jobs like crates, boxes, and flooring.

Where it grows
Magnolia grows along the southeast Atlantic coast of the United States, stretching from North Carolina to Texas.

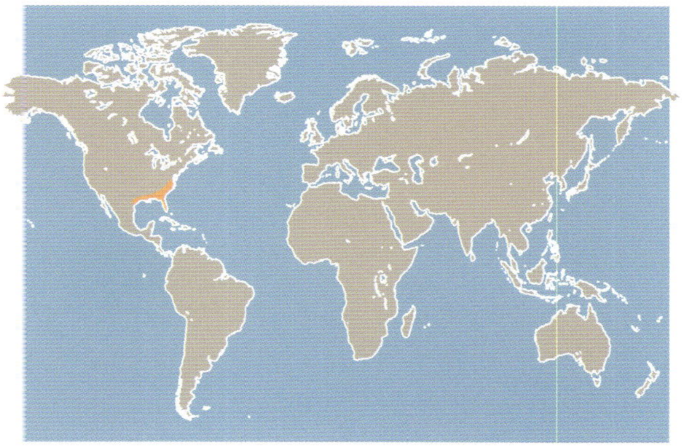

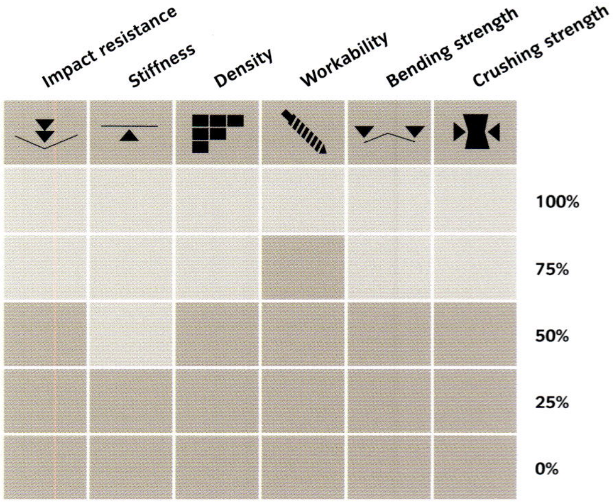

AT A GLANCE

Impact resistance is a measure of the wood's toughness. It describes its resistance to suddenly applied shock loads.

Stiffness is a measure of the wood's elasticity. It is considered in conjunction with bending strength.

Density is measured as specific gravity, the ratio of the density of a substance to that of water.

Mansonia altissima	Family: *Triplochitonaceae*	**MANSONIA**	Hardwood

Growth

Mansonia is also known as bété (Ivory Coast and Cameroon), aprono (Ghana), and ofun (Nigeria). It grows to a height of about 30m (100ft) with a diameter of 2–2½ft (0.6–0.8m).

Appearance

The sapwood is creamy white, while the heartwood varies from dark gray-brown to mauve-brown, with a strong purple tint. It often has lighter or darker bands, but fades with maturity to a dull, pale purplish brown. Mansonia is usually straight grained, sometimes interlocked, and the texture is fine, smooth, and even.

Properties

The wood weighs on average 37lb/ft^3 (590kg/m^3) when seasoned, and dries fairly rapidly and well with some distortion in the length. There is medium shrinkage in service. Mansonia has high bending strength, low stiffness, medium shock resistance, and high crushing strength. It has a good steam-bending rating only if there are no knots. It is best to bend this timber green. It works easily with both hand and machine tools, with only a slight blunting effect on cutters. Mansonia produces a fine machine dust that is highly irritating to the skin, nose, eyes, and throat. Good dust extraction, face masks, and barrier creams are necessary. It screws and nails without difficulty, glues well, takes stain and polish, and can be brought to an excellent finish. The sapwood is rarely liable to attack by powder post beetle. The heartwood is very durable and extremely resistant to preservation treatment, and the sapwood is permeable.

Uses

Mansonia is an excellent timber for high-quality cabinets and furniture making, chairs, radio and television cabinets, interior joinery, shop and office fittings, and pianos and musical instruments. It is a good turnery wood for fancy bowls and the like. It is also used in the car industry for window cappings, dashboards, and fascias. Selected logs are sliced for decorative veneers for cabinets, marquetry, and paneling.

Where it grows

Mansonia occurs in tropical west Africa, mainly in southern Nigeria, the Ivory Coast, and Ghana.

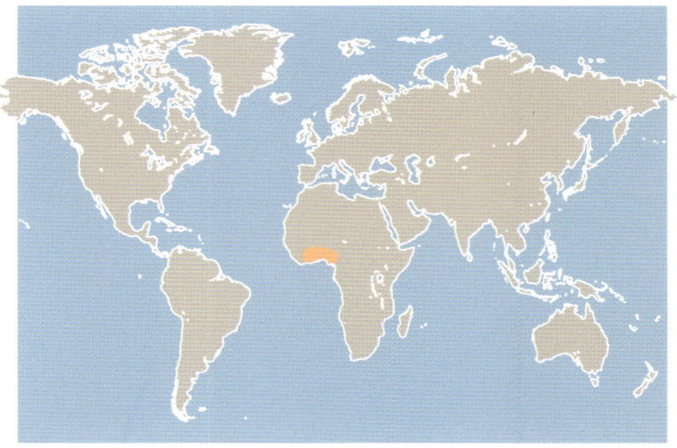

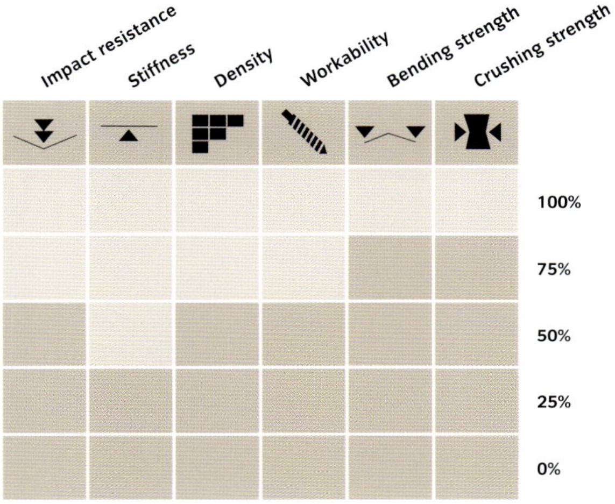

Workability describes how easy a wood is to work and whether it has a significant blunting effect on tools.

Bending strength is also known as maximum bending strength. Pressure is applied to each end of a board until it cracks.

Crushing strength is the ability of wood to withstand loads applied to the end grain, a critical test for wood used as short columns or props.

Metopium brownii | Family: *Anacardiaceae* | **CHECHEN** | Hardwood

Growth
Named after the 19th-century British botanist Robert Browne, chechen is also known as chechem and Honduras walnut. Although it is a member of a nut-bearing family, it is more commonly associated with the cashew than the walnut. The tree varies greatly in size, from no more than a shrub to a moderate 50ft (15m) specimen. The bark is notoriously poisonous, but that is not true of the lumber.

Appearance
Reminiscent of aged mahogany, chechen is dark brown with a wavy striped grain, with an appearance you either love or hate. The pale yellow sapwood contrasts heavily with the heartwood, which often exhibits reds, greens, and golds and has a superb luster. The patterning can be very attractive, especially when plain sawn. Fine to medium in texture, the wood is uniform in density.

Properties
Very hard and strong, chechen is relatively heavy at 53lb/ft^3 (850kg/m^3) when seasoned. Although the bark is considered poisonous, the dust is not; otherwise, very little is known about this species, except that it can chip when surfaced and tends not to blunt tools too severely. Screws and nails require pre-boring because chechen is so hard, but polishing is simple and the results are superb.

Uses
Chechen is used locally in construction, and is increasingly being used in other parts of the world for instruments, furniture, cabinets, and turnery.

Where it grows
Chechen grows in a band across Central America and the Caribbean, from Mexico to Jamaica.

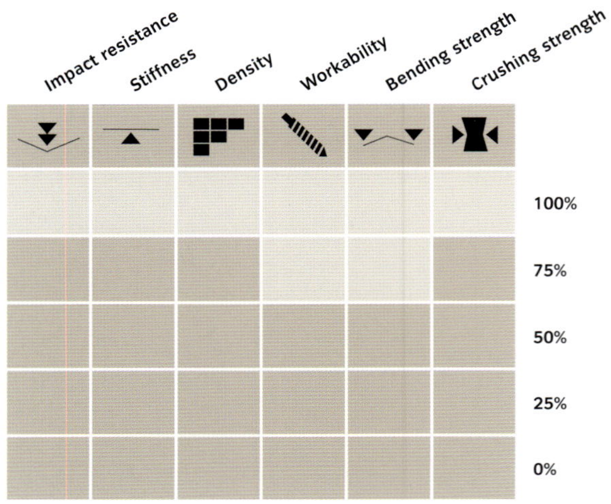

AT A GLANCE

Impact resistance is a measure of the wood's toughness. It describes its resistance to suddenly applied shock loads.

Stiffness is a measure of the wood's elasticity. It is considered in conjunction with bending strength.

Density is measured as specific gravity, the ratio of the density of a substance to that of water.

Microberlinia brazzavillensis | Family: *Leguminosae* | **ZEBRANO** | Hardwood

Growth
Microberlinia brazzavillensis is also known as zingana (Cameroon and Gabon); allene, ele, and amouk (Cameroon); and zebrawood (UK and US).

Appearance
On quartered surfaces, the heartwood has a light golden yellow background, with narrow regular and parallel veining of dark brown to almost black producing a zebra-striped appearance. On flat sawn or rotary cut surfaces, this gives the wood a wild streaked pattern. The grain is interlocked or wavy, and the texture is coarse with a lustrous surface.

Properties
The weight of zebrano averages 46lb/ft^3 (740kg/m^3) when seasoned. The wood is difficult to dry because of the alternate hard and soft grain and is liable to distortion. It is stable in service. This hard, heavy, dense wood is high in all strength properties and is noted for its very high stiffness. It is not suitable for steam bending. Zebrano can be worked readily with both hand and machine tools, but it is difficult to obtain a smooth finish because of the nature of the grain. Care is required in gluing and a clear filler should be used in polishing, when the surface can be brought to an excellent finish. The wood is nondurable and resistant to preservative treatment, but the sapwood is permeable.

Uses
Zebrano is commonly supplied as sliced decorative veneers, usually quarter-cut to avoid buckling because of the alternating hard and soft grain. It is used for inlays and marquetry on cabinets and furniture in the form of crossbandings. Veneers kept in stock tend to buckle, and it is advisable to keep them weighted down. Zebrano in the solid is used for turnery for brush backs, and small turned items such as fancy handles and tool handles. It is also used in sculpture and wood carving.

Where it grows
This distinctive is chiefly found in west Africa in Cameroon and Gabon.

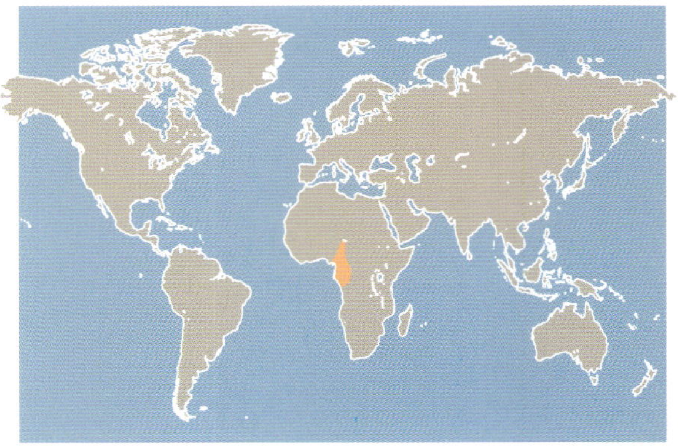

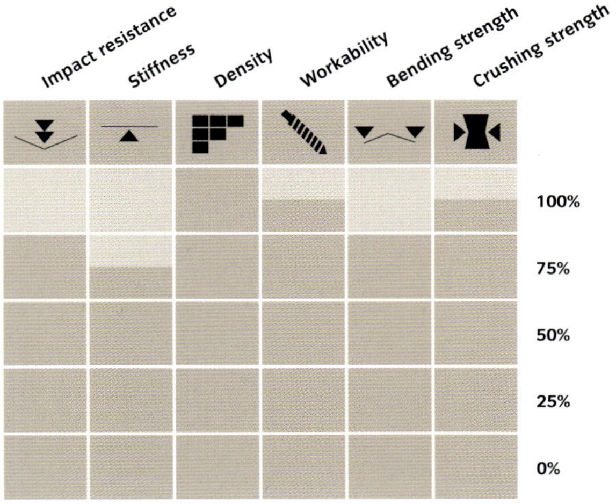

Workability describes how easy a wood is to work and whether it has a significant blunting effect on tools.

Bending strength is also known as maximum bending strength. Pressure is applied to each end of a board until it cracks.

Crushing strength is the ability of wood to withstand loads applied to the end grain, a critical test for wood used as short columns or props.

Millettia laurentii | Family: *Leguminosae* | **WENGE** | Hardwood

Growth
Wengé is also known as palissandre du Congo (Congo); dikela, mibotu, bokonge, and tshikalakala (Zaire); awong (Cameroon); and nson-so (Gabon). A very closely related species, *Millettia stuhlmannii* Taub., produces a wood commonly known as panga-panga in Mozambique. Trees reach about 60ft (18m) in height with a diameter of 2ft (0.6m).

Appearance
The sapwood of wengé is whitish and clearly defined from the heartwood. The heartwood is dark brown, with close black veining and alternate closely spaced whitish bands of light and dark parenchyma tissue, which produces a very decorative figure. The wood is straight grained and has an irregular, coarse texture.

Properties
Wengé weighs 52–62lb/ft^3 (830–1000kg/m^3), and panga-panga weighs 50lb/ft^3 (800kg/m^3) when seasoned. Both dry very slowly and require care to avoid surface checking, but generally the degrade is minimal. The wood is stable in service. Wengé has high bending strength and resistance to shock loads, and is especially noted for its shock resistance and medium stiffness. It has a poor steam-bending rating, but high resistance to abrasion. This durable wood works readily with both hand and machine tools, but cutters should be kept very sharp. It requires pre-boring for nailing. Resin cells in the wood structure can interfere with gluing and polishing, but filling is the answer for a very good finish. The wood is durable and extremely resistant to preservative treatment.

Uses
Wengé has a high natural resistance to abrasion, and is thus excellent for flooring for public buildings, or where there is heavy pedestrian traffic. The dark chocolate-brown makes for a dark floor, but this is not a disadvantage for certain types of hotel, showroom, and boardroom. It is also used for all forms of interior and exterior joinery and general construction work. It makes a very good turnery wood and is ideal for wood sculpture. Selected logs are sliced for decorative veneers for cabinets and architectural paneling.

Where it grows

Wengé occurs mainly in Zaire, Cameroon, and Gabon. The closely related species panga-panga occurs in Mozambique.

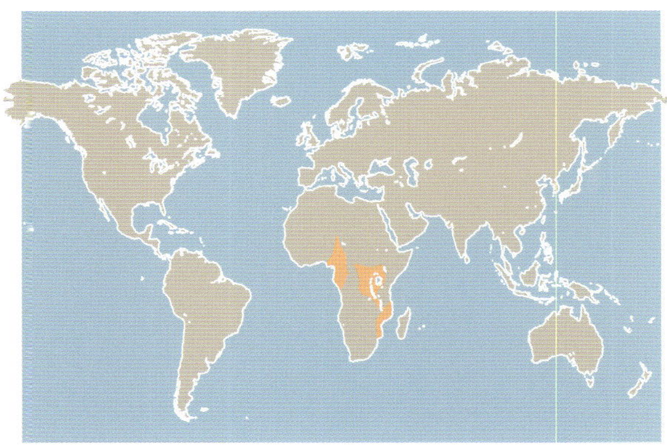

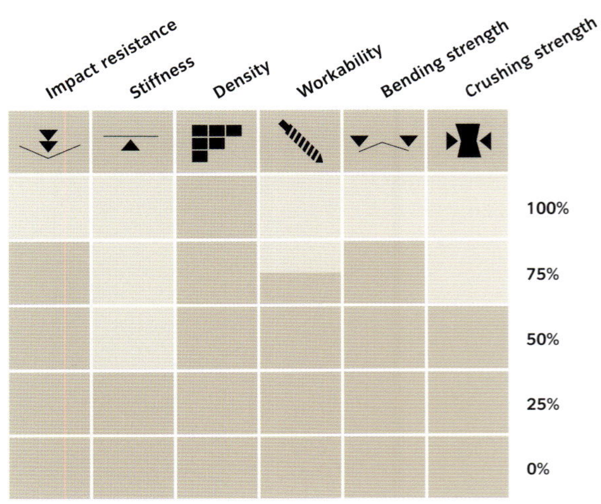

AT A GLANCE

Impact resistance is a measure of the wood's toughness. It describes its resistance to suddenly applied shock loads.

Stiffness is a measure of the wood's elasticity. It is considered in conjunction with bending strength.

Density is measured as specific gravity, the ratio of the density of a substance to that of water.

Mitragyna ciliata | Family: *Rubiaceae* | **ABURA** | Hardwood

Growth
Abura grows to a height of over 100ft (30m), with a diameter of 3–5ft (1–1.5m). Related species include *Mitragyna stipulosa* and *M.rubrostipulara*, which grow in Uganda and are sold as nzingu.

Appearance
The rather wide, plain sapwood of abura is not clearly defined from the heartwood, which varies from a pale yellow or pinkish brown to tones of orange-red and light brown. The irregular gray-brown, spongy heart may have occasional streaks of dark red-brown in large logs and can give the appearance of stained sapwood. The grain of abura is mostly straight, but sometimes interlocked and occasionally spiral. The texture is moderately fine and very even.

Properties
Abura varies from 29 to 43lb/ft^3 (460 to 690kg/m^3) in weight, but averages 35lb/ft^3 (560kg/m^3) when seasoned. Abura air and kiln dries rapidly and very well. The wood is very stable, with small movement in service when dry. It has very low stiffness, medium crushing strength, and low shock resistance, with a very poor steam-bending classification. It works well and cleanly with hand and machine tools, but is sometimes siliceous and the blunting effect on cutting edges can be moderate or severe. Machining is satisfactory but cutting edges must be kept sharp to prevent a wooly surface. The timber glues well, stains easily, and can be brought to a very good finish. Pre-boring is advised for nailing. Abura is perishable and liable to insect attack, but the sapwood is permeable.

Uses
Abura is one of the best west African timbers for moldings. It is extensively used for interior joinery and furniture framings, edge lippings, and drawer sides; its abrasive qualities make it ideal for decorative, hard-wearing flooring. Specialist uses include pattern making and vehicle bodywork; it is utilized for oil vats and laboratory fittings, and battery and accumulator boxes because it is acid-resistant. It is rotary cut for plywood and sliced for decorative veneers suitable for cabinets and paneling.

Where it grows
Abura occurs in the wet coastal swamp forests of tropical west Africa, from Sierra Leone and Liberia to Cameroon and Gabon.

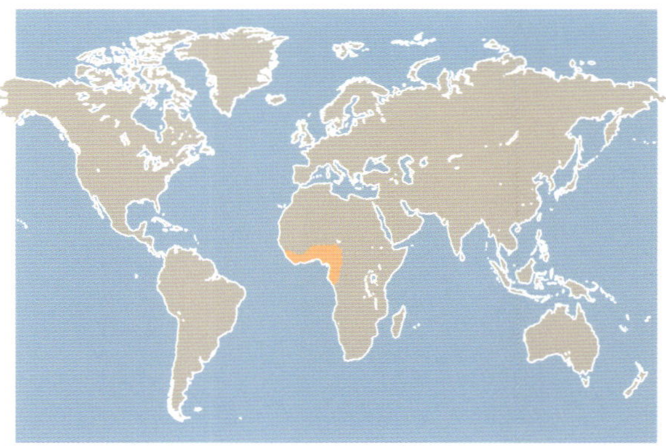

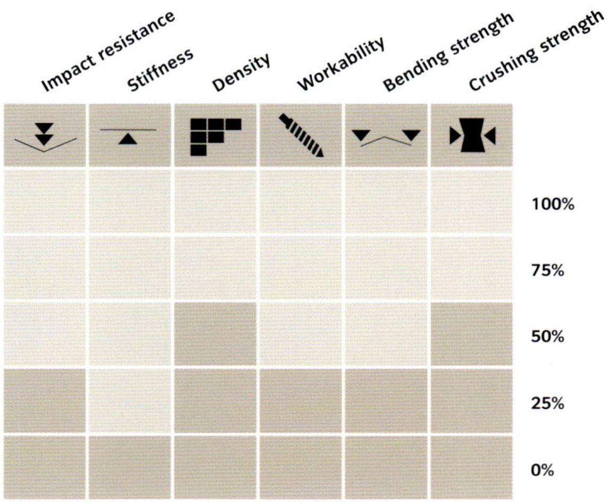

Workability describes how easy a wood is to work and whether it has a significant blunting effect on tools.

Bending strength is also known as maximum bending strength. Pressure is applied to each end of a board until it cracks.

Crushing strength is the ability of wood to withstand loads applied to the end grain, a critical test for wood used as short columns or props.

Myroxylon balsamum	Family: *Leguminosae*	**BALSAMO**	Hardwood

Growth

Balsamo grows relatively tall, up to 100ft (30m), with a straight, clean trunk that tends to be fairly slender at no more than 3ft (1m) in diameter. It is a useful lumber, but sadly there are too few examples left, although it has been reported that it can be grown in plantations. It is tapped for balsam.

Appearance

There is great variety to balsamo, although it is usually a consistent chocolate-brown. The grain is often straight and indistinct, but the patterning can also be striped with slightly lighter bands, and there is great contrast between the heartwood and the much paler sapwood. You can also find some ripple marks from the interlocking grain. It has some of the look of Cuban mahogany (*Swietenia mahoganii*), especially when finished, but is not quite as red.

Properties

Balsamo is very heavy at up to 65lb/ft^3 (1040kg/m^3) when seasoned. It seasons well and is moderately stable once dry. Coarse textured but uniform, balsamo is durable and you can see the glitter of silica in the grain that correctly indicates the abrasive nature of the lumber and the dulling effect it can have on cutting edges. It can also be difficult to use, though it has a great luster and finishes well.

Uses

Balsamo lumber is versatile and used for furniture and cabinet making, as well as for utility purposes.

Where it grows

Balsamo grows down the west coast of Central America and across South America.

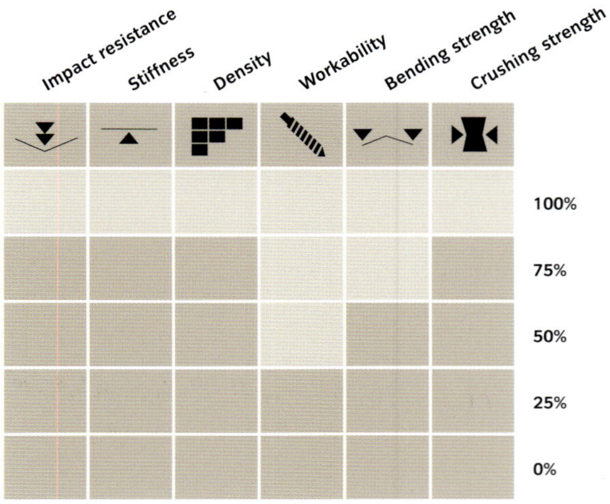

AT A GLANCE

Impact resistance is a measure of the wood's toughness. It describes its resistance to suddenly applied shock loads.

Stiffness is a measure of the wood's elasticity. It is considered in conjunction with bending strength.

Density is measured as specific gravity, the ratio of the density of a substance to that of water.

Nesogordonia papaverifera	Family: *Tiliaceae*	**DANTA**	Hardwood

Growth

Danta grows to a height of 90–100ft (27–30m) above a sharp buttress, and with a diameter of 2–2½ft (0.6–0.8m). It is also known as kotibé (Ivory Coast); otutu (Nigeria); olborbora (Gabon); ovoué (Cameroon); eprou (Ghana); and tsanya (Zaire).

Appearance

The sapwood is very pale brown with a pinkish tinge, and clearly defined from the heartwood, which is a dark reddish brown mahogany color. Danta has a narrowly interlocked grain that produces a striped figure when cut on the quarter. Sometimes small, round pin knots or dark streaks of scar tissue can spoil the appearance of danta, and the wood has a greasy feel. The texture is fine.

Properties

Danta averages about 46lb/ft^3 (740kg/m^3) in weight when seasoned. The wood dries well but rather slowly, with little degrade. There is medium movement in service. It has high bending and crushing strengths, low stiffness, and medium resistance to shock loads, with a moderate steam-bending rating. The wood works easily with both hand and machine tools, with a tendency to pick up on quartered surfaces. It requires pre-boring for screwing or nailing but glues well, and can be brought to an excellent finish. It is liable to attack by powder post beetle, and the heartwood is durable to marine borers.

Uses

Danta is a very strong and elastic timber. It is widely used for furniture, cabinet making, interior and exterior joinery, shop fitting, and bench tops. It has excellent resistance to abrasion and is ideal for decorative flooring. Specialist uses include etching timber for graphic art; a turnery wood for tool handles; stylish rifle- and gunstocks; strong framing for truck, coach, and wagon carriage vehicle bodywork; and boat building bentwork. When treated with preservative, it is used for telegraph cross arms and railway sleepers. Selected logs are sliced for decorative veneers for cabinets and panels.

Where it grows
Danta occurs in the mixed deciduous forests of southern Nigeria, the Ivory Coast, and Ghana.

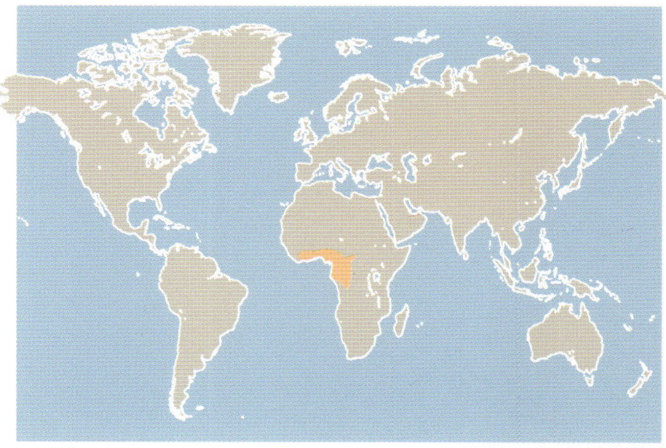

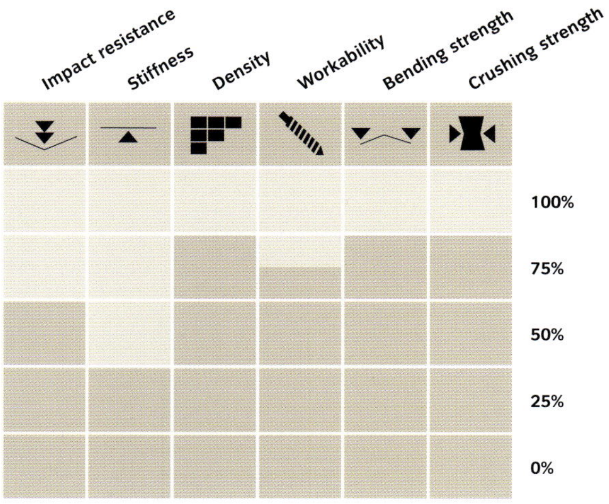

Workability describes how easy a wood is to work and whether it has a significant blunting effect on tools

Bending strength is also known as maximum bending strength. Pressure is applied to each end of a board until it cracks.

Crushing strength is the ability of wood to withstand loads applied to the end grain, a critical test for wood used as short columns or props.

Nothofagus cunninghamii | Family: *Fagaceae* | **TASMANIAN MYRTLE** | Hardwood

Growth

Tasmanian myrtle grows up to 100–130ft (30–40m) tall, occasionally up to 200ft (60m), with a diameter of 2–3ft (0.6–1m). It is also known as myrtle beech, myrtle, and Tasmanian beech, but it is not a true myrtle (*Myrtus spp.*) or beech (*Fagus spp.*).

Appearance

The pink to reddish brown heartwood is separated from the narrow white sapwood by a zone of intermediate color. The grain is straight to slightly interlocked, often wavy, with a very fine, uniform, even texture.

Properties

Tasmanian myrtle weighs an average of 45lb/ft^3 (720kg/m^3) when seasoned. The lighter sapwood dries readily and well, but the darker heartwood is liable to honeycombing, severe internal checking, and collapse. This can be restored by reconditioning. There is small movement in service. The wood has medium bending strength and stiffness, high crushing strength, and low resistance to shock loads, with a good steam-bending classification. It works readily with both hand and machine tools, but has a moderate blunting effect on cutting edges. It has good holding properties for nailing or screwing, glues satisfactorily, and can be stained and polished to a good finish. The heartwood is nondurable and the sapwood is liable to attack by powder post beetle, but is permeable for preservation treatment.

Uses

This very versatile timber is used locally for similar purposes to beech. It appears extensively in cabinets, furniture, interior joinery, and moldings; it is very popular for domestic flooring and parquetry blocks. As a turnery wood, it is used for brush backs, bobbins, and handles; it is also employed for shoe heels and food containers, butter boxes, and so on. Other applications include motor vehicle bodywork and, when treated, exterior heavy construction and joinery, and bridge and wharf decking. It is rotary cut for plywood and laminated work, and sliced for decorative veneers for cabinets and doors.

Where it grows

This Australian timber, closely related to northern hemisphere beech (*Fagus spp.*), occurs in Tasmania and Victoria.

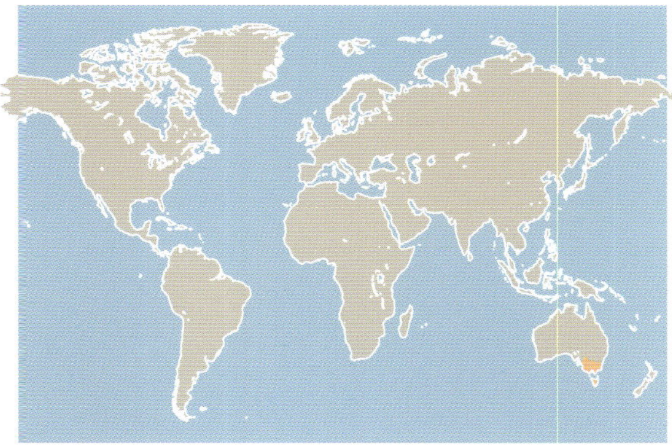

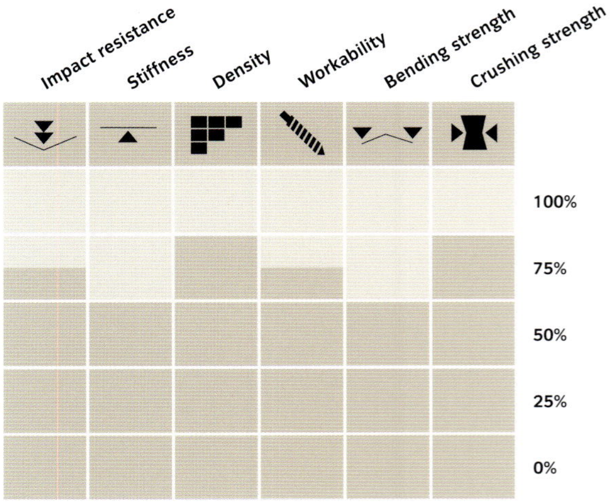

AT A GLANCE

Impact resistance is a measure of the wood's toughness. It describes its resistance to suddenly applied shock loads.

Stiffness is a measure of the wood's elasticity. It is considered in conjunction with bending strength.

Density is measured as specific gravity, the ratio of the density of a substance to that of water.

Nothofagus spp. | Family: *Fagaceae* | **NEW ZEALAND BEECH** | Hardwood

Growth

New Zealand beech grows to approximately 100ft (30m) in height, with a diameter of about 2–5ft (0.6–1.5m). It includes three species: *Nothofagus menziesii*, which is known as silver beech and southland beech; *N.fusca*, known as red beech; and *N.truncata*, known as hard beech and clinker beech. None of these three species is a true beech (*Fagus spp.*).

Appearance

The inner heartwood is a uniform pink-brown in color. Silver beech has a narrow sapwood, and an intermediate zone of salmon-pink false heartwood (commercially regarded as sapwood) separates the sapwood and true heartwood. It is mostly straight grained, sometimes curly, with a fine, even texture.

Properties

Silver beech weighs about 33–46lb/ft^3 (530–740kg/m^3), red beech weighs 44lb/ft^3 (700kg/m^3), and hard beech weighs 48lb/ft^3 (770kg/m^3) when seasoned. The wood dries fairly easily; there is a tendency to end splitting, but as a general rule distortion is comparatively slight. There is small movement in service. These woods have medium bending and crushing strengths, low stiffness and resistance to shock loads, and a good steam-bending classification. Silver beech and red beech work easily with both hand and machine tools, except where irregular grain is present on quartered stock, when a reduction in the cutting angle is recommended. Silica in the ray cells of hard beech causes severe dulling of tools. They stain and glue well, and can be brought to a good finish. Silver beech is nondurable, but red and hard beech are both durable. They are liable to attack by the common furniture beetle and powder post beetle. They are all extremely resistant to preservative treatment.

Uses

These timbers are used in New Zealand for cabinets and furniture, interior and exterior joinery, and moldings. Their abrasive qualities make them suitable for domestic flooring. They are also good turnery woods used for tool handles, bobbins, shoe heels, and brushware, and have many specialist uses such as boat building, building construction, food containers, butter boxes, laundry boxes, and vehicle bodywork. Logs are rotary cut for plywood and sliced for decorative veneers for furniture and paneling.

Where it grows

This group of trees grows in New Zealand.

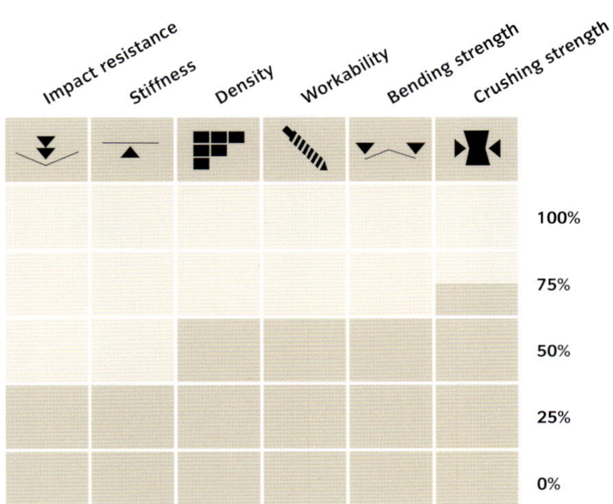

Workability describes how easy a wood is to work and whether it has a significant blunting effect on tools.

Bending strength is also known as maximum bending strength. Pressure is applied to each end of a board until it cracks.

Crushing strength is the ability of wood to withstand loads applied to the end grain, a critical test for wood used as short columns or props.

Ochroma pyramidale | Family: *Bombacaceae* | **BALSA** | Hardwood

Growth
The word balsa (Spanish for raft) was given to the wood by early colonists when they found the native Indians using it to make rafts. The tree grows rapidly to a height of 70ft (21m), with a diameter of about 2ft (0.6m). It reaches maturity in 12–15 years, then deteriorates rapidly.

Appearance
The bulk of commercial timber is the sapwood, which is white to oatmeal in color, often with a pinkish or yellow tinge. The central core of heartwood is pale brown. It is straight grained, and the texture is fine, even, and lustrous.

Properties
The weight ranges between 5 and 16lb/ft³ (80 and 250kg/m³), averaging 10lb/ft³ (160kg/m³) when seasoned. It is a very difficult wood to dry and should be converted immediately after it is felled. Kiln drying of converted stock is much preferred to air drying in order to minimize splitting and warping. It is stable in use. Balsa is the weakest of all commercial timbers in all categories, and has a very poor steam-bending rating. It is easy to work with both hand and machine thin-edged tools if they are kept sharp. Gluing is the best way to fasten balsa. It can be stained and polished but is very absorbent. The timber is perishable and liable to insect attack, but is permeable for preservation treatment.

Uses
Balsa is highly valued for heat insulation in refrigerated ships, cold stores, and so on; and for buoyancy in life belts, rafts, floats, buoys, and water sports equipment. It is valued for its resilience in protective packaging, its lightness in model making and theatre props, and for its sound and vibration insulation. Balsa is used for corestock in lightweight metal-faced sandwich construction sheets for laminated aircraft floors and partitions.

Where it grows
Balsa occurs from Cuba to Trinidad and from southern Mexico through Central America to Brazil. The bulk of the world's lightest wood comes from Ecuador. Supplies also come from India and Indonesia, where it has been planted.

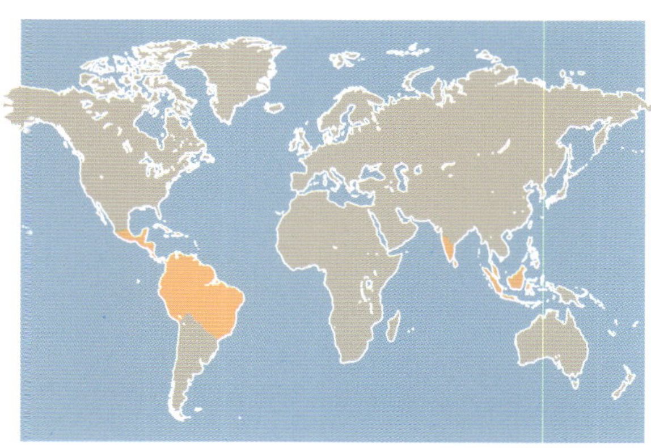

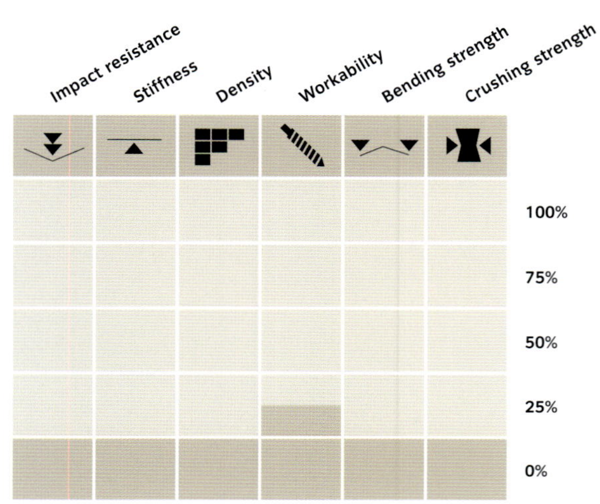

AT A GLANCE

Impact resistance is a measure of the wood's toughness. It describes its resistance to suddenly applied shock loads.

Stiffness is a measure of the wood's elasticity. It is considered in conjunction with bending strength.

Density is measured as specific gravity, the ratio of the density of a substance to that of water.

Ocotea bullata	Family: *Lauraceae*	**STINKWOOD**	Hardwood

Growth

Stinkwood is also known as Cape olive and Cape laurel (because of its origins in the Cape Peninsula area of South Africa), stinkhout, and umnukane. It grows to a height of 60–80ft (18–24m), with a diameter of 3–5ft (1–1.5m).

Appearance

The heartwood varies from an even straw shade to gray-brown and very dark reddish brown mottled with yellow, maturing to almost black. The grain varies from straight to interlocked or spiral; the surface displays exceedingly fine but pronounced medullary rays, and the texture is moderately fine and uniform. Stinkwood has an unpleasant odor when freshly worked—from where it gets its name—but this does not persist when it is dried.

Properties

Stinkwood varies in weight according to its color, the light type weighing an average of 42lb/ft^3 (670kg/m^3) and the dark types approximately 50lb/ft^3 (800kg/m^3) when seasoned. The dark wood is more difficult to dry, but the lighter type dries fairly rapidly, with little degrade. There is considerable shrinkage in service. Stinkwood has medium bending and crushing strengths and stiffness, and high resistance to shock loads. It is not used for steam bending. The wood works fairly easily with both hand and machine tools, but has a severe blunting effect on cutting edges. Stinkwood requires pre-boring for nailing, and glues without difficulty. Smooth surfaces are obtained by scraping and sanding before polishing to an excellent finish.

Uses

This timber is highly prized in South Africa for high-class cabinets and furniture, especially Dutch designs of period furniture from the 17th, 18th, and 19th centuries. It is also used for light structural work and interior joinery. Its resilient qualities make it suitable for light domestic flooring and vehicle bodies. As a turnery wood, it is utilized for tool handles and fancy goods. There is a wide range of specialist uses, including ladders, sporting goods, wheelwrighting, agricultural implements, and toys. It is excellent for battery separators. Selected logs are sliced for decorative veneers for cabinets and panels.

Where it grows

Stinkwood occurs in South Africa, from the forested country of the Cape Peninsula, northward to Natal and eastern Transvaal.

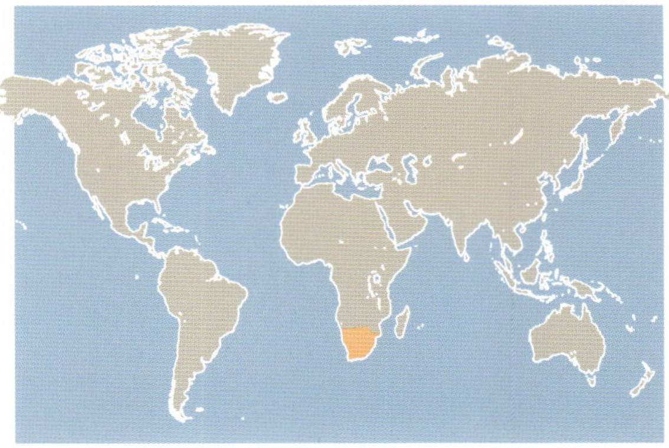

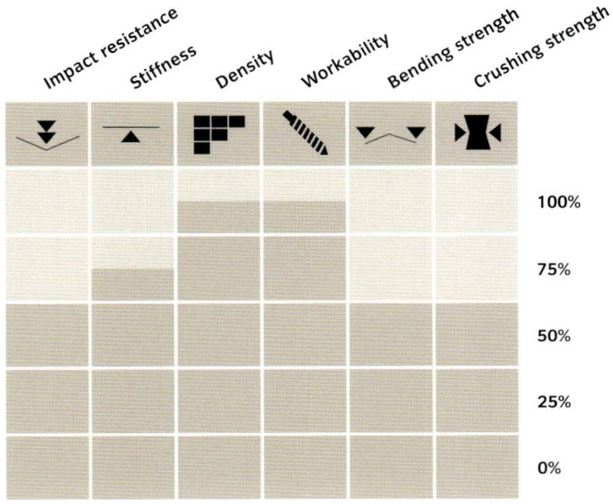

Workability describes how easy a wood is to work and whether it has a significant blunting effect on tools.

Bending strength is also known as maximum bending strength. Pressure is applied to each end of a board until it cracks.

Crushing strength is the ability of wood to withstand loads applied to the end grain, a critical test for wood used as short columns or props.

Ocotea rodiaei	Family: *Lauraceae*	**GREENHEART**	Hardwood

Growth

This evergreen tree grows to between 70 and 130ft (21 and 40m) in height, with a straight cylindrical bole approximately 50–80ft (15–24m) long and about 3ft (1m) in diameter.

Appearance

Greenheart has pale yellow-green sapwood that is about 1–2in (2.5–5cm) wide. It shades gradually into the heartwood, which varies from yellowish green through light olive, dark olive, and orange-brown to dark brown. The heartwood is often marked with black streaks. Local distinction between color varieties (black, brown, yellow, or white greenheart) has no bearing on the wood's properties. The grain varies from straight to interlocked, while the texture is fine, uniform, and lustrous.

Properties

The weight of greenheart averages about 64lb/ft^3 (1030kg/m^3) when seasoned. It dries very slowly and with considerable degrade, especially in the thicker sizes. Once dry, there is medium movement in service. This wood has exceptional strength in all categories, with a moderate steam-bending rating. It is moderately difficult and dangerous to work because poisonous splinters fly from the interlocked, cross, or end grain; the difficult grain affects many machining operations. Pre-boring is essential for screwing or nailing. A fine, smooth, lustrous surface can be obtained. Gluing results are variable; staining is rarely necessary but the wood polishes well. It is very durable, and immune to marine borers. Greenheart is extremely resistant to preservative treatment.

Uses

This is one of the world's major timbers for marine and ship construction. It is used for revetments, docks, locks, fenders, braces, decking, groynes, lock gates, pier decking and handrails, jetties, piling, bridges, and wharf and harbor work. In ship construction it appears as engine bearers, planking, gangways, fenders, stem posts, and sheathing for whalers. Other special uses include heavy-duty factory flooring, chemical vats, and filter press plates and frames. It is good for turnery of all kinds, billiard cue butts, fishing rods, and the central laminae of longbows.

Where it grows
Greenheart is the major commercial wood of Guyana, where it is known as demerara greenheart, and occurs to a limited extent in Surinam and Venezuela.

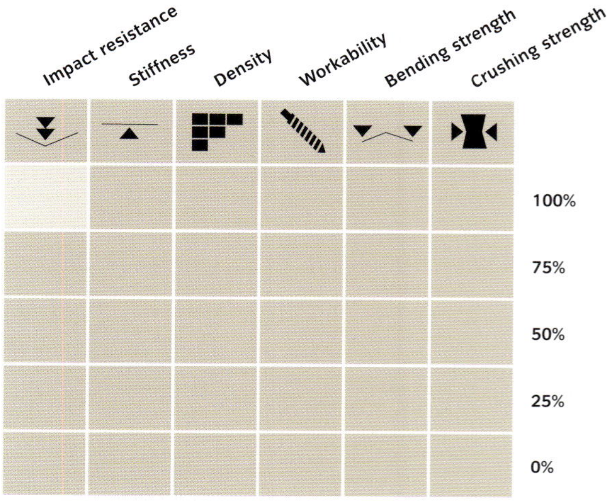

AT A GLANCE

Impact resistance is a measure of the wood's toughness. It describes its resistance to suddenly applied shock loads.

Stiffness is a measure of the wood's elasticity. It is considered in conjunction with bending strength.

Density is measured as specific gravity, the ratio of the density of a substance to that of water.

Olea spp. | Family: *Oleaceae* | **OLIVEWOOD** | Hardwood

Growth

The olive tree *Olea europaea* is grown in the Mediterranean for its edible fruit and olive oil, and is usually small and misshapen. Commercial timber comes from Africa and includes *O.hochstetteri*, which produces east African olive, also known as musheragi in Kenya, and *O.welwitschii* (Knobl.) Gilg. & Schellenb., which provides loliondo in Tanzania and elgon olive in Kenya. Olivewood grows to about 80ft (24m) in height, is heavily fluted and crooked, and has a diameter of 1½–2½ft (0.5–0.8m).

Appearance

The sapwood is pale creamy yellow and quite plain, but the heartwood has a pale brown background with very attractive irregular markings of mid-brown to dark brown and blackish streaks. The grain is straight to shallowly interlocked and the texture is very fine and even.

Properties

O.hochstetteri weighs an average of approximately 55lb/ft³ (880kg/m³), and *O.welwitschii* weighs about 50lb/ft³ (800kg/m³) when seasoned. The wood is rather refractory and needs to be air dried slowly, especially because internal checking or honeycombing may occur in thicker pieces if drying occurs too quickly. It can be kiln dried successfuly. There is considerable movement in service. The wood has excellent strength in every category. The sapwood may be bent to a small radius, but because of resin exudation olivewood has only a moderate steam-bending classification. The wood is rather difficult to work because the interlocked grain affects machining. There is high resistance in cutting, with a moderate blunting effect on tools. It requires pre-boring for nailing. The wood glues well, and can be brought to an excellent finish. The heartwood is moderately durable and resistant to preservative treatment, but the sapwood is permeable.

Uses

This very attractive timber has a good resistance to abrasion and makes an excellent decorative flooring for public buildings. Olivewood is used for furniture, cabinets, and paneling and is ideal for turnery, for tool and fancy handles, and bowls. Olivewood is popular for sculpture and carving, and logs are sliced for decorative veneers.

Where it grows

The olive tree is grown in the Mediterranean mainly for fruit and olive oil. Commercial timber comes from Kenya, Tanzania, and Uganda.

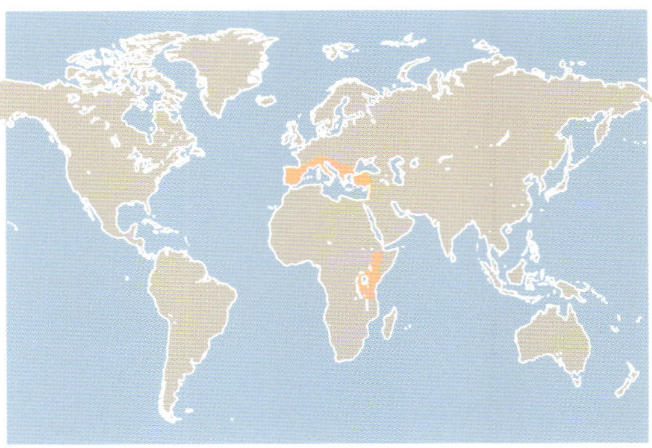

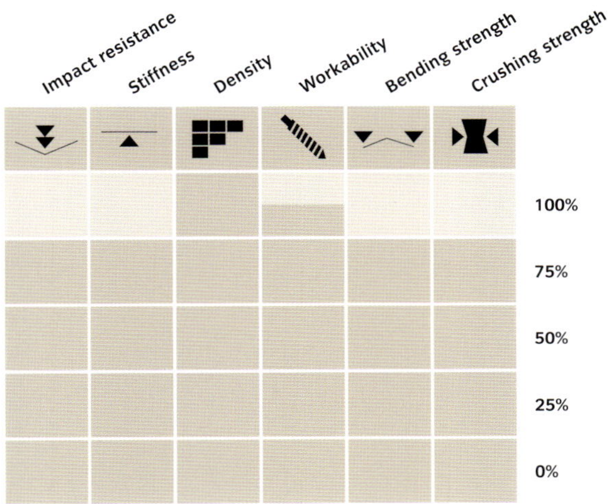

Workability describes how easy a wood is to work and whether it has a significant blunting effect on tools.

Bending strength is also known as maximum bending strength. Pressure is applied to each end of a board until it cracks.

Crushing strength is the ability of wood to withstand loads applied to the end grain, a critical test for wood used as short columns or props.

Paratecoma peroba | Family: *Bignoniaceae* | **WHITE PEROBA** | Hardwood

Growth

White peroba is also known as peroba de campos, ipé peroba, peroba amarella, peroba branca, and ipé claro (Brazil); and golden peroba (UK). It should not be confused with *Aspidosperma peroba*, which produces rosa peroba. It reaches a height of 130ft (40m), with a straight symmetrical bole and a diameter of about 5ft (1.5m).

Appearance

The white to yellowish sapwood is clearly defined from the heartwood, which is a pale golden olive-brown, but with yellow, greenish, or red shading. The grain is commonly interlocked or wavy, and the texture is medium and uniform, often with a lustrous surface. The grain of quartered surfaces produces a narrow striped or roe figure.

Properties

The weight of white peroba averages about 47lb/ft^3 (750kg/m^3) when seasoned. The wood dries easily with only negligible splitting, and distortion is not serious. There is medium movement in service. The wood has a medium bending strength, low stiffness and shock resistance, and high crushing strength. It has a moderate steam-bending classification. The material works readily with both hand and machine tools, and planes easily to a smooth, silken finish. Fine machine dust can cause skin irritation and splinters are poisonous. White peroba has good holding properties, glues satisfactorily, and can be brought to a good finish. The very durable heartwood is resistant to insect and fungal attack, and is also resistant to preservative treatment.

Uses

In its native Brazil, this very attractive timber is used extensively for high-class furniture and cabinet making. It is also used for interior and exterior joinery and in building construction; it is ideal as a pleasing heavy-duty flooring to withstand continuous traffic. Specialized uses include framing and floors for vehicle bodywork, and decking and flooring for boat building. It is also suitable for making vats for storing foodstuffs and chemicals. Selected logs are sliced for decorative veneers for cabinets and paneling.

Where it grows

White peroba grows in the coastal forests of Brazil.

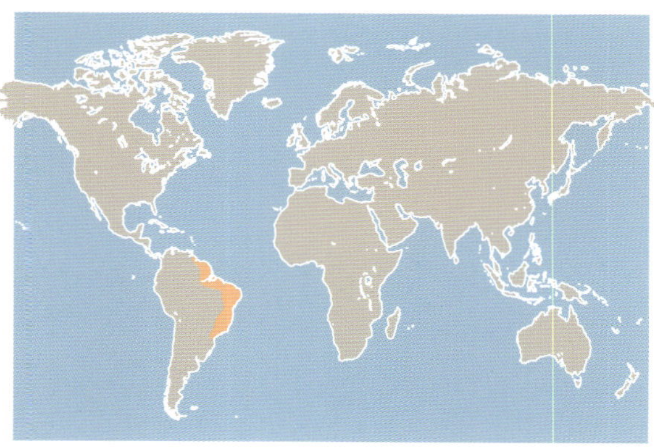

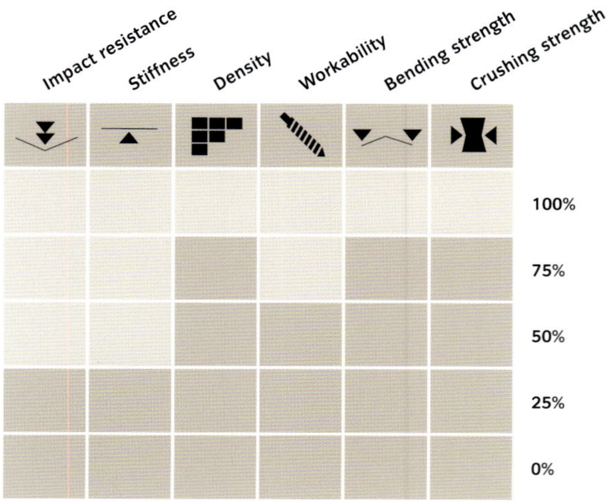

AT A GLANCE

Impact resistance is a measure of the wood's toughness. It describes its resistance to suddenly applied shock loads.

Stiffness is a measure of the wood's elasticity. It is considered in conjunction with bending strength.

Density is measured as specific gravity, the ratio of the density of a substance to that of water.

Peltogyne spp.	Family: *Leguminosae*	**PURPLEHEART**	Hardwood

Growth

The species of commercial importance in the Caribbean are *Peltogyne pubescens* Benth., *P.porphyrocardia* Griseb., and *P.venosa* (Vahl) Benth var. *densiflora* (Spruce) Amsh. They are known as amaranth and violetwood in the US. *P.venosa* from the Guianas is also important in the Amazonas of Brazil and other areas of South America; it is known as koroboreli, saka, and sakavalli (Guyana); purperhart (Surinam); pau roxo, nazareno, and morado (Venezuela); tananeo (Colombia); and amarante (Brazil). The semi-deciduous trees reach a height of 125–150ft (38–45m), with a diameter of 2–4ft (0.6–1.2m).

Appearance

The timber has a white to cream sapwood. The heartwood is bright purple on exposure to light, then matures into a dark purplish brown. It is generally straight grained, but sometimes wavy or interlocked with a moderate to fine, uniform texture.

Properties

Purpleheart averages about 54lb/ft^3 (860kg/m^3) in weight when seasoned. The wood dries fairly rapidly with little degrade, and there is little movement in service. The timber has high bending and crushing strength, high stiffness, and medium resistance to shock loads. It has a moderate steam-bending rating. It is rather difficult to work, with a moderate to severe blunting effect on tools. It requires pre-boring for nailing, but glues well and polishes easily. Spirit finishes tend to remove the purple color. The sapwood is liable to insect attack. The heartwood is very durable and extremely resistant to preservative treatment, but the sapwood is permeable.

Uses

Purpleheart is used locally as a cabinet and furniture wood, but also for heavy outdoor constructional work, including bridges, freshwater piling, and dock and harbor work. It makes an attractive flooring. It is used for sculpture, carving, and turnery for tool handles and small fancy items. Specialized uses include boat building, gymnasium apparatus, diving boards, skis, wheelwrighting, billiard cue butts, vats for chemicals, and filter presses. It is also sliced for decorative veneers.

Where it grows

Purpleheart is widely distributed in tropical America from Mexico down to southern Brazil.

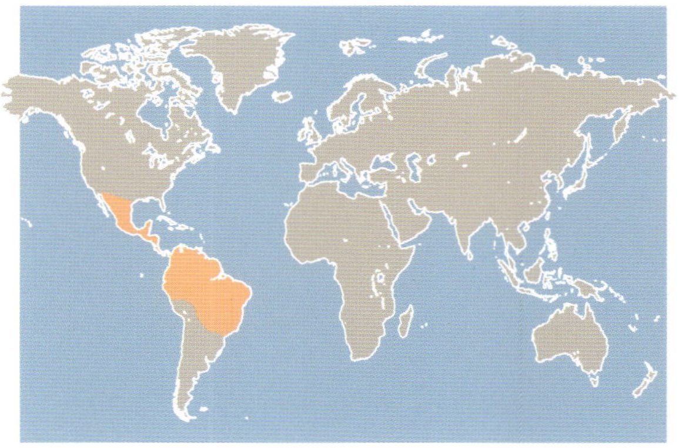

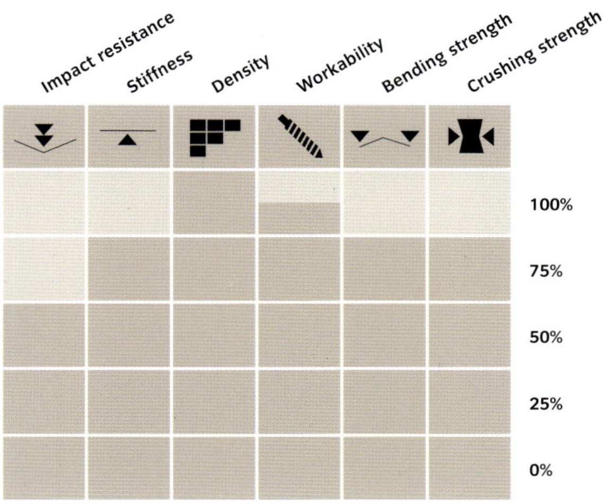

Workability describes how easy a wood is to work and whether it has a significant blunting effect on tools.

Bending strength is also known as maximum bending strength. Pressure is applied to each end of a board until it cracks.

Crushing strength is the ability of wood to withstand loads applied to the end grain, a critical test for wood used as short columns or props.

Pericopsis elata	Family: *Leguminosae*	**AFRORMOSIA**	Hardwood

Growth

Afrormosia is also known as assamela (Ivory Coast); kokrodua (Ghana and Ivory Coast); ayin and egbi (Nigeria); and andejen (Cameroon). It reaches a height of 150ft (45m) and a diameter of about 3ft (1m).

Appearance

The creamy buff sapwood is well defined from the heartwood, which is golden brown when freshly felled and darkens on exposure. The grain varies from straight to interlocked, which produces a rope-striped figure on quartered surfaces. The texture is moderately fine but without the oiliness of teak (*Tectona grandis*). The wood is liable to blue mineral stains if it comes into contact with iron or iron compounds in damp conditions because of its high tannin content.

Properties

The wood weighs about 43lb/ft^3 (690kg/m^3) when seasoned, and dries slowly but well, with little degrade. There is exceptionally small movement in service. It has medium stiffness, high crushing strength, medium shock resistance, and a moderate steam-bending rating. The interlocked grain can affect machining. Tipped saws should be used because there is a moderate blunting effect on tools. Pre-boring is required for nailing and screwing. Afrormosia glues well and takes a good finish. It is very durable, resistant to both fungi and termites, and extremely resistant to preservative treatment.

Uses

Afrormosia was originally used as a substitute for teak in the furniture industry for framing and fittings, and the edge lippings and facings of panels. Today it is used extensively in its own right where a very attractive, strong, stable, and durable wood is required. It appears in high-class furniture and cabinet making, chairs, interior joinery, stairs, shop and office fitting, and agricultural implements. It makes an attractive floor, and is also used for exterior joinery, boat building, and marine piling. Selected logs are sliced for decorative veneers for furniture, flush doors, and wall paneling.

Where it grows

Afrormosia occurs in Ghana, the Ivory Coast, Zaire, and Nigeria.

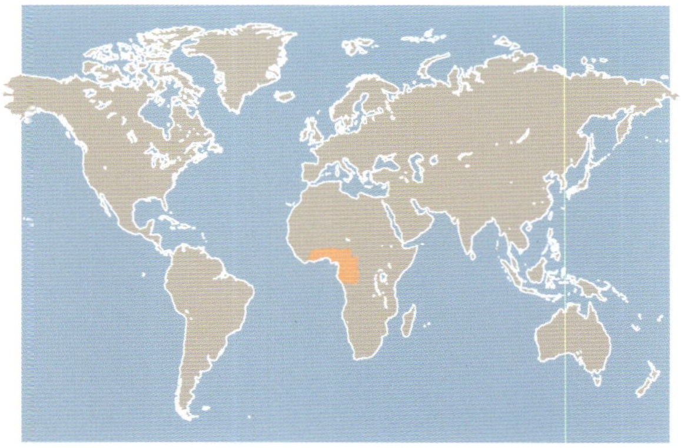

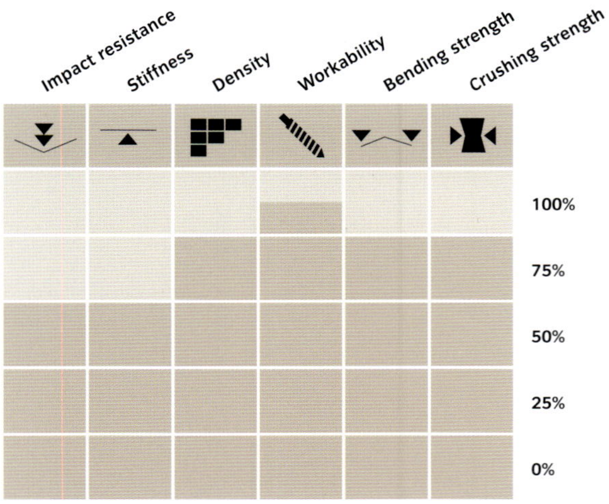

AT A GLANCE

Impact resistance is a measure of the wood's toughness. It describes its resistance to suddenly applied shock loads.

Stiffness is a measure of the wood's elasticity. It is considered in conjunction with bending strength.

Density is measured as specific gravity, the ratio of the density of a substance to that of water.

Phoebe porosa | Family: *Lauraceae* | **IMBUIA** | Hardwood

Growth
Imbuia is also known as imbuyia, amarela, canella imbuia, and embuia (Brazil); and as Brazilian walnut (US and UK). It grows to about 130ft (40m) in height, with a diameter of about 6–7ft (1.8–2m).

Appearance
The beige sapwood is clearly defined from the heartwood, which varies from olive-yellow to chocolate-brown, frequently variegated. The grain may be straight but sometimes wavy or curly, with a fine to medium texture and a high luster. It has a spicy, resinous scent and taste, most of which is lost in drying.

Properties
The weight is about 41 lb/ft^3 (660kg/m^3) when seasoned. The wood air dries rapidly and care is needed to avoid a tendency to warp. It should be kiln dried slowly to avoid degrade. There is small movement in service. Imbuia has medium to low strength in all categories, with a very low steam-bending classification, but it is chiefly used for its decorative qualities where strength is not important. It works easily with both hand and machine tools, with only a slight blunting effect on cutting edges, and finishes very smoothly. The machining dust can be an irritant to the eyes, nose, and throat. The wood has good holding properties, glues without problems, stains and polishes easily, and can be brought to an excellent finish. The durable heartwood resists insect attack and is moderately resistant to preservative treatment, but the sapwood is permeable.

Uses
Finished imbuia is similar in appearance to walnut (*Juglans spp.*), and for many years it has been marketed as Brazilian walnut. In Brazil, it is considered to be one of the most valuable woods for high-class cabinets and furniture, and superior interior joinery for paneling and shop and bank fitting. It also makes a high-grade decorative flooring for light traffic. Among its specialized uses are sculpture and carving, turnery for handles and fancy bowls, rifle butts, and gunstocks. Sliced highly decorative veneers are exported for cabinets and architectural paneling.

Where it grows
Imbuia grows in the southern areas of Brazil.

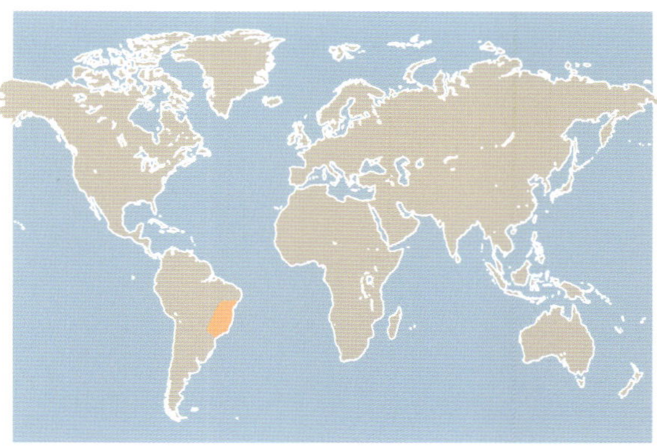

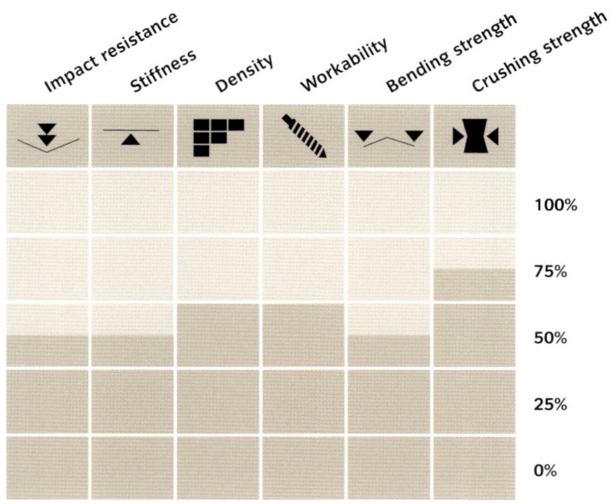

Workability describes how easy a wood is to work and whether it has a significant blunting effect on tools.

Bending strength is also known as maximum bending strength. Pressure is applied to each end of a board until it cracks.

Crushing strength is the ability of wood to withstand loads applied to the end grain, a critical test for wood used as short columns or props.

Picea abies	Family *Pinaceae*	**EUROPEAN SPRUCE/WHITEWOOD**	Softwood

Growth

Picea abies reaches an average height of 120ft (37m) and a diameter of 2½–4ft (0.8–1.2m). In the mountains of Rumania it reaches a height of 200ft (60m) with a 5–6ft (1.5–1.8m) diameter. It is also known as white deal, common spruce, and Norway spruce, as well as Baltic, Finnish, and Russian whitewood, according to the country of origin.

Appearance

The color varies from almost white to pale yellow-brown, with a natural luster. The annual rings are clearly defined. The wood is straight grained and has a fine texture.

Properties

P. abies weighs an average of 29lb/ft^3 (460kg/m^3) when seasoned. It dries rapidly and well, with some risk of distortion. It has low stiffness and resistance to shock loads, medium bending and crushing strength, and a very poor steam-bending rating. There is medium movement in service. It works easily with both hand and machine tools, holds screws and nails well, glues satisfactorily, and takes stains, paints, and varnishes for a good finish. The sapwood is liable to attack by the common furniture beetle; the nondurable heartwood is resistant to preservative treatment.

Uses

Norway spruce provides traditional Christmas trees from its thinnings. The best-quality spruce comes from the most northerly regions, but trees grown at the same latitude will produce different qualities according to the altitude. It is used for interior building work, carcassing, domestic flooring, general carpentry, boxes, and crates. Small logs are used in the round for masts, pit props, and ladder strings. Spruce from central and eastern Europe produces excellent quality tone woods for piano and other keyboard instrument soundboards, and the bellies of violins, lutes, guitars, and so on, because of its unsurpassed resonance qualities. It is used in the manufacture of pulp and paper, and in Germany the bark is stripped and used for tannin extraction. It is also utilized for the production of plywood.

Where it grows
This wood occurs throughout Europe, with the exception of Denmark and the Netherlands, into western Russia.

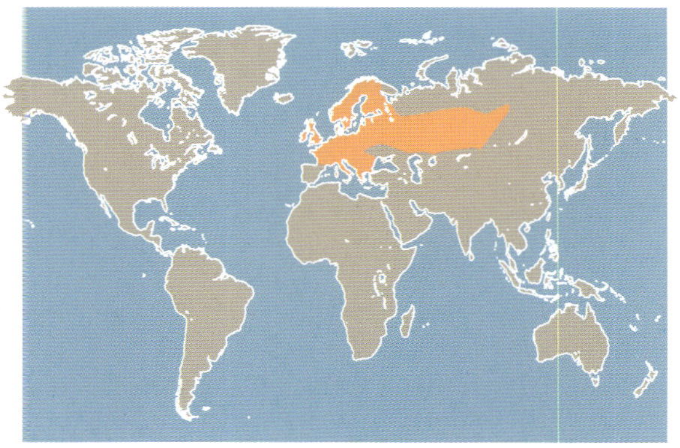

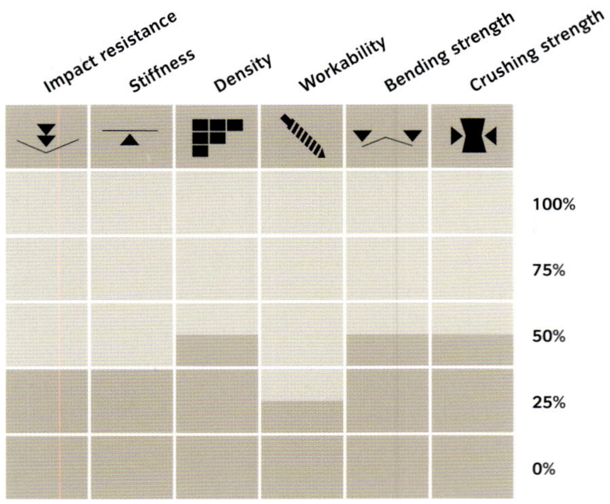

AT A GLANCE

Impact resistance is a measure of the wood's toughness. It describes its resistance to suddenly applied shock loads.

Stiffness is a measure of the wood's elasticity. It is considered in conjunction with bending strength.

Density is measured as specific gravity, the ratio of the density of a substance to that of water.

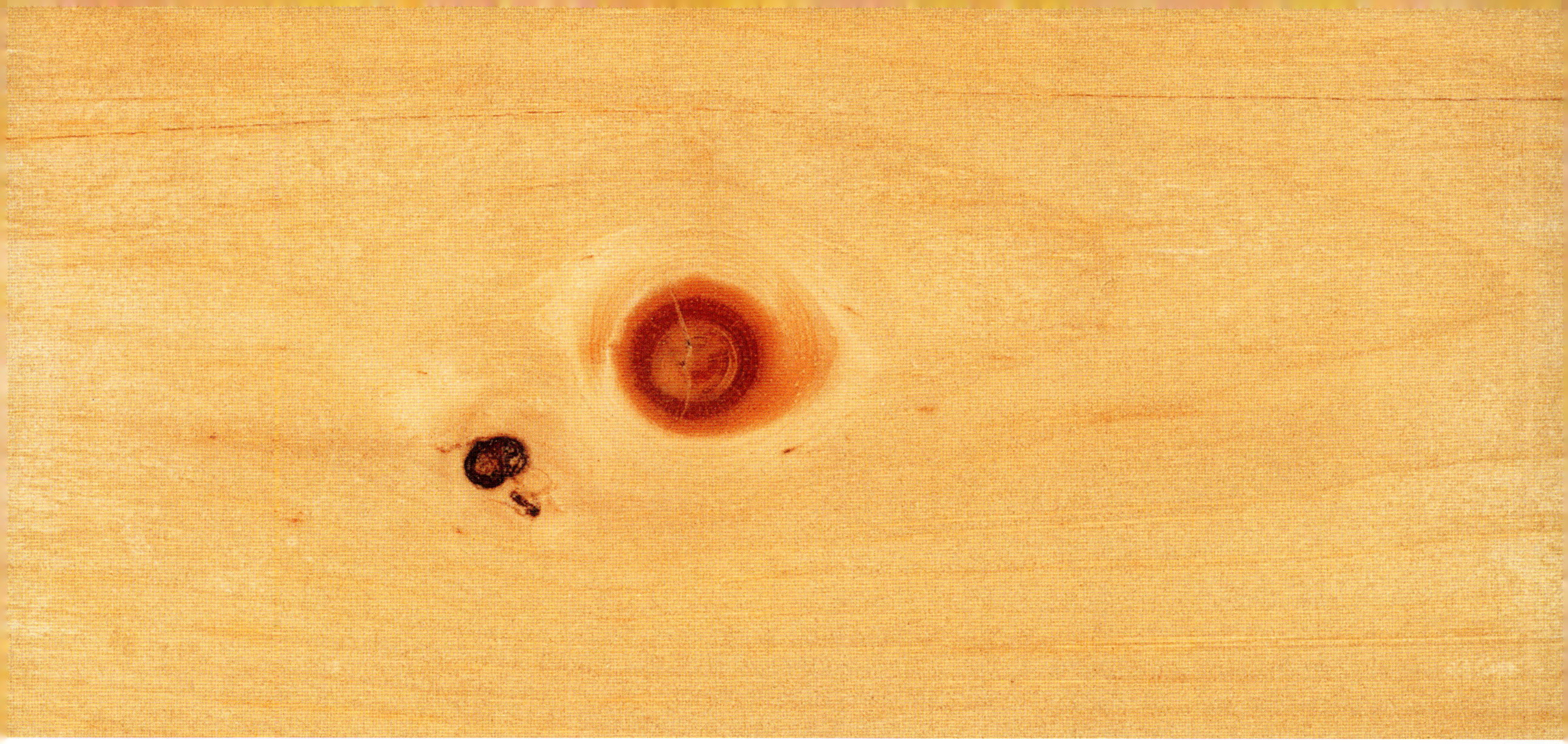

Pinus monticola | Family: *Pinaceae* | **WESTERN WHITE PINE** | Softwood

Growth

Western white pine reaches 75–120ft (23–37m) in height, with a diameter of about 3ft (1m) or more. It is also called Idaho white pine in the US because it grows most abundantly in the state of Idaho. Closely related species include *Pinus contorta* Dougl., producing lodgepole pine, which is also known as contorta pine (UK); and *P.banksiana* Lamb., providing jack pine, which is also known as princess pine and Banksian pine (Canada and US).

Appearance

The sapwood is white; the heartwood is only slightly darker and varies from a pale straw color to shades of reddish brown. Fine brown lines caused by resin ducts appear on longitudinal surfaces. It is straight grained, with an even, uniform texture. Yellow pine (*Pinus strobus*) is always called white pine in Canada and the US, although there are differences in weight and marking.

Properties

The wood weighs about 28lb/ft^3 (450kg/m^3) when seasoned. It dries readily and well, with little checking or warping, and has a slightly higher shrinkage rating than yellow pine. There is little movement in service. This low-density timber has rather low strength properties, and is not suitable for steam bending. The material works easily with both hand and machine tools, takes screws and nails without difficulty, glues satisfactorily, and takes paint and varnish well. The wood is nondurable, liable to beetle attack, and moderately resistant to preservative treatment, but the sapwood is permeable.

Uses

Western white pine is chiefly used for interior joinery for doors and windows, interior trim, fitments, shelving, and light and medium building construction. Specialized uses include furniture and cabinets, boat and ship building, pattern making, drawing boards, domestic wooden ware, and match splints. It is rotary cut for plywood and corestock, and selected logs are sliced for decorative paneling veneers.

Where it grows

This tree grows in the mountain forests of western Canada and the western United States, from sea level up to over 10,000ft (3000m). It occurs south down to the Kern River in California and east into northern Montana; it is most abundant in northern Idaho.

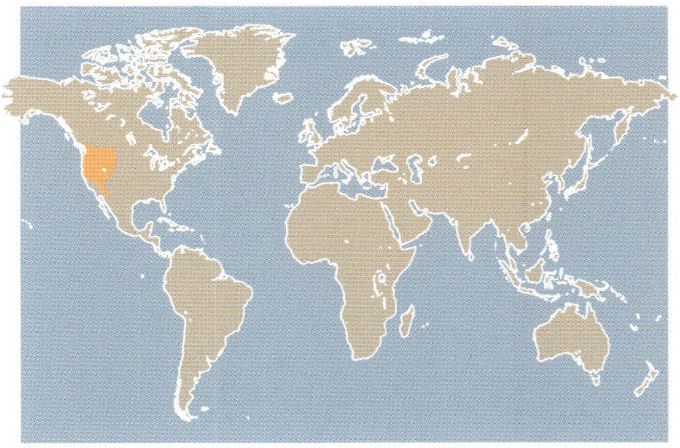

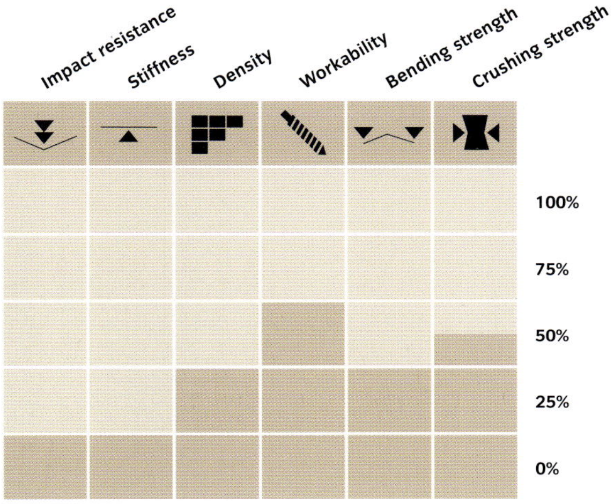

Workability describes how easy a wood is to work and whether it has a significant blunting effect on tools.

Bending strength is also known as maximum bending strength. Pressure is applied to each end of a board until it cracks.

Crushing strength is the ability of wood to withstand loads applied to the end grain, a critical test for wood used as short columns or props.

Pinus ponderosa | Family: *Pinaceae* | **PONDEROSA PINE** | Softwood

Growth

Ponderosa pine reaches an average height of 100ft (30m), with a diameter of about 2ft (0.6m). However, it can grow to much larger dimensions, reaching up to 170ft (52m) in height with a 4ft (1.2m) diameter. It is known by a number of different names, including western yellow pine (US and Australia); bird's eye pine, knotty pine, and British Columbia soft pine (Canada); and Californian white pine (US).

Appearance

Mature trees have a very thick, pale yellow sapwood that is soft, non-resinous, and uniform in texture. The heartwood is orange to reddish brown, with prominent dark brown resin duct lines on longitudinal surfaces. The heartwood is considerably heavier than the sapwood.

Properties

Ponderosa pine weighs about 32lb/ft^3 (510kg/m^3) when seasoned. It dries easily and well with little degrade, but the wide sapwood is susceptible to fungal and blue staining if the wood is not carefully piled during air drying. There is very little movement in service. It has medium bending and crushing strength, low stiffness and shock resistance, and a poor steam-bending rating. The timber works easily with both hand and machine tools, but resin exudation tends to clog cutters and saws. The wood can be glued satisfactorily, takes screws and nails without difficulty, and if it is treated to remove the surface gumminess, gives good results when painted and varnished. The heartwood is nondurable and moderately resistant to preservative treatment, but the sapwood is permeable.

Uses

The valuable sapwood is used in the United States for pattern making. The heartwood is used for kitchen furniture, building construction, window frames, doors, general carpentry, packing cases, crates, and pallets. When treated, it is used for sleepers, poles, and posts. Logs are rotary cut for veneers and sliced for knotty pine paneling.

Where it grows

Ponderosa pine occurs in the drier regions of southern British Columbia and from Montana, western Nebraska, and Texas into Mexico and west to the Pacific coast. It also grows in southeast Australia, New Zealand, and South Africa.

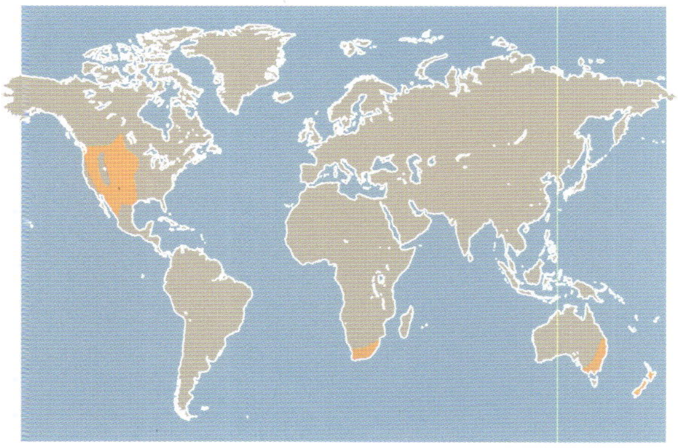

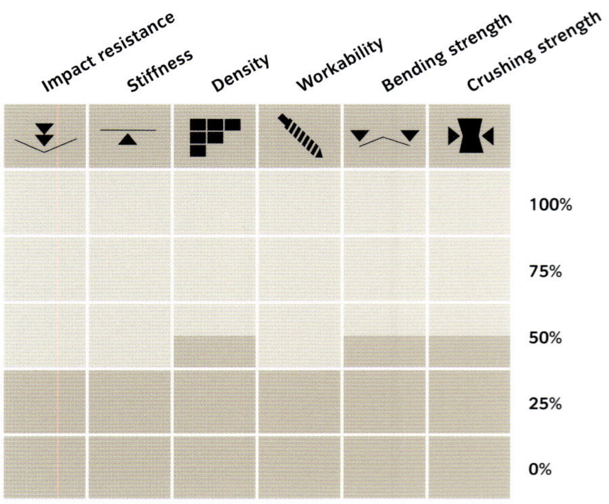

AT A GLANCE

Impact resistance is a measure of the wood's toughness. It describes its resistance to suddenly applied shock loads.

Stiffness is a measure of the wood's elasticity. It is considered in conjunction with bending strength.

Density is measured as specific gravity, the ratio of the density of a substance to that of water.

Pinus spp.	Family: *Pinaceae*	**AMERICAN PITCH PINE**	Softwood

Growth
Pitch pine is the heaviest commercial softwood. *Pinus palustris* is also known as longleaf pine, Florida longleaf yellow pine, and Georgia yellow pine; *P.elliottii* is also known as slash pine, longleaf yellow pine, and longleaf (US), and as Gulf coast pitch pine and longleaf pitch pine (UK). The heaviest timber is shipped as pitch pine, the lighter wood as southern pine. They grow to a height of 100ft (30m) and a diameter of 2–3ft (0.6–1m).

Appearance
The creamy pink sapwood is quite narrow, and contrasts with the heartwood, which is yellow-red to reddish brown, with a wide conspicuous growth ring figure, especially in fast-grown timber. It is very resinous and has a coarse texture.

Properties
The weight for seasoned American pitch pine varies from about 41 to 43lb/ft^3 (660 to 690kg/m^3). The wood dries well with little degrade and is stable in service. It has high bending and crushing strength, high stiffness, and medium resistance to shock loads. It is not suitable for steam bending because of the wood's high resin content. American pitch pine can be worked readily with both hand and machine tools, but resin can be troublesome in clogging cutters and saw teeth. It holds screws and nails firmly, glues without difficulty, and takes paint and other finishes satisfactorily. The timber is moderately durable, although beetle damage is sometimes present. The heartwood is resistant to preservative treatment, but the sapwood is permeable.

Uses
The timber is used for heavy construction work, truck and railway wagons, ship building, exterior joinery, piling, dock work, bridge building, decking, and chemical vats. Lower grades are used for interior joinery, general building, domestic flooring, crates, and pallets. The timber is rich in resinous secretions and also produces the largest percentage of the world's rosin and turpentine.

Where it grows
American pitch pine grows through the southern United States in a curve from Virginia through Florida to the Gulf.

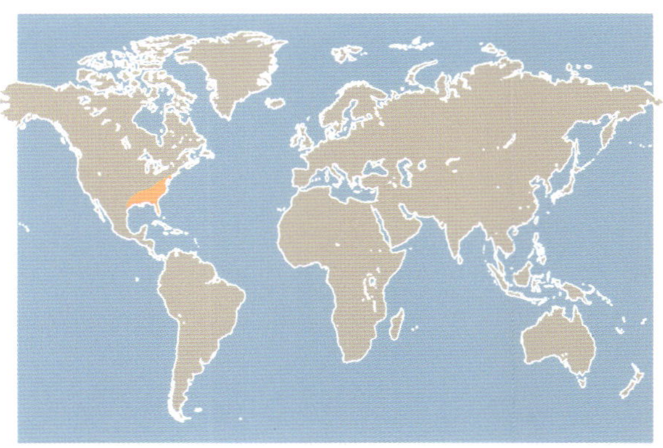

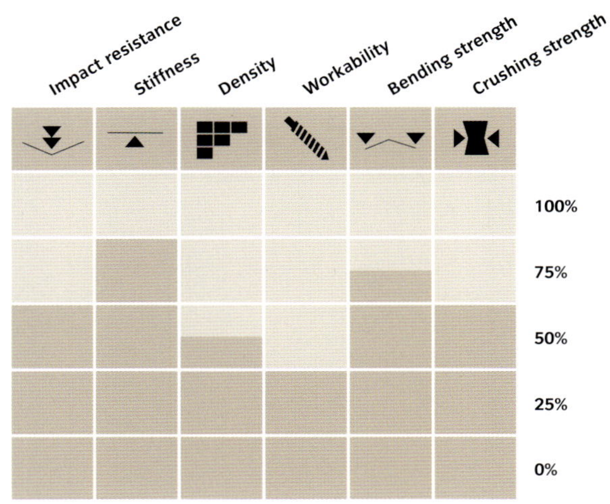

Workability describes how easy a wood is to work and whether it has a significant blunting effect on tools.

Bending strength is also known as maximum bending strength. Pressure is applied to each end of a board until it cracks.

Crushing strength is the ability of wood to withstand loads applied to the end grain, a critical test for wood used as short columns or props.

Pinus strobus	Family: *Pinaceae*	**YELLOW PINE**	Softwood

Growth
Pinus strobus can reach a height of 150ft (45m) and a diameter of about 5ft (1.5m), but it tends to average about 100ft (30m) in height and 2–3ft (0.6–1m) in diameter. It is also known as white pine, eastern white, cork, and soft pine (Canada and US); northern white and northern pine (US); and Quebec yellow, Quebec pine, and Weymouth pine (UK).

Appearance
The sapwood is white and the heartwood varies from a light straw-brown to a light reddish brown. The wood is not very resinous; the ducts appear as thin brown lines on longitudinal surfaces but the growth rings are inconspicuous. Yellow pine is straight grained and the texture very fine and even.

Properties
The weight of yellow pine varies from approximately 24 to 26lb/ft^3 (390 to 420kg/m^3) when seasoned. The wood dries fairly rapidly and well, but care needs to be taken when air drying in order to avoid sap stains. Yellow pine has extremely low shrinkage and is a very stable wood in service. The timber is weak in all strength properties, and is not suitable for steam bending. It works very easily with both hand and machine tools, has good screw- and nail-holding properties, glues satisfactorily, and can be brought to an excellent finish. Yellow pine is susceptible to attack by the common furniture beetle. The heartwood is nondurable and resistant to preservative treatment, but the sapwood is permeable and can be treated successfully.

Uses
Yellow pine, with its low shrinkage and extreme stability in use, is particularly suited for engineers' pattern making for very fine detail, and drawing boards, doors, and similar high-class work. It is also used for sculpture and carving, and for high-class interior joinery, cabinet and furniture making, shelving, and interior trim. Specialized uses include parts for stringed instruments such as guitars, organ parts, ship and boat building, and light construction. Second-growth timber is much coarser in texture and usually knotty. It is used for match splints, packaging containers, and wood flour.

Where it grows
Yellow pine species occur in Canada and the US from Newfoundland to the Manitoba border and south to north Georgia.

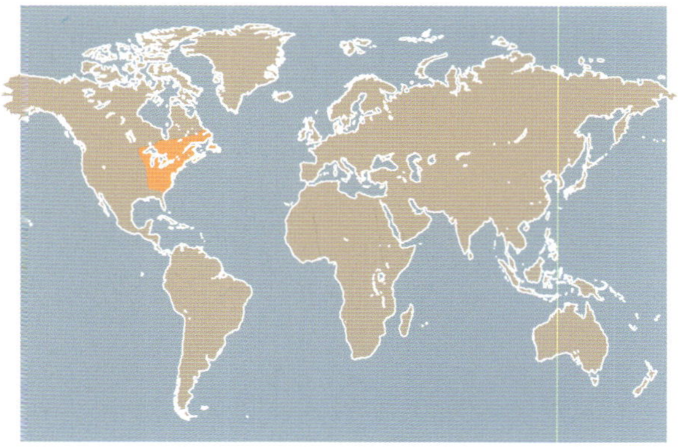

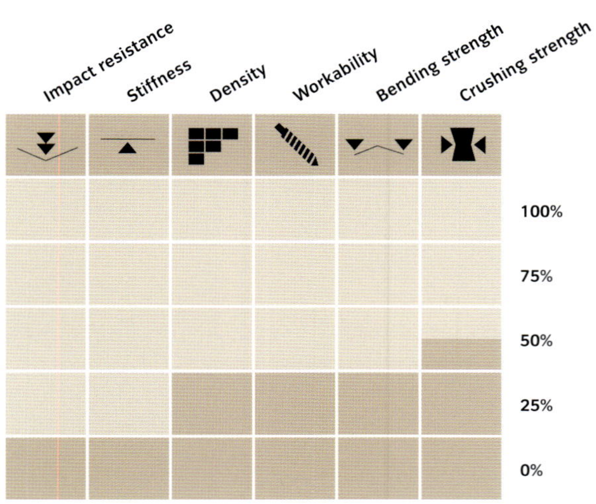

AT A GLANCE

Impact resistance is a measure of the wood's toughness. It describes its resistance to suddenly applied shock loads.

Stiffness is a measure of the wood's elasticity. It is considered in conjunction with bending strength.

Density is measured as specific gravity, the ratio of the density of a substance to that of water.

Pinus sylvestris	Family: *Pinaceae*	REDWOOD/SCOTS PINE	Softwood

Growth

In good conditions *Pinus sylvestris* reaches 130–140ft (40–43m) in height, with a diameter of 2–3ft (0.6–1m). In the UK, imported timber is known as redwood, red deal, or simply red in the north, and yellow deal or yellow in the south. Homegrown timber is called Scots pine, red pine, Norway fir, and Scots fir. Other names include Baltic, Finnish, Swedish, Archangel, Siberian, and Polish pine.

Appearance

The knotty wood has a mildly resinous heartwood of pale red-brown, distinct from the paler creamy white to yellow sapwood, with clearly marked annual rings. The texture varies from the slowly grown fine grain of northern Russia to the coarser and denser wood of northern Europe.

Properties

The weight of seasoned timber is about 32lb/ft^3 (510kg/m^3). It dries very rapidly and well, although it has a tendency to develop blue sap stain while drying. There is medium movement in service and the timber is stable in use. The wood has low stiffness and resistance to shock loads, low to medium bending and crushing strength, and a very poor steam-bending rating. It works easily with both hand and machine tools. It holds nails and screws well, but gluing can be troublesome because of the wood's resin content. The wood can be stained, painted, or varnished to a good finish. It is liable to attack by the common furniture beetle. The heartwood is nondurable and moderately resistant to preservative treatment, but the sapwood is permeable.

Uses

The best grades are used for furniture, interior joinery, turnery, and vehicle bodies. Other grades are employed for building construction and carcassing. When treated, redwood is extensively used for railway sleepers, telegraph poles, piles, and pit props. Logs are cut for plywood and sliced for decorative veneers. It is also used in the chemical wood pulp industry.

Where it grows

This common commercial softwood occurs from the Sierra Nevada in Andalusia and the mountains of western Spain, through the Maritime Alps, Pyrenees, the Caucasus, and Transylvanian Alps, up into western Siberia.

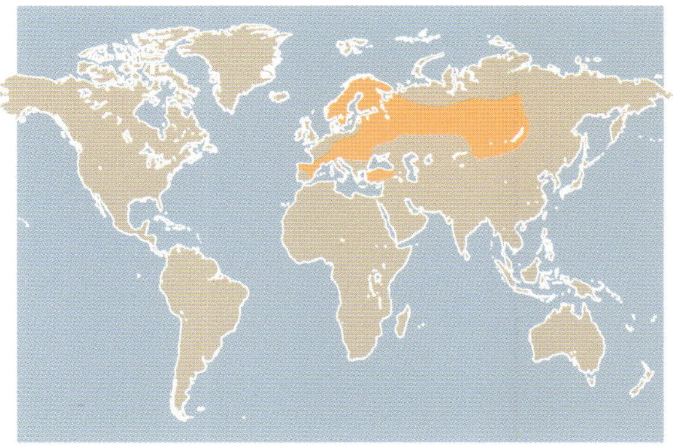

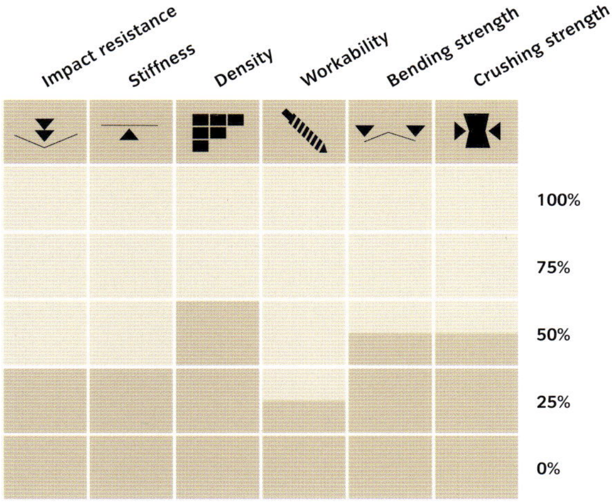

Workability describes how easy a wood is to work and whether it has a significant blunting effect on tools.

Bending strength is also known as maximum bending strength. Pressure is applied to each end of a board until it cracks.

Crushing strength is the ability of wood to withstand loads applied to the end grain, a critical test for wood used as short columns or props.

Piratinera guianensis | Family: *Moraceae* | **SNAKEWOOD** | Hardwood

Growth
Snakewood is also known as leopard wood (US); letterwood (UK); amourette (France); bourra courra (Guyana); letterhout (Surinam); and palo de oro (Venezuela). It grows to about 80ft (24m) in height and about 1–3ft (0.3m–1m) in diameter.

Appearance
Snakewood is one of the most expensive woods in the world, and gets its name from the dark red to reddish brown snakeskin appearance of the heartwood. It has irregular black striped markings and dark spots like a leopard or hieroglyphic characters—hence the name letterwood. These dark spots and areas are the result of variations in the gummy deposits that fill the cell cavities. It is irregular grained, but the texture is moderately fine.

Properties
Snakewood is extremely hard and weighs 81lb/ft^3 (1300kg/m^3) when air dried. The wood is difficult to dry with a tendency to degrade, and there is medium movement in service. The material is exceptionally strong in all categories, and is not suitable for steam bending. It is very difficult to work, and has a severe blunting effect on cutting edges. It needs care in gluing and finishing because of the resin content, but can be polished to a smooth and beautiful finish. It is a very durable wood, immune to insect attack, and extremely resistant to preservative treatment.

Uses
Snakewood is a superb turnery wood for walking sticks, drumsticks, fishing rod butts, fancy handles for cutlery and umbrellas, fancy trinkets, and brush backs. It is used for violin bows and is the traditional wood for native archery bows. Selected logs are sliced for decorative veneers for cabinets or sawn for inlay work.

Where it grows
Snakewood occurs in Central and tropical South America, from the Amazon region of Brazil through Guyana, Venezuela, Colombia, and Panama, southern Mexico, and the West Indies. Commercial supplies come mainly from Guyana, French Guiana, and Surinam.

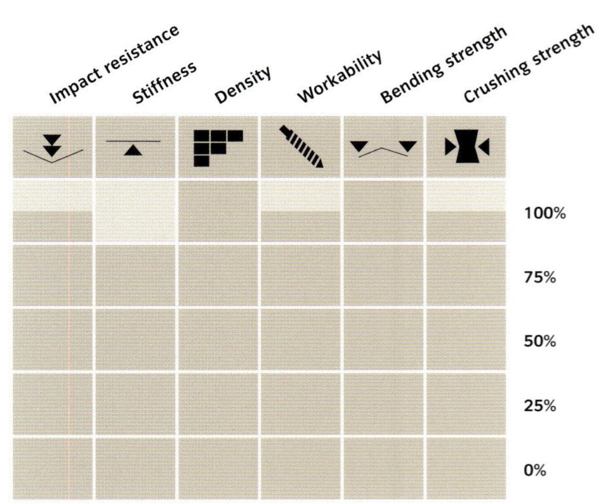

AT A GLANCE

Impact resistance is a measure of the wood's toughness. It describes its resistance to suddenly applied shock loads.

Stiffness is a measure of the wood's elasticity. It is considered in conjunction with bending strength.

Density is measured as specific gravity, the ratio of the density of a substance to that of water.

Platanus hybrida | Family: *Platanaceae* | **EUROPEAN PLANE** | Hardwood

Growth

The related species *Platanus orientalis* produces eastern plane tree, which occurs in southeast Europe, Turkey, and Iran; *P. occidentalis* produces American plane, known as sycamore or buttonwood in the US. Both have been hybridized to produce *P. hybrida*, which is also known as London plane or English plane in the UK. It grows to a height of 100ft (30m), with a diameter of 3ft (1m).

Appearance

The sapwood is not very distinct from the heartwood, which is light reddish brown with darker, conspicuous broad rays on quartered material. These produce a very decorative flecked figure, and such wood is sold as lacewood. The wood is straight grained, with a fine to medium texture.

Properties

European plane averages about 39lb/ft^3 (620kg/m^3) in weight when seasoned. It air dries fairly rapidly, is prone to splitting, and has a tendency to distort. It is stable in service and has medium strength in all categories except for low stiffness, which earns it a very good steam-bending classification. The timber works well with both hand and machine tools, and has only a moderate blunting effect on cutting edges. Sharp cutters are required when planing or molding, and there is a tendency to bind on saws. It screws and nails without difficulty, takes glue well, and can be brought to an excellent finish. The sapwood is liable to attack by the common furniture beetle. The heartwood is perishable but permeable to preservation treatment.

Uses

This highly decorative wood is used for the interiors of high-class cabinets and furniture, joinery, carriage interiors, light construction, door skins, and paneling; and in turnery for striking handles of tools and fancy handles. Logs are sliced for decorative veneers for cabinets and paneling. For inlay and marquetry work, the veneers are treated as harewood, when the background becomes silver gray and the flecked rays retain their original color.

Where it grows

This tree occurs throughout Europe.

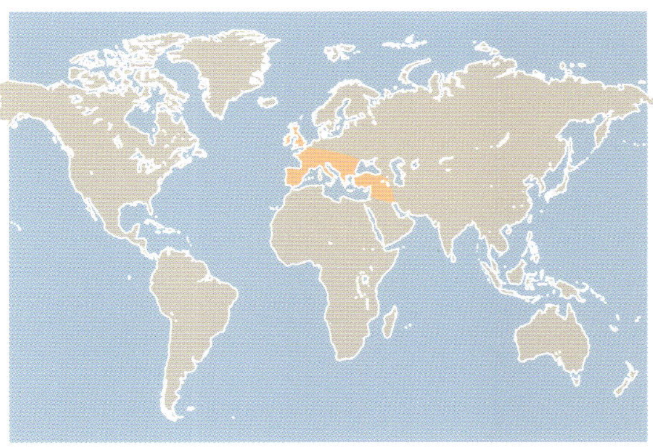

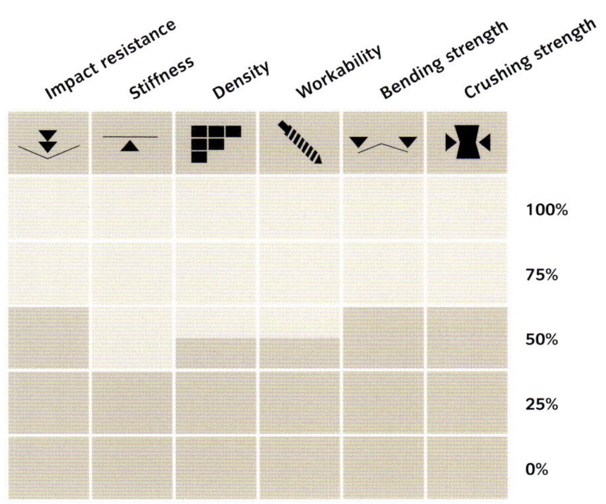

Workability describes how easy a wood is to work and whether it has a significant blunting effect on tools.

Bending strength is also known as maximum bending strength. Pressure is applied to each end of a board until it cracks.

Crushing strength is the ability of wood to withstand loads applied to the end grain, a critical test for wood used as short columns or props.

Podocarpus spp. | Family: *Podocarpaceae* | **PODO** | Softwood

Growth

Podo is produced principally by *Podocarpus gracilior* Pilg; *P.milanjianus* Rendle, which is found at higher altitudes; and *P.usambarensis* Pilg., which grows at lower altitudes. The latter two woods attain a height of 100ft (30m) or more, with a diameter of 2½–4ft (0.8–1.2m). *P.gracilior*, growing to a much larger diameter, is also known as yellow wood (South Africa and British Honduras); kahikatea, miro, and matai (New Zealand); and manio (Chile).

Appearance

There is only a very slight distinction between the sapwood and the heartwood of podo, which are light yellow-brown. The wood has no clearly defined growth rings, giving it a uniform texture. It is straight grained.

Properties

Podo weighs 32–39lb/ft^3 (510–620kg/m^3) when seasoned. It dries fairly rapidly, with a pronounced tendency to distort. There is medium movement in service. It has medium bending and crushing strength, low stiffness and resistance to shock loads, and a moderate steam-bending rating. The wood works easily with both hand and machine tools, although the wood is brittle. It requires pre-boring for nailing, but holds screws well and glues satisfactorily. It does not take stain uniformly, but can be painted or varnished well. The wood is liable to insect attack and is nondurable, but is permeable for preservation treatment.

Uses

Podo is used where durability is not of major importance for joinery and interior fittings in building construction, scaffold planks and boards, fascia boards, flooring and framing, kitchen furniture, and moldings. It is also used for turnery and, when treated, for weatherboards and boat building. *P.gracilior* is rotary cut for good-quality plywood and sliced for decorative veneers. *P.milanjianus* is used for low-grade plywood and corestock for laminated boards.

Where it grows

Podo grows in east Africa, including Kenya, Uganda, Ethiopia, Tanzania, Zambia, and Zimbabwe. It also occurs in Central America, Chile, and parts of Australasia.

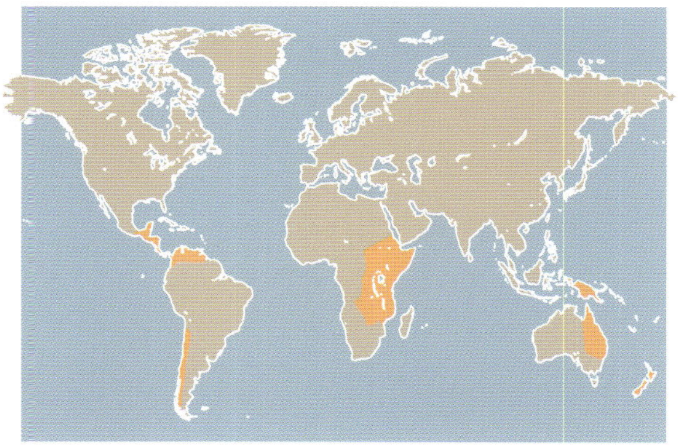

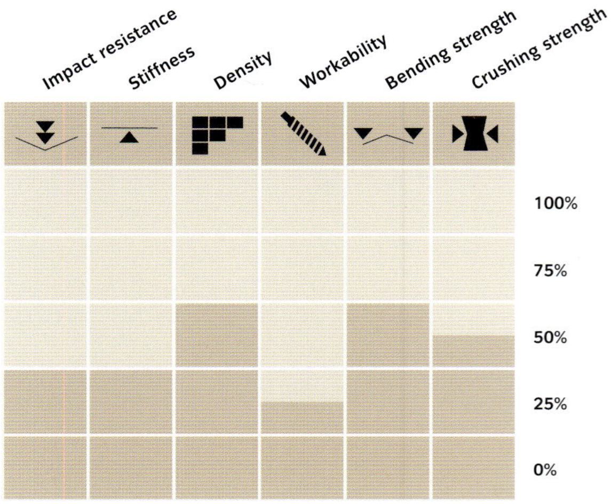

AT A GLANCE

Impact resistance is a measure of the wood's toughness. It describes its resistance to suddenly applied shock loads.

Stiffness is a measure of the wood's elasticity. It is considered in conjunction with bending strength.

Density is measured as specific gravity, the ratio of the density of a substance to that of water.

Podocarpus totara	Family: *Podocarpaceae*	**TOTARA**	Softwood

Growth

Podocarpus totara grows to an average height of 70ft (21m), with a diameter of approximately 2–5ft (0.6–1.5m). However, it often reaches 130ft (40m). The related species *P.hallii* grows to 24–60ft (7–18m) in height.

Appearance

P.totara is a straight-grained wood of medium reddish brown with a fairly fine, even texture. *P.hallii* tends to have interlocked or wavy grain. In common with other softwoods that grow in the southern hemisphere, the growth rings of totara are not clearly defined.

Properties

Totara weighs 30lb/ft^3 (480kg/m^3) when seasoned. The wood dries fairly rapidly and well, and there is little degrade and only small movement in service. It has low bending strength and resistance to shock loads, but medium crushing strength, making it more suitable for columns and posts than beams and joists. It has a moderate steam-bending classification. The timber works easily with both hand and machine tools. *P.hallii* is more difficult to machine because of its interlocked grain. Both species hold screws and nails without difficulty. Care is needed in gluing, and the resin content requires special treatment before painting to be sure of a good finish. The wood has natural durability and a high resistance to decay, but is liable to attack by the common furniture beetle. The heartwood is resistant to preservative treatment, but the sapwood is permeable.

Uses

Totara is the only softwood that is resistant to attack by marine borers, which makes it a very important wood in its native New Zealand for docks, wharf and harbor work, and bridges. It has specialized uses in ship and boat building and for chemical vats. It is also widely used for flooring, cladding, and shingles, and for all work in contact with the ground. It is the traditional wood for Maori carvings and canoe building. Logs of *P.hallii* that have a more interlocked and wavy grain are sliced for decorative veneers and exported to Europe for pianos, cabinets, and paneling.

Where it grows

Totara occurs only in New Zealand.

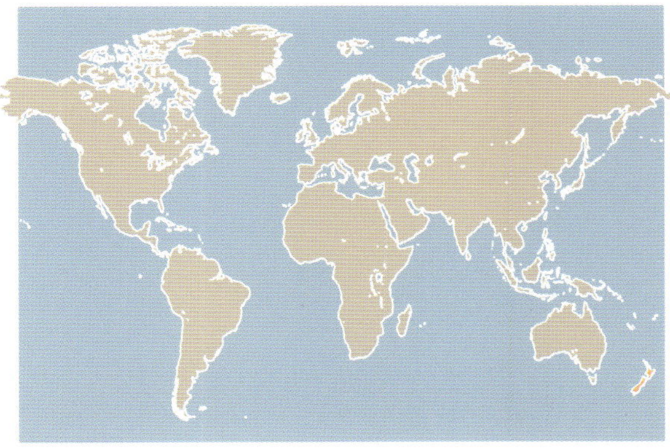

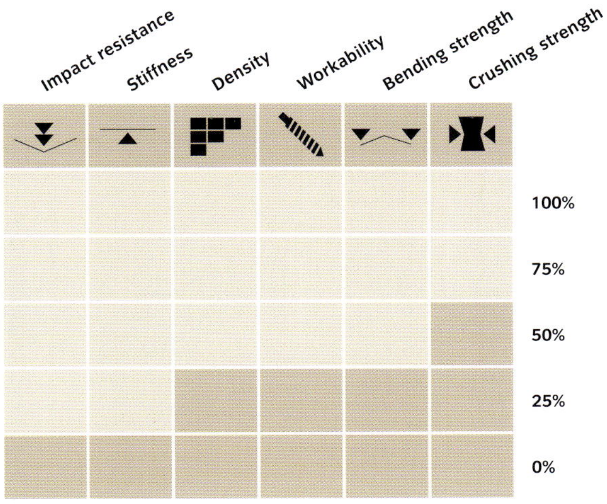

Workability describes how easy a wood is to work and whether it has a significant blunting effect on tools.

Bending strength is also known as maximum bending strength. Pressure is applied to each end of a board until it cracks.

Crushing strength is the ability of wood to withstand loads applied to the end grain, a critical test for wood used as short columns or props.

***Populus* spp.** | Family: *Salicaceae* | **POPLAR** | Hardwood

Growth

The principal commercial species of northern temperate regions are: *Populus nigra* L., which produces black poplar or European black poplar (Europe); *P.canadensis* Moench. var. *serotina*, which provides black Italian poplar (Europe); *P.robusta* Schneid, which produces black poplar or robusta (Europe); *P.tremula* L., which provides European, English, Finnish, or Swedish aspen, according to the country of origin; *P.balsamifera* L. syn. *P.tacamahaca* Mill., which produces Canadian poplar, also known as tacamahac poplar and balsam poplar (US), and as balm poplar and black poplar (Canada). The black poplars reach a height of 100–115ft (30–35m), with a diameter of 3–4ft (1–1.2m) or more. Aspen grows to around 60–80ft (18–24m) in height.

Appearance

The heartwood, not clearly defined from the sapwood, varies from creamy white to very pale straw, and in some species to pale brown or pink-brown. It is usually straight grained and rather wooly, but has a fine, even texture.

Properties

Poplar averages 28lb/ft^3 (450kg/m^3) in weight when seasoned. The wood dries fairly rapidly and well with little degrade, and there is medium movement in service. It has low bending strength, very low stiffness and shock resistance, medium crushing strength, and a very poor steam-bending rating. It works easily with hand or machine tools, but very sharp and thin-edged cutters are required. Poplar holds screws and nails well, and glues easily. Staining can be patchy, but the wood can be painted or varnished to a satisfactory finish. Logs are liable to attack by beetles and wood boring caterpillars (*Cossidae*). The sapwood, which constitutes a large proportion of the tree, is perishable but permeable for preservative treatment.

Uses

Poplar is much less liable to splinter than softwoods and selected grades are used for interior joinery, furniture framing, toys, and turnery. Logs are rotary cut for plywood and corestock and sliced for veneers. It is the main timber for match splints, wood wool, chip baskets, and punnets. It also comes in for rough use for truck floors, packing cases, crates, and pallets.

Where it grows

Poplar grows in the northern temperate regions of the world, from Canada and the northern United States to Europe, and across Asia to China.

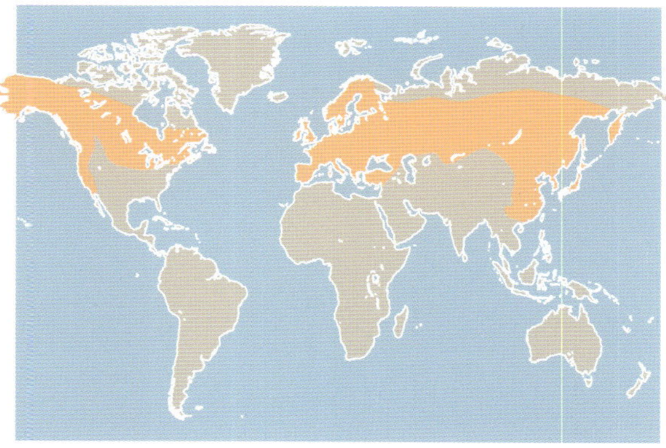

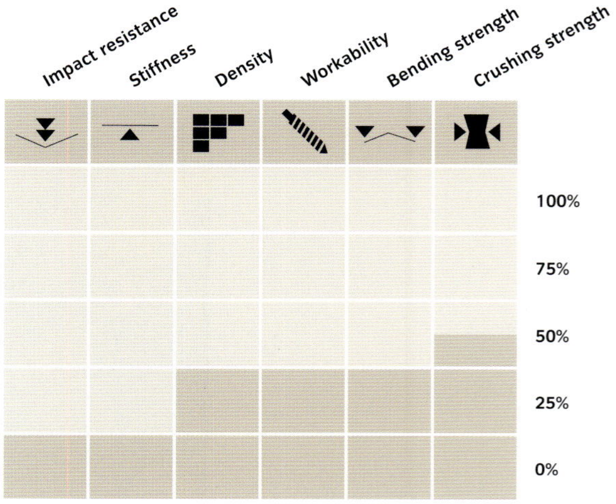

AT A GLANCE

Impact resistance is a measure of the wood's toughness. It describes its resistance to suddenly applied shock loads.

Stiffness is a measure of the wood's elasticity. It is considered in conjunction with bending strength.

Density is measured as specific gravity, the ratio of the density of a substance to that of water.

Populus tremuloides | Family: *Salicaceae* | **CANADIAN ASPEN** | Hardwood

Growth
Canadian aspen grows to a height of 40–60ft (12–18m) or more, with a diameter of 8–12in (20–30cm).

Appearance
The sapwood is not distinct from the heartwood, which is creamy white to very pale biscuit. It is mostly straight grained, occasionally wavy, and inclined to be wooly. Sometimes pink, orange, and golden streaks are visible; the texture is fine and even.

Properties
The weight of Canadian aspen averages 28lb/ft³ (450kg/m³) when seasoned. The wood dries easily, but is inclined to warp and twist in drying, and distort unless care is taken in piling. There is small movement in service. It has low bending and crushing strength, low stiffness, medium resistance to shock loads, and a very poor steam-bending rating. It works easily with both hand and machine tools, but tends to bind and tear on the saw. Very sharp, thin-edged tools are needed. The timber holds screws and nails without difficulty and glues well, but on wooly surfaces staining may be patchy. The surface can be painted or varnished to a good finish. The wood is nondurable and extremely resistant to preservative treatment.

Uses
This timber has a wide range of different uses, including furniture interiors and fitments, brake blocks for iron wheels, vehicle bodies and the bottoms of trucks, wagons, food containers, chip and fruit baskets, boxes, packing cases, crates and pallets, wood wool, and match splints. It is used in North America and Canada for veneer for matches, for chip and fruit baskets and punnets, and for wood, pulp, and paper manufacture. It is also rotary cut for plywood and used as corestock for laminated boards and chipboard. Selected logs are sliced for highly decorative veneers for paneling.

Where it grows
This tree, one of the most widely distributed in North America, occurs in the Lake and Rocky Mountain states of Canada, from Newfoundland and Nova Scotia to Alaska, and south along the Appalachians through New England to Minnesota.

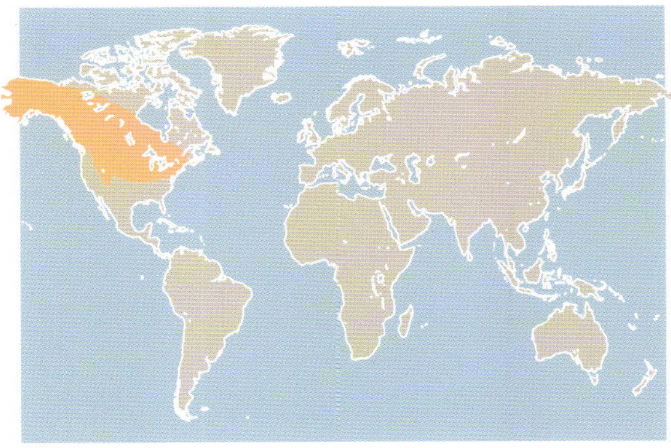

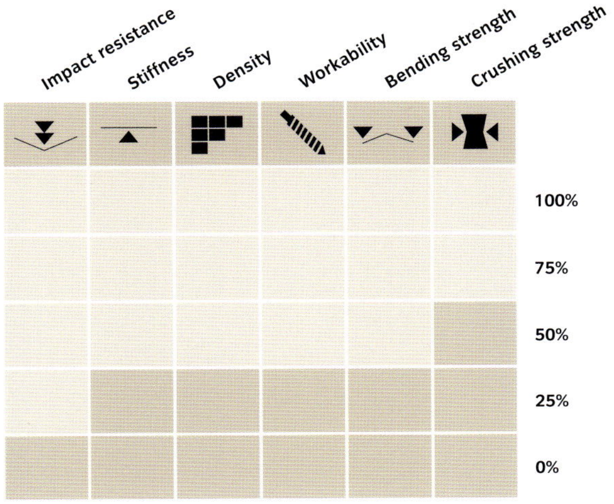

Workability describes how easy a wood is to work and whether it has a significant blunting effect on tools.

Bending strength is also known as maximum bending strength. Pressure is applied to each end of a board until it cracks.

Crushing strength is the ability of wood to withstand loads applied to the end grain, a critical test for wood used as short columns or props.

***Prunus* spp.** | Family: *Rosaceae* | **CHERRY** | Hardwood

Growth

Prunus serotina Ehrh. produces American cherry, also known as black cherry (Canada and US) and cabinet cherry (US). *P. avium* L. syn. *Cerasus avium* Moench. provides European cherry, also known as gean, mazzard, cherry, and wild cherry (UK). European cherry grows to a height of 60–80ft (18–24m), with a diameter of about 2ft (0.6m). American cherry reaches a height of 100ft (30m).

Appearance

The creamy pink sapwood of *P. avium* is clearly defined from the heartwood, which is a pale pinkish brown maturing to red-brown. *P. serotina* is a darker red-brown, with narrow brown pith flecks and small gum pockets. Both have straight grain and a fairly fine, even texture.

Properties

The weight of *P. avium* is 38lb/ft^3 (610kg/m^3), while *P. serotina* is 36lb/ft^3 (580kg/m^3) when seasoned. The wood dries fairly rapidly, with a strong tendency to warp and shrink and with medium movement in service. It has medium bending and crushing strengths, medium shock resistance, low stiffness, and a very good steam-bending rating. It works well with both hand and machine tools, with a moderate blunting effect on cutting edges, but cross-grained timber tends to tear in planing. The wood holds screws and nails well, glues easily, and takes stain and polishes to an excellent finish. It is moderately durable; the sapwood is liable to attack by the common furniture beetle, but is almost immune to attack by powder post beetle. The heartwood is moderately durable and resistant to preservative.

Uses

European cherry has a handsome figure and color, and is used for cabinet and furniture making, carving and sculpture, and decorative turnery for domestic ware, shuttle pins, toys, and parts of musical instruments. American cherry is used for pattern making, tobacco pipes, boat interiors, and backing blocks for printing plates. Both types are rotary cut for plywood and sliced for decorative veneers for cabinets and panels.

Where it grows

Cherry occurs in the United States from Ontario to Florida and from the Dakotas to Texas. It is also native to Europe, and occurs in the mountains of north Africa.

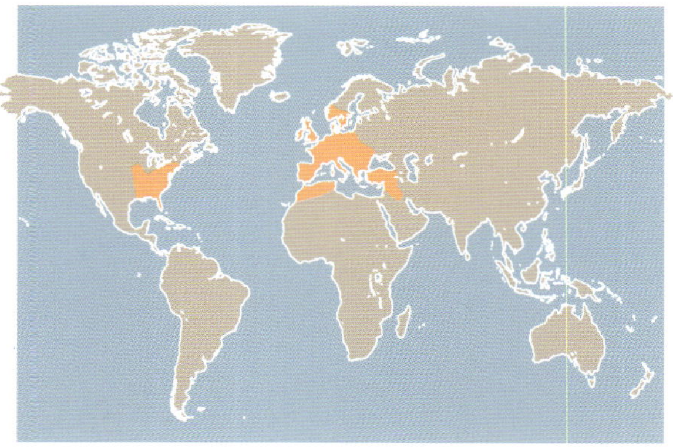

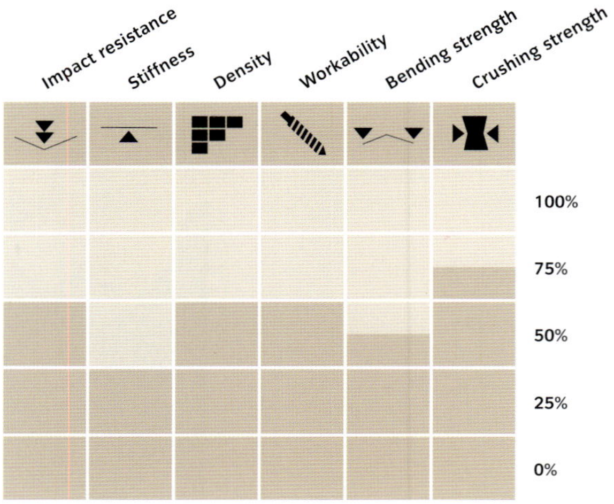

AT A GLANCE

Impact resistance is a measure of the wood's toughness. It describes its resistance to suddenly applied shock loads.

Stiffness is a measure of the wood's elasticity. It is considered in conjunction with bending strength.

Density is measured as specific gravity, the ratio of the density of a substance to that of water.

Pseudotsuga menziesii	Family: *Pinaceae*	**DOUGLAS FIR**	Softwood

Growth

This softwood, not a true fir (*Abies spp.*), is also known as Oregon pine (US) and British Columbia pine and Columbian pine (UK). In Canada and the United States, trees reach a height of 300ft (92m), averaging 150–200ft (45–60m), and 3–6ft (1–1.8m) in diameter. The bole is clear of branches for about two-thirds of its height, yielding a very high percentage of timber clear of knots and other defects.

Appearance

The sapwood is slightly lighter in color than the heartwood, which is a light reddish brown. There is a prominent growth ring figure on plain-sawn surfaces or rotary cut veneers. The grain is mostly straight, but often wavy or spiral. The texture is medium and uniform.

Properties

Douglas fir weighs 33lb/ft^3 (530kg/m^3) when seasoned. The wood dries fairly rapidly and well without much warping, but knots tend to split and loosen. Resin canals also tend to exude and show as fine brown lines on longitudinal surfaces. Douglas fir is stable in service, has high bending strength, stiffness, and crushing strength, medium resistance to shock loads, and a poor steam-bending rating. The wood works readily with both hand and machine tools. Cutters should be kept very sharp because there is a moderate blunting effect. It is subject to beetle attack, is moderately durable, and is resistant to preservative.

Uses

This is the world's most important source of plywood. In the solid, large baulks are used for heavy construction work, laminated arches, roof trusses, beams, interior and exterior joinery, dock and harbor work, marine piling, ship building, mining timber, railway sleepers, cooperage for vats, and tanks for chemical plants, breweries, and distilleries. Selected logs are sliced for decorative veneers for paneling.

Where it grows

Douglas fir occurs in abundance in British Columbia, Washington, and Oregon, through Wyoming to southern New Mexico, and west to the Pacific coast. It has been introduced to the UK, Australia, and New Zealand.

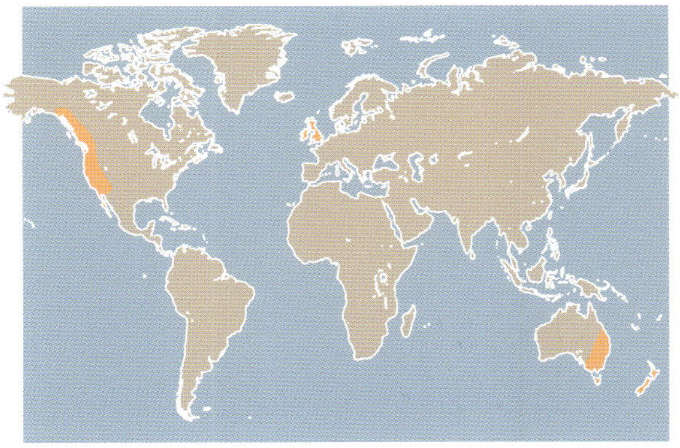

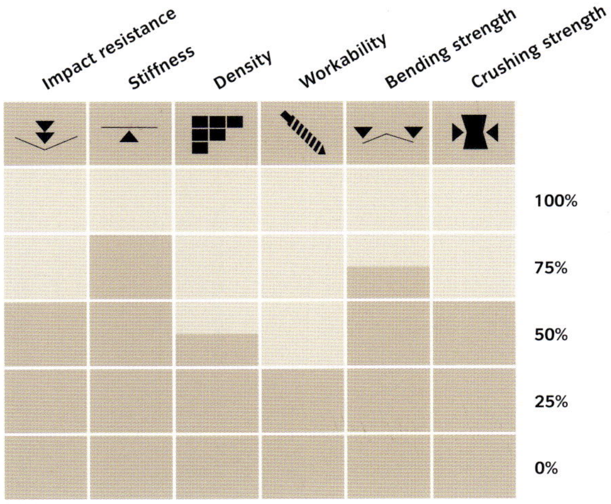

Workability describes how easy a wood is to work and whether it has a significant blunting effect on tools.

Bending strength is also known as maximum bending strength. Pressure is applied to each end of a board until it cracks.

Crushing strength is the ability of wood to withstand loads applied to the end grain, a critical test for wood used as short columns or props.

Pterocarpus angolensis | Family: *Leguminosae* | **MUNINGA** | Hardwood

Growth
Muninga grows to a height of 50ft (15m), sometimes reaching 70ft (21m), with a diameter of 2ft (0.6m). It is known by several other names in its native Africa, including mninga (Tanzania); ambila (Mozambique); mukwa (Zambia and Zimbabwe); and kiaat, kajat, and kajatenhout (South Africa).

Appearance
The oatmeal-colored sapwood of muninga is clearly defined from the heartwood, which matures into a deep golden brown with irregular darker chocolate-brown or dark red markings, sometimes marred with white spots or blotches. Although occasionally straight, the grain is often irregularly interlocked, which produces an attractive figure on quartered surfaces. The texture is fairly coarse and uneven.

Properties
Muninga averages about 39lb/ft^3 (620kg/m^3) in weight when seasoned; the timber from Zimbabwe is softer and weighs only 34lb/ft^3 (540kg/m^3). The wood has excellent drying properties and dries fairly slowly, especially in thicker sizes, with only a slight tendency to surface checking. It is exceptionally stable in use. This timber has medium bending strength, very low stiffness, low shock resistance, a high crushing strength, and a moderate steam-bending classification. It works easily with both hand and machine tools, but with a tendency for the irregular grain to pick up when planing. It has good holding properties, glues well, and can be brought to an excellent finish. The sapwood is liable to attack by powder post beetle. The heartwood is very durable and resistant to preservative treatment.

Uses
Muninga, a very attractive wood, is excellent for turnery and is also used for carving and wood sculpture, high-class joinery, and, in both solid and veneer forms, for furniture, cabinets, and paneling. It makes an excellent flooring with moderate resistance to wear and is suitable for domestic use, especially over underfloor heating systems.

Where it grows
Muninga occurs in the savannah forests of Tanzania, Zambia, Angola, Mozambique, Zimbabwe, and South Africa.

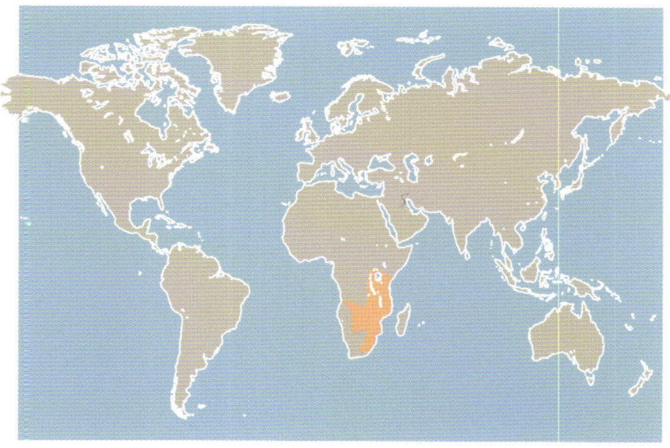

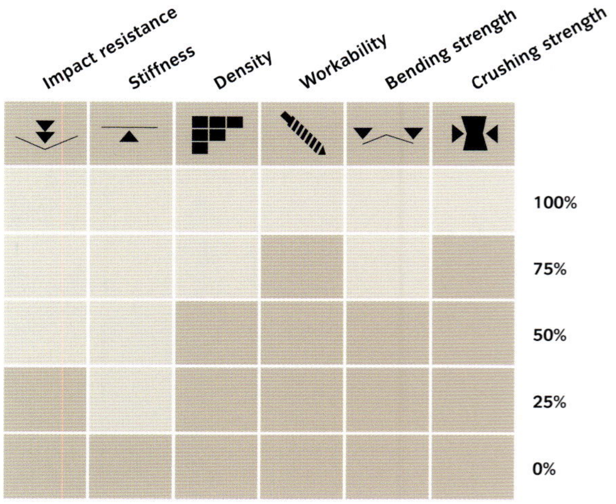

AT A GLANCE

Impact resistance is a measure of the wood's toughness. It describes its resistance to suddenly applied shock loads.

Stiffness is a measure of the wood's elasticity. It is considered in conjunction with bending strength.

Density is measured as specific gravity, the ratio of the density of a substance to that of water.

Pterocarpus dalbergoides | Family: *Leguminosae* | **ANDAMAN PADAUK** | Hardwood

Growth
Andaman padauk is also known as Andaman redwood and vermillion wood in the US. It grows to a height of 80–120ft (24–37m), with very large buttresses and a diameter of 2½–3ft (0.8–1m), with a clean bole up to 40ft (12m).

Appearance
The narrow sapwood is fawn-gray, while the handsome heartwood varies from yellowish pink with darker red lines to a rich, almost blood-red crimson hue. It may also be reddish purple with darker purple lines, sometimes with darker red or black streaks. Both types mature into a handsome reddish brown. The grain is usually interlocked, with a medium to coarse texture, producing an attractive roe or curly figure on quartered surfaces.

Properties
Andaman padauk weighs an average of about 48lb/ft^3 (770kg/m^3) when seasoned. The wood kiln dries without undue degrade and is exceptionally stable in use. This heavy, dense timber has medium bending strength, low stiffness, low shock resistance, and a high crushing strength. It is not suitable for steam bending. There is high resistance in cutting and the wood has a moderate blunting effect on tools, especially when planing interlocked grain on quartered surfaces. It requires pre-boring for nailing, but holds screws well and glues satisfactorily. The wood can be brought to an excellent finish. It is very durable, and is noted for its high resistance to decay. The heartwood is moderately resistant to preservative treatment, but the sapwood is permeable.

Uses
This very attractive timber is used for high-class cabinets, furniture, and billiard tables. It is ideal for interior joinery, especially for shop and bank fittings, and counters subject to wear. It is also popular for turnery for fancy handles and brush backs, and for wood sculpture and carving. It is highly valued for exterior joinery and for boat building; it makes a hard-wearing and attractive domestic flooring. Logs are sliced for decorative veneers for cabinets and paneling. *Pterocarpus macrocarpus* produces Burma padauk, weighing 53lb/ft^3 (850kg/m^3) and used for similar purposes.

Where it grows
This tree grows only in the Andaman Islands.

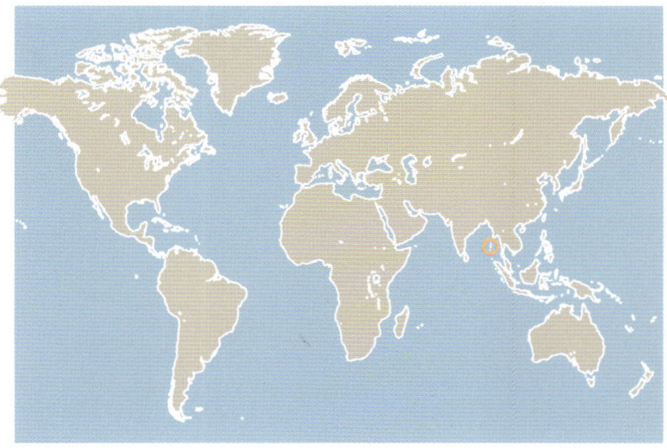

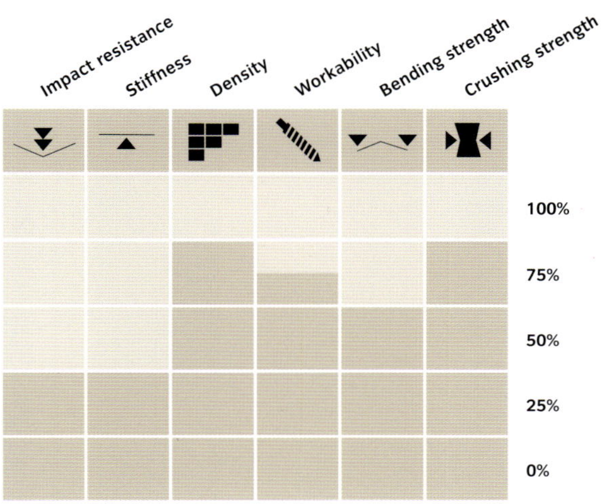

Workability describes how easy a wood is to work and whether it has a significant blunting effect on tools.

Bending strength is also known as maximum bending strength. Pressure is applied to each end of a board until it cracks.

Crushing strength is the ability of wood to withstand loads applied to the end grain, a critical test for wood used as short columns or props.

Pterocarpus indicus	Family: *Leguminosae*	**NARRA**	Hardwood

Growth

Narra is also known as red or yellow narra in the US, depending on its color, and as Solomons padauk or Papua New Guinea rosewood, depending on its country of origin. It grows to a height of 130ft (40m), with a diameter of about 7ft (2m).

Appearance

The light straw-colored sapwood is quite clearly defined from the valuable heartwood, which varies from golden yellow to brick-red. Red narra comes from slow-growing, ill-formed trees; timber from Cagayan, which is generally harder and heavier, is blood-red. The wood produces a wide range of very attractive figures from a combination of terminal parenchyma and storied elements, and irregularities such as mottle, fiddleback, ripple, and curl from wavy, interlocked, crossed, and irregular grain. The texture is moderately fine.

Properties

When seasoned, the weight averages about 41lb/ft^3 (660kg/m^3), but darker wood is heavier. The wood dries fairly slowly but reasonably well, the red requiring more care than the yellow. Narra wood is very stable in use and has medium strength in all categories. Straight-grained wood works well with both hand and machine tools, with only a slight dulling effect on cutters; irregular grain requires a reduced cutting angle for best results. Narra takes screws and nails without difficulty, glues easily, and can be polished to an excellent finish. It is resistant to fungal and insect attack, is very durable, and is resistant to preservative treatment.

Uses

Narra is extensively used locally for high-class cabinets, furniture, and joinery, including interior trim for houses, boats, and paneling. It makes a very good flooring timber. Specialized uses include sculpture and carving, cases for scientific instruments, parts for musical instruments, and sports goods. It is ideal for turnery of all kinds. It is sliced for decorative veneers for cabinets and paneling. The trade name amboyna is restricted to the highly valued and beautiful amboyna burl veneers.

Where it grows

Narra occurs throughout southern and southeast Asia. It is found extensively in the Philippines and is abundant in Cagayan, Mindoro, Palawan, and Cotabato.

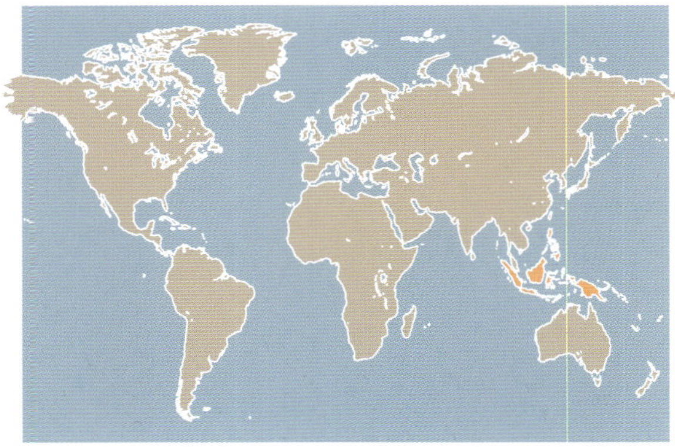

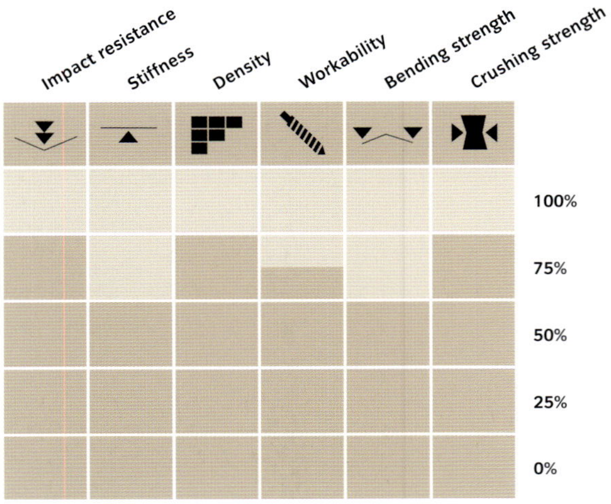

AT A GLANCE

Impact resistance is a measure of the wood's toughness. It describes its resistance to suddenly applied shock loads.

Stiffness is a measure of the wood's elasticity. It is considered in conjunction with bending strength.

Density is measured as specific gravity, the ratio of the density of a substance to that of water.

Pterocarpus soyauxii | Family: *Leguminosae* | **AFRICAN PADAUK** | Hardwood

Growth
African padauk grows to a height of about 100ft (30m) and a diameter of 2–3ft (0.6–1m), with wide buttresses and a divided bole. It is also known as camwood and barwood (UK).

Appearance
When freshly cut, the heartwood is a very distinctive, vivid blood-red color maturing to dark purple-brown with red streaks. The heartwood is sharply demarcated from the straw-colored sapwood. The grain is straight to interlocked, and the texture varies from moderate to very coarse.

Properties
African padauk weighs 40–50lb/ft^3 (640–800kg/m^3) when seasoned and dries very well with the minimum of degrade. The wood is very dense, with high bending and crushing strengths, and medium stiffness and resistance to shock loads, but it is not suitable for steam bending. It is exceptionally stable in service. The timber works well with both hand and machine tools, with only a slight blunting effect on cutting edges. It holds nails and screws without difficulty, glues easily and well, and can be polished to an excellent finish. The wood is very durable and renowned for its resistance to decay. It is also moderately resistant to preservative treatment.

Uses
African padauk is world famous as a dye wood, but it is also extensively used for high-class cabinets, furniture, and interior joinery. It is an excellent turnery wood, and is used for knife and tool handles as well as fancy turnery. It is also very good for carving and sculpture. Other specialized uses include electrical fittings and spirit levels. It is an ideal boat-building wood. In Africa it is used for making paddles, oars, and agricultural implements. Its abrasive qualities make it a good heavy-duty flooring of very attractive appearance, suitable for heavy pedestrian traffic, especially where underfloor heating is installed because it has such good dimensional stability. Selected logs are sliced for decorative veneers for cabinets and paneling.

Where it grows
This tree occurs in central and tropical west Africa.

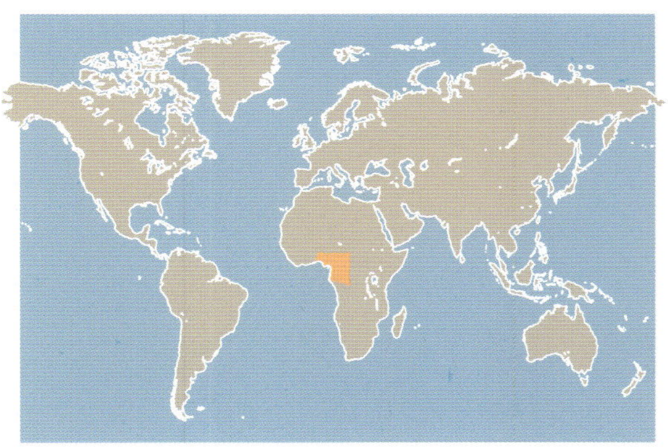

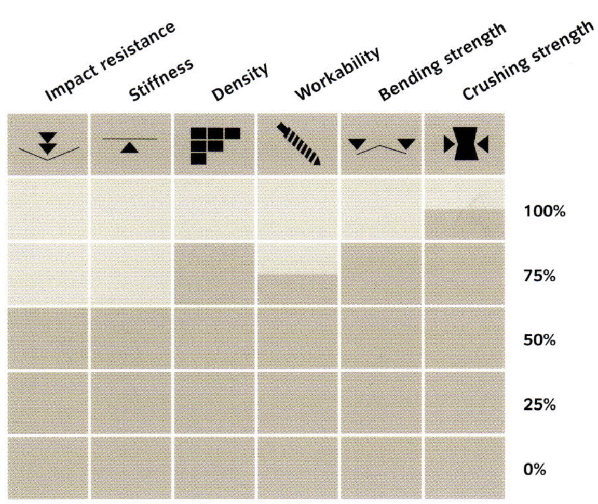

Workability describes how easy a wood is to work and whether it has a significant blunting effect on tools.

Bending strength is also known as maximum bending strength. Pressure is applied to each end of a board until it cracks.

Crushing strength is the ability of wood to withstand loads applied to the end grain, a critical test for wood used as short columns or props.

Pterygota spp.	Family: *Sterculiaceae*	**AFRICAN PTERYGOTA**	Hardwood

Growth

Pterygota bequaertii De Wild. is known as koto (Ivory Coast) and grows to a height of 75–100ft (23–30m). *P.macrocarpa* K. Schum, known as ware or awari (Ghana) and kefe or poroposo (Nigeria), grows to 120ft (37m). The diameter above the heavy buttresses is 1½–4ft (0.5–1.2m).

Appearance

Both sapwood and heartwood are creamy white, with a gray tint and a shallowly interlocked grain, with small knot clusters and a moderately coarse texture. Quarter-sawn surfaces display a flecked ray figure.

Properties

The weight of African pterygota is 33–47lb/ft^3 (530–750kg/m^3) at 12 percent moisture content. When seasoned, the average for *P.bequaertii* is 41lb/ft^3 (660kg/m^3), and the average for *P.macrocarpa* is 35lb/ft^3 (560kg/m^3). Both types dry fairly rapidly, and are prone to blue and gray fungal staining. Care is needed to avoid surface checking and extension of original shakes; cupping may also occur but distortion is usually small. There is medium movement in service. These medium-density woods possess medium bending and crushing strengths, low stiffness, and low to medium resistance to shock loads, but have a very poor steam-bending classification. The wood works easily with both hand and machine tools, provided cutting edges are kept sharp, because there is a medium blunting effect on tools. The timber glues easily, but there is a tendency for the wood to split when nailed near the edges. The grain needs filling in order to produce a good finish. This perishable species is permeable for preservative treatment.

Uses

African pterygota is used for furniture fitments, interior joinery, and carpentry, as well as for packaging, boxes, crates, and pallets. Logs are rotary cut into corestock and backing veneer for plywood, and sliced for decorative veneers. Pterygota veneers require very careful handling because they are brittle and split easily.

Where it grows
Both species of African pterygota are found in the rainforests of Nigeria and Cameroon.

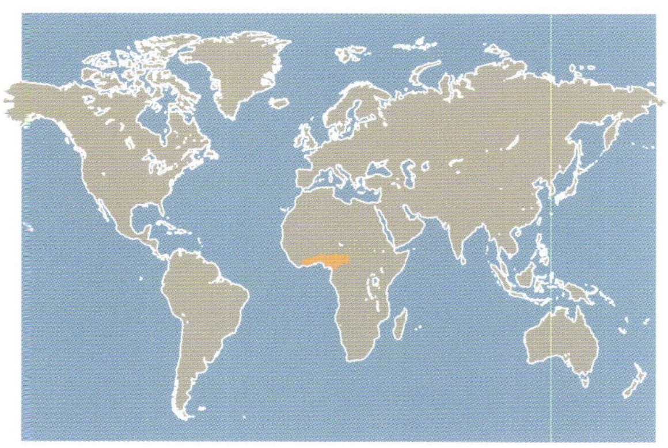

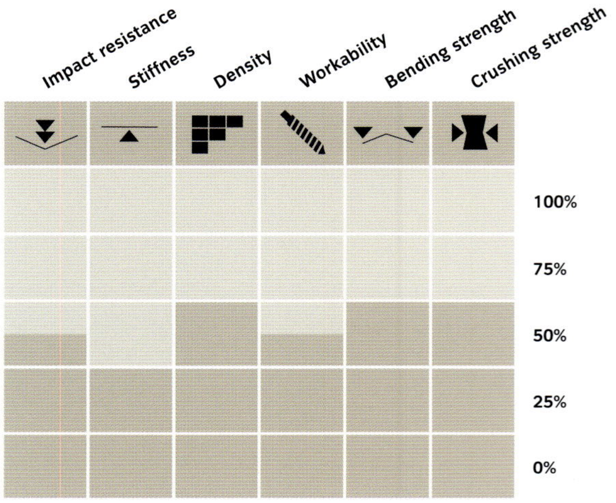

AT A GLANCE

Impact resistance is a measure of the wood's toughness. It describes its resistance to suddenly applied shock loads.

Stiffness is a measure of the wood's elasticity. It is considered in conjunction with bending strength.

Density is measured as specific gravity, the ratio of the density of a substance to that of water.

Pyrus communis | Family: *Rosaceae* | **PEAR** | Hardwood

Growth
There are numerous varieties of pear tree, all of which derive from the wild pear tree, with harsh, inedible fruit. Trees grown for commercial timber reach 30–40ft (9–12m) in height, although sometimes up to 60ft (18m), with a diameter of 1–2ft (0.3–0.6m), but often with poor stem form.

Appearance
The sapwood is pale yellow-apricot, and the heartwood varies from flesh tone to a pale pinkish brown. Very minute pores and vessel lines account for an unusual uniformity and a very fine, even, and smooth texture. The rays are faintly visible on quartered surfaces as tiny flecks of a deeper tone than the ground tissue. Grain is straight, sometimes irregular, which can produce a handsome mottled figure.

Properties
Pear weighs 43–44lb/ft^3 (690–700kg/m^3) when seasoned. It dries slowly, but with a definite tendency to warp and distort where irregular grain is present. The wood is strong, tough, and stable in use, but its strength is relatively unimportant since it is available only in small sizes. It is not used for steam bending. Pear machines well but is moderately hard to saw, and has a fairly high blunting effect on cutters, which should be kept very sharp. The wood glues well, and gives excellent results with stain and polish. It is perishable, but permeable for impregnation.

Uses
Pear has excellent turning properties, and is used for fancy goods, wooden bowls, the backs and handles of brushes, umbrella handles, and measuring instruments such as set squares and T-squares. It is excellent for carving and sculpture because of the very fine grain, and also for musical instruments such as recorders. It is stained black for violin fingerboards, and utilized for laps for polishing jewels for clocks and watches. It is sliced for decorative veneers for cabinets, paneling, marquetry, and inlay work.

Where it grows
The pear tree originated in southern Europe and western Asia, but is now widespread across Europe. Today, commercial timber comes from old orchards in Italy, Switzerland, France, Germany, and the Tyrol.

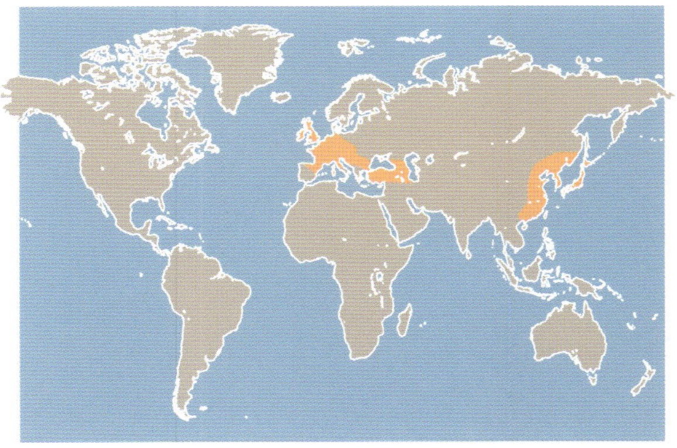

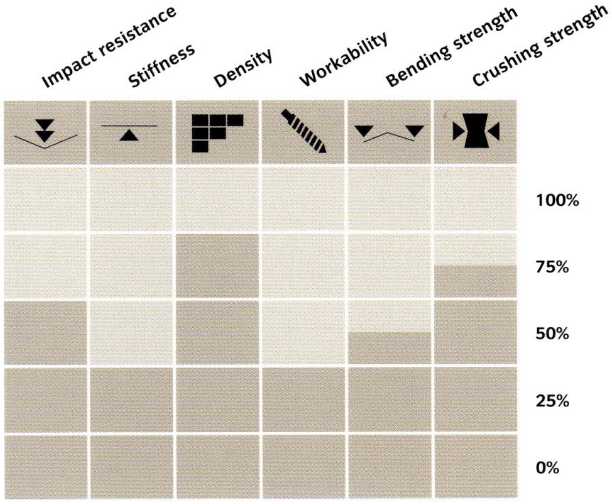

Workability describes how easy a wood is to work and whether it has a significant blunting effect on tools.

Bending strength is also known as maximum bending strength. Pressure is applied to each end of a board until it cracks.

Crushing strength is the ability of wood to withstand loads applied to the end grain, a critical test for wood used as short columns or props.

Quercus alba | Family: *Fagaceae* | **AMERICAN WHITE OAK** | Hardwood

Growth

The genus *Quercus* produces the true oaks and has more than 200 different species. The white oak is one of the finest trees of North America, both for looks and for its lumber. It grows to about 80ft (24m) in height, with a diameter of no more than 3ft (1m). It often has a wonderfully clean trunk and a generous crown. It is famous for producing blemish-free lumber of the highest quality, if perhaps a bit uninteresting by European white oak standards. Related species include *Q.prinus* (chestnut oak), *Q.lyrata* (overcup oak), and *Q.michauxii* (swamp chestnut oak).

Appearance

The heartwood of American white oak is a consistent tan to straw color, with very little sapwood. The straightness of the grain, which is so useful for woodworkers, diminishes the appearance a little, but there is still interesting patterning from the medullary rays on quarter-sawn surfaces, and the potential for flame figure on plain-sawn sides. It provides an excellent compromise between the wildness of European oak and the bland, beech-like appearance of red oak.

Properties

Not only is American white oak attractive, but it is also moderately strong and certainly has potential for bending. It is relatively heavy at $47lb/ft^3$ ($750kg/m^3$) when seasoned, but not unduly so, and is not particularly dense. It has the added advantage of being very durable, both to damp and insects, and is used extensively for outdoors projects. The texture is consistent, and somewhere between medium and coarse. Trees grown farther south tend to have wider growth rings, which make the lumber stronger. As with all oak species, the wood reacts with ferrous metals, undermining the strength of steel fittings and staining the wood.

Uses

American white oak is used in virtually every way you can imagine. From joinery, interior trim, and flooring to furniture and cabinet making, white oak has become one of the first species woodworkers turn to, especially now that it can be acquired from certified, sustainable sources. It is also used in construction, maritime work, and coach building.

Where it grows
American white oak grows down the eastern side of North America from Canada to Florida.

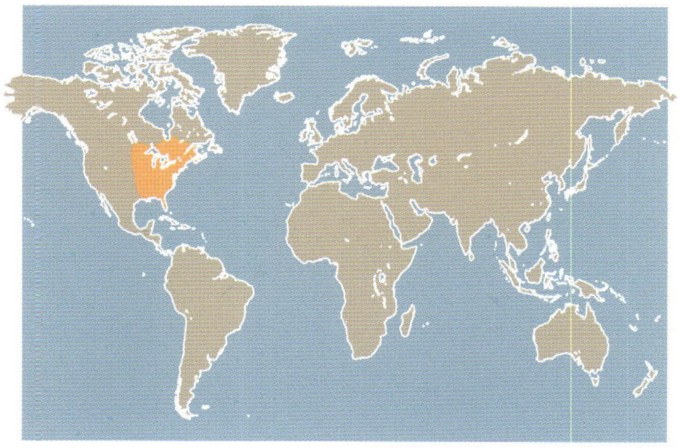

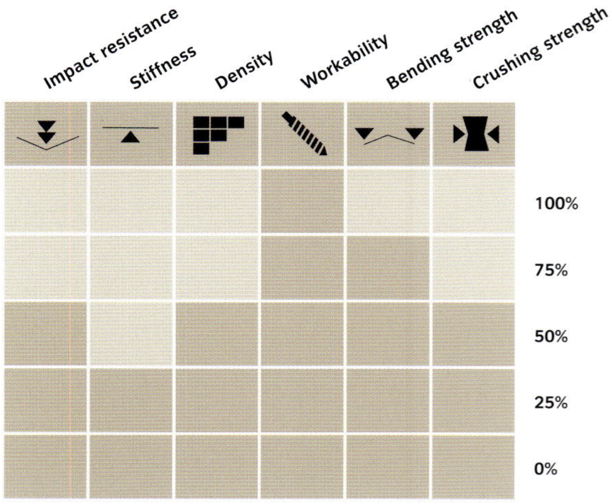

AT A GLANCE

Impact resistance is a measure of the wood's toughness. It describes its resistance to suddenly applied shock loads.

Stiffness is a measure of the wood's elasticity. It is considered in conjunction with bending strength.

Density is measured as specific gravity, the ratio of the density of a substance to that of water.

Quercus rubra | Family: *Fagaceae* | **AMERICAN RED OAK** | Hardwood

Growth

American red oak is more abundant in Canada than in the United States, and grows to a height of 60–70ft (18–21m), with a diameter of 3ft (1m). *Quercus rubra* is sometimes known as northern red oak (Canada and US), while the related species *Q.falcata* var. *falcata* is variously known as southern red oak and Spanish oak (US).

Appearance

Red oak outwardly resembles the white oak, except that the heartwood varies from biscuit-pink to reddish brown. The grain is usually straight; southern red oak is coarser textured than the northern variety. Red oak has a less attractive figure than white oak because of its larger rays. There is a considerable variation in the quality of red oak; northern red oak grows comparatively slowly and compares favorably with northern white oak, while red oak from the southern United States grows faster and produces a harder, heavier wood.

Properties

The average weight of red oak is 48lb/ft^3 (770kg/m^3) when seasoned. It dries slowly, and care is needed in air and kiln drying to prevent degrade. There is medium movement in service. This dense wood has medium bending strength and stiffness, high shock resistance and crushing strength, and a very good steam-bending classification. It usually offers a moderate blunting effect on cutting edges, which should be kept sharp. The wood requires pre-boring, and gluing results are variable, but red oak takes stain well and polishes to a good finish. The wood is nondurable, moderately resistant to preservative treatment, and unsuitable for exterior work.

Uses

Red oak is too porous for tight cooperage purposes and its lack of durability and drying problems limit its use. However, it is good for domestic flooring, furniture fitments, interior joinery, and vehicle construction. Logs are rotary cut for plywood manufacture and sliced for decorative veneers. Another related species, Persian red oak (*Q.castaneaefolia*), is impermeable and used for barrel staves.

Where it grows

American red oak is distributed across the eastern part of Canada and North America.

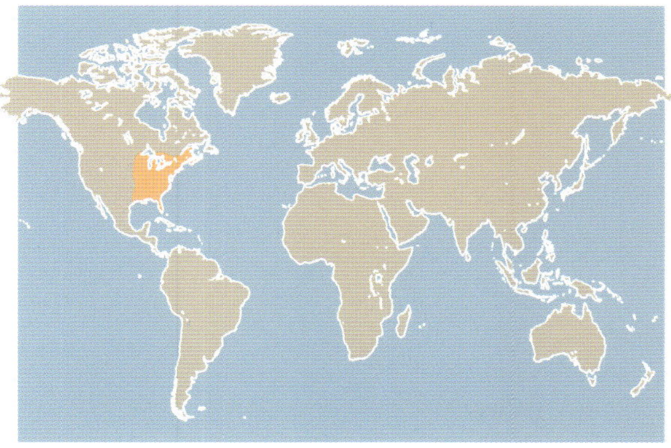

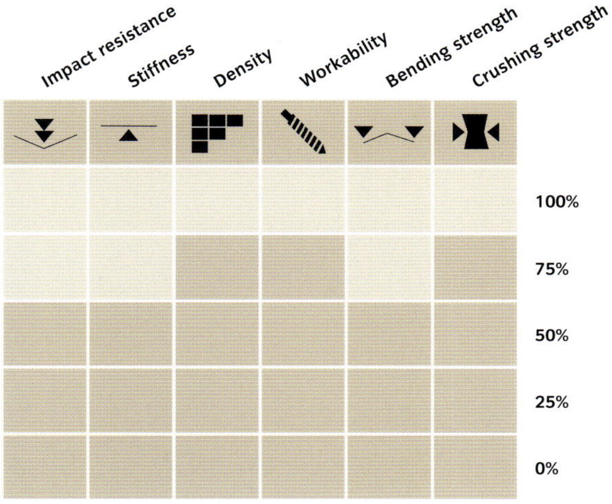

Workability describes how easy a wood is to work and whether it has a significant blunting effect on tools.

Bending strength is also known as maximum bending strength. Pressure is applied to each end of a board until it cracks.

Crushing strength is the ability of wood to withstand loads applied to the end grain, a critical test for wood used as short columns or props.

Quercus spp.	Family: *Fagaceae*	**EUROPEAN WHITE OAK**	Hardwood

Growth
The principal species producing European white oak are: *Quercus petraea*, known as sessile oak and durmast oak (UK), and English, French, Polish, and Slavonian oak, according to the country of origin; and *Q.robur*, providing pedunculate oak (UK). The related species *Q.mongolica* produces Japanese white oak. European white oaks grow to 60–100ft (18–30m) in height and 4–6ft (1.2–1.8m) in diameter.

Appearance
The sapwood is lighter than the heartwood, which is light tan or yellow-brown, usually straight grained, but often irregular or cross-grained. It has a characteristic silver-grained figure on quartered surfaces because of broad rays, and has a moderately coarse texture.

Properties
European white oak weighs between 45 and 47lb/ft³ (720 and 750kg/m³) when seasoned. Volhynian, Slavonian, and Japanese oaks are a little lighter at 41–42lb/ft³ (660–670kg/m³). European white oak air dries very slowly and displays a tendency to split and check. This dense wood has moderately high bending and crushing strengths, low stiffness and resistance to shock loads, and a very good steam-bending rating. White oak is corrosive to metals, and liable to develop blue stains in damp conditions. Machining is generally satisfactory and the wood can be brought to an excellent finish. It is durable but liable to beetle attack. The heartwood is extremely resistant to preservative treatment, although the sapwood is permeable and can be preserved satisfactorily.

Uses
One of the world's most popular timbers, white oak is ideal for furniture and cabinet making. It is used for boat building, dock and harbor work, vehicle bodywork, high-class interior and exterior joinery, and flooring. It is excellent for ecclesiastical sculpture and carving, and also tight cooperage for whisky, sherry, and brandy casks. It is sliced for decorative veneers.

Where it grows
Most white oaks occur in the temperate regions of the northern hemisphere; in warmer climates they grow in the montane forests. White oaks occur in Europe and parts of Asia, including Japan.

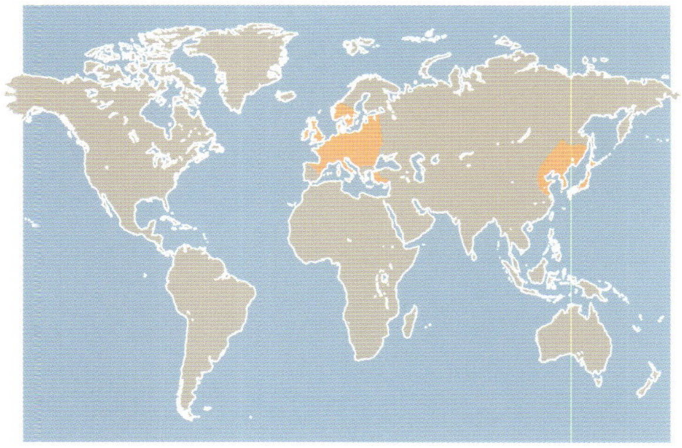

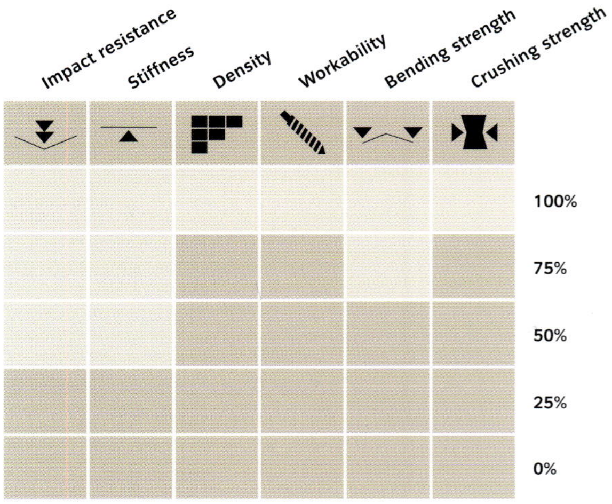

AT A GLANCE

Impact resistance is a measure of the wood's toughness. It describes its resistance to suddenly applied shock loads.

Stiffness is a measure of the wood's elasticity. It is considered in conjunction with bending strength.

Density is measured as specific gravity, the ratio of the density of a substance to that of water.

Salix spp.	Family: *Salicaceae*	**WILLOW**	Hardwood

Growth

Salix alba produces white willow and common willow (UK); *S.fragilis* provides crack willow (Europe and north Asia); *S.alba* var. *coerulea* produces cricket-bat willow and close-bark willow; and *S.nigra* provides black willow (US). The weeping willow thrives in wet acidic soil near streams and rivers. Many species are either pollarded or cut very low to induce long, slender shoots known as osiers that are used for basket- and wickerwork. Willows grow to a height of 70–90ft (21–27m), with a diameter of 3–4ft (1–1.2m).

Appearance

The timber has a white sapwood and a creamy white heartwood with a pink tinge. It is typically straight grained, with a fine, even texture.

Properties

Willow weighs an average of 28lb/ft^3 (450kg/m^3) when seasoned, although cricket-bat willow weighs only 21–26lb/ft^3 (340–420kg/m^3) when dry. Willow dries well and fairly rapidly, and degrade is minimal, but it often retains pockets of moisture and special care is needed in checking the moisture content. Crack willow splits badly in conversion. The timber is stable in use. Willow has low bending and crushing strength, very low stiffness and resistance to shock loads, and a poor steam-bending rating. It works easily by both hand and machine, with a slight blunting on tools; sharp cutters are needed to avoid wooliness. The wood takes nails and glues well, and can be stained and brought to an excellent finish. Willow is perishable and liable to attack by powder post and common furniture beetles. The heartwood is resistant to preservation treatment, but the sapwood is permeable.

Uses

Selected butts of cricket-bat willow are used for cleft cricket-bat blades. Other willows are used for artificial limbs, clogs, flooring, brake blocks in colliery winding gear, toys, sieve frames, flower trugs, vehicle bottoms, boxes, and crates. Osiers are grown for wickerwork, fruit baskets, and fruit punnets. Pollarded shoots are used for stakes and wattle hurdles. Willow is sliced for attractive moiré and mottled figured veneers for architectural paneling, and treated as harewood for marquetry work.

Where it grows

The main commercial species of willow occur in Europe, western Asia, and the United States.

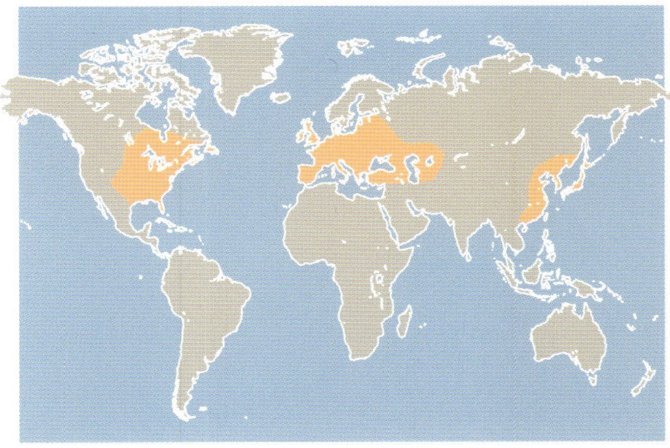

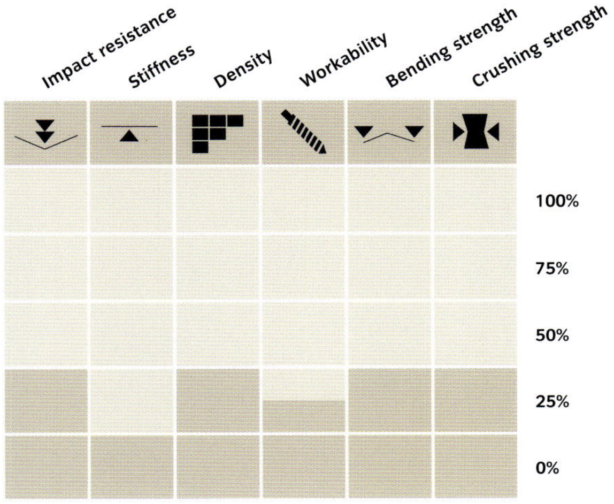

Workability describes how easy a wood is to work and whether it has a significant blunting effect on tools.

Bending strength is also known as maximum bending strength. Pressure is applied to each end of a board until it cracks.

Crushing strength is the ability of wood to withstand loads applied to the end grain, a critical test for wood used as short columns or props.

Sequoia sempervirens | Family: *Taxodiaceae* | **SEQUOIA** | Softwood

Growth

The greatest living organism on earth is *Sequoia gigantea* Decne., commonly known as the Californian big tree, giant redwood, and Wellingtonia. A protected species whose dimensions are unequalled, its wood is of no commercial value. Its cousin *S.sempervirens* Endl., however, produces the commercially traded sequoia, also known as the Californian redwood and coast redwood. This massive tree reaches 200–340ft (60–104m) in height, with a diameter of 10–15ft (3–4.5m).

Appearance

The sapwood of the sequoia is white and the heartwood is a dull reddish brown, with a distinct growth-ring figure. It is straight grained, and the texture varies from fine to coarse.

Properties

The average weight of the sequoia is 26lb/ft^3 (420kg/m^3) when seasoned. The wood air dries fairly rapidly and well with little degrade, and is stable in use. It has low bending and crushing strength, low resistance to shock loads, very low stiffness, and a poor steam-bending rating. It works easily with both hand and machine tools, but it is prone to splintering. Sharp tools are needed to reduce chip-bruising. It takes nails well, but alkaline adhesives should be avoided because they cause stains. Sequoia provides a good finish. It is invaluable for use in exposed situations for its durability, and is resistant to preservative treatment.

Uses

The excellent durability of sequoia makes it ideal for wooden pipes, flumes, tanks, vats, silos, and slats in water-cooling towers. It is also used for coffins. It is extensively employed for posts, interior and exterior joinery, organ pipes, exterior cladding and shingles, and the windows and doors of buildings. The cinnamon-colored, very thick bark is used in the manufacture of fiberboard. Logs are rotary cut for plywood faces, and selected logs are sliced for highly valued veneers. The extremely attractive burls are marketed as vavona burl.

Where it grows

Sequoia occurs in the United States in southern Oregon and northern California.

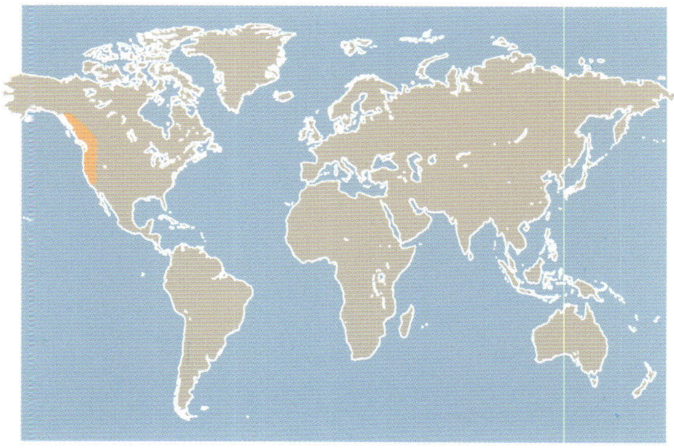

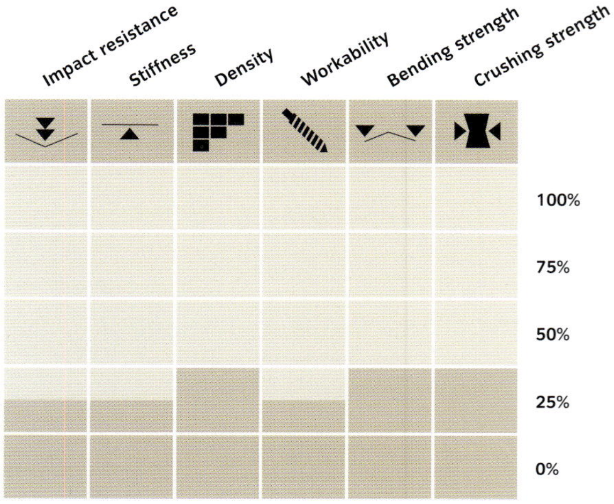

AT A GLANCE

Impact resistance is a measure of the wood's toughness. It describes its resistance to suddenly applied shock loads.

Stiffness is a measure of the wood's elasticity. It is considered in conjunction with bending strength.

Density is measured as specific gravity, the ratio of the density of a substance to that of water.

Shorea spp. | Family: *Dipterocarpaceae* | **RED MERANTI/SERAYA/LAUAN** | Hardwood

Growth

Meranti, seraya, and lauan vary in color and density and are organized into two groups as follows: a light red group comprising light red meranti, light red seraya, and white lauan; and a dark red group comprising dark red meranti, dark red seraya, and red lauan. These trees reach 200–230ft (60–70m) in height and 3–5ft (1–1.5m) in diameter.

Appearance

The following details about appearance can only be very general because of the number of different species included in the light red and dark red groups. However, in the first group, the color is generally pale pink to red; in the second group, it is medium to dark red-brown with white resin streaks. Both have interlocked grain and a rather coarse texture.

Properties

The light red timbers of the first group have an average weight of 34lb/ft^3 (540kg/m^3), while the dark red woods of the second group weigh about 42lb/ft^3 (670kg/m^3) on average when seasoned. Drying is usually fairly rapid, without serious degrade. Both timbers are stable in use, but the first light red group is much weaker than the darker red timbers. Both types have medium bending and crushing strengths, low stiffness and shock resistance, and a poor steam-bending rating. They work well with both hand and machine tools, hold screws and nails satisfactorily, can be glued easily, and produce a good finish when filled. The light red timbers are nondurable, and the dark red group are moderately durable and resistant to impregnation.

Uses

The light red timbers are used for interior joinery, light structural work, domestic flooring, cheap furniture, and interior framing. The dark red group is used for similar purposes, plus exterior joinery, cladding, shop fitting, and boat building. Logs of both groups are used for plywood manufacture and sliced for decorative veneers for cabinets and paneling.

Where it grows

A large number of species of the genus *Shorea* occur in southeast Asia. Meranti grows in Malaya, Sarawak, and Indonesia; seraya in Sabah; and lauan in the Philipp nes.

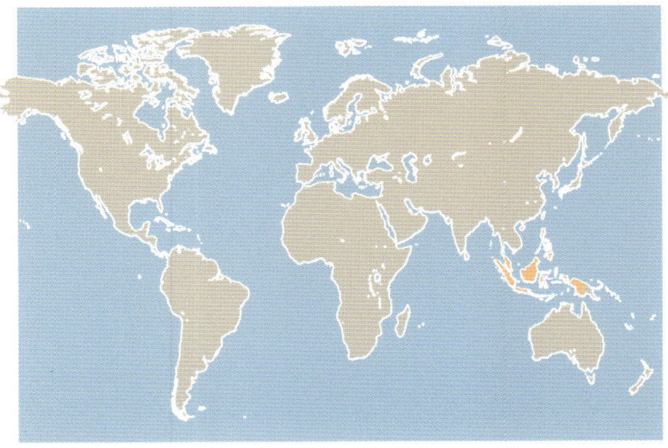

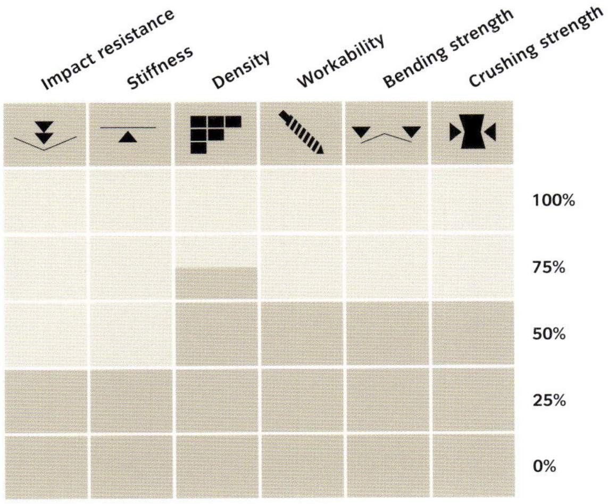

Workability describes how easy a wood is to work and whether it has a significant blunting effect on tools.

Bending strength is also known as maximum bending strength. Pressure is applied to each end of a board until it cracks.

Crushing strength is the ability of wood to withstand loads applied to the end grain, a critical test for wood used as short columns or props.

Shorea spp. | Family: _Dipterocarpaceae_ | **WHITE/YELLOW MERANTI/SERAYA** | Hardwood

Growth
White meranti occurs in west Malaysia, Sarawak, Brunei, and Sabah, and is also known as lun and lun puteh in Sarawak, and as melapi in Sabah. Note that white meranti is not the equivalent of white seraya or white lauan. Yellow meranti of Malaysia is also known as meranti damar hitam, and yellow meranti of Brunei and Sarawak as lun and lun kuning. Yellow seraya of Sabah is known as seraya kacha and selangan kacha. Trees grow to 200ft (60m) in height and 3–5ft (1–1.5m) in diameter.

Appearance
The texture is moderately coarse but even. Yellow meranti and yellow seraya sapwood is lighter in color and distinct from the heartwood, which is light yellow-brown and matures to a dull yellow-brown. They have shallowly interlocked grain and moderately coarse texture. The sapwood of white meranti is well defined, and the heartwood matures to a much lighter golden brown.

Properties
Yellow meranti and yellow seraya weigh 30–42lb/ft^3 (480–670kg/m^3), and white meranti weighs 41lb/ft^3 (660kg/m^3) when seasoned. Yellow meranti and yellow seraya dry slowly but well, apart from a tendency to cup, and brittleheart is sometimes present. They have low bending strength and shock resistance, medium crushing strength, very low stiffness, and a moderate steam-bending rating. White meranti dries without serious degrade, has medium strength in all categories, and a very poor steam-bending rating. All three timbers are stable in use. Yellow meranti and yellow seraya work satisfactorily, but the silica in white meranti has a severe blunting effect on tools, making tipped saws a necessity. They all hold nails and screws well, glue easily, and when filled provide a good finish. They are moderately durable and the sapwood is permeable.

Uses
Both yellow and white timbers are used for light construction, interior joinery, furniture, and flooring. White meranti is also used for exterior joinery, ship and boat planking, shop fitting, and carriage framing. Logs are cut for plywood and veneers.

Where it grows
The name meranti is applied to timbers from Malaysia, Sarawak, and Indonesia; seraya refers to timber from Sabah.

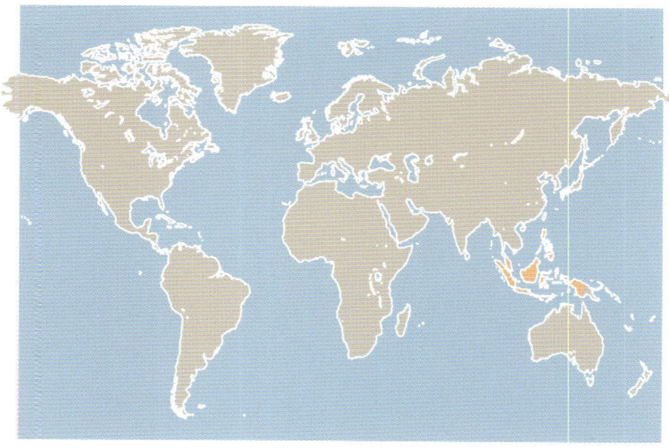

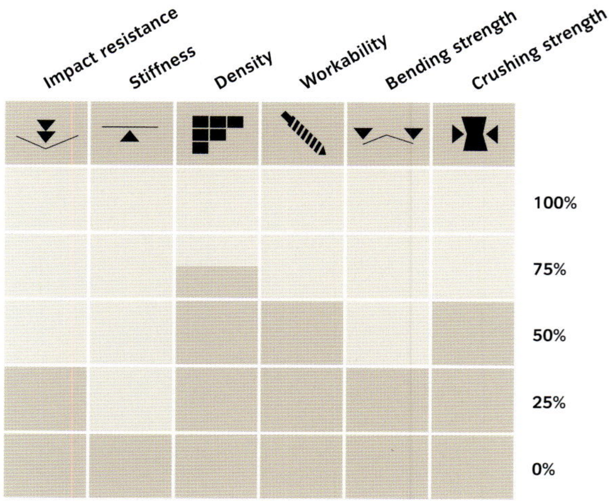

AT A GLANCE

Impact resistance is a measure of the wood's toughness. It describes its resistance to suddenly applied shock loads.

Stiffness is a measure of the wood's elasticity. It is considered in conjunction with bending strength.

Density is measured as specific gravity, the ratio of the density of a substance to that of water.

***Swietenia* spp.** | Family: *Meliaceae* | **AMERICAN MAHOGANY** | Hardwood

Growth
Cuban or Spanish mahognay (*Swietenia mahoganii* Jacq.) was brought to Europe by the Spanish in the late 16th century. Since the 18th century it has been the most cherished cabinet wood in the world and is now rare. Forest trees grow to 150ft (45m) in height, but plantation trees average 100ft (30m) with a diameter of 4–6ft (1.2–1.8m). Today, commercial supplies are of *S.macrophylla* King.

Appearance
The sapwood is yellowish white; the heartwood varies from pale red to dark red-brown in heavier timber. It is mostly straight grained, but pieces with interlocked or irregular grain produce a highly valued figure on quartered surfaces. It has a moderately fine to medium uniform texture.

Properties
The average weight of American mahogany is 34lb/ft^3 (540kg/m^3) when seasoned. The wood can be air or kiln dried rapidly and well without any risk of warping or checking, but tension wood and gelatinous fibers can result in high longitudinal shrinkage. The timber is stable in use. It has low bending strength, very low stiffness and shock resistance, medium crushing strength, and a moderate steam-bending rating. This is one of the best woods to use with either hand or machine tools, and sharp cutting edges will overcome wooliness. American mahogany holds nails and screws well, glues satisfactorily, and gives an excellent finish. Liable to insect attack, this timber is durable and extremely resistant to preservative treatment.

Uses
American mahogany goes into high-class cabinets and reproduction furniture, chairs, paneling, interior joinery, domestic flooring, exterior joinery, boat building, pianos, and burial caskets. It is excellent for carving, engravers' blocks, engineers' patterns, molds, and dies. It is cut for plywood and sliced to produce a wide range of fiddleback, blister, roe, striped, curl, and mottled figures in veneer for cabinets and paneling.

Where it grows
American mahogany occurs from southern Mexico south along the Atlantic coast from Belize to Panama, including Colombia, Venezuela, Peru, Bolivia, and Brazil. The timber is named after its country of origin.

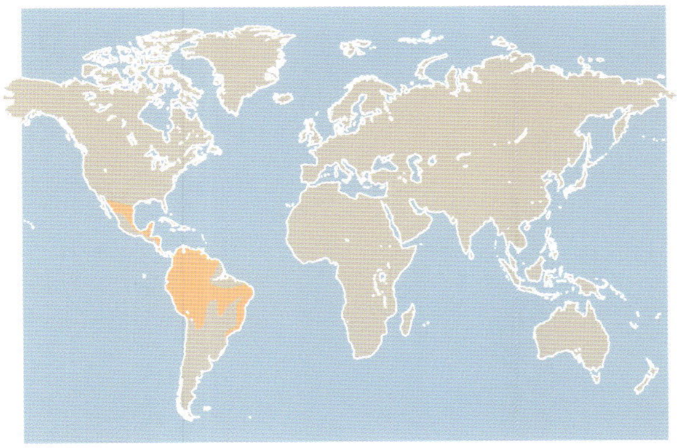

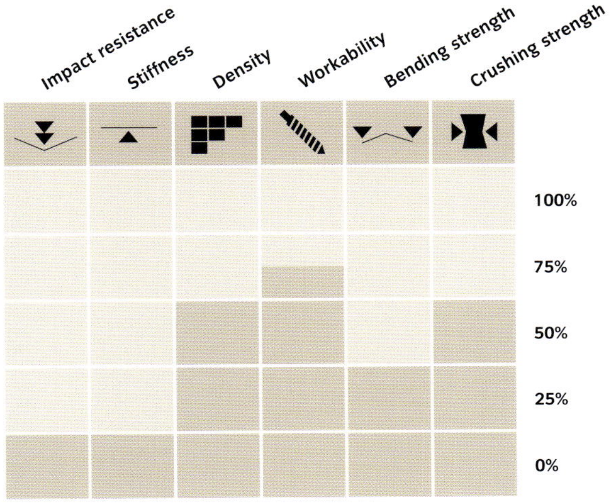

Workability describes how easy a wood is to work and whether it has a significant blunting effect on tools.

Bending strength is also known as maximum bending strength. Pressure is applied to each end of a board until it cracks.

Crushing strength is the ability of wood to withstand loads applied to the end grain, a critical test for wood used as short columns or props.

Tabebuia spp. | Family: *Bignoniaceae* | **IPE** | Hardwood

Growth

Known most commonly as ipe, but also as lapacho, ironwood, greenheart, and many other names, this tall tree, which reaches upward of 150ft (45m) in height, represents a group of species that includes *Tabebuia heptaphylla*, *T.chrysanthak*, *T.serratifolia,* and *T.guayacan*, as well as *T.ipe* itself. The common name of greenheart does not connect this species to the more famous greenheart, *Ocotea rodiaei*.

Appearance

Ipe is not a particularly attractive lumber, having an awkward stripey figure and a nondescript chocolate-brown color, although the range of colors does vary from light brown to darker bands. The sapwood is yellow-white, but because there are so many species grouped within the ipe collection of timbers, the color of both sapwood and heartwood cannot be relied upon for consistency.

Properties

Ipe is a very heavy timber, weighing up to 75lb/ft³ (1200kg/m³) when seasoned. It is very durable in every way, and is stable once dry, with seasoning moderately easy and quick. The species is generally counted as strong and hard. The grain is essentially straight, but also interlocking, so ipe can be a difficult lumber to use, especially with its uneven texture that ranges from fine to medium, and that is coarse at times. The fibers tend to tear badly when the wood is sawn across the grain, and it is fairly brittle. The dust can also irritate, and the lumber can dull cutting blades quickly.

Uses

Ipe is used most extensively in construction work, especially for maritime purposes, but is also employed for flooring, decking, and handles. It is not particularly popular for decorative work.

Where it grows

Ipe is randomly found across South America and Central America, plus the Caribbean.

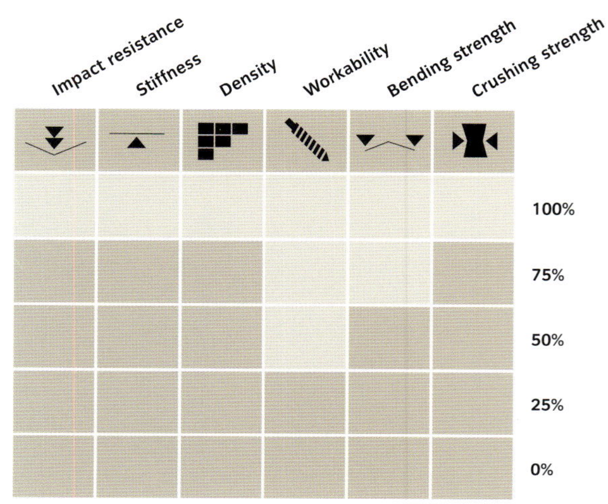

AT A GLANCE

Impact resistance is a measure of the wood's toughness. It describes its resistance to suddenly applied shock loads.

Stiffness is a measure of the wood's elasticity. It is considered in conjunction with bending strength.

Density is measured as specific gravity, the ratio of the density of a substance to that of water.

Taxus baccata | Family: *Taxaceae* | **YEW** | Softwood

Growth
Yew grows to a height of 40–50ft (12–15m), with a short twisted or fluted bole, and often consists of several vertical shoots that have fused together to form multiple stems.

Appearance
The heartwood varies from orange-brown streaked with darker purple, to purplish brown with darker mauve or brown patches, and clusters of in-growing bark. The irregular growth pattern produces wood of varying ring widths that combine with narrow widths of dense latewood to give a highly decorative appearance.

Properties
Yew is among the heaviest and most durable of softwood timbers, and weighs 42lb/ft^3 (670kg/m^3) when seasoned. The wood dries fairly rapidly and well, with little degrade if care is taken to avoid shakes developing or existing shakes from opening. Distortion is negligible and it is stable in use. This hard, compact, and elastic wood has medium bending and crushing strength, with low stiffness and resistance to shock loads. Straight-grained air-dried yew is one of the best softwoods for steam bending, even though it is inclined to check during drying. It works well in most hand and machine operations, but when irregular, curly, or cross grain is present, it tears easily. Nailing requires pre-boring and the oiliness of the wood sometimes interferes with gluing, but it stains satisfactorily and provides an excellent finish. Yew is durable, but not immune from attack by the common furniture beetle; it is resistant to preservative treatment.

Uses
For many centuries, yew was prized for the English archer's longbow. It is an excellent turnery and carving wood, and is used for reproduction furniture making, interior and exterior joinery, garden furniture, fences, and gate posts. It is the traditional wood for Windsor chair bentwood parts. It is sliced for highly decorative veneers and burls.

Where it grows
The yew is widely distributed through Algeria, Asia Minor, the Caucasus, northern Iran, the Himalayas, Burma, and Europe.

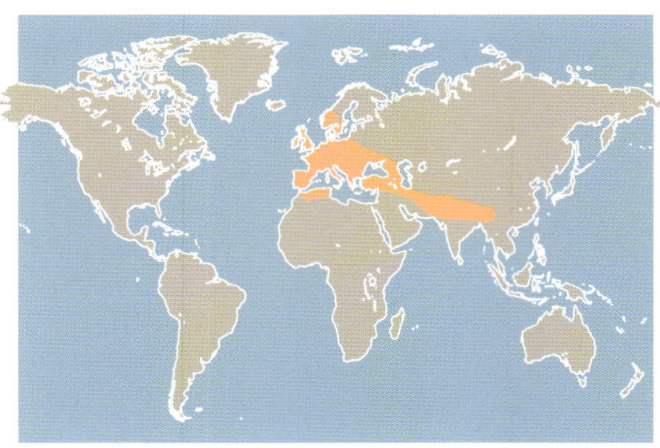

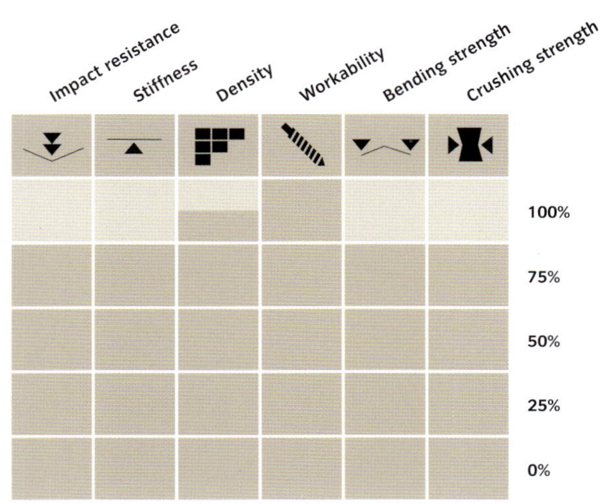

Workability describes how easy a wood is to work and whether it has a significant blunting effect on tools.

Bending strength is also known as maximum bending strength. Pressure is applied to each end of a board until it cracks.

Crushing strength is the ability of wood to withstand loads applied to the end grain, a critical test for wood used as short columns or props.

Tectona grandis | Family: *Verbenaceae* | **TEAK** | Hardwood

Growth

In the most favorable locations, *Tectona grandis* grows to between 130 and 150ft (40 and 45m) in height, with a diameter of approximately 6–8ft (1.8–2.4m). However, most teak averages at just 30–35ft (9–11m) in height, with a diameter of about 3–5ft (1–1.5m).

Appearance

True Burma teak has a narrow, pale yellow-brown sapwood and a dark golden brown heartwood, darkening on exposure to mid- or dark brown. Other types of teak have a rich brown background color with dark chocolate-brown markings. The grain is mostly straight in Burma teak, and wavy in Indian teak from Malabar. The texture is coarse and uneven and it feels oily to the touch.

Properties

Teak weighs 38–43lb/ft^3 (610–690kg/m^3), averaging 40lb/ft^3 (640kg/m^3) when seasoned. The wood dries rather slowly, and there is small movement in service. Teak has medium bending strength, low stiffness and shock resistance, high crushing strength, and a moderate steam-bending classification. It works reasonably well with both hand and machine tools, and has a moderately severe blunting effect on cutting edges, which must be kept sharp. Machine dust can be a severe irritant. Pre-boring is required for nailing, it glues well, and can be brought to an excellent finish. The timber is very durable.

Uses

Teak enjoys a well-deserved reputation for its strength and durability, stability in fluctuating atmospheres, and its excellent decorative appearance. Its vast number of uses include furniture and cabinet making, decking for ship and boat building, deck houses, handrails, bulwarks, hatches, hulls, planking, oars, and masts. It is also used for high-class joinery for doors, staircases, and paneling, and externally for dock and harbor work, bridges, sea defenses, and garden furniture. It makes a very attractive flooring. Good chemical resistance enables it to be used for laboratory benches, fume ducts, and vats. It is cut for all grades of plywood and decorative veneers.

Where it grows

Teak is indigenous to Burma and grows extensively throughout India, Thailand, Indonesia, and Java. It has also been introduced into Malaysia, Borneo, the Philippines, tropical Africa, and Central America.

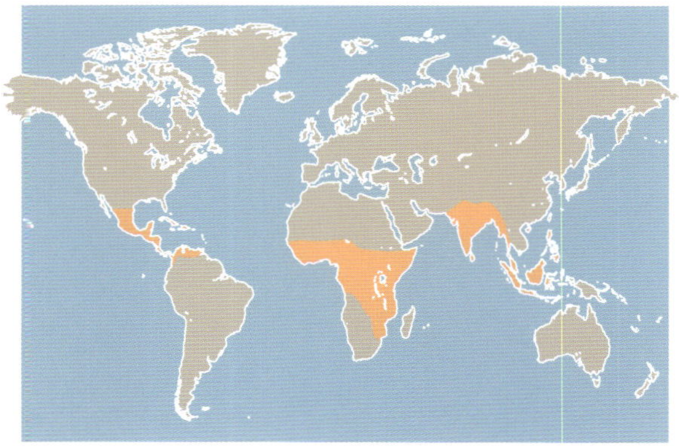

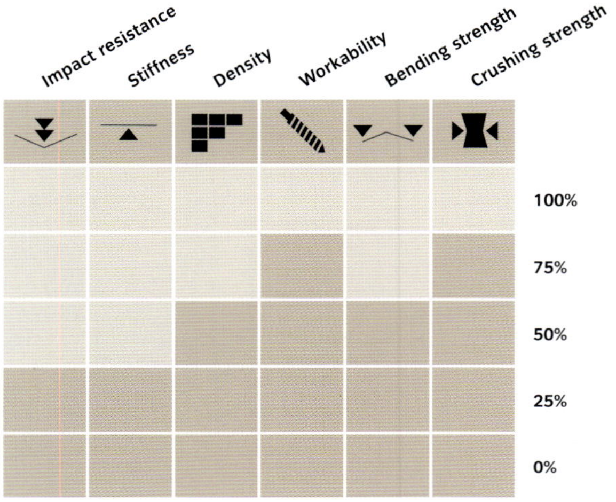

AT A GLANCE

Impact resistance is a measure of the wood's toughness. It describes its resistance to suddenly applied shock loads.

Stiffness is a measure of the wood's elasticity. It is considered in conjunction with bending strength.

Density is measured as specific gravity, the ratio of the density of a substance to that of water.

Terminalia bialata	Family: *Combretaceae*	**INDIAN SILVER GRAYWOOD**	Hardwood

Growth

The species *Terminalia bialata* produces a pale wood known as white chuglam, as well as the darker, highly figured Indian silver graywood. The tree attains a height of 100–160ft (30–48m), with a diameter of 2½–5ft (0.8–1.5m).

Appearance

The sapwood, which may comprise the whole tree, is a uniform grayish yellow in color—this is white chuglam. In other logs, there is a false heartwood of gray to smoky yellow-brown, or sometimes olive to nut-brown, banded with darker brown streaks. This highly ornamental marbled effect is described as Indian silver graywood. The grain in both is usually straight, but sometimes wavy. The texture is medium.

Properties

T.bialata averages 42lb/ft^3 (670kg/m^3) in weight when seasoned. The wood air dries very well, with some tendency for end splits and checks to develop. Conversion while the timber is green and prompt storage under cover for air drying will prevent appreciable degrade. Kiln drying is trouble free. There is small movement in service. This dense timber has medium strength in all categories, but a poor steam-bending classification. It works easily with hand and machine tools, and produces a smooth finish on straight-grained surfaces. It holds nails and screws well, can be glued satisfactorily, and can be brought to a good finish with stains and polishes. The figured timber is moderately durable. The sapwood is liable to attack by powder post beetle. Indian silver graywood is extremely resistant, and white chuglam moderately resistant to preservative treatment.

Uses

The highly figured Indian silver graywood is used for all kinds of decorative work for furniture, cabinets, and high-class joinery, including decorative paneling in public buildings, railway coaches, and ocean liners. The plainer white chuglam is used in India for flooring and interior joinery, including staircases, as well as mathematical instruments, boat fittings, plain furniture, edge lippings, and tea chests. Selected logs of Indian silver graywood are sliced for highly decorative veneers.

Where it grows

Terminalia bialata occurs in the Andaman Islands.

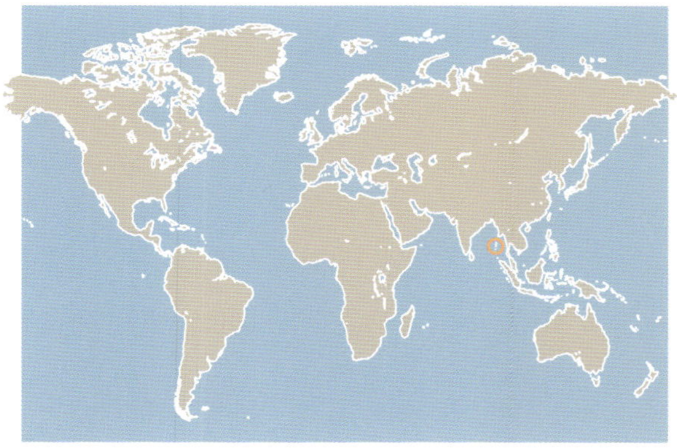

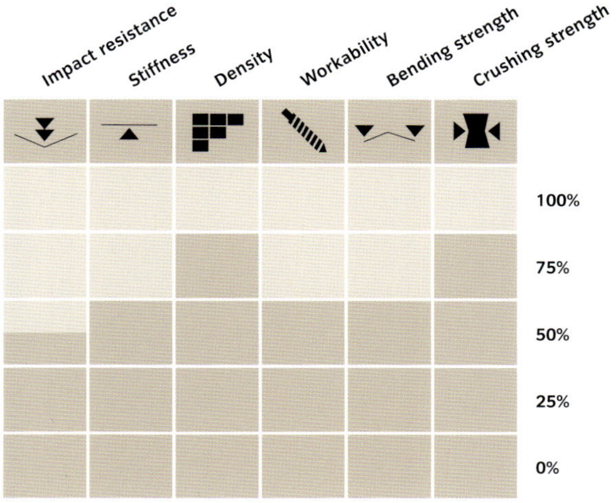

Workability describes how easy a wood is to work and whether it has a significant blunting effect on tools.

Bending strength is also known as maximum bending strength. Pressure is applied to each end of a board until it cracks.

Crushing strength is the ability of wood to withstand loads applied to the end grain, a critical test for wood used as short columns or props.

Terminalia ivorensis | Family: *Combretaceae* | **IDIGBO** | Hardwood

Growth

Idigbo grows to 150ft (45m) in height and a diameter of 3–4ft (1–1.2m), with a clean cylindrical bole for 70ft (21m) above the broad, blunt buttresses. It is also known as framiré (Ivory Coast) and emeri (Ghana).

Appearance

There is little distinction between the sapwood and heartwood, which are plain pale yellow to light pinkish brown. The grain is straight to slightly irregular, with a medium to fairly coarse, uneven texture.

Properties

The weight of idigbo is variable due to lightweight brittleheart, especially in large overmature logs. It averages 34lb/ft^3 (540kg/m^3) when seasoned, and dries rapidly and well with little distortion. There is small movement in service. The wood has medium density, low bending strength, very low stiffness, medium crushing strength, very low shock resistance, and a very poor steam-bending classification. The wood works easily with both hand and machine tools, with little dulling effect on cutting edges, but is prone to pick up the grain on quartered surfaces. It has good screw- and nail-holding properties, glues well, takes stain readily, and, when filled, provides a good finish. The timber contains a natural yellow dye that may leach out and stain fabrics in moist conditions; also its high tannin content will cause blue mineral stains to appear if the wood comes into contact with iron or iron compounds in the damp. It is slightly acidic and will corrode ferrous metals. The sapwood is liable to attack by powder post beetle; the heartwood is durable and extremely resistant to preservative treatment.

Uses

Idigbo is very useful for furniture and fine interior and exterior joinery, such as window and door frames, cladding, shingles, carpentry, and building construction. It makes a good domestic flooring. Logs are rotary cut for plywood and sliced for decorative paneling veneers.

Where it grows

Idigbo grows in central west Africa, including equatorial Guinea, Sierra Leone, Liberia, the Ivory Coast, Ghana, and southern Nigeria.

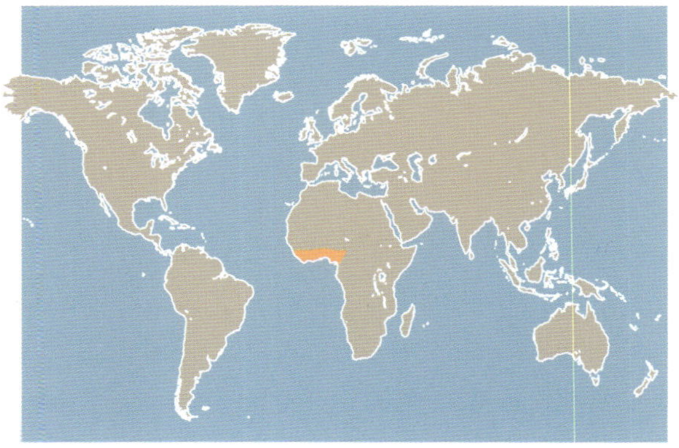

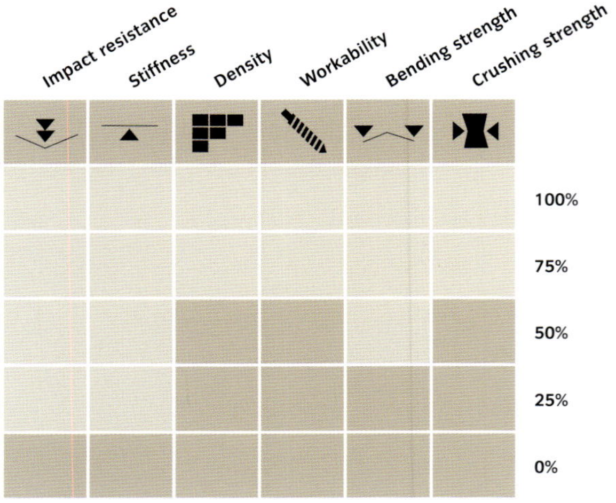

AT A GLANCE

Impact resistance is a measure of the wood's toughness. It describes its resistance to suddenly applied shock loads.

Stiffness is a measure of the wood's elasticity. It is considered in conjunction with bending strength.

Density is measured as specific gravity, the ratio of the density of a substance to that of water.

Terminalia spp.	Family: *Combretaceae*	**INDIAN LAUREL**	Hardwood

Growth

Indian laurel is derived from three main species: *Terminalia alata* Roth., *T.coriacea* W & A., and *T.crenulata* Roth. It is also known as taukkyan (Burma), and as asna, mutti, and sain (India). Indian laurel is not a true laurel (*Laurus spp.*). It reaches a height of 100ft (30m) with a straight bole of 40–50ft (12–15m) and a diameter of 3ft (1m).

Appearance

The sapwood of Indian laurel is reddish white and is sharply defined from the heartwood, which varies from light brown with very few markings or finely streaked with darker lines, to dark brown banded with irregular darker brown streaks. The grain is fairly straight to irregular and coarse textured.

Properties

The weight of Indian laurel averages about 53lb/ft³ (850kg/m³) when seasoned. It is a highly refractory timber to dry, and is prone to surface checking, warping, and splitting; it must be dried slowly to avoid degrade. There is small movement in service. It is very dense, has medium bending strength, shock resistance, and stiffness, high crushing strength, and a poor steam-bending classification. It is rather difficult to work with hand tools and moderately hard to machine, especially when interlocked grain is present. It is difficult to nail but holds screws well and glues firmly. The wood requires filling for a good finish, which is best achieved with oil or wax. The sapwood is subject to attack by the powder post beetle but the heartwood is moderately durable and resistant to preservative treatment. The sapwood is permeable for treatment.

Uses

This is one of India's most valuable woods, used extensively for furniture and cabinet making, and high-class interior joinery for paneling, doors, and staircases. It is an excellent turnery wood for tool handles, brush backs, and police batons. It is used in India for boat building and, when treated, for posts and pit props, and harbor and dock work. Logs are sliced into flat-cut or quartered highly decorative veneers for cabinets and paneling.

Where it grows

Indian laurel occurs throughout India, west Pakistan, Bangladesh, and Burma.

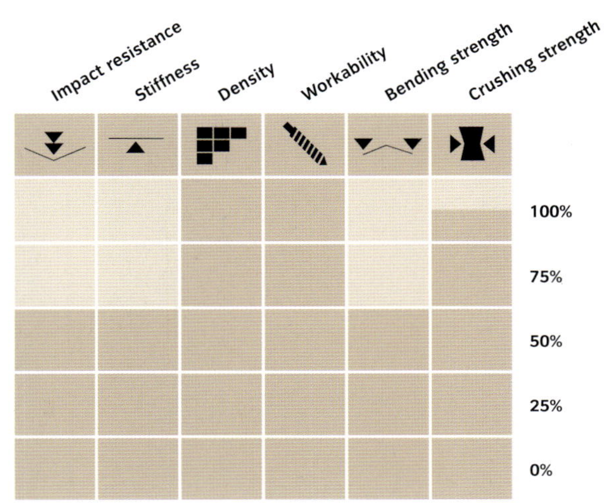

Workability describes how easy a wood is to work and whether it has a significant blunting effect on tools.

Bending strength is also known as maximum bending strength. Pressure is applied to each end of a board until it cracks.

Crushing strength is the ability of wood to withstand loads applied to the end grain, a critical test for wood used as short columns or props.

Terminalia superba | Family: *Combretaceae* | **AFARA/LIMBA** | Hardwood

Growth
The pale yellow-brown to straw-colored heartwood is known as light afara or light limba. Heartwood with gray-black streaked markings is known as dark afara, dark limba, or limba bariolé, and as korina in the US. It reaches a height of 150ft (45m) and about 5ft (1.5m) in diameter. Above the buttress the bole is straight and cylindrical for 90ft (27m).

Appearance
The sapwood and heartwood of this tree are uniformly pale straw to light yellow-brown, but some logs have an irregular dark heart with gray-brown or almost black streaks and markings. The timber is straight and close grained, but often wavy. The texture is moderately coarse but even.

Properties
The weight is 30–40lb/ft³ (480–640kg/m³), averaging 34lb/ft³ (540kg/m³) when seasoned. This medium-density timber has low bending strength and stiffness, but medium crushing strength. Care is needed in air drying because there is a tendency for the heart- or brashwood to split and shake, but kilning is rapid with little or no degrade and there is only small movement in service. The wood works well with both hand and machine tools, but a low cutter angle is required when planing irregular grain to prevent tearing. It glues well, provides an excellent finish when filled, and requires pre-boring for nailing or screwing. The wood is nondurable, and the sapwood is liable to attack by the powder post beetle and blue sap stain. The heartwood has moderate resistance to preservative treatment.

Uses
The light-colored wood is widely used in furniture production and interior joinery, shop and office fitting, and coffins. The blackish streaked heartwood produces very attractive face veneers for paneling and furniture, flush doors, and marquetry. It is also a good turnery wood. Both are used for plywood manufacture. The grayish-brown type is used for corestock and light construction work, such as school equipment.

Where it grows
This tree occurs throughout west Africa, from Cameroon to Sierra Leone.

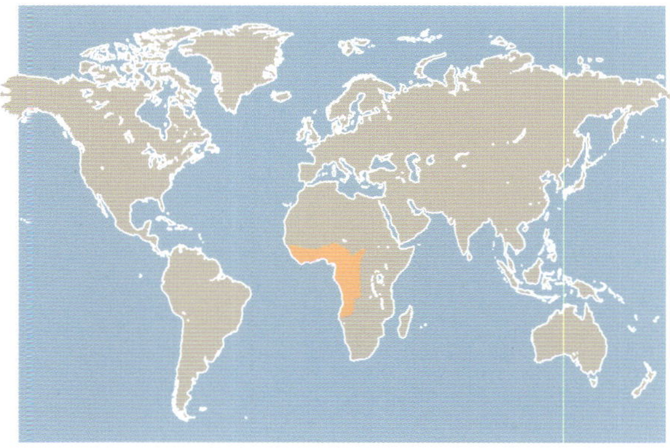

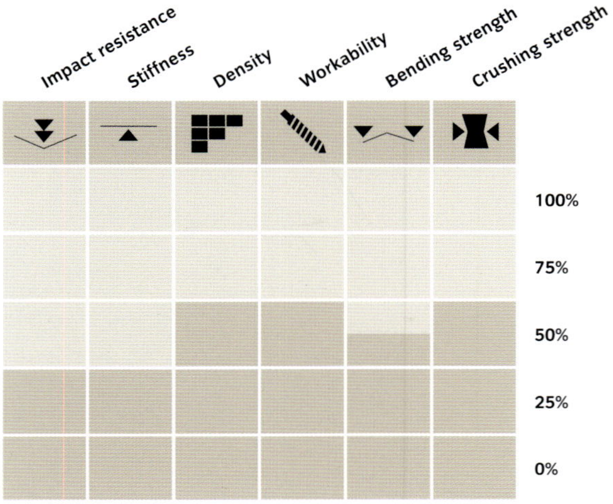

AT A GLANCE

Impact resistance is a measure of the wood's toughness. It describes its resistance to suddenly applied shock loads.

Stiffness is a measure of the wood's elasticity. It is considered in conjunction with bending strength.

Density is measured as specific gravity, the ratio of the density of a substance to that of water.

Tetraclinis articulata	Family: *Cupressaceae*	**THUYA BURL**	Softwood

Growth

Unusually this species is famed not for its lumber, but for burls that grow on the rootstock. The tree itself rarely grows very high, because cutting or fire stunts its growth but stimulates burls to develop underground. These are then cut away from the root system. An evergreen tree, it tends to grow in dry regions, and may reach 50ft (15m) in height, but not often. Thuya burl can be harvested as coppice, but is now under great threat in the small areas where it grows.

Appearance

Most burls tend to be random in their patterning, with swirls of varying sizes and density. Thuya burl also varies in character, but can be more regular, rather like a dark, overdeveloped bird's eye maple. It is golden brown in color, almost red sometimes, with darker pips or spots. Some of the most common patternings that occur are known as tiger, panther, peacock, and parsley, describing the style of mottling, spiral, or ripple in the wood.

Uses

Thuya burl is now only available as a veneer, such is its rarity. It is not used in any structural way, although the few solid pieces that very rarely appear on the market are prized by turners for making ornaments, bowls, and boxes. As a veneer, it is used in the production of high-quality furniture and cabinets.

Where it grows

Thuya burl grows in north Africa and southern Spain.

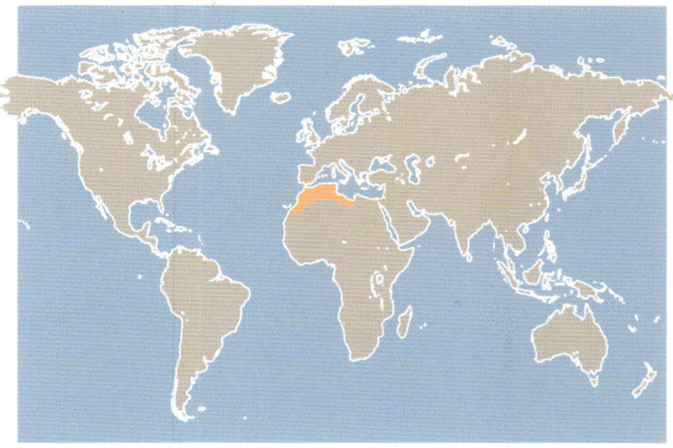

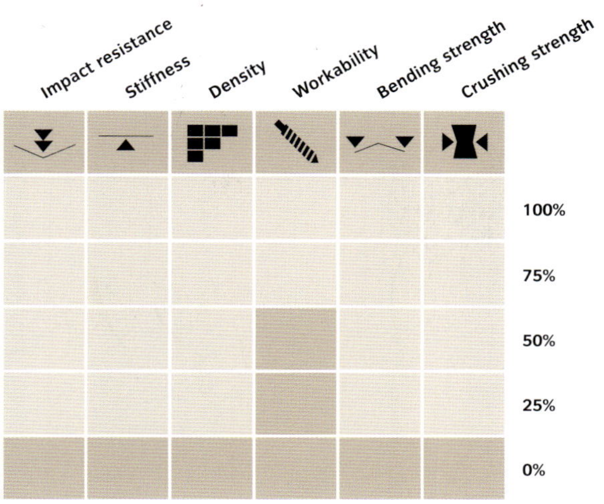

Workability describes how easy a wood is to work and whether it has a significant blunting effect on tools.

Bending strength is also known as maximum bending strength. Pressure is applied to each end of a board until it cracks.

Crushing strength is the ability of wood to withstand loads applied to the end grain, a critical test for wood used as short columns or props.

Thuya plicata | Family: *Cupressaceae* | **WESTERN RED CEDAR** | Softwood

Growth

The western red cedar is also commonly known as giant arbor vitae (US), red cedar (Canada), and British Columbia red cedar (UK). It grows to a height of 150–250ft (45–76m), with a diameter of 3–8ft (1–2.4m). Despite its common name, it is not a true cedar (*Cedrus spp*).

Appearance

The sapwood is white, in contrast with the heartwood, which varies from dark chocolate-brown in the center to a salmon-pink outer zone that matures to a uniform reddish brown. Once dry and exposed, the timber weathers to silver gray, which makes it a particularly attractive prospect for shingles, weatherboard, and timber buildings. The wood is non-resinous, straight grained, and has a prominent growth-ring figure. It has a coarse texture and is rather brittle.

Properties

Western red cedar weighs about 23lb/ft^3 (370kg/m^3) when seasoned. Thin sizes dry readily with little degrade, but thicker stock requires careful drying. There is very small shrinkage in changing atmospheres, and stability in service. The wood has low strength in all categories and a very poor steam-bending classification. It works easily with both hand and machine tools, with little dulling effect on cutting edges. Cutters should be kept very sharp. It has fairly good nailing properties but galvanized or copper nails should be used, because the wood's acidic properties cause corrosion of metals and black stains in the wood in damp conditions. Western red cedar can be glued easily and nailed satisfactorily, and takes stains of the finest tint without fading. It can be polished to an excellent finish. The sapwood is liable to attack by powder post beetle; the heartwood is durable and resistant to preservative treatment.

Uses

This softwood is extensively used in the solid for greenhouses and sheds, shingles, exterior weatherboarding, and vertical cladding. It also goes into beehives, and is used in the round for poles and fences.

Where it grows

Western red cedar occurs from Alaska south to California, and east from British Columbia to Washington, Idaho, Montana, and the northern Rockies. It has also been introduced in the UK and New Zealand.

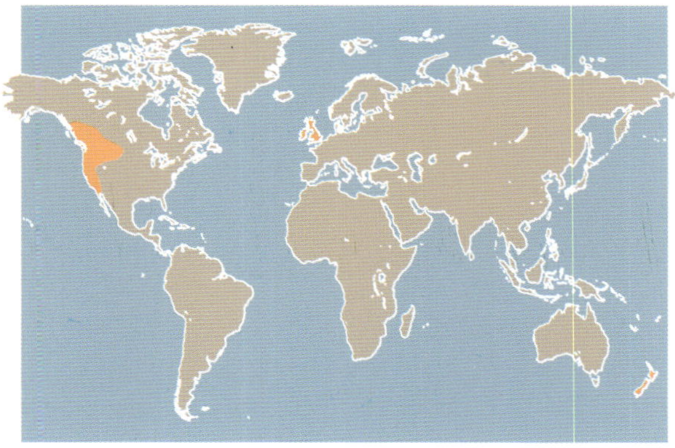

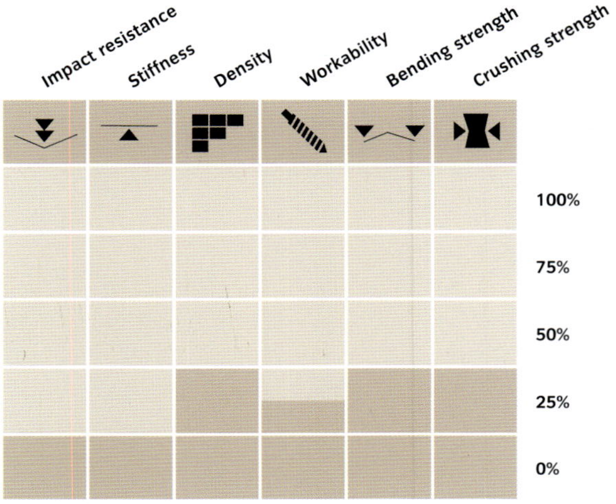

AT A GLANCE

Impact resistance is a measure of the wood's toughness. It describes its resistance to suddenly applied shock loads.

Stiffness is a measure of the wood's elasticity. It is considered in conjunction with bending strength.

Density is measured as specific gravity, the ratio of the density of a substance to that of water.

Tieghemella heckelii | Family: *Sapotaceae* | **MAKORE** | Hardwood

Growth
Makoré is also known as agamokwe (Nigeria), and as baku and abaku (Ghana). *Tieghemella africana* is a very similar species that grows in Cameroon and Gabon, where it is known as douka. These trees attain a height of approximately 120–150ft (37–45m), with a diameter of about 4ft (1.2m).

Appearance
The heartwood varies from pale blood-red to reddish brown, and the sapwood is slightly lighter. Some logs have irregular veins of darker color. Most timber is straight grained, but selected logs provide a broken stripe or mottle and a very decorative moiré or watered silk appearance, with a high natural luster. The texture is much finer and more even than mahogany.

Properties
The average weight of makoré is 39lb/ft^3 (620kg/m^3) when seasoned, and it dries at a moderate rate with little degrade. There is small movement in service. The timber has medium bending and crushing strength, low stiffness and shock resistance, and a moderate steam-bending rating. The silica content causes severe blunting of cutting edges, and when working with dry wood, tungsten carbide-tipped saws are required. Machine dust is an irritant to the eyes, nose, and throat, and efficient dust extraction is essential. The wood tends to split in nailing, but takes glue well and stains and polishes to an excellent finish. It tends to develop blue stains if it comes into contact with iron or iron compounds in damp conditions. The sapwood is liable to attack by powder post beetle. The heartwood is very durable and extremely resistant to preservation treatment.

Uses
Makoré is used for doors, table legs, chairs, fittings, superior interior joinery, and paneling, and for exterior joinery for cladding, doors, sills, and thresholds. Specialized uses include framing for vehicles and carriages, boat building, laboratory benches, and textile rollers. It is an excellent turnery wood and makes a good flooring. Logs are peeled for veneers for marine-quality plywood, and sliced for highly decorative veneers.

Where it grows
Makoré occurs in Sierra Leone, Nigeria, the Ivory Coast, Ghana, and Liberia.

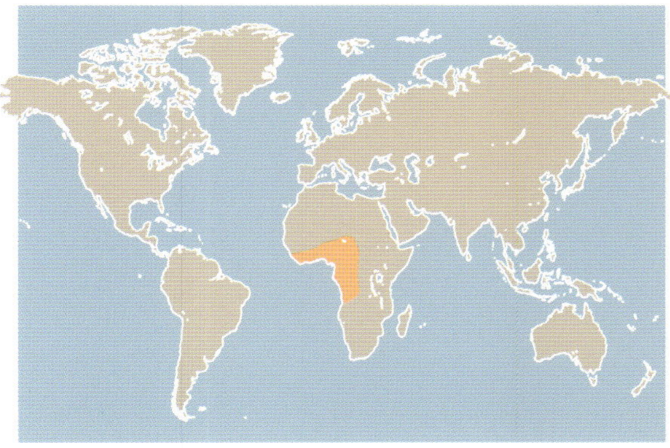

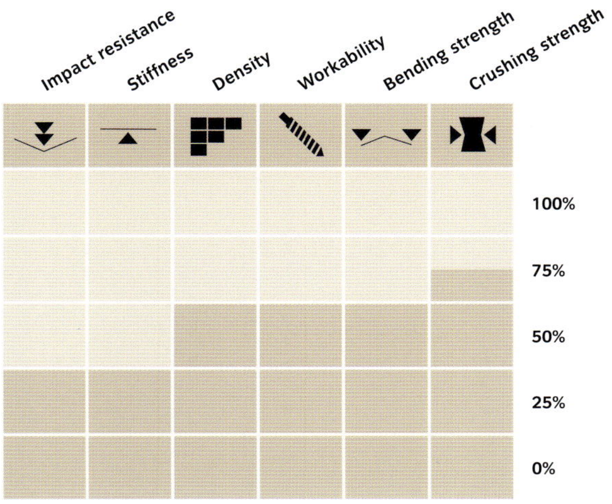

Workability describes how easy a wood is to work and whether it has a significant blunting effect on tools.

Bending strength is also known as maximum bending strength. Pressure is applied to each end of a board until it cracks.

Crushing strength is the ability of wood to withstand loads applied to the end grain, a critical test for wood used as short columns or props.

Tilia spp.	Family: *Tiliaceae*	**LIME/BASSWOOD**	Hardwood

Growth

There are several closely related species of *Tilia*. *T.vulgaris* produces the European lime or linden tree; *T.americana* provides American lime or American basswood; and *T.japonica* produces Japanese lime or Japanese basswood. All three species attain an average height of between 65 and 100ft (20 and 30m), with a diameter up to 4ft (1.2m).

Appearance

There is no distinction between the sapwood and heartwood in any of the three species. Both are a creamy white color when the tree is first felled maturing to a pale brown when dried. The wood has a straight grain, a fine, uniform texture, and is soft, weak, odorless, and free from any taints.

Properties

The weight of European lime is 34lb/ft^3 (540kg/m^3) when seasoned. American basswood and Japanese lime are 26lb/ft^3 (420kg/m^3) when seasoned. All three species dry fairly rapidly, with little degrade, and only a slight tendency to distort. There is medium movement in service. The wood has low to medium bending and crushing strength, low stiffness and shock resistance, and a poor steam-bending rating. It works easily with both hand and machine tools, but needs thin-edged sharp tools for a smooth finish. The wood nails and glues well, and can be stained and polished satisfactorily for a good finish. The sapwood is liable to attack by the common furniture beetle. The heartwood is perishable, but is permeable to preservative treatment.

Uses

Lime/basswood resists splitting in any cutting direction and is ideal for carving, cutting boards for leather work, pattern making, and so on. Hat block manufacturers regard it as an alternative to alder (*Alnus spp.*). Other specialized uses include artificial limbs, piano sounding boards, and harps. It is a good turnery wood for broom handles and bobbins, and is used for beehive frames, flat paintbrush handles, cask bungs, toys, clogs, and dairy and food containers. It is rotary cut for corestock and plywood. Selected logs are sliced for decorative veneers for marquetry and architectural paneling.

Where it grows

Lime/basswood grows in Canada, the eastern United States, Europe, and parts of Asia.

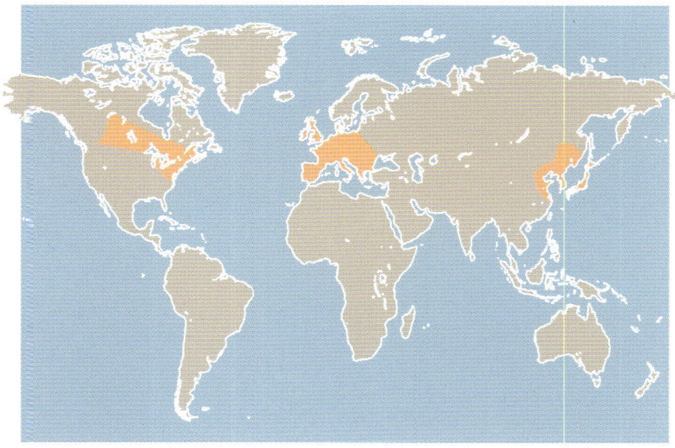

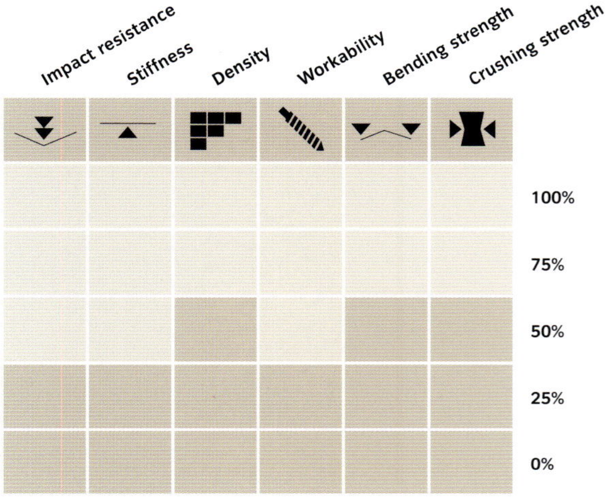

AT A GLANCE

Impact resistance is a measure of the wood's toughness. It describes its resistance to suddenly applied shock loads.

Stiffness is a measure of the wood's elasticity. It is considered in conjunction with bending strength.

Density is measured as specific gravity, the ratio of the density of a substance to that of water.

Triplochiton scleroxylon | Family: *Triplochitonaceae* | **OBECHE** | Hardwood

Growth

Triplochiton scleroxylon is known by a number of different names in its native west Africa: arere (Nigeria), wawa (Ghana), samba (Ivory Coast), and ayous (Cameroon and Zaire). It attains a height of between 150 and 180ft (45 and 55m), with a diameter of around 3–5ft (1–1.5m), and a clean cylindrical bole free from branches up to 80ft (24m).

Appearance

There is little distinction between the sapwood and heartwood, both of which are a creamy yellow to pale straw color. The grain is interlocked, producing a striped appearance on quartered stock, and the texture is moderately coarse but even. The wood has an attractive natural luster.

Properties

Obeche weighs 24lb/ft^3 (390kg/m^3) when seasoned. It dries very rapidly and easily, with no tendency to split or for shakes to extend, but slight distortion may occur. There is small movement in service. The wood has low bending and crushing strength, very low stiffness and shock resistance, and a moderate to poor steam-bending classification. It works easily with both hand and machine tools, with only a slight blunting effect on cutting edges. Sharp cutters with a reduced sharpness angle are recommended. The wood nails easily but has poor holding qualities. It glues well, but requires a light filling to obtain a good finish. This nondurable timber tends to blue stain if it comes into contact with iron compounds in moist conditions. The sapwood is liable to attack by the powder post beetle. The heartwood is perishable and resistant to preservative treatment, but the sapwood is permeable.

Uses

Where durability and strength are relatively unimportant, obeche is used for whitewood furniture and fitments, interior rails, drawer slides and linings, cabinet framing, interior joinery, moldings, sliderless soundboards for organs, and in model making. It is rotary cut for constructional veneer for corestock and backing veneer for plywood, and it is sliced for decorative striped veneers. Blue-stained obeche is particularly sought by marquetry craftsmen.

Where it grows

This tree occurs throughout west Africa, including Nigeria, Ghana, the Ivory Coast, Cameroon, and Zaire.

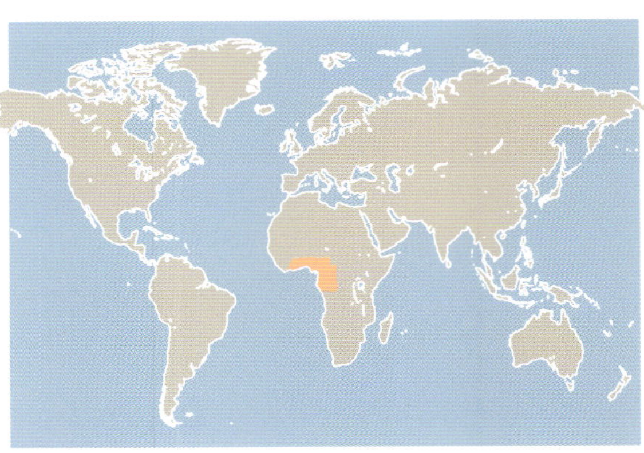

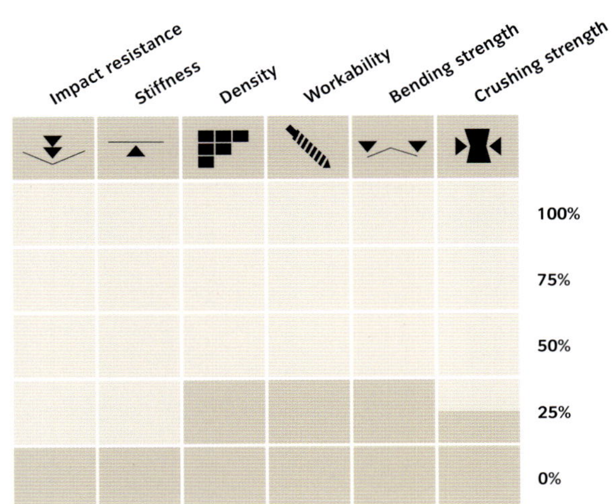

Workability describes how easy a wood is to work and whether it has a significant blunting effect on tools.

Bending strength is also known as maximum bending strength. Pressure is applied to each end of a board until it cracks.

Crushing strength is the ability of wood to withstand loads applied to the end grain, a critical test for wood used as short columns or props.

Tsuga heterophylla | Family: *Pinaceae* | **WESTERN HEMLOCK** | Softwood

Growth

Also known as Pacific hemlock and British Columbian hemlock, this tree grows to a height of 200ft (60m), with a diameter of 6–8ft (1.8–2.4m).

Appearance

The heartwood is a cream color with a very pale brown cast. Darker latewood bands often produce a well-marked growth-ring figure with purplish lines. It is straight grained with a fairly even texture, and is somewhat lustrous.

Properties

Western hemlock weighs 30lb/ft^3 (480kg/m^3) when seasoned. The initially high moisture content of this wood demands careful drying to avoid surface checking and ensure uniform drying in thick stock. Distortion is minimal. There is small movement in service. The wood has medium bending and crushing strength, low hardness and stiffness, and a moderate steam-bending rating. It works readily with both hand and machine tools, with little dulling of cutting edges. It can be glued, stained, painted, or varnished to a good finish. It should be pre-bored for nailing near the ends of dry boards. Damage by *Siricid* wood wasps is sometimes present. The sapwood of seasoned timber is liable to attack by the common furniture beetle. Dark brown or black resinous scars (known as black check) are also sometimes found, caused by fly larvae (*Syrphidae*). Western hemlock is not durable or resistant to decay. The heartwood is resistant to preservative treatment.

Uses

Western hemlock, regarded as one of the most valuable North American timbers, is exported to all parts of the world in large baulk dimensions for use in general building construction, joists, rafters, studding, interior and exterior joinery, doors, floors, fitments, suspended ceilings, and vehicle bodywork. It is widely used for wood turnery, broom handles, and for packaging cases, crates, and pallets. It is also treated for railway sleepers. Logs are cut into veneers for plywood and decorative paneling. The timber is also used for quality newsprint pulp.

Where it grows

This softwood tree occurs in Alaska, British Columbia, northern Washington, Idaho, and on the western slopes of the Cascades.

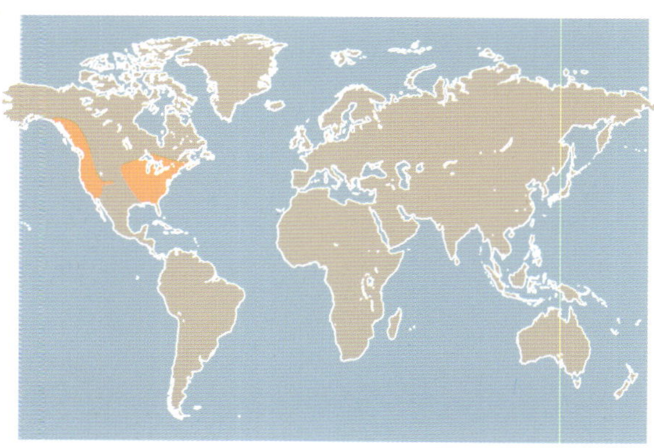

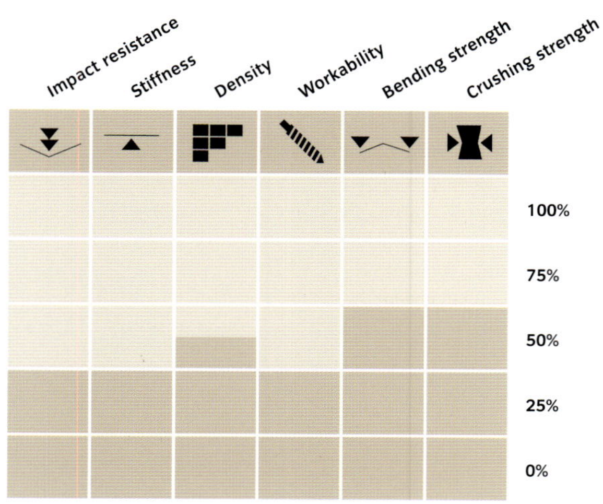

AT A GLANCE

Impact resistance is a measure of the wood's toughness. It describes its resistance to suddenly applied shock loads.

Stiffness is a measure of the wood's elasticity. It is considered in conjunction with bending strength.

Density is measured as specific gravity, the ratio of the density of a substance to that of water.

Turreanthus africanus | Family: *Meliaceae* | **AVODIRE** | Hardwood

Growth

Avodire is also known as African satinwood. Although this species is part of the mahogany family, the two woods bear little resemblance to each other, at least in color. *Turreanthus africanus* grows to no more than 100ft (30m) in height, but it is rare to find a very long section of clean stem to harvest good lumber. The genus is named after a 17th-century Italian botanist called Turro.

Appearance

Avodire heartwood is a creamy yellow color that shines superbly. The color gradually darkens to a more golden hue, and within the straight grain you can often notice ghostly ribbons of shimmering lighter and darker wood. The patterning can be mottled or striped. A key quality of avodire is its natural high luster, which gives it a splendid shine. Its texture is fine and even, although the grain can be interlocking.

Properties

Avodire is of medium weight at 34lb/ft^3 (540kg/m^3). It dries rapidly, but can twist and warp, and there is a risk of splitting and checking, especially around knots. However, it is stable once dry, although not particularly durable. Despite its interlocking grain, it is not a difficult species to work and the results can be very successful.

Uses

Avodire is popular with shop fitters, because it is lightweight but finishes well and can take a good edge. It is also used for joinery, and as a decorative veneer for paneling, doors, and cabinets.

Where it grows

Avodire is grown along the tropical belt in west Africa, including Sierra Leone and the Ivory Coast, and it currently appears to be plentiful and in no danger.

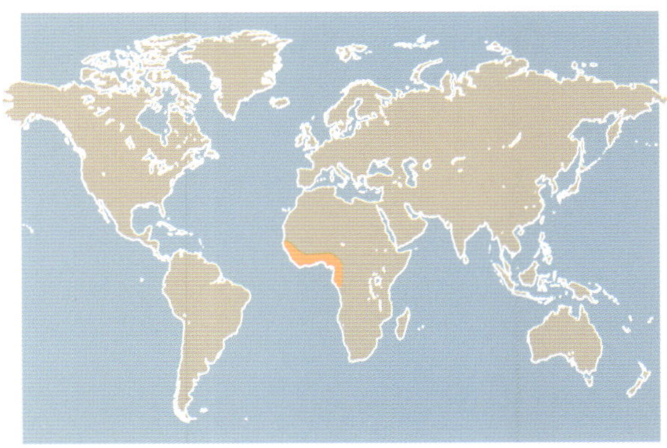

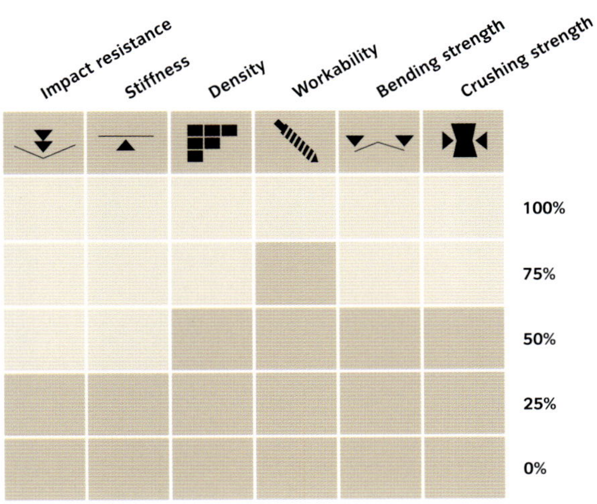

Workability describes how easy a wood is to work and whether it has a significant blunting effect on tools.

Bending strength is also known as maximum bending strength. Pressure is applied to each end of a board until it cracks.

Crushing strength is the ability of wood to withstand loads applied to the end grain, a critical test for wood used as short columns or props.

Ulmus spp. | Family: *Ulmaceae* | **AMERICAN ELM** | Hardwood

Growth

There are three main species of American elm in the *Ulmus* genus. *U.americana* L. produces white elm, which is also known as water elm, swamp elm, and American elm. *U.fulva* Michx. provides slippery elm, also known as soft elm, red elm, and slippery barked elm. *U.thomasii* Sarg. produces rock elm, also known as cork elm, hickory elm, and cork bark elm. American elms average 50–80ft (15–24m) in height, with a diameter of 1–4ft (0.3–1.2m).

Appearance

The heartwood is medium to light reddish brown, and the sapwood is slightly paler. Rock elm is straight grained with a moderately fine texture. White elm is sometimes interlocked and the texture coarse and rather wooly.

Properties

White elm weighs about 36lb/ft^3 (580kg/m^3) when seasoned; slippery elm is a little heavier. Rock elm weighs between 39 and 49lb/ft^3 (620 and 780kg/m^3) when seasoned. All species dry readily with minimum shrinkage. American elms have medium bending and crushing strength and very low stiffness. White elm has high resistance and rock elm very high resistance to shock loads. All species have very good steam-bending ratings. The timbers work fairly easily with only a moderate blunting effect on tools. They take nails without splitting, glue satisfactorily, and provide an excellent finish. The sapwood is liable to attack by powder post beetle but is resistant to fungus. American elm is nondurable and moderately resistant to preservative treatment.

Uses

American elm is used in boat and ship building for stem posts, ribs, general framing, gunwales, bilge stringers, keels, rubbing strips, and components that are completely submerged in water. It is also employed for underwater parts in dock and harbor work. Other uses include wheel hubs, blades of ice hockey sticks, agricultural implements, chair rockers, gymnasium equipment, bentwork for vehicle bodies, and ladder rungs. The wood is excellent for turnery, and is sliced for decorative veneers and burls.

Where it grows

American elm grows in eastern and central parts of the United States. Different species also occur in Canada, reaching as far west as Saskatchewan, and as far south as Quebec and Ontario.

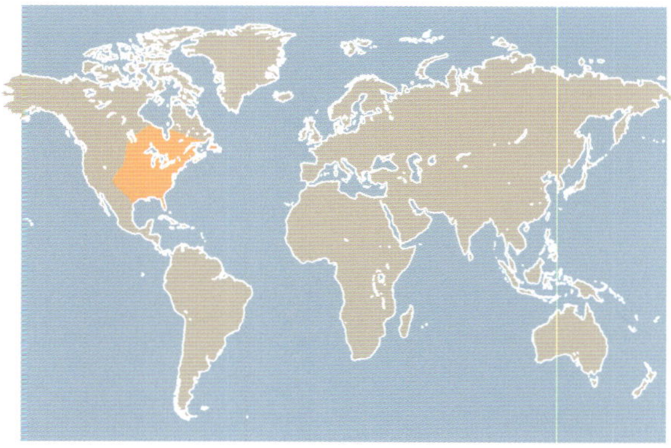

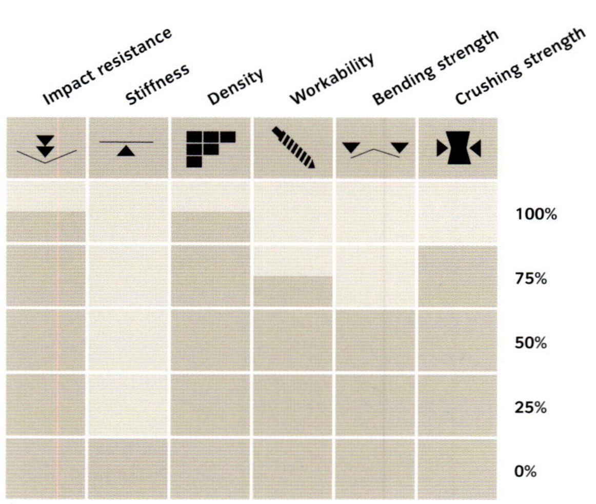

AT A GLANCE

Impact resistance is a measure of the wood's toughness. It describes its resistance to suddenly applied shock loads.

Stiffness is a measure of the wood's elasticity. It is considered in conjunction with bending strength.

Density is measured as specific gravity, the ratio of the density of a substance to that of water.

***Ulmus* spp.** | Family: *Ulmaceae* | **EUROPEAN ELM** | Hardwood

Growth

English elm (*Ulmus procera*) is also known as red elm and nave elm. Smooth-leaved elm (*U.carpinifolia*) is the common elm of Europe, known as French elm or Flemish elm. There is also Dutch elm (*U.hollandica*), and wych elm (*U.glabra*), also known as Scotch elm, mountain elm, and white elm. All these elms reach an average height of 120–150ft (37–45m), with a diameter of 3–5ft (1–1.5m), except wych elm, which grows to 100–125ft (30–38m) tall and up to 5ft (1.5m) in diameter.

Appearance

The heartwood is usually a dull brown, often with a reddish tint, and is clearly defined from the paler sapwood. The heartwood has distinct and irregular growth rings, giving the wood a rather coarse texture. It is cross-grained and of irregular growth, which provides some very attractive figure. Wych elm has a greenish tinge. Continental European elms are usually more straight grained than English elm.

Properties

European elms weigh approximately 34lb/ft^3 (540kg/m^3) when seasoned; wych elm weighs about 42lb/ft^3 (670kg/m^3). The wood dries fairly rapidly, with a strong tendency to distort. It has low bending and crushing strength, with very low stiffness and resistance to shock loads. All elms have a very good steam-bending rating. The wood can be difficult to work, tending to pick up in planing and bind on the saw, but it takes nails well, glues satisfactorily, and provides a good finish. The sapwood is liable to attack by powder post beetle and common furniture beetle. Elm is nondurable, moderately resistant to preservative treatment, and the sapwood is permeable.

Uses

The Rialto bridge in Venice stands on elm piles. Elm is used for boat and ship building, dock and harbor work, weatherboards, gymnasium equipment, agricultural implements, vehicle bodywork, ladder rungs, coffins, and the seats of Windsor chairs. It makes an attractive flooring. It is also used for meat chopping blocks, and as a turnery wood for bowls. It is sliced for highly decorative veneers, and elm burls are used for cabinets and paneling.

Where it grows
European elm grows in the temperate climates of Europe.

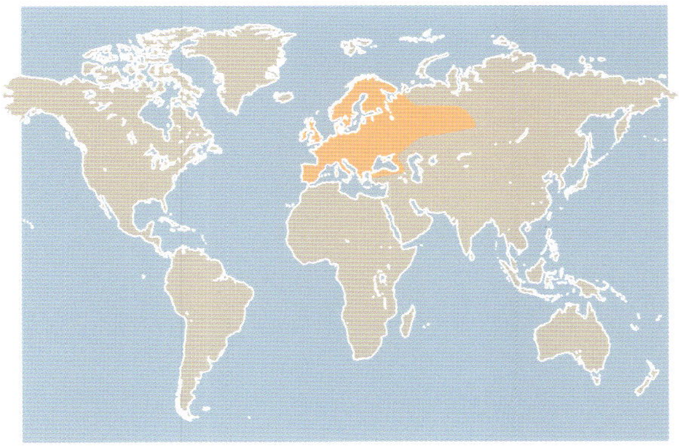

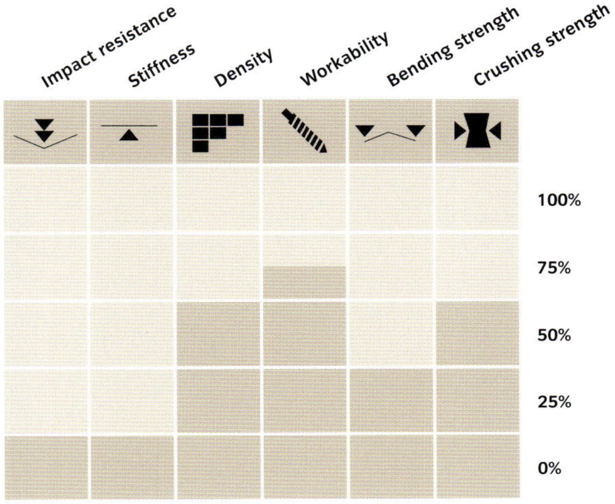

Workability describes how easy a wood is to work and whether it has a significant blunting effect on tools.

Bending strength is also known as maximum bending strength. Pressure is applied to each end of a board until it cracks.

Crushing strength is the ability of wood to withstand loads applied to the end grain, a critical test for wood used as short columns or props.

GLOSSARY

Angiosperm A class of plant whose seeds are borne inside an ovary.

Apical meristem The growing point of tissues of living wood cells capable of repeated division, found at the tip of the stem.

Bast The soft, fibrous layer of phloem tissue that forms between the bark and the inner cell structure.

Bole The lower section of the stem or trunk of a tree, from above the root-butt to the first limb or branch.

Burls (burrs) Abnormal, wart-like growths or excrescences often produced by stooling. Irritation or injury causes stunted growth that develops into a contorted, gnarled mass of dense woody tissue that produces a highly decorative appearance of tightly clustered dormant buds, each with a darker pith.

Calyx A whorl of usually green leaves, known as sepals, forming the outer part of a bud or flower.

Cambium An active layer of cells that divides to produce new tissues. Vascular cambium produces xylem on the inside of the stem and phloem on the outside, below the bark.

Catkin A dropping spike, or cat's tail, of scalybracted, stalkless flowers.

Collapse Irregular and excessive shrinkage of timber during drying.

Compression wood Timber from part of a conifer that has been under compression, such as below a branch or on the concave side of a bent tree. The cells are shorter than normal and thicker walled. The wood is usually of a dark color.

Cork A layer of dead cells on the outside of a stem or root that protects the inner tissues against damage; particularly well developed in the cork oak tree.

Corolla The ring of petals forming the conspicuously colored part of the flower.

Cortex The part of a tree's bark between the endodermis and the epidermis.

Cotyledon A seed leaf that becomes the first leaf of the embryo plant.

Crotches (curl) Figure of the grain produced by suitable conversion from the junction of a branch with the stem of the tree, or between two branches. The wood fibers suffer from either compression or tension, being distorted by the weight of the limb.

Cuticle The impervious outer coating of the epidermis that prevents damage and water loss.

Dicotyledon In the embryo stage, dicotyledons have two cotyledons in the seed. Dicotyledons include all broad-leaved trees and most shrubs.

Diffuse-porous Where the pores are diffused or scattered across the growth ring, so that there is little difference between the pores in the earlywood and latewood zones. Also, where is the gradual change in size and distribution across the growth ring.

Doat or dote Localized patches of incipient decay or rot in timber.

Earlywood The early part of a growth ring, consisting of pale inner wood with thin walls, formed in the spring and early summer. Also known as springwood.

E.M.C. Equilibrium moisture content: the moisture content at which wood is stable and in equilibrium with the humidity of its surroundings.

Endocarp The inner layer of the pericarp.

Endodermis The inner layer of the cortex.

Endosperm The nutritive tissue around the embryo of a seed.

Epidermis The layer of cells just beneath the protective cuticle.

False heartwood Dark innerwood caused by disease or fungal attack.

Fibers The longitudinal thick-walled wood elements in hardwoods whose function is to provide strength. The weight and hardness of wood is proportional to the amount of wood fiber in the tree.

Figure The pattern on the longitudinal surface caused by variations in the color; the arrangement of tissues such as the grain, rays, branches, and contortions around knots; irregularity and interlacing of fibers. Abnormal figure is due to external defects, such as insect attack, decay, reaction wood wounds, and pollarding.

Flitch A section of a log trimmed and prepared for conversion into veneers, or part of a converted log suitable for further conversion.

F.S.P. Fiber saturation point: the point at which the cell walls are fully saturated but the cells contain no "free" moisture. Shrinkage will occur with additional seasoning below this point. The physical properties of wood do not change when the moisture content is above F.S.P.

Girdling Cutting through the cambium layer around the circumference of a growing tree to terminate its growth before felling.

Grain The direction of the wood fibers relative to the long axis of the tree or piece of wood.

Growth ring The area of growth, comprising earlywood and latewood, by which a tree increases in diameter every year.

Gymnosperm Cone-bearing softwoods with seeds that are exposed or naked—not enclosed in an ovary.

Honeycombing Checks in the interior of wood, invisible on the surface, caused by case hardening in seasoning.

Hypocotyl Part of the embryo seeding below the cotyledons.

Latewood The darker portion of a growth ring, consisting of denser wood with thicker walls, forming in mid- and late summer. Also known as summerwood.

Lenticel A pore on the trunk or branch that breathes and shows a white mark on the bark.

Lignin An important chemical constituent of cellular tissue that has a hardening, binding function in the cell walls of xylem and gives wood its basic character.

Mesocarp The middle layer of the pericarp.

Mesophyll The inner tissue of a leaf.

Moisture content Moisture exists in the cell walls and cell spaces of heartwood, and in the cell contents of sapwood. The strength and stiffness of wood varies in almost inverse ratio to the changes in moisture content.

Monocotyledon Monocotyledons have only one first seed leaf, or cotyledon, and include palms and all grasses.

Montane forests Forests that occur in mountainous regions.

Movement The dimensional changes in timber after it has been air- or kiln-dried, caused by variations in atmospheric conditions (see also Shrinkage).

Net veins See Reticulate veins.

Node The slightly swollen part of a stem from which a shoot, leaf, or whorl of leaves arises.

Osmosis The tendency of dissimilar liquids and gases to diffuse through a membrane or porous structure.

Ovary The part of the flower containing the ovules.

Ovate Egg-shaped, broadest below the middle.

Ovule Young seed within the ovary.

Parenchyma Wood's soft tissue concerned with the distribution and storage of carbohydrates. It is composed of thin-walled, brick-shaped cells with pits that may be axial or radial.

Pedicel The stalk of a flower or fruit.

Peduncle The stalk of a flower or inflorescence.

Pericarp The seed vessel or wall of the developed ovary.

Periderm The tissues of the cork cambium and the outer bark.

Petiole A leaf stalk

Phloem Vascular tissue that transports food materials made by the plant. Also known as bast or inner bark.

Photosynthesis The process by which carbohydrates are synthesized from carbon dioxide and water in the presence of sunlight and chlorophyll.

Pistil Female flower organs comprising ovary, style, and stigma.

Pith The middle core of parenchyma in a stem, around which all future growth takes place. It ceases to function after the sapling stage. Also known as the heart of the medulla.

Pith flecks These are not connected with the pith, but are irregular, discolored streaks caused by insect attack. Wound parenchyma forms on the occluding insect tunnels and cross-sections appear as flecks on converted timber.

Pits Parts of the cell wall in wood tissue that remain thin during the thickening of the cell walls and serve as a link between the cells for the transmission of sap.

Plumule The rudimentary stem in an embryo plant.

Pollarding The continuous looping of the top, or poll, of the tree to encourage fresh growth. The succession of new shots, or knurls, forms highly decorative burls (burrs).

Pollination The transfer of pollen from the male anther of a flower to the female stigma.

Rays A vertical sheet of tissue formed radially across the growth rings of trees, consisting chiefly of parenchyma cells. Rays allow the transmission of sap. There are two types of rays: medullar rays (also known as primary rays) that extend from the bark to the medulla, or pith, of the tree; and vascular rays that do not reach the pith.

Radicle The first tiny root sprouting from a seed.

Reaction wood The name given to either tension wood or compression wood, caused by the distortion of natural growth in trees.

Respiration This is the reverse of photosynthesis. In respiration, organic matter is broken down into carbon dioxide and water with the release of energy.

Reticulate veins Veins that resemble the threads of a net (the smaller veins in most dicotyledons).

Ring-porous Where there is a distinct contrast in size and number of the pores in different parts of the growth ring, with larger pores in the earlywood producing a well-marked boundary between the earlywood and latewood zones.

Sapwood The outer region of the tree trunk composed of living xylem cells that transport water throughout the tree.

Savannah Extensive grassy treeless plains in tropical and subtropical regions, usually covered with low vegetation.

Sepal One of the individual segments of the calyx.

S.G. Specific Gravity: the relative weight of substance compared with that of an equal volume of water. The S.G. of air-dried hardwoods varies between 0.45 and 1.4 approximately, and the S.G. of softwoods varies from about 0.25 to 0.8 at 15 percent moisture content.

Shake A split or separation between adjacent layers of fibers caused by wind, thunder, frost, lack of nutrition, felling, or faulty seasoning. There are compound, cross, cup, ring, heart, radial, shell, star, or thunder shakes.

Shrinkage The dimensional change in wood between its "green" state and after seasoning by air- or kiln-drying to its equilibrium moisture content, which varies with local conditions and conditions of end use.

Stipule A growth, mostly leafy, at the base of the petiole that is often shed early.

Stomata Breathing pores chiefly found on the undersurface of leaves. Each pore, or stoma, is usually controlled by two guard cells.

Stooling Throwing out shoots from a tree stump to produce a second growth from the original roots, in a similar way to pollarding.

Tannin An acidic substance distilled from the bark, wood, and excrescences of many species of trees and used for converting hide into leather.

Tension wood A term given to wood in which the cells are thin-walled and abnormally long. This can occur in parts of deciduous trees that are under tension; for example, on the convex side of leaning trees.

Texture The texture in hardwoods depends on the size and distribution of the wood elements and to a lesser extent on the rays. Texture varies in different species and according to the rate of growth and may be coarse, fine, medium, uniform, smooth, even, or uneven.

Tracheids Often called wood fibers, these are narrow, vertically elongated tubular wood cells with rounded ends and bordered pits on their side walls. They form the bulk of the wood of conifers and correspond to the fibers in hardwoods.

Transpiration Water loss from the leaves by evaporation, especially through the stomata.

Vascular tissue The living tissue that conducts water and food substances through the tree, and provides mechanical support. It is composed chiefly of xylem, which forms the wood, and phloem, which forms the bast.

Vessels Found only in hardwood and also known as pores, vessels are elongated cells arranged one on top of another with their ends missing, and are well-perforated, forming continuous pipe-like tubes for conducting water through the tree.

Whorl Three or more leaves in a circle from a node; also used to describe a circle of branches or branchlets.

Xylem Basic wood tissue, comprising long cells with thickened walls by which water and mineral salts are transported through the tree.

INDEX

Common names are generally used in this index. Latin names are listed alphabetically on pages 36–37. The main text entries for each wood are indicated in **bold**.

CREDITS

Quarto would like to thank and acknowledge the following for supplying photographs and illustrations reproduced in this book. All other photographs and illustrations are the copyright of Quarto Publishing plc. While every effort has been made to credit contributors, Quarto would like to apologize should there have been any omissions or errors—and would be pleased to make the appropriate correction for future editions of the book.

Key: ***l*** left, ***r*** right, ***t*** top, ***b*** bottom

11tl	L. Clarke / CORBIS
15r	Maurice Nimmo; Frank Lane Picture Agency / CORBIS
19t	Gunter Marx Photography / CORBIS
19r	Darrell Gulin / CORBIS
19b	Wolfgang Kaehler / CORBIS
20b	Paul A. Souders / CORBIS
21t	Chinch Gryniewicz; Ecoscene / CORBIS
21r	Michael & Patricia Fogden / CORBIS
21b	Paul A. Souders / CORBIS
24l & r	FSC International
25tl	Wolfgang Kaehler / CORBIS
25tr	Barry Jordan www.highwaygold.co.uk
26br	Dan Lamont / CORBIS
27t	Jean Heguy / CORBIS
29l	P.A.L. Foundation
29br	Ecotimber
30b	Layne Kennedy / CORBIS
33t	Stéphane Choquet and Annabel Gaitskell / Gécé Associés http://gece.associes.free.fr

Quarto would also like to acknowledge the individual contributions of the five experts who wrote the text in this book.

Lucinda Leech and Bill Lincoln, pages 18–25
Jane Marshall and Aidan Walker, pages 26–33
Bill Lincoln and Nick Gibbs, pages 34–187